ANTISEMITISM AND XENOPHOBIA
IN GERMANY AFTER UNIFICATION

ANTISEMITISM AND XENOPHOBIA IN GERMANY AFTER UNIFICATION

Edited by Hermann Kurthen,
Werner Bergmann, and Rainer Erb

New York   Oxford
OXFORD UNIVERSITY PRESS
1997

Oxford University Press

Oxford   New York
Athens   Auckland   Bangkok   Bogota   Bombay   Buenos Aires
Calcutta   Cape Town   Dar es Salaam   Delhi   Florence   Hong Kong
Istanbul   Karachi   Kuala Lumpur   Madras   Madrid   Melbourne
Mexico City   Nairobi   Paris   Singapore   Taipei   Tokyo   Toronto

and associated companies in
Berlin   Ibadan

Copyright © 1997 by Oxford University Press, Inc.

Published by Oxford University Press, Inc.
198 Madison Avenue, New York, New York 10016

Oxford is a registered trademark of Oxford University Press

Library of Congress Cataloging-in-Publication Data
Antisemitism and xenophobia in Germany after unification / edited by
Hermann Kurthen, Werner Bergmann, Rainer Erb.
     p.   cm.
Includes bibliographical references.
ISBN 0-19-510485-4. — ISBN 0-19-511010-2 (pbk.)
1. Antisemitism—Germany.   2. Xenophobia—Germany.   3. Germany—
Politics and government—1990–   4. Germany—Ethnic relations.
I. Kurthen, Hermann.   II. Bergmann, Werner.   III. Erb, Rainer, 1945–   .
DS146.G4A49   1997
305.892'4043—DC20   96-33656

9 8 7 6 5 4 3 2 1

Printed in the United States of America
on acid-free paper

Acknowledgments

The editors are grateful for institutional support from the Center for Research on Antisemitism (Zentrum für Antisemitismusforschung) of the Technische Universität Berlin and its chair, Wolfgang Benz, including the financial support for translations by Allison Brown. Staff members of the center, Angelika Königseder and Alexander Piccolruaz, also helped to prepare the chronology in the appendix. Gerald R. Kleinfeld at Arizona State University helped to obtain funding from the German Studies Association of America to allow the German editors to discuss drafts at GSA meetings in Washington, D.C., and Dallas. For their willingness to provide survey data and printed material, we thank the Spiegel Verlag in Hamburg, the Emnid-Institut in Bielefeld, D3 Systems (David Jodice), and David Singer of the American Jewish Committee in New York. The editors are also very grateful to Kay Losey at the English Department of the University of North Carolina at Chapel Hill for her comments and proofreading support on various drafts of the introduction, the conclusion, and the appendix. Also, Bonita Samuel's help reading and correcting drafts at the Institute for Research in Social Science at UNC has been important to the timely completion of this project. Peter Merkl, Konrad Jarausch, Siegfried Mews, Heike Trapp, and Stefan Immerfall also provided useful suggestions. Finally, we appreciate the support and patience of the staff of Oxford University Press, in particular, our production editor, Paula Wald.

Contents

Abbreviations

ADL	Anti-Defamation League
AJC	American Jewish Committee
B90	Bündnis 90/Die Grünen (Alliance 90/Green Party)
CCJG	Zentralrat der Juden in Deutschland (Central Council of Jews in Germany)
CDU	Christlich Demokratische Union (Christian Democratic Union)
CIS/USSR	Commonwealth of Independent States (former Soviet Union)
CSU	Christlich Soziale Union (Christian Social Union)
DVU	Deutsche Volksunion (German People's Union)
EU	European Union
FAP	Freiheitliche Deutsche Arbeiterpartei (Free Worker Party)
FBI	Federal Bureau of Investigation
FDJ	Freie Deutsche Jugend (Free German Youth)
FDP	Freie Demokratische Partei (Free Democratic Party)
FFD	Freundeskreis Freiheit für Deutschland (Freedom for Germany Circle)
FRG	Bundesrepublik Deutschland (Federal Republic of [West] Germany)
GDR	Deutsche Demokratische Republik ([East] German Democratic Republic)
IfD	Institut für Demoskopie
IHR	Institute for Historical Review
JCA	Jüdischer Kulturverein (Jewish Cultural Association)
KPD	Kommunistische Partei Deutschlands (Communist Party of Germany)
NATO	North Atlantic Treaty Organization
NPD	Nationaldemokratische Partei Deutschlands (National Democratic Party of Germany)

NSDAP	Nationalsozialistische Deutsche Arbeiterpartei (National Socialist German Workers' Party)
PDS	Partei des Demokratischen Sozialismus (Party of Democratic Socialism, former SED)
PLO	Palestine Liberation Organization
REP	Republikaner Partei (Republican Party)
SED	Sozialistische Einheitspartei Deutschlands (Socialist Unity Party of Germany)
SPD	Sozialdemokratische Partei Deutschlands (Social Democratic Party of Germany)
SRP	Sozialistische Reichspartei (Socialist Reich Party)
UN	United Nations

Contributors

BRIGITTE BAILER-GALANDA is a native of Vienna. After studying economics and social science at Vienna University, she received a doctoral grant in history and finished her Ph.D. in 1992. Since 1979 she has worked as a researcher at the Austrian Resistance Archive in Vienna. In 1992 Bailer-Galanda received the Austrian Käthe-Leichter state award for her research on the persecution and resistance of the Jews in Austria between 1934 and 1945, postwar Austrian right-wing extremism, and the so-called restitution *(Wiedergutmachung)* for victims of National Socialism. She has assisted in the preparation of many publications of the Austrian Resistance Archive and coedited *Ein teutsches Land: Die "rechte" Orientierung des Jörg Haider* (Vienna: Lücker, 1987), *Die neue Rechte: Jörg Haider—ein Politiker der neuen oder der ganz alten Art* (Vienna: Zukunft Verlag, 1987), *Alte und neue Rechte: Rechtsextremismus und Rechtstrend* (Vienna: Zukunft Verlag, 1992), *Amoklauf gegen die Wirklichkeit: NS-Verbrechen und "revisionistische" Geschichtsschreibung* (Vienna: Dokumentationsarchiv, 1992), *Wiedergutmachung—Kein Thema: Österreich und die Opfer des Nationalsozialismus* (Vienna: Lücker, 1993), and *Handbuch des österreichischen Rechtsextremismus* (Vienna: Deuticke, 1994).

WERNER BERGMANN is a native of Celle (Lower Saxony). He studied social sciences, education, and philosophy at Hamburg University, where he completed his Ph.D. in 1979. After graduation, he worked briefly as a teacher before becoming assistant professor at the Center for Research on Antisemitism, Technical University of Berlin, in 1984. Bergmann has published numerous books and internationally acclaimed articles about antisemitism in Germany. He coedited *Error without Trial: Psychological Research on Antisemitism* (Berlin: Walter de Gruyter,

1988), *Die Nachtseite der Judenemanzipation: Der Widerstand gegen die Integration der Juden in Deutschland, 1780–1860* (Berlin: Metropol, 1989), *Antisemitismus in der politischen Kultur nach 1945* (Opladen: Westdeutscher Verlag, 1990), *Neonazismus und rechte Subkultur* (Berlin: Metropol, 1994), and *Schwieriges Erbe: Der Umgang mit Nationalsozialismus und Antisemitismus in Österreich, der DDR und der Bundesrepublik Deutschland* (Frankfurt am Main: Campus, 1995).

MANFRED BRUSTEN is a native of North Rhine–Westphalia. He has studied sociology, economics, and social psychology at the University of Münster and was a Fulbright scholar at the University of California at Berkeley. He finished his Ph.D. in sociology at the University of Bielefeld in 1974, where he worked for some years as a research and teaching assistant. Since 1975 he has been professor of the sociology of deviance and social control at Wuppertal University. He began his career studying issues like the administration of juvenile welfare, deviant behavior and stigmatization within schools, and police interrogation and police deviance. He has coedited or written a number of works, including *Jugend: Ein soziales Problem?* (Opladen: Westdeutscher Verlag, 1982) and *Youth Crime, Social Control, and Prevention* (Pfaffenweiler: Centaurus, 1986). Since the mid-1980s he has become more interested in Holocaust research and comparative attitudinal research on pupils and university students in Germany and Israel. He edited a 1947 report of a Jewish medical doctor from Berlin (H. W. Wollenberg) who witnessed the atrocities in "forced-labor camps" in Silesia: . . . *und der Alptraum wurde zum Alltag* (Pfaffenweiler: Centaurus, 1992). In recent years, his interest has shifted to victims of Nazi state terror: German-born Jews in Australia.

RAINER ERB is a native of Hamburg. He studied sociology and religious sciences at the Free University of Berlin, where he was also a research assistant and received his Ph.D. in 1983. He worked as a researcher at the Center for Research on Antisemitism in Berlin until 1995, when he joined the Moses-Mendelssohn Center for European-Jewish Studies at the University of Potsdam (near Berlin). Erb has published extensively on the history and sociology of the current articulation of antisemitism, on research in prejudice, on Christian-Jewish relations since the eighteenth century, and on right-wing extremism and violence. He coedited *Antisemitismus in der politischen Kultur nach 1945* (Opladen: Westdeutscher Verlag, 1990), *Antisemitismus in der Bundesrepublik Deutschland: Ergebnisse der empirischen Forschung von 1946 bis 1989* (Opladen: Leske & Budrich, 1991), *Antisemitism in Germany: The Post-Nazi Epoch from 1945 to 1995* (New Brunswick: Transaction, forthcoming), *Neonazismus und rechte Subkultur* (Berlin: Metropol, 1994), and he edited *Die Legende vom Ritualmord: Zur Geschichte der Blutbeschuldigungen gegen Juden* (Berlin: Metropol, 1993).

WOLFGANG G. GIBOWSKI was born in Mannheim, Germany. He studied economics at the University of Heidelberg. He was then a postgraduate student of Professor Rudolph Wildenmann's at the University of Mannheim, where he studied political science and election behavior. He is president of the German Studies Association in the U.K. Gibowski is currently ministerial director and deputy head of the German Federal Press and Information Office in Bonn. Prior to 1990, he was a director of the Forschungsgruppe Wahlen (Research Group on Elections) in Mannheim, where he conducted the national monthly "Politbarometer" broadcast on ZDF-TV and projected forecasts for national, state, and local elections in Germany as well as European parliamentary elections. Gibowski has published extensively on electoral behavior in Germany, survey methods, and public opinion in such journals as *Aus Politik und Zeitgeschichte* and *Zeitschrift für Parlamentsfragen.* He also has coauthored numerous chapters in books, the most recent being "Germany's General Election in 1994: Who Voted for Whom?," in *Germany's New Politics,* edited by David P. Conradt et al. (Providence, R.I.: Berghahn, 1995), pp. 105–130.

HERMANN KURTHEN was born in Stuttgart (Baden-Württemberg). He acquired a B.A. in political science and two M.A.s in sociology and political economy at the Free University of Berlin before receiving his Ph.D. in 1984 in social science. He then became a researcher at the Berlin Forschungsstelle Arbeitsmigration, Flüchtlingsbewegungen und Minderheitenpolitik (Research Center on Labor Migration, Refugee Movements, and Minority Policies). Kurthen taught and conducted research in Berlin, Canada, and the United States. He has been awarded grants from the German Research Fund and the German Marshall Fund of the United States. From 1991 to 1993 he was awarded a German Academic Exchange Service lectureship as adjunct associate professor of German studies at the University of North Carolina at Chapel Hill. His teaching and research interests are in the fields of minority politics; immigration; and multiculturalism, ethnic relations and stratification, labor migration, and antidiscrimination. He coauthored *Ausländerbeschäftigung in der Krise?: Die Beschäftigungschancen und -risiken ausländischer Arbeitnehmer am Beispiel der West Berliner Industrie* (Berlin: Sigma, 1989) and authored *Politische Ökonomie und Persönlichkeitstheorie: Aneignung und Individualität in der bürgerlichen Gesellschaft* (Cologne: Pahl Rugenstein, 1985). Forthcoming is a volume on welfare state incorporation of immigrant minorities in Germany and the United States.

ANNA J. MERRITT received her B.A. at Smith College and is currently associate director of the Institute of Government and Public Affairs at the University of Illinois at Urbana-Champaign. A longtime Berlin observer, she has translated and coedited such books as *Public Opinion in Occupied Germany: The OMGUS Surveys, 1945–1948* (Urbana: University of Illinois Press, 1970) and *Public Opinion in Semi-Sovereign Germany: The HICOG Surveys, 1949–1955* (Urbana: University of Illinois Press, 1980).

RICHARD L. MERRITT was born in Portland, Oregon. He received his Ph.D. at Yale University and is currently professor of political science and research professor in communications at the University of Illinois at Urbana-Champaign. Merritt has taught at Yale University and was a visiting professor in Berlin and South Africa. He has lectured at major universities and government institutions on five continents. He has also served as vice president of the International Studies Association and International Political Science Association. Merritt has published over 100 articles and 50 reviews in scholarly journals and books. His research focuses on international political communication and postwar German polities. He co-edited *Public Opinion in Occupied Germany: The OMGUS Surveys, 1945–1948* (Urbana: University of Illinois Press, 1970) and *Public Opinion in Semi-Sovereign Germany: The HICOG Surveys, 1949–1955* (Urbana: University of Illinois Press, 1980) and authored *Democracy Imposed: U.S. Occupation Policy and the German Public, 1945–49* (New Haven, Conn.: Yale University Press, 1995).

ELLIOT NEAMAN is a native of Vancouver, British Columbia, and studied sociology at the University of British Columbia (B.A. 1979) and history and philosophy at the Free University of Berlin (M.A. 1985). He received his Ph.D. in history at the University of California, Berkeley, in 1992. Since 1993 he has been assistant professor of history at the University of San Francisco. His area of research is European cultural pessimism in the twentieth century. He has authored numerous articles on German intellectual history, most notably in *New German Critique* and *Critical Review,* and has written at length on the situation in Germany since 1989 in *Tikkun* and *Dissent.* He is on the board of editors at *Tikkun.* Forthcoming is his book *A Dubious Past: Ernst Jünger and the Politics of Literature after Nazism* with the University of California Press.

WILFRIED SCHUBARTH is a native of East Germany. He is currently a research assistant in educational sciences at the Technical University of Dresden. Prior to that, he was employed at the German Youth Institute in Munich and at the Leipzig Central Institute for Youth Research. His fields of research concern youth and right-wing extremism, xenophobia, and violence in East Germany. He has coedited several volumes, including *Der antifaschistische Staat entläßt seine Kinder: Jugend und Rechtsextremismus in Ostdeutschland* (Cologne: PapyRossa, 1992), *Jugend Ost. Zwischen Hoffnung und Gewalt* (Opladen: Leske & Budrich, 1993), *Schule, Gewalt und Rechtsextremismus* (Opladen: Leske & Budrich, 1993), and *Gewalt an Schulen* (Opladen: Leske & Budrich, 1996).

HOLLI A. SEMETKO was born in Trenton, Michigan. She received a B.A. in political science and economics from Albion College in 1980. She then attended the London School of Economics and Political Science, where she received an M.S. in political sociology in 1981 and a Ph.D. in political science in 1987. She was awarded the Samuel H. Beer Prize for the best dissertation in British politics, 1987–1989. In the spring of 1994, Semetko was a research fellow at the Joan Shorenstein Center on the Press, Politics and Public Policy, Kennedy School of Government, Harvard University. She is professor and chair of audience and public opinion research, Faculty of Political and Social Sciences, University of Amsterdam, as well as associate professor of communications and political science at Syracuse University. Semetko is also chair of the International Political Science Association's Research Committee on Political Communication and serves on the editorial boards of *Political Communication* and *The Harvard International Journal of Press/Politics.* Her research interests include the influence of the media on election campaigns, on public opinion about foreign affairs in advanced industrial societies, and on politics in societies in transition. She has published numerous articles in journals and books. She coauthored *The Formation of Campaign Agendas: A Comparative Analysis of Party and Media Roles in Recent American and British Elections* (Hillsdale, N.J.: Lawrence Erlbaum, 1991) and *Germany's "Unity Election": Voters and the Media* (Cresskill, N.J.: Hampton, 1994). Currently, Semetko is writing a book comparing her studies of recent elections in Germany, Spain, Britain, and the United States.

FREDERICK D. WEIL completed his Ph.D. in sociology at Harvard University in 1981. He has received extensive grants and fellowships to study in Germany at the ZUMA (Center for Survey Research in Mannheim) and the University of Heidelberg. After serving as research associate and lecturer at Harvard, he was an assistant professor at the Department of Sociology at the University of Chicago from 1981 to 1987. He is currently associate professor of sociology at Louisiana State University. Weil has edited or written about twenty publications. His main area of concern is in the comparative realm, for example, public opinion in Western democracies on antisemitism, political culture, and issues of democratization. Weil has recently edited *Research on Democracy and Society,* volume 1, *Democratization in Eastern and Western Europe* (Greenwich, Conn.: JAI Press, 1993), and volume 2, *Political Culture and Political Structure: Theoretical and Empirical Studies* (Greenwich, Conn.: JAI Press, 1994).

JULIANE WETZEL is a native of Munich. She received her Ph.D. in history at Munich University in 1987. Between 1987 and 1991, she was employed at the Munich Institute for Contemporary History, and since that time she has worked as a researcher at the Center for Research on Antisemitism in Berlin. She has published works on Jewish persecution, Jewish postwar history in Germany, and right-wing extremism in an international perspective. Wetzel has published over twenty articles, as well as *Jüdisches Leben in München, 1945–1951* (Munich: Kommissionsverlag Uni-Druck, 1987), and she coedited *Meine Vertreibung aus Prag: Erinnerungen an den Prager Aufstand 1945 und seine Folgen* (Munich: Oldenbourg, 1991) and *Lebensmut im Wartesaal: Die jüdischen DPs im Nachkriegsdeutschland* (Frankfurt am Main: Fischer Taschenbuch Verlag, 1994).

ANTISEMITISM AND XENOPHOBIA IN GERMANY AFTER UNIFICATION

HERMANN KURTHEN, WERNER BERGMANN, AND RAINER ERB

Introduction

Postunification Challenges to German Democracy

The collapse of the Communist regime in the German Democratic Republic (GDR) and the opening of the Berlin Wall on November 9, 1989, were welcomed around the world. But the rapid unification of East and West Germany brought ambivalent reactions, especially from Germany's European neighbors. On the one hand there were fears of the political and economic dominance of a united Germany in the center of Europe. On the other hand recollections of the devastating consequences of German national unification movements of the past were rekindled. Voices were heard even within Germany that warned of the emergence of a new sense of nationalism that would slacken ties to Western democracies and promote a new chapter of German assertiveness—one that would seek, for example, to repress memories of World War II and the Holocaust. Such anxiety was directed in particular toward East Germans because very little was known of their political attitudes. Because they had lived under the conditions of a second dictatorship, they were expected to harbor antidemocratic, authoritarian, and intolerant views. In response to these fears, numerous empirical studies were begun in 1990 in the former GDR on voter profiles, issues regarding the political culture, and attitudes toward foreigners. One study focused on antisemitism (defined as an unfavorable and hostile attitude and evaluation of Jews); another concerned xenophobia (i.e., an unduly fearful, hostile, or contemptuous attitude toward foreigners). The surveys' findings were surprising to many because they revealed only slight differences in levels of antisemitism and xenophobia between East and West Germans. Though hostility toward foreigners was, indeed, somewhat stronger among East Germans, respondents in the East displayed far less willingness to vote for right-wing extremist parties, and they were much less antisemitic than westerners.

Attitudes toward foreigners, as other studies and opinion polls have shown, are less uniform than the term *foreigner* itself suggests. In fact, opinions about different groups vary to a great degree. Migrant laborers (formerly guest workers) from the Mediterranean periphery and Turkey, many of them in Germany for more than two decades, are more accepted and integrated than asylum seekers and refugees from civil wars. Foreigners from Africa, Asia, Eastern Europe, and Russia experience more social distance than persons from the European Union (EU), North America, or Australia. The immigration of ethnic German resettlers from Eastern Europe and the former Soviet Union posed the fewest integration problems because of the immigrants' willingness to fully blend into their "fatherland." Nevertheless, these resettlers have also contributed to feelings of immigration pressure by the indigenous population. German Jews and Sinti (Gypsies) born in Germany are frequently counted as aliens even though they are full-fledged citizens.

When a wave of violence against asylum seekers began in 1991 with pogrom-like actions in East Germany and media reports of neo-Nazi marches (Husbands 1991), the findings of the previously mentioned public opinion surveys were quickly forgotten and the events were regarded as symptoms of dangerous developments in Germany. Antiasylant riots such as the one in Rostock in August 1992, the arson attack on the "Jewish barrack" at the Sachsenhausen concentration camp memorial, the Rudolf Hess memorial march in Wunsiedel, the arson murders of Turkish families in Mölln and Solingen, and the attack on the Lübeck synagogue seemed to confirm warnings of the political consequences of German unification.

With Germany's lingering past in their minds, a broad national and international audience responded to these postunification developments in united Germany. Influential commentators raised their concerns in editorial columns. Newspapers were flooded with letters to the editor that questioned the reliability of German democracy after unification. Observers in Germany and abroad used the passive and indecisive actions of politicians and police to draw parallels to the end phase of the Weimar Republic in the early 1930s, shortly before the rise of Adolf Hitler and his National Socialist movement. In the eyes of these critics, attacks on immigrant minorities duplicated the persecution of the Jews 50 years previously. Some commentators even raised the prospect of a rising Fourth Reich (Mead 1990, Sana 1990) that would repeat the crimes and mistakes of the past. Jewish authors expressed their fears about "the escalation of terror in Germany" and asked, "Is it time to leave?" (Neaman 1993).

Other frequent questions were, Is the outburst of hatred and violence a specific German phenomenon or only the work of some young thugs? To what extent do these events after unification represent an attitude change in the German population as a whole? Are prejudice and hateful acts confined to a small group of young skinheads (mostly uneducated, unemployed, and lower-class youth) or to a handful of *ewig Gestrigen* (reactionaries attached to the past) on the far Right? Why is resentment also significantly higher among older, lower-class, and authoritarian segments of the population? Is it true that even within respected democratic parties, signs of subtle and openly aired resentment have emerged and that antisemitism and xenophobia are becoming culturally acceptable again? Can the right-wing intellectual scene that refers to revisionist history, *völkisch* cultural traditions, and nationalist identity rhetoric gain respectability among the cultural elite? Can the

Right exploit the ambivalent attitudes toward Germany's dealing with the past that are found among considerable percentages of respondents? These respondents do not deny the existence of camps and the Holocaust, but they reject responsibility for the acts of their parents and grandparents and express fears that remembrance is exploited by Jews. How widespread and threatening are these developments and do remedies exist to counter them?

The shrillness of some alarmist cries and suspicions has obscured a sober assessment of the origins, dynamics, and outcomes of the escalation of violence and resentment. This passionate concern, repeated over and over, must be confronted with the same intensive sociological and political research that was undertaken in the years following unification in order to distinguish fact from fiction. For example, it was found that by and large an adolescent subculture was—and still is—responsible for xenophobic violence (Willems et al. 1993). But public opinion surveys and the results of numerous elections at the national and regional levels since 1991 have proven that racist neo-Nazi and antisemitic propaganda and xenophobic fears exploited in election campaigns by far right-wing parties did not receive significant and persistent public support. The two largest right-wing parties, the German People's Union (Deutsche Volksunion [DVU]) in the northern states of West Germany and the "Republikaner" Party (REP) in the southern states, enjoyed notable election successes only for a short period (see Falter 1994; see also the chronology in the appendix).

Nevertheless, the undeniable fact of an upsurge of violence and resentment has been interpreted by many observers as a general shift to the Right and a rise in xenophobia and antisemitism. Among the extremist right-wing fringe, xenophobia and antisemitism are closely linked, although their ideological roots, motivations, and expressions differ. Extremists perceive immigrants as a threat to ethnocultural identity and racial homogeneity of the German collective; Jews are hated because they question the image of an untainted national past as witnesses and victims of the Holocaust. Foreigners correspond to the underclass stereotype of being lazy, dirty, deviant, and promiscuous. Jews are depicted as a small but powerful group that pushes its political and financial interests behind the scenes.

Among the general public, the strength of and linkage between both patterns of prejudice are less pronounced. Views about the 7 million immigrants are less restrained by taboos than are views about Jews. Foreigners are openly rejected because of social competition in the workplace, housing, education, welfare, and social security. In contrast, the public image of the comparatively small group of Jewish citizens (about 50,000) is nourished by remaining elements of traditional religious and economic antisemitism and resentments that are the result of reparations, collective guilt, and public commemorations of the Holocaust.

Closer analysis, documented in this volume, reveals the activation of prejudices and the emergence of a xenophobic protest movement in the aftermath of the 1989–90 upheavals. This movement exploited the advantages of a democratic society and the historically and politically unique opportunity of the unification crisis to use violence and resentment (Jaschke 1993, Bergmann and Erb 1994c). The goal was to achieve and reaffirm a supposedly ethnocultural homogeneity—as expressed in the slogan "Germany for the Germans" and the often-repeated mantra

"Germany is not an immigration society"—thereby clinging to a concept of nationhood and identity that was no longer a reality owing to the increasing pluralism and diversity that was transforming German society into a multiethnic and multicultural entity (Kurthen and Minkenberg 1995).

Several factors combined to facilitate the development and activation of a violent and primarily xenophobic subculture. First, media and politicians on the Right focused on, stimulated, and dramatized the large, unprecedented wave of immigration supposedly flooding Germany. The influx of hundreds of thousands of asylum seekers, ethnic Germans, and East Germans coming into West Germany and, later, the distribution of refugees in the East German new *Länder* according to a federal quota system were seen as creating social problems in employment, housing, integration, welfare, and education. Thus this influx became the focus of strong public attention. Second, politicians, the government, and administrations on all levels were embarrassed by the actions of extremists and wished this contentious issue would simply disappear. Therefore they initially ignored or downplayed the threat posed by the upsurge of extremist violence and popular resentment. Only after public polarization and rising broad protests, both from within and outside Germany, did they feel obligated to establish policies and take actions against extremism and its sources. Third, the political conflict between the governing conservative-liberal coalition and the social-democratic and Green Party opposition blocked for almost a year any effective government action in legislating political asylum, action that was central to quelling abuse of the very liberal West German asylum legislation and in addressing public discontent about inefficient policies. Fourth, institutions of social control in the eastern German states virtually collapsed. These factors all proved advantageous for violent groups, a situation that in turn triggered new actions in both parts of Germany.

The conditions for mobilization of eastern German youth by the right-wing political spectrum were more favorable than in the West, because counterforces in eastern Germany in the form of a left-wing youth culture had lost their legitimacy and the citizens' movement had suffered burnout from unproductive debates at "round-table" discussions during unification and thus were not an attractive alternative for young people seeking action. Xenophobic activities and violence were able to increase quickly in number and degree. A subculture of young men with prescribed modes of dress, music, and behavior emerged as part of an international right-wing-oriented skinhead youth scene whose members were inclined to act out their often unpolitically rooted hatred and prejudice against poorer and weaker groups, such as immigrant minorities, but also against gays, Left and anarchist "Autonome" youth gangs, the elderly, homeless, disabled, and East Europeans. The youth of the offenders, the type of actions they took, their use of weaponry (baseball bats and Molotov cocktails), and their provocative, utterly embarrassing to Germans, use of Nazi salutes and slogans support the fact that they represented not a broad social mass movement but a right-wing youth movement.

What suddenly became visible had been known to researchers of youth and right-wing extremism since the mid-1980s—a movement that attempts to ignore fundamental principles of democracy and human rights. The movement's supporters encompass unpolitical, alcoholic thugs and bigots but also rabble-rousers, whose belief system is based on nationalist, racist, or authoritarian and state-centered totalitarian ideologies. The extremist fringe ranges from nationalist intellectuals (the New Right) and a multitude of legal or illegal parties, groups, and factions to militant neo-Nazis and violent youth gangs, in particular antiforeigner skinheads.

Right-wing extremism, which primarily had existed until then in small and hidden organizations and informal groups, expanded its sphere by recruiting young members of the hooligan and skinhead subcultures. Tapping these groups served to significantly increase the number of violent crimes with right-wing extremist motives even before 1990.[1] The sensational success of the "Republikaner" Party at the polls in January 1989 brought the growth of right-wing extremism in West Germany into the public consciousness. Antiforeigner and antiasylum-seeker violence that exploded in 1991–92 corresponded to the rising numbers of immigrants and the confusing asylum debate (Kurthen 1995). Particularly in the former GDR, violence reached unparalleled heights in 1992. In contrast, violent antisemitic incidents started to rise but with a time lag and at a comparatively much lower level of intensity, incident structure, and different background of perpetrators. In 1990 the 38 counted antisemitic acts were composed of 9 involving arson or explosive acts, 4 involving bodily injury, and 25 involving property damage, such as graffiti. Of 39 cemetery desecrations, half were of proven right-wing origin (see Merkl 1994: 478, n. 37). Although xenophobically motivated violence declined after 1993 following bold public and political moves against extremists and reform of the asylum law that curbed immigration, antisemitic incidents were on the rise till 1994 and fell since then. According to police reports, antisemitic acts consisted mainly of slander, hate propaganda, public incitement, graffiti, and other nonviolent damage to property (see chapter 2). Overall, however, the wave of violence seems to have reached its apex and to be on the decline (see table 1.1).

Of particular interest is the sudden increase of violence in the East German states. Little was known about right-wing extremism in the former Communist state; since the early 1980s, the youth culture in the GDR was divided into a variety of subgroups, including right-wing extremist groups as well as peace and environmental groups and punks. Youth research in East Germany, concentrated in Leipzig, observed that since the late 1970s young people's identification with the socialist state declined and a small but growing minority of youth supported a fascist model of society. Following the spectacular and controversially debated attack by neo-Nazis in East Berlin on people attending a rock concert in the Church of Zion in 1987, it was no longer possible for GDR authorities to continue their practice of avoiding public and international reactions by disallowing any publicity of right-wing radical and antisemitic incidents. The increased violence that followed the political upheaval of 1989–90 was thus not solely a consequence of the collapse, transformation, and restructuring of a socialist society; rather, it had already formed its roots in the former GDR.

Serious East German social science research about this phenomenon only became possible after unification and the opening of archives (see chapter 6). For example, the former state party, the Socialist Unity Party (Sozialistische Einheitspartei Deutschlands [SED]); the state youth organization, Free German Youth

TABLE 1.1. Right-Wing Extremism, Immigration, and Violence against Foreigners and Jews in Germany, 1980–1994

	1980	1981	1982	1983	1984	1985	1986	1987	1988	1989	1990	1991	1992	1993	1994	1995
Asylum seekers (in thousands)	108	49.4	37.4	19.7	35.3	73.8	99.7	57.4	103	121	193	256	438	323	127	128
Membership of right-wing parties, extremist organizations, skinheads, etc. (in thousands)	19.8	20.3	19	20.3	22.1	22.1	33.1	25.2	28.3	35.9	32.2	39.8	41.9	41.5	36.6	30.1
Membership of "Republikaner" Party (in thousands)	—	—	—	—	—	2	4	5	8.5	25	20	20	23	23	20	16
Total Right incidents	1,643	1,824	2,510	1,347	1,154	1,754	1,281	1,447	1,607	1,853	1,848	3,884	7,684	10,561	7,952	7,896
Right antiforeigner incidents	—	—	—	—	—	—	—	—	—	516	389	2,720	4,746	5,580	3,491	2,468
Right antisemitic incidents	263	323	479	239	191	200	250	330	350	267	208	367	627	656	1,366	1,155
Right violent antiforeigner acts	60	45	43	32	36	50	117	98	103	146	152	1,255	2,000	1,609	860	540
Violent antisemitic acts with presumed Right background (mostly cemetery desecrations)	—	—	—	17	12	—	—	—	—	58	59	84	83	72	41	27
Right violent acts in West Germany	113	92	88	76	91	123	189	195	193	264	273	999	1,774	1,482	989	837[d]
Right violent acts in East Germany	—	—	—	—	—	—	—	—	—	—	367	493	865	750	500	
Total Right incidents per million[a]	27.4	30.4	41.8	22.4	19.2	29.2	21.3	24.1	26.8	30.9	23.1	47.9	94.9	130.3	96.9	96.3
Right antiforeigner incidents per million	—	—	—	—	—	—	—	—	—	8.6	4.9	33.6	58.6	68.9	42.6	30.1
Right antisemitic incidents per million[b]	4.3	5.3	7.9	3.9	3.2	3.3	4.1	5.5	5.8	4.5	2.6	4.6	7.8	8.1	16.6	14.1
Right violent acts per million in West Germany[c]	1.8	1.5	1.5	1.3	1.5	2.1	3.3	3.3	3.2	4.3	4.6	16.4	28.6	22.8	15.2	10.2[d]
Right violent acts per million in East Germany	—	—	—	—	—	—	—	—	—	—	2.1	29	54.1	46.9	31.3	

Sources: Bundesministerium des Innern 1993, 1994, 1995, and own calculations (population basis since 1990 United Germany).

[a]Comparable incident figures (total/per million) exist for France 1990 (722/12.77), for Austria 1992 (429/55.3), and for the United Kingdom 1991 (7,882/136.9). See Bundesminister des Innern 1993: 77 ff. New Jersey (U.S.A.), in comparison, reported over a thousand hate crimes, mostly directed against blacks, Muslims, and Asians (about 130 per million). Los Angeles County reported 672 incidents, 60% of them against gay men, blacks, and Jews in 1991 (about 75 per million; see Merkl 1994: 431).

[b]The German figures compare with antisemitic incidents (total/per million) in 1991: United States (1,879/7.6), Denmark (40/7.7), and Canada (251/11.4). In 1993 the figures for the United States were 1,867/7.5. For 1992, the ADF reported 1730 antisemitic acts (6.9 per million), including 758 acts of harassment, assaults and threats, and 927 acts of vandalism (arson, bombings, cemetery desecrations, etc.). Data from Anti-Defamation League 1993b and Merkl 1994: 431. The FBI reported 4,755 incidents in the United States in 1991 (18.9), among which over 72% involved ethnic or racial background. The U.S. data are not nationally representative because only one-fifth of localities reported to the FBI. See Merkl 1994: 474, footnote 11.

[c]The German figures compare with extreme right-wing violent incidents (total/per million) in other Western countries: Switzerland 1991 (77/11.6), France 1991 (91/1.6), Sweden 1992 (32/3.7), Hungary 1992 (91/8.6). Data from Bundesminister des Innern 1993: 77 ff.

[d]Includes data for East and West Germany.

(Freie Deutsche Jugend [FDJ]); and the Ministry for State Security (Stasi) had undertaken some investigations about the type and extent of neo-Nazi support and youth violence in the end phase of the GDR. Existing groups provided a core for the establishment of local right-wing groups after the opening of the border in the fall of 1989. West German neo-Nazis saw these groups as potential recruits. Contacts between eastern and western groups developed quickly. Within a short period of time, the right-wing subculture in East Germany had assumed the styles and behavior of its western counterparts. Simultaneously, ideology was transferred from West to East, and violence from East to West. West German neo-Nazis who visited their East German comrades could share not only their ideology but also their greater political experience and ways of dealing with journalists; on the other hand the violent actions in East Germany served as a model for West Germany.

The 1991–93 wave of mainly xenophobic violence, representing a protest movement built on historically unique conditions, was considerably dampened after 1993 by the responses of government and society catching up with events. The banning of organizations, harsher criminal prosecution, public protests, and the ability of the political system to take action in the area of unrestricted immigration through the asylum law contributed to restrict a further upsurge of attacks and prejudice. The failures of right-wing parties at postunification German polls and the stability of attitudes of Germans toward Jews, other ethnic minorities, and asylum seekers (confirmed by public surveys) support the idea that the violence represented a situational escalation rather than a reversal of the trend toward a more liberal, tolerant, and open-minded society. Stability of democratic orientations can be assumed because surveys showed a large majority of Germans expressing concern about the growth of right-wing extremism and antisemitic tendencies. Particularly after the Mölln anti-Turkish arson attack, the Germans clearly dissociated themselves from right-wing extremists and expressed overwhelming solidarity with the victims. In fact, this event proved crucial to delegitimizing the right-wing xenophobic violence and rhetoric of parties such as the REP. Consequently, there was less widespread fear within Germany that a Nazi Party could ever regain power. In April 1995, three-quarters of polled Germans felt such an event was impossible, in contrast to opinions outside Germany, where 44% of U.S.-Americans believed it to be possible.

The impact of these concerned and sometimes extremely critical foreign reactions on German domestic policy cannot be underestimated. Ever since U.S. High Commissioner John McCloy declared in 1949 that Germans' attitudes toward Jews represented the touchstone for German democracy, antisemitism has been interpreted not as an expression of a group conflict, but always as a destabilization of the democratic culture and as a lack of motivation in drawing the correct consequences from the Nazi past. For example, inciting racial hatred and denial of the Holocaust are punishable as a crime in Germany, whereas they are a legal part of freedom of speech in other countries. The social and political elite in Germany also respond very quickly and consistently to antisemitic incidents; this is not true to the same degree with respect to xenophobia.

In the history of the FRG, the years 1989 to 1993 represent the third postwar wave of right-wing extremism, which followed periods of right-wing-party success in the early 1950s by the Socialist Reich Party (Sozialistische Reichspartei [SRP]) and in the mid-to-late 1960s by the German National Democratic Party (National-demokratische Partei Deutschlands [NPD]). These waves all followed a typical course. The surprising early success of Right extremism was perceived as a threat to German democracy; reluctant political and social counterreactions ultimately always succeeded in marginalizing extremism. During its success phase, the right-wing camp was represented by a single party, which later splintered into numerous competing smaller parties and groups after experiencing failure.

Although the success and failure of right-wing extremist parties can be explained by so-called sociological crisis theories, this is not true for the increase in antisemitic incidents. The latter are related neither to economic cycles nor to electoral success of right-wing parties, which cautiously try to avoid appearing anti-Jewish because of the public ostracism imposed on antisemites and the fear of legal repercussions. Aside from often apolitical vandalism and adolescent incidents (e.g., swastika daubing) triggered by single, isolated events—then heavily exploited and imitated by antisemites—a series of politically initiated antisemitic incidents in the past were usually closely tied to phases of increased public discourse and public discontent regarding issues related to Germany's Nazi past (e.g., reparation payments and Holocaust remembrance issues). The current phase deviates from this pattern as antisemitic harrassment and crimes increased at the same time that a wave of xenophobic violence occurred in postunification Germany. One explanation points to the fact that leaders of right-wing and extremist parties in Germany have directed the disappointment of their fellow travelers over the electoral failures of their cause after 1993 at Jewish representatives, organizations, and influence. Anti-Jewish attacks were used to motivate the remaining supporters, whereas neo-Nazis, who have no voter constituency to consider, attack Jews as their ideologically defined enemy. Such a worldview does not consider Jews to be one minority among many. Whereas most of the immigrants and ethnic minorities in Germany are rejected predominantly as a social burden and for reasons of economic competition, Jews are regarded as powerful and anti-German "wire-pullers." Jews are accused of manipulating the German elite in order to prevent the development of a self-confident German nation out of vindictiveness for unique Nazi crimes, which are in their monstrosity denied by extremists. Jews supposedly direct immigration waves to Germany to weaken the national substance and force Germany to become integrated in broad supra- or international entities and coalitions that curb national sovereignty and self-determination. In their hatred of Jews, minorities, and immigrants; in their contempt for federal agencies and politics; and in their paranoid fears of worldwide conspiracies of a one-world government, and so on, extremists in Germany share similar beliefs as those in other countries, such as the United States. From the perspective of antisemitism research it is obvious that the traditional stereotype of the world Jewish conspiracy has been adapted to the situation following the collapse of communism. The United States is the only remaining world power, a government that—according to the traditional stereotype—is run by Jews on Wall Street, in Hollywood, in the media, and elsewhere. For the more dangerous segment of right-wing ideologues, antisemitism is also anti-Americanism.

In order to accurately assess antisemitic resentment and prejudice over the last four years, it is necessary to retrace its history in the FRG and in the former GDR, a history that goes back to 1945.

The horrified reactions to the extent of Nazi extermination politics with respect to the Jews, the discredited Nazi ideology after 1945, and the denazification and reeducation policies of the Allies all led, at least among the intelligentsia, to a rejection of hypernationalism and antisemitism. This was not true to the same extent for the population at large; it can thus be assumed that into the late 1960s there was a discrepancy between public opinion and individual attitudes.

Findings of U.S. Military Government surveys conducted in 1946 and an evaluation of newspaper reports indicated an almost unbroken persistence of antisemitism in the late 1940s and early 1950s (see Merritt and Merritt 1970, 1980). This was expressed with an openness and brutality that seems unfathomable today; it was primarily aimed directly against Jewish citizens. The public support for the acquittal of Nazi film director Veit Harlan, director of the notoriously antisemitic propaganda film *Jew Süss,* was indicative of the anti-Jewish sentiment of the early 1950s, as was the public opposition to restitution of Jewish property, to reparations policy in general, and to the surge of cemetery desecrations. The process of making antisemitism a public taboo and denying it a public forum had already begun, but it still had far to go at the end of the 1950s. The wave of antisemitic incidents in the winter of 1959–60, which triggered worldwide outrage, marked a turning point in German attitudes toward Jews because a broad base of the German population opposed this vandalist rioting. (Now we know from Stasi archives that some incidents had been provoked by Communist undercover actions from the East.) Concrete steps were taken and changes occurred in schools, academia, churches, and the law against inciting racial hatred. The process of bringing the issue into the German public arena and dealing with it was furthered by such closely followed events as the Adolf Eichmann trial in Jerusalem (1961), the Auschwitz trial in Frankfurt (1963–65), and the literary debate on the Holocaust—for example, such plays as *The Deputy* (1963) by Rolf Hochhuth, *The Investigation* (1965) by Peter Weiss, and *Jöel Brandt* (1965) by Heiner Kipphardt.

A 1974 antisemitism study showed an obvious decline in antisemitic stereotypes as compared with the 1940s and 1950s (Silbermann 1982). This shift can be traced largely to the younger generations who were socialized after 1945 (born 1935 and later), not to any significant changes in attitudes among the older generations. This trend has continued ever since; representative surveys conducted in the late 1980s determined that approximately 15% of the population was explicitly anti-Jewish; among those 50 years of age and younger, the figure was clearly less, at 6%. The success of coping with the past, spreading knowledge, and reeducating the public is also apparent in the fact that today only 17% percent in western Germany and 5% in eastern Germany regard the number of Holocaust victims to be exaggerated (Golub 1994), whereas a majority (in then West Germany) supported that statement in the early 1950s (63% considered the figure of 5 million murdered Jews to be either somewhat or greatly exaggerated in 1954 [see Emnid-Institut 1954]).

Also there is a common consent of anti-antisemitism among the German elite. The media, churches, unions, academia, political parties, educational institutions, and so on, have socially isolated and marginalized antisemitism among right-wing extremists. Topics of public controversy and survey results demonstrate that a shift has taken place in the motives for antisemitism in Germany—to a secondary anti-semitism. The issue is no longer mainly one of group conflict over scarce resources (jobs, housing, political influence), but the specifically German problem of having to live with a damaged national identity. The "antisemitic" affairs of the 1980s—the failed attempt of Ronald Reagan and Helmut Kohl at Bitburg in May 1985 to reconcile former enemies at the graves of soldiers (including some young Waffen-SS conscripts); the controversy surrounding the performance of Rainer Werner Fassbinder's play *Garbage, the City, and Death* in the fall of 1985; the so-called historians' debate about the historical legacy of the Holocaust in comparative perspective; and the stylistically insensitive commemorative speech by then Bundestag president Philipp Jenninger on the occasion of the fiftieth anniversary of the Reichskristallnacht (Night of Broken Glass) in 1988—all became scandals not because they were intentionally anti-Jewish but because they were seen as unacceptable, offensive attempts to deal with or to overcome the past. Regarding West Germany, one can speak of a tenacious process of dismantling prejudices and anti-Jewish attitudes to raise awareness and sensitivity, in short, a collective learning process that has been going on for decades and that has not yet been completed (see chapter 3). However, with regard to xenophobia, this process is much less advanced.

In the self-image of the GDR as well as in its research, antisemitism played a role only in the early history of its socialist society. It was regarded as eliminated once expropriation of the means of production from private ownership supposedly removed the foundation of prejudice and greed in society. In addition, it was believed that constantly propagated Communist antifascism in the media, education, public events, speeches, and so on and strict prohibition of any deviating and extremist opinion would prevent any reawakening of antisemitism or ethnic or national hatred. The task of observing public opinion and individuals was reserved for state security services. In the socialist GDR, social science survey research was rarely or at best superficially conducted. Attitudes toward Jews were never the subject of a survey. Antisemitic incidents were either not perceived as such, were regarded as the result of Western provocation, or were dealt with internally, quietly, and without publicity. The policy of the GDR leadership toward Jews and Jewish congregations can best be described by quoting the demand that Count Clermont-Tonnère had made in 1789: "Nothing for the Jews as a nation; everything for the Jews as people." Although persecuted Jews received state compensation as "victims of fascism" and Jewish congregations received financial support from the state, contact with Jews outside the country, above all with Israel and Jewish organizations in the United States, was prohibited (Maser 1995). Claims made by individuals or congregations for the return of "Aryanized" property were not recognized. Stalinist campaigns and trials against "Jewish conspirators" took place in 1952 in East Germany in much less prominent and oppressive form. At that time many Jews, especially those in the ruling classes, hastily left the country (Herf 1994). East Germany participated in the anti-Israel politics of the Eastern bloc by supporting Israel's enemies and Arab terrorists. News coverage of events in the Middle East was not only done exclusively from the perspective of the Arab states but also included anti-Zionist rhetoric carrying traditional antisemitic stereotypes. Foreign policy interests led the GDR leadership to allow Jewish communities to intensify their foreign contacts starting in 1986–87, especially to Jewish organizations in the United States. These contacts were supposed to serve the function of opening the door for Erich Honecker, SED leader and head-of-state, who wanted to cap his political career with a state visit to the United States. At meetings with representatives of international Jewish organizations in 1988 in East Berlin, the GDR leadership mentioned for the first time the possibility of paying reparations. In view of this historical burden of guilt, the first freely elected parliament in East Germany (Volkskammer) unanimously approved the following declaration in April 1990: "We ask the forgiveness of Jews throughout the world. We ask forgiveness of the people of Israel for the hypocrisy and hostility of official GDR policy toward the state of Israel and for the continued persecution and humiliation of Jewish citizens in our country after 1945."

A look at the development of antisemitism over the past 50 years of West and East German history is necessary to gain a firm basis from which to evaluate the present. The sometimes sensational and moralistic focus of the mass media and event-oriented scientific research on current developments, especially when they concern collective violence with deadly consequences, runs the risk of misinterpreting short-term developments as long-term trends (Dudek 1994: 292). When, for example, political one-sidedness of the entire justice system is concluded from a poor, extremist trial decision that is worthy of criticism or when revisionist views of a prominent historian are regarded as a new majority opinion of German historiography, then isolated events are generalized and wrongly interpreted as an indication of attitudinal changes in the population at large and among the political elite. News coverage refers by definition to current events and appraises them from the present perspective. But this runs the danger of ignoring historical origins, hidden social processes, and structural conditions. It is the task of research to place current developments within a larger time frame and chain of causes, and thus conduct multilevel analyses of antisemitism and racism that take into account the complexity of the phenomena.

The attention given to postunification events by concerned writers, journalists, politicians, and academics in Germany and abroad indicates the existence of a strong interest in events in united Germany. At the same time, however, it also reveals a lack of detailed knowledge and thorough analysis of the extent and imminent danger of antisemitism and xenophobia in Germany, particularly among the English-speaking public.

A review of English-language literature on the subject confirms that there are currently few publications that explain antisemitism and xenophobia in postunification Germany in a comparatively detailed and complete manner. Nearly all existing publications have excluded East Germany and are outdated in their coverage of most recent events, surveys, and research findings in Germany. Though as a reaction to the dramatic changes in Central and Eastern Europe after 1989 several international conferences have attempted to get a grasp on the consequences of these revolutions few have covered antisemitism and xenophobia. Only one conference in the fall of 1992 on antisemitism in Europe covered developments in Germany (see *Patterns of Prejudice* 1993). Scholarly literature and research has focused in the past on two types of analysis: international comparative research and research concentrating on Germany. Bauer and Rosensaft 1988 and Gilman and Katz 1991 are examples of research in comparative perspective. However, they do not specifically discuss the relationship between antisemitism and xenophobia but address the issue of antisemitism more from historical, cultural, religious, and literary viewpoints. Michael Curtis and particularly Helen Fein have approached the sociological and political contexts of modern antisemitism, but some of their findings need to be updated and tested again. Thus, in this volume we shall refer to some of the earlier findings and theories that have been discussed by Curtis (1986) and Fein (1987) and apply them to Germany based on the most recent polls and studies. With regard to research on Germany, Benz (1992a, 1993a, 1995a, 1995b), Rabinbach and Zipes (1986), Bergmann and Erb (1990), and Bergmann, Erb and Lichtblau (1995) recently presented volumes that deal with the history of antisemitism in postwar Germany. Stern (1991) has concentrated on a history of the cultural and political dimension of antisemitism and philosemitism in postwar West Germany only. Relatively few investigators—like Silbermann (1982), Silbermann and Sallen (1992), Silbermann and Schweps (1986), Bergmann and Erb (1990, and 1991a), Butterwegge and Isola (1990), Butterwegge and Jäger (1992), Farin and Seidel-Pielen (1992), Merkl and Weinberg (1993), Björgo and Witte (1993), Kowalsky and Schroeder (1994)—have specifically dealt with questions of persisting postunification German xenophobia and antisemitism based on the most recent empirical studies. Before 1989 most data and analyses were limited to West Germany. It was only after the fall of the Berlin Wall that empirical surveys were able to cover attitudes of East Germans toward Jews and the Holocaust (Jodice 1991, Wittenberg, Prosch, and Abraham 1991, 1995, Emnid-Institut 1992, Golub 1994, Brusten 1995). Studies of GDR German youth also included questions about antisemitism (Förster et al. 1993). Some surveys deliberately compared opinions in East and West Germany, thus allowing researchers to test with sufficient accuracy hypotheses about the extent and links of xenophobia and antisemitism after unification.

In reviewing the existing literature and our own research about the origins and dynamics of, and remedies for, postunification antisemitism and xenophobia, at least three areas of analysis influenced our selection of authors and chapters and the structure of this book.

1. The overall demographic distribution of behavior, attitudes, and voting patterns within the East and West German population.
2. Antisemitic and xenophobic milieus, movements, groups, and organizations;

ideology and discriminatory actions aimed at specific victim groups; the violence of such groups (against people, property, community facilities, and symbols); and, finally, the demographic profiles of the offenders.
3. The institutional, political, and societal background of postunification events, such as, for example, the perceptions and responses of decision-making bodies in government, administration, political parties, and the judiciary, as well as the substantial public reaction, expressed, for example, at public events, anti-Nazi counterdemonstrations, and vigils by hundreds, thousands, and hundreds of thousands of Germans in the East and the West. In addition, one has to take into account the opinions and actions of targets of resentment and violence, that is, of minorities and their communities and representatives. Finally, we have to consider the media's news coverage, including foreign public opinion and media reports.

Developments in each one of these areas should not be projected onto another, as each has its own structure and logical development. Aggressive, openly displayed antisemitism by certain fringe groups might very well increase considerably at a particular moment in time without necessarily signifying corresponding changes in the political system, the elite, or public opinion (Epstein 1993). Findings can vary depending on what methodological and theoretical framework and what comparative standards are chosen for the analysis.

In order to offer a complex picture of the situation since German unification and to document the profound changes taking place in Germany, we present recent articles based on qualitative and quantitative data that deal with central aspects of the aforementioned areas. The intention is to collect genuine historical, sociological, and political science research; to make comparisons; to give answers to the questions raised earlier; and to draw conclusions about issues of strong public interest. The sources on which these contributions are based include official statistics and polls; interviews with experts; media reports; analyses of secondary sources, documents, and literature; and ethnographic materials. We combined German and American perspectives using different sociological, political, and historical approaches and methods. The inclusion of different views and disciplines provides more objective and richer insights into recent research in and about Germany. It also gives readers a chance to compare findings and make up their own minds about the state of affairs. In any case, the contributors to this volume demonstrate that the issue at hand is more complex than some media reports and academic observers have suggested. Inappropriate, simplified, and overgeneralized analysis can lead to the wrong application of remedies and the failure of well-intended measures of prevention. In the worst case it is counterproductive and promotes what it pretends to avoid.

This volume is unique, even within the German-speaking world. It includes not only most recent survey and case study research about antisemitism and xenophobia (chapters 2–5) but also validated assessments of specific social forces, movements, groups, and organizations that propagate hate and prejudice (chapters 6–9). Responses from Germany, from the German Jewish community, and from the media abroad are included, as well as an analysis of the reactions and remedies to effectively overcome antisemitism and xenophobia (chapters 10–13). The volume ends with an appendix that contains an updated and detailed account of antisemitic incidents in united Germany between 1989–90 and 1994.

With the objective of assessing the origins of, the extent of, and the remedies to antisemitism and xenophobia in postunification Germany, the contributions are organized into three parts corresponding to the analytical distinctions between research areas described previously.

Part I explores empirical facts and findings regarding the origins and the extent of antisemitism and xenophobia in East and West Germany. Does the outburst of antisemitic and xenophobic violence after unification indicate persistent changes in the attitudes of Germans as a whole (chapter 2)? How are current attitudes toward Jews and minorities linked with the perception of the past? Can increased knowledge about and attitudes toward the Holocaust curb antisemitism (chapter 3)? How can the current levels of knowledge of, interest in, and emotional attachment to the Holocaust and remembrance (e.g., among student populations in East and West Germany) be compared (chap. 4)? Are extremist antidemocratic attitudes interrelated with antisemitism and hostility toward foreigners? Is German democracy stable enough to cope with these new threats (chapter 5)?

Part II examines the roots and motives of groups and organizations that propagate antisemitism and xenophobia. This part focuses on sources of prejudice and violence. Why have extreme right-wing rhetoric and symbols become so attractive to marginalized youth subcultures (chapter 6)? How strongly are antisemitism and xenophobia embedded in the programs and politics of extremist and right-wing parties, groups, and organizations (chapter 7)? Has unification sped up an increasing legitimization of reactionary elements of German political culture that relate to the Third Reich and the Holocaust, leading to the infiltration of a New Right discourse into the young intelligentsia of Germany in both East and West (chapter 8)? What are the main tools and arguments of revisionist propaganda, and how much of an inroad have they made into the public (chapter 9)?

Part III investigates national and international perceptions of, and reactions to, antisemitism and xenophobia. This part explores reactions and remedies to postunification events. How did German society respond to rising violence and prejudice against Jews and foreigners (chapter 10)? Chapter 11 deals with the impact of unification on the largest Jewish community in united Berlin. What challenges confronted Jewish unity and how did the community respond? The next chapter gives a view from outside. How has the image of Germany changed in the U.S. media in light of postunification antisemitism and xenophobia (chapter 12)? The part ends with concluding remarks and outlines further research topics and questions (chapter 13), followed by a chronology of antisemitic and extreme right-wing events in Germany after unification in 1989/90 (appendix).

NOTE

Parts of this chapter were translated from German by Allison Brown and Hermann Kurthen.

1. The fact that German police sources label incidents as having a "right-wing" background is not in every case evidence of neo-Nazi political motives or proof that "right-wing" incidents were planned and organized by such political groups. According to German police reports in 1992, the right-wing violent subculture represented 1,600 neo-Nazis and about 5,000 skinheads (the latter not including anti-racist Sharpskins and left-wing Redskins). The statistics do not report how many incidents and violent acts had spontaneous and local character involving turf fights, sexual jealousies, xenophobia, roving mobs, soccer hooligans, youth gangs, drunks, and unaffiliated individuals. Evidence from research and court trials suggest that a large portion of all reported incidents had a rather apolitical origin. During the height of violent anti-foreigner incidents in the first half of 1992, about 9% of 1,443 reported incidents were arson, 12% were attacks on person, and the rest were other offenses such as robbery, graffiti, and other property damage and threats, insults, and other forms of harassment. In 1992 8% of all violent right-wing attacks were directed against the police or other public agencies (see Merkl 1994: 445–46, 478, n. 39). The poor education, young age, and lower-class background of offenders point at weak social control in dysfunctional families and communities. Kids from these milieus tend to join youth subcultures and use shock, provocation, and violence as means of self-expression and identification. Labeling them without differentiation as incorrigible Nazi hoodlums plays into the hands of political extremists waiting to recruit them for their own purposes (see Merkl 1994: 452 ff.).

FACTS AND FINDINGS ABOUT ANTISEMITISM AND XENOPHOBIA IN UNITED GERMANY

WERNER BERGMANN

Antisemitism and Xenophobia in Germany since Unification

Various phenomena may be analyzed in order to ascertain the extent and sig-nificance of antisemitism in society: public opinion; the attitude of the intel-lectual elite; treatment by the media; antiminority activities; government treatment of Jews and antisemites in politics, the courts, and education; the ideology and activities of right-wing organizations, and the like. The results vary according to the chosen subject of the analysis. I shall concentrate on public attitudes toward Jews and foreigners on the one hand and on open, sometimes violent acts of antisemitism and xenophobia on the other; I shall also examine the connections between the two. Antisemitism and xenophobia will be treated separately. Al-though they correlate highly with each other, I believe they vary in terms of mo-tives, prevalence, and public acceptance.

    1. Motives: Rejection of Jews in Germany today must be viewed within the context of attitudes toward National Socialism and German history. Guilt, respon-sibility, and reparations are the major issues involved, in contrast to questions of entitlement to civil rights and welfare services or feelings of cultural isolation, which influence attitudes toward migrant laborers in Germany. Right-wing extrem-ism always couples antisemitism with xenophobia, though each serves a different function: Jews are challenged as a politically influential group that is suspected of being behind state and media attacks on the right-wing. Foreigners *(Ausländer)*, on the other hand, are considered competitors, providing a present and concrete embodiment of the "enemy." The prejudices against middle-class, socially inte-grated Jews as a group tend to involve accusations that they have too much influ-ence and financial strength. Migrant laborers and asylum seekers—who occupy the lowest rung on the labor market ladder—are subjected to the same prejudices that make up the negative image of the working class (lazy, loud, having a lot of children, sexually promiscuous).

2. Prevalence: Antisemitism and xenophobia are not equally prevalent in society. Although it is true that most antisemites are xenophobic, forming an ideologically right-wing hard core, opposition to certain immigrant groups or immigration · in general often does not include rejection of Jews, especially among younger generations (see Bergmann 1992).[1] Group resentment based on actual or feared social competition and conflict is less relevant when it comes to attitudes toward Jews and Blacks. Prejudice against these traditional scapegoats is based rather on ethnocultural distance, traditional prejudice, and racism; but resentment is less prevalent among the public than is xenophobic hostility toward Turks and Arabs. The relatively low level of social distance from Jews can be explained by the lack of social conflicts with this relatively small and invisible group. But more important is the impact of decades of an emerging public taboo against antisemitism, postwar education about the history of antisemitism, and empathy with the fate of persecuted Jews. Such a public awareness does not exist for other minority groups. Thus, Jews have lost their traditional scapegoat role, whereas resentment of other groups is more tolerated today. This analysis raises the question, Are xenophobic persons not necessarily antisemitic? However, both strong antisemites and extremists (i.e., persons with deep ideologically rooted prejudices) tend to score high in their rejection of foreigners and non-Germans, regardless of ethnic, cultural, or other differences.

Among East Germans in particular, there is a considerable discrepancy between attitudes toward Jews and those toward foreign nationals. East Germans are clearly less antisemitic than West Germans, but more xenophobic.

3. Acceptance: Tolerance of antisemitic or xenophobic opinions and incidents varies considerably in politics, the media, and public opinion. Whereas antisemitic statements are considered taboo and quickly lead to public censure, this is not equally true with respect to xenophobia.

Antisemitism in Public Opinion

West Germany

The relationship between Germans and Jews, which received little attention in the 1970s, returned to the public eye in the form of various scandals in the mid-80s. The Bitburg affair, the Fassbinder and Jenninger scandals, insults leveled at Jews by Christian Democratic Party (Christlich-Demokratische Union [CDU]) officials, and the historians' debate *(Historikerstreit)* about the uniqueness of the Holocaust in history led to heated public debates. For the first time since the early 1970s, surveys on antisemitism in the population were carried out in 1986, 1987, and 1989 (Institut für Demoskopie 1986, 1987, Bergmann and Erb 1991a, Emnid-Institut 1989), and they yielded the same results: about 15% of the West German population was strongly antisemitic, with great discrepancies between generations, reflecting their different political socialization. This is confirmed by three important surveys in the late 1980s (Institut für Demoskopie 1986, 1987, Emnid-Institut 1989), despite their use of different questions, rating methods, and category hierarchies.[2]

In comparison to research findings from the 1950s, one could speak of a slow but steady decline in anti-Jewish attitudes in West Germany. A second important factor was education level; whereas 20% of those with less schooling were antisemitic, the figure was only 5% for those with a college education. As the number of those old enough to have been actively involved in the Nazi period continues to decrease, the attitudes of subsequent generations are also becoming more and more similar, so that the dominant influence of age is disappearing. In particular, differences between the 18 to 29-year-old group and the 30 to 50-year-old group are negligible (see table 2.1).

The GDR and the East German States

No studies on antisemitism exist for East Germany prior to 1990, so we do not know which periods brought a decline in antisemitic prejudice or the factors that influenced the changes. Some empirical findings from the time before the Berlin Wall fell, however, verify the existence of right-wing extremism among adolescents in the socialist GDR (German Democratic Republic). In 1988, the Central Institute for Research on Youth in Leipzig found that about 10–15% of all young people sympathized with Nazi ideology (H. Müller 1991, Friedrich and Schubarth 1991). In 1988 and 1989, there were approximately thirty cases annually, involving sixty offenders, in which charges were pressed for neo-Nazi activities.

Two surveys were conducted at the end of 1990, both of which confirmed that East Germans were less antisemitic in all areas of prejudice than West Germans (Wittenberg, Prosch, and Abraham 1991, Jodice 1991). A comparative study conducted in late 1991 determined a West-East ratio of 16% versus 4% of Germans with antisemitic attitudes (*Der Spiegel* 1992: 70 f.).[3] Additional studies from 1994 have confirmed these findings. The data also show that these differences generally apply to attitudes toward World War II, Nazism, and the Holocaust (Forsa 1994, Golub 1994). Since 1945 such viewpoints have been closely tied in both parts of Germany to the attitudes toward Jews (see also chaper 3). Respondents in East Germany generally demonstrated more specific knowledge of National Socialism, rejecting it more decisively and tending less toward rationalization. These data are confirmed by election results that show only minimal support for ultraright-wing parties in the new federal states (the best election result for the "Republikaner" Party in 1994 was 1.4% in the state assembly elections of Saxony-Anhalt). The

TABLE 2.1. Antisemitic Attitudes by Age Group, 1949–1991

Age Group	1949	Age Group	1991 West Germany	1991 East Germany
18–30	26%	16–24	12%	6%
30–50	23%	25–35	13%	3%
50–65	25%	36–49	14%	4%
		50–64	22%	3%
65+	17%	65+	23%	6%
N	2,000	N	1,875	947

Sources: IfD 1949, Emnid-Institut 1992.

only attitudinal dimension in which East Germans showed a negative deviation from West Germans was in their attitudes toward Israelis and Zionism, thus showing the negative impact of decades of anti-Israeli propaganda and policies by the GDR leadership. Although Germans in the East rejected Jews less often than those in the West did (8% vs. 13%), they more often "did not want to have much to do with Israelis" (16% vs. 11%). In 1990, young people in the eastern German city of Jena clearly showed even stronger rejection (26%) than the adults did (Wittenberg, Prosch, and Abraham 1995).[4] This result, of course, begs the question why antisemitic attitudes have declined more sharply in the former GDR than in the Federal Republic of Germany, where, after all, the goal of postwar re-education was actively pursued. There are three possible explanations for this.

1. The presence of a dogmatic ideology centered around antifascism was able to eradicate dissenting prejudices and worldviews more thoroughly than the open, wide range of ideologies that coexist in a pluralistic society, even if that society generally rejects and opposes extreme right-wing ideas. In the GDR, fundamental reference points were antifascism, resistance, and the idea of socialism. The Jews and the Holocaust do not—and never did—play anything similar to the role they did in the FRG. The generation that built up East Germany in the 1950s and 1960s at least could be expected to faithfully support a humanist-oriented form of antifascism and thus reject antisemitism.

2. State doctrine in the GDR treated antisemitism and neofascism as the problems of capitalist countries, thus exonerating its population of any historical responsibility for Nazi fascism. East Germans accepted this; in the words of writer Stephan Hermlin, they lived in the belief that "half the German population were antifascists during the Nazi period." This freedom from guilt appears to explain why East Germans are less antisemitic and show less rejection of memories of the Holocaust. They feel free of the need to deal with questions concerning their share of guilt and responsibility, issues which, I believe, represent an essential motive for post-Holocaust antisemitism among West Germans today.[5]

3. It is possible that the psychoanalytic model, which theorizes that something can be overcome by being worked through, does not apply to societies as a whole. Antifascism as proclaimed by the East German state made it impossible to constantly reiterate antisemitic ideas. Consequently, the handing down of anti-Jewish stereotypes was effectively blocked. In West Germany, on the other hand, the very intense preoccupation with Nazism in schools and public life meant that, like it or not, prejudices about Jews were also communicated. This is particularly apparent with regard to religious anti-Judaism, which virtually disappeared in the atheistic GDR.

As in the case of West Germany, the main factors that influenced the different manifestations of antisemitism in the GDR are level of education and generational cohort (i.e., age group). Because of the very different educational systems and occupational structures in the Federal Republic and East Germany, it is difficult to compare the effects of education and employment history on the adoption of antisemitic attitudes. Individuals in the GDR were not as clearly separated by education, income, employment, and status differences as were individuals in the FRG, so that it might be expected that attitude differences among East Germans would be less clearly related to level of education or employment. The empirical findings confirm this assumption. As in western Germany, formal schooling in eastern Germany has a positive effect, that is, those with a college education very rarely express negative attitudes toward Jews, whereas the corresponding figure for those having completed only the regular 10 years of schooling (polytechnic high school) is above the population average. However, the distinctions between different education and employment groups are less than in western Germany.

Political orientation, measured according to plans to vote for a particular party or a self-evaluation on a 10-point Left-Right scale, showed a significant correlation to attitudes toward Jews. As expected, antisemitism is widespread among those with extreme right-wing views, though left-wing extremists, in keeping with their anti-Zionism and critical attitudes on religion, also rejected Jews more often than those located at the center of the political spectrum. The same pattern applies for both eastern and western Germany. An evaluation of voter intentions showed that right-wing extremists consider the "Republikaner" to be "their" party; two-fifths of the voters in both East and West Germany are antisemitic (see table 2.2). More than half of all eastern "Republikaner" voters are under 35 years of age, whereas three-quarters of western "Republikaner" Party voters are over 35 years of age. Otherwise, the distribution of antisemitism among voters of other parties corresponds to the expected Right-Left pattern in both East and West.

The age distribution of antisemites in 1991 in East Germany was different from that in West Germany (see table 2.1); as in the latter, the older age groups were more antisemitic than the middle cohorts of 35- to 64-year-olds. In the youngest age group—socialized and educated primarily in the 1980s, a time when young people showed growing skepticism toward and rejection of the official myths and propaganda of the GDR (Friedrich and Griese 1991)—an increase in antisemitic prejudice can be observed between 1990 and 1992.

Differences in political attitudes between age cohorts have also been observed in West Germany. In the 1960s, surveys already showed that generations socialized after 1945 display less antisemitism. Accordingly, significant differences in the early 1990s were found to exist only between respondents above and below age 50. Differences within the 16–49 age group are negigible. Also, with time proceed-

TABLE 2.2. Antisemitic Respondents within the Electorate in East and West Germany in 1991 according to Party Preference (N = 2,822)

Party Preference	West Germany		East Germany	
	Antisemites	Nonantisemites	Antisemites	Nonantisemites
REP	38%	62%	40%	60%
CDU/CSU	19	81	5	95
FDP	18	82	4	96
SPD	13	87	3	97
B90/Green	10	90	0	100
PDS	5	95	0	100

Source: Spiegel 1992.

ing, the cohort differences by and large become smaller and insignificant. For example, in the 1991 Emnid-Institut survey (1992), antisemitic attitudes by age were distributed as follows: ages 16–24 (12%), 25–35 (13%), 36–49 (14%), 50–64 (22%), and 65 and over (23%).

Compared with West Germany, age effects in East Germany—though existing—are almost ignorable (Bergmann and Erb, 1995). In 1991, antisemitism was exhibited among the 16–24 age group by 6% of all respondents, among the 25–64 age groups by 3%, and among respondents older than age 65 by 6%. East-West differences have to be explained by political socialization. In the GDR, subtle or open antisemitism and Nazi propaganda were publicly banned from speeches, newspapers, books, brochures, movies, songs, and so on and were replaced by socialist anti-fascist campaigns. In contrast, postwar education in the FRG was based on a somewhat ambiguous anti-Communist and antitotalitarian consensus that allowed for the continuing existence of prewar ideology and resentment.

As our data show—confirmed by the first public opinion survey about prejudice in East Germany in 1990—young adults and adolescents in East Germany proved more susceptible to xenophobic and antisemitic slogans (Wittenberg, Prosch, and Abraham 1991) than the middle-aged cohorts. Studies of youths 14 years of age and older show strong political polarization into right- and left-wing camps in the new states, whereas political ties to the democratic center parties are weak. Antisemitic statements meet with approval from 12% among 14- to 25-year-olds in Saxony and Saxony-Anhalt but were more often rejected (71%) than other xenophobic items (29% approval; 45% rejection). A negative trend is evident between different age groups, however, as the 14- to 18-year-olds displayed the greatest degree of antisemitism: 14% agree with the old anti-Jewish slogan, "The Jews are Germany's misfortune" ("Die Juden sind Deutschlands Unglück"), which is far more than among those in the 20 to 25 age group (1%). Youth researchers in Leipzig, who conducted a study on young people in 1990, repeated their study in 1992 and determined that right-wing extremist orientations, xenophobia, and the inclination toward violence had increased among German adolescents in the East during those two years (Förster et al. 1993).[6] In a youth survey conducted in 1993 in Brandenburg, as many as 25% of the students at comprehensive high schools agreed strongly or somewhat with the above-mentioned anti-Jewish slogan (see Sturzbecher, Dietrich, and Kohlstruck 1994). This Brandenburg youth study also used the statement, from the 1991 Spiegel-sponsored Emnid-Institut survey, "Jews are partly to blame for the persecution and hate against them" ("Die Juden sind mitschuldig, wenn sie gehaßt und verfolgt werden"). In Brandenburg 25% of 17- to 18-year-old respondents and 32% aged 15 to 16 agreed with this statement, whereas in the representative Emnid poll on a 6–point Likert scale only 10% of East German respondents aged 18 to 24 expressed strong or some support for that opinion (Emnid-Institut 1992; table 2.5).

Gender and education shape this anti-Jewish potential: of male apprentices (persons enrolled in a training or apprenticeship program for a blue-collar occupation), 33% reject Jews (female apprentices: 10%), compared to 16% of male high school students (4% of the girls) in the eleventh and twelveth grades. The rejection of foreigners by German youth in the former GDR also increased sharply (by about

10%) between 1990 and 1992. Young people in eastern Germany also lead the statistics in Europe with regard to xenophobia.

The situation is different in western Germany. In a survey conducted in December 1992, the Infas-Institut (Institut für angewandte Sozialforschung) presented young people in Schleswig-Holstein with a similar statement, "The Jews are a people who bring nothing but disaster" ("Die Juden sind ein Volk, von dem nur Unheil ausgeht"). Compared to eastern German youth, in the west only 5.1% of respondents aged 14 to 18 and 4.2% aged 19 to 24 expressed support for this statement.

Public Opinion Trends since Unification

The 1990 public opinion surveys contradicted the pessimism of an assertive united Germany moving "back to the future" (Mearsheimer 1990) or the phantom of a "Fourth Reich" promoting noisy nationalism, antisemitism, and racism. But optimism was soon questioned by the wave of xenophobic violence, neo-Nazi demonstrations, and antisemitic attacks that happened in particular between 1991 and 1993. However, the often repeated speculation that the escalating wave of violence corresponded with a dramatic increase of resentment in public opinion cannot be corroborated. First, sociopsychological findings about the relationship between attitudes and actions confirm that manifest behavior is greatly dependent on situational circumstances (see Willems et al. 1993). Second, violent actions of the extremist fringe did not reflect attitudes of the majority. Rather, arson and brutal assaults led to an isolation of the violent activists and their propaganda of hate and contempt.

A series of public opinion surveys validated that attitudes in Germany remained stable. The German public has shown increasing concern about the growth of antisemitism since 1990. Jodice found that in 1990 14% of all Germans perceived antisemitism a "very serious problem" (Jodice 1991: table 10a). This percentage grew to 26% in 1994 (Golub 1994: table 5). Both surveys also revealed stability or a slight decline in antisemitism, according to the responses to several questions that are believed to be indicative of antisemitism (see tables 2.3–2.5).

According to findings of these youth studies and public surveys, antisemitism has not gained significance in the population at large but has, indeed, become more widespread and radicalized within a particular subpopulation: ultraright-wing

TABLE 2.3. "Now, as in the past, Jews exert too much influence on world events"

Sample	Year	Agree Strongly	Agree Somewhat	Disagree Somewhat	Disagree Strongly	Don't Know
West Germany	1990	12%	32%	27%	11%	18%
	1994	11	23	32	14	19
East Germany	1990	3	17	38	19	24
	1994	3	16	33	19	29

Sources: Jodice 1991, Golub 1994.

TABLE 2.4. "Jews are exploiting the National Socialist Holocaust for their own purposes"

Sample	Year	Agree Strongly	Agree Somewhat	Disagree Somewhat	Disagree Strongly	Don't Know
West Germany	1990	13%	32%	25%	11%	19%
	1994	18	26	25	13	18
East Germany	1990	4	16	34	21	25
	1994	4	15	36	20	24

Sources: Jodice 1991, Golub 1994.

adolescents—particularly less educated, right-wing-oriented male manual laborers. This finding is corroborated by media reports of antisemitic actions, as well as criminological evaluations of offenses. The particular susceptibility of youth in eastern Germany is rooted above all in the far-reaching and crisis-ridden transformation processes going on in the new states, which required radical reorientation (see chapter 6). In addition, the antisemitic wave can be explained by dramatic societal transformations at a time when public debate on issues of political asylum and immigration emerged, thus offering easy scapegoats.

Xenophobia in Public Opinion

Since the early 1980s, West German governments have hovered uneasily between limitation and integration—between rejecting asylum seekers and immigrants on the one hand and granting "foreigners" equal treatment in society on the other hand. West German policies changed dramatically from 1978 to 1982. This was accompanied by a polarization in public opinion that resulted in what could be referred to as "a shift from a receptive society to a rejectionist one" (Bade 1992); thus it became a society that started to articulate the presence of "foreigners" as a "problem." In 1980, the number of asylum seekers (107,818) rose for the first time. Although this number sank by more than half in the following year, it was sufficient to unleash a debate on asylum rights in 1980–81, which took on distorted proportions through gross exaggeration of the figures. The subject of asylum was then thrown into the same pot as the problems of labor migrants living in Germany, and the resulting soup was stirred (Thränhardt 1993). Starting in 1986,

TABLE 2.5. "Recently someone said: 'Today in the aftermath of German unification, we should not talk so much about the Holocaust, but should rather draw a line through the past'"

Sample	Year	Correct	Incorrect	Don't Know/No Answer
West Germany	1990	65%	27%	8%
	1994	56	29	15
East Germany	1990	44	47	9
	1994	36	54	10

Sources: Jodice 1991, Golub 1994.

the asylum and foreigner debates surged once again, in the face of the increasing number of asylum seekers—rising to over 100,000—and also through the "Republikaner" Party's antiforeigner election campaigns. It is important to recognize that this debate was structured and dramatized by distinctions made between those who were considered "genuine" political refugees, which supposedly represented a small minority of the total applicants for asylum, and the masses of "pseudo" asylum seekers. Parallel to these developments, right-wing parties ("Republikaner," Nationaldemokratische Partei Deutschlands [NPD], and Deutsche Volksunion [DVU]) gained popularity.

The socialist GDR officially welcomed foreigners and claimed that the population expressed no hostilities toward foreign nationals;[7] in fact, the status of resident aliens was less than equal. Conflicts with Polish visitors, resentment of preferential treatment of de facto guest workers from "brotherly" socialist countries, and the findings of surveys conducted immediately after the Wall came down indicate the existence of a pronounced ethnocentrism in the East German population before 1990.

The Asylum Debate and Immigration

Because of the economic and psychological problems that developed in its wake, German unification did not give rise to national euphoria, as had been feared, but led instead to a depression that exposed the limits of political effectiveness. The virulent asylum debate in 1989 in West Germany and the related rise in right-wing extremism were placed on the back burner during the process of unification, and the ultraright parties achieved disappointing 1990 election returns, above all in the former GDR. The situation changed in 1991, however, when the political parties continued their perennial conflict by placing the issue of the asylum article 16 of the Federal Basic Law (the West German constitution) back on the agenda. The legal right to asylum (by far the most generous in the Western hemisphere) and right-wing extremism were issues of greatest concern to the population in October 1992: 50% of the respondents to an IfD Survey mentioned the asylum issue and 44% the issue of right-wing extremism (IfD 1992a). At the same time the political disputes gave voters—a majority of whom were also in favor of restrictive legislation[8]—the impression that politicians were incapable of resolving the issue. Almost two-thirds of the population in 1991–92 felt that "politicians were not seriously attempting to solve the problem" (IfD 1992a). This debate gave violent extremists the impression that expressing hate and contempt through action had some legitimization and support among the public. The combination of perceived pressure of an unprecedented immigration situation, the seemingly incapability of traditional political parties to resolve the issue at hand, and an assumed xenophobic public consensus certainly contributed to the poisoned atmosphere in Germany in the summer and fall of 1992.[9] Political incompetence—not a general political shift to the Right—was primarily responsible for the rise of hostility toward asylum seekers, Turks, and other immigrants (Leenen 1992).

Surveys yielded mixed findings with respect to the distribution of xenophobic attitudes (table 2.6). Surprisingly, some opinion polls on the attitudes of West Ger-

TABLE 2.6. Disapproving Attitudes toward "Guest Workers" in West Germany,
1980–1990

	Should Try to Adapt Better	Should Be Sent Back	Should Be Prohibited from Political Activity	Should Abide Endogamy
1980	66%	52%	51%	44%
1984	61	42	47	34
1988	57	36	38	33
1990	51	31	36	34

Source: ALLBUS Survey 1980, 1984, 1988, 1990.
Note: The following questions were asked:
"Guest workers should try to adapt their lifestyle a little better to that of the Germans."
"If jobs get short, the guest workers should be sent back to their native countries."
"Guest workers should be prohibited from any political activity at all in Germany."
"Guest workers should marry people from their own countries."

mans toward foreigners suggest that antipathy receded between 1980 and 1990 (Allgemeine Bevölkerungsumfrage [ALLBUS] 1980–90, IPOS [Institut für praxis-orientierte Sozialforschung] 1987–91).

From 1990 on, the debate about asylum and immigration came to a halt and deepened public discontent and polarization (Kurthen 1995). On the one hand the proportion of western Germans willing to halt the immigration of asylum seekers altogether declined from 30% in 1990 to 23% in 1992, but fewer respondents supported unrestricted entry (1990, 19%; 1992, 13%). A considerable majority (65%) preferred a policy that limited entry of so-called economic refugees, as was discussed in the public arena at that time. Eastern Germans were less supportive of such a limitation than their western counterparts. About 5% fewer eastern Germans supported a complete halt of asylum seekers who wished to enter the country.[10] This figure represents the only deviation from opinions of western Germans; eastern Germans advocated stronger and broader restrictions on other groups of immigrants from the European Community (EC) and from non-EC countries.[11] Foreign nationals in the new federal states in the East were seen as unwanted competitors in a situation of economic turmoil.[12]

Other surveys, such as the Eurobarometer survey, differ somewhat from the findings mentioned earlier. For both, eastern and western Germany, the Eurobarometer data show an increase in the number of those in favor of reducing the rights of non-EC foreigners in Germany from 1990 to 1992. In the West, the number increased from 21% in 1990 to 44% in 1992; in the east, the increase was smaller: from 22% to 37%. This suggests a drastic increase in xenophobia in both parts of Germany.

Using the Eurobarometer data from 1988 and 1992, Fuchs, Gerhards, and Roller (1993) ascertain a strong increase in negative evaluations of non-EC foreigners for all West European countries. They also refer to a significant correlation among rejection of foreigners, group size, and cultural distance, as well as a correlation between the sending and the host countries. Their findings support the assumption that xenophobia is likely to exist in Germany and Western Europe for some time, nurtured by the presence of large immigrant minorities, social competition, and lingering racist and nationalist attitudes.

But some contradictions of these survey findings remain and are difficult to explain (Hill 1993: 45). On methodological grounds, Hill favors the findings from ALLBUS and IPOS surveys that do not suggest a dramatic change in attitudes toward foreigners. This interpretation is supported by two Emnid-Institut surveys (Emnid—Institut 1989, 1992). The 1992 survey (using the same like–dislike scales as in March 1989) was conducted at the end of 1991—at the height of the so-called asylum debate—and surprisingly shows a significant decrease in antipathy toward asylum seekers and Turks.[13] Since it seems unlikely that attitudes would shift so drastically for the better, we assume that one has to take into account a context bias. Further investigation is needed to test the hypothesis that respondents used opinion polls to air their current anger or hope. The more positive findings of the Emnid surveys may indicate a desire for a political solution or opposition and distancing from the vigilante justice of the violent fringe rather than a significant change in negative attitudes or stereotypes toward foreigners in general. Or did the violence, indeed, galvanize the public and create a stable attitude shift toward more awareness and tolerance?

Another field of contention is the role of authoritarianism. Recent studies did not find any differences between young people from East and West Berlin (aged 16–21) with respect to the extent of right-wing and authoritarian attitudes. They did, however, find differences in attitudes toward foreign nationals. In a study of Berlin youth in 1991, those from the eastern part of the city revealed slightly more negative attitudes than those from the western sector (31% compared to 24% of young people from West Berlin agreed with the statement, "Foreigners should leave Germany as quickly as possible" (Oesterreich 1993). This manifestation of right-wing extremism and xenophobia among eastern German youth could be seen as a reaction to radical political changes and not as an expression of a "deformed GDR personality."[14]

This hypothesis was corroborated in 1993 when the 1991 Oesterreich study (1993) was repeated. The increasing effects of the unification crisis led to an 11% rise in xenophobia among young people in East Berlin, as compared to 1991. There was a slight decrease during this same period among young people in West Berlin (Oesterreich 1994). As in findings on antisemitism, East German youth were found to be especially xenophobic, so that the age distribution in East and West varied significantly. Another survey found that in East Berlin, the cohorts under 34 years of age were more ethnocentric than those aged 35–64, whereas in West Berlin the age groups under 50 were the least ethnocentric (Stöss 1993a). In other words, right-wing attitudes tend to increase with age in West Germany, whereas in East Germany young people (in addition to those over 65) can be called xenophobic.[15]

These studies suggest that the succession of political generations in the former GDR is different from the western part of Germany. The oldest generation (over 65) in both parts of Germany was raised during the Nazi period and most frequently displays right-wing and xenophobic attitudes. The antifascist socialization in the GDR seems to have had its greatest impact on the middle generations (ages 35–64), who, in the period of reconstruction, more strongly identified with the "antifascist state" than the younger cohorts, who showed a more tenuous commitment to their state, as evidenced by the development of a right-wing youth culture in the 1980s. In West Germany, on the other hand, the most definitive difference in terms of attitudes is between those below age 50 and those over 50.

Aside from age, education has an influence on xenophobic attitudes. The less educated tend to be more ethnocentric. Political identification is another important factor. People who identify with the political Right are more often ethnocentric than those on the Left. This holds true for the old and the new federal states alike. For the new states only, the place of residence has a significant influence on ethnocentrism: respondents living in smaller and more rural communities are more often in favor of putting a stop to immigration. Unemployment only moderately influences the degree of xenophobia in the new states, whereas in western Germany, unemployment does not appear to have any impact at all on xenophobia, calling into question narrow socioeconomic theories that explain xenophobia simply with labor market deprivation and competition.

Violence against Jews and Foreigners

Of course, the relative stability in attitudes seems to contradict the violence that has been directed at foreigners and Jews in Germany in the last five years. An attitudinal analysis can only partly explain this phenomenon. Drawing conclusions about behavior on the basis of the existence of a particular attitude is only possible to a limited extent. Xenophobic and antisemitic attitudes are far more widespread than an inclination toward violence, which in turn is more widespread than actual violent attacks.

The discrepancy between attitudes and behavior becomes especially visible when the age distribution of right-wing extremist attitudes is analyzed relative to participation in xenophobic or antisemitic activities. Whereas ultraright-wing and anti-Jewish attitudes are most prevalent among older Germans of both genders, virtually all those responsible for violent crimes are young men. According to an analysis of 758 convictions of participants in right-wing extremist acts of violence since 1991, 78% of the offenders were between 14 and 20 years old, only 3% were over 30, and only 1% were female. Of these offenders, 9% were either members of an ultraright-wing party or organization or had contact with one, and 30% belonged to the skinhead scene (Bundesministerium des Innern 1995, Willems et al. 1993). In an evaluation of the education and career level of offenders, most were found to have had little education, that is, 78% attended *Hauptschule* (equivalent to junior high school); 10% attended *Realschule* (basic high school), and half of them were still in school or job training; approximately 29% had not completed any vocational training whatsoever or had quit such a program at least once. In other words, this is a problem concerning less-educated young men, basically a peripheral group in danger of marginalization.

Studies on participation in different types of political protest revealed a definitive increase of inclination toward and tolerance of violence in the early 1990s in

Germany. Tolerance of violence among adolescents in the new eastern states is higher and more often accompanied by a right-wing political orientation than it is in western Germany (see Hoffmann-Lange 1995a: 73). This stronger ideological foundation in the former GDR is less a result of insecurity in coping with new postunification demands than it is the result of an attitudinal pattern that combines nationalism, xenopobia, and a pseudo-Darwinist ideology of violence and struggle with anomie and a delegitimization of the state monopoly of power. In contrast, in western Germany the propensity toward violence in 1992 was still more strongly associated with left-wing supporters (70% on the Left vs. 52% on the Right had thought about violent means in achieving their political aims). But in eastern Germany, the inclination to participate in illegal activity was greater among right-wing (84%) than among left-wing respondents (71%) (Hoffmann-Lange 1995a; see also Willems et al. 1993). In the early 1990s, within the context of immigration and xenophobia, a new violent potential developed that was directed against weaker social groups, above all immigrants. Thus there was not only a rise in tolerance toward using violence in achieving political aims but also a new, right-wing violent fringe was formed, made up in part of young people who combined violent youth crime with a right-wing political orientation. Neo-Nazi organizations attempted to recruit members from this potentially violent youth scene, especially in eastern Germany, and to integrate these cliques of adolescents into right-wing networks (Bergmann and Erb 1994c, Bergmann 1994c).

The fact that sensational actions directed against homes of asylum seekers (Hoyerswerda, Rostock, Quedlinburg) were even possible in 1991–92 in the new federal states (sometimes lasting for days) and that most xenophobic activity took place in the states of Brandenburg and Mecklenburg–West Pomerania (also in the East), can be attributed to the favorable opportunity structure. Owing to the extensive breakdown of police authority, especially in rural areas, and the reorganization of the judicial system, conditions served to encourage violent, right-wing criminals because the risk of getting apprehended and convicted was relatively low. In addition, setting up accommodations for asylum seekers in overwhelmed eastern German communities led to local conflicts that seemed to legitimize the violent actions of young people against these homes. However, this opportunity structure had changed by late 1992. Since then the overwhelming majority of Germans and the public have expressed clear opposition to violence against foreigners or their homes.[16] Bans on organizations, coordinated investigations, searches and seizures, countless criminal proceedings, and high sentences for xenophobic crimes have had a perceptible impact on the right-wing scene. The number of serious acts of violence and other forms of extremist right-wing violations of law thus decreased in 1993–94.[17]

The number of illegal actions motivated by right-wing sentiments fluctuated in the years 1980 to 1990—between 1,300 and 1,900—most of them so-called propaganda offenses (i.e., the use of swastikas, and the Nazi salute, dissemination of neo-Nazi literature, etc.). No increase after this period could be observed, except that violent crimes increased slightly starting in 1989 (1988, 193; 1989, 253; 1990, 309) before "mushrooming" in 1991 (1,492), peaking in 1992 (2,639), and declining ever since (1993, 2,232; 1994, 1,489; 1995, 837), though they remained well above the level in the 1980s. About one-third of these crimes were committed in eastern Germany and two-thirds in western Germany; that is, relative to population, an above-average number of crimes took place in the GDR.

In 1991, among violent thugs, foreigners were considered public enemy number one; more recently, there has been a shift to more diffuse targets of attack. From 1993 to 1994, the number of violent crimes motivated by xenophobia declined by 50% (1,609 to 860); right-wing extremist acts that victimized other groups (disabled, homosexuals, homeless) rose from 394 to 493; and violent antisemitic incidents fell from 1993 (72) to 1994 (41) and again to 1995 (27). Typical offenses in 1991–93, such as killings, arson, and disturbing the peace, went down considerably in 1994; the decline in property damage and assault cases, however, was not as great. When analyzing violations of the law other than violent crimes, above all in the area of public incitement to racial hatred and propaganda offenses, one can see that these infractions have decreased to a lesser extent than violent crimes. This can be traced to the fact that because of increased police and judicial activity, offenders have taken to lesser crimes, refraining from the more serious ones. These developments indicate that collective acts of violence, (e.g., the attacks on homes for asylum seekers) that were common in the 1991–92 wave of violence, have become rarer and have given way to a more diffuse form of everyday violence in small groups.

Anti-Jewish incidents have increased sharply since the second half of 1992 (1991, 367; 1992, 627; 1993, 656; 1994, 1,366; 1995, 1,155). This increase in the number of general antisemitic offenses can be partly attributed to the greater awareness of the public, who are now reporting offenses of this nature more often, and to the improved categorizing of these incidents by the police authorities.[18]

Thus one could say that antisemitism clearly follows on the heels of xenophobia. This indicates that such attacks are not the result of spreading antisemitic attitudes; on the contrary, Jews and Jewish institutions, as well as other groups, are becoming targets in the course of a wave of violence that is primarily xenophobic in nature. The time lag in the rise of antisemitic hate propaganda and public incitement offenses indicates different sources and groups of perpetrators. Antiforeigner violence was started and carried out mostly by youngsters. But those responsible for anonymous and slanderous pamphlets, letters, phone calls, and so on are more likely to be extremist, antisemitic fanatics, some even older people who have been activated by the wave of violence and hatred.

A minority of youths have combined xenophobia and antisemitism into a complex of hatred of everything appearing "foreign." The mobilization of right-wing extremism, which can also be observed in other European countries, has thus led to a wavelike increase in manifestations of antisemitism since 1991.

Most of the incidents included in the figures mentioned herein are propaganda offenses (graffiti and poster hanging), followed by slander, libel, and threats of violence. Physical attacks on Jews have been rare. In the seven cases of bodily injury reported in 1993, most of the victims were non-Jewish Germans who were either mistaken for Jews or were attacked after expressing positive attitudes toward Jews. Incidents of arson or firebombing, as well as other forms of damage to property, have been almost exclusively directed toward monuments, memorials, or Jewish cemeteries. They are therefore intended as an iconoclastic redefinition of these artworks or institutions more than attacks against existing Jewish communities. This is in contrast to the attacks on homes for asylum seekers, which are obviously directed against the residents living there.[19] However, Jewish communities have been subjected to telephone threats and defamatory letters. These appear to be exceptional incidents, according to a nonrepresentative study conducted by Alphons Silbermann and Herbert A. Sallen in 1990. A large percentage of Jews questioned, considered many Germans to be antisemitic, but hardly any of them had personally experienced discrimination at work or in their communities (Silbermann and Sallen 1992, 47).

In assessing the development of violence, it is important to take into account the escalation process and the fact that such incidents often occur in waves. The monthly statistics on desecration of Jewish buildings and cemeteries for the period from January 1992 to February 1993 clearly reflect that anti-Jewish actions followed phases of xenophobic mobilization; for example, the highest figures for violence occurred from October to December 1992 after the antiforeigner violence in Rostock. Such short-term swings do not provide conclusive information as far as longer-term, stable levels of antisemitic violence are concerned. It is more significant that there has been an annual average of slightly over 30 desecrations in the Federal Republic since 1986, compared to only 15 to 20 in the preceding years. The escalation to 40 incidents in 1990–91, 62 in 1992, 68 in 1993, 68 in 1994, and 40 in 1995 started from an already existing level. (The number of criminal acts in 1985 was as high as it would again become in 1991.) Half of the cemetery desecrations each year have had a right-wing extremist background. Most of the remaining desecrations are probably acts of right-wing sympathizers or imitations by apolitical lunatics. Similar waves of antisemitism have often emerged in the FRG and other countries (see Epstein 1993), without reversing or even interrupting the long-term trend toward a decline in antisemitism.

Such waves of violence have almost always been triggered by isolated antisemitic attacks and are seldom the result of more general political events. By publicly opposing such actions, politics and the media have served to inhibit these waves. A different situation prevails with regard to xenophobia. Here, clear relationships can be observed with economic conditions (or at least the subjective perception of them), the number of immigrants, and above all discourse in politics and the media. In contrast to antisemitism, the issue of "foreigners" is a less tabooed subject in political and social debate, for it allows the public expression of negative opinions about "the foreigners." Such statements by media or politicians would never be tolerated if made about Jews; in that case, anyone making such statements would suffer a withdrawal of public respect.

NOTES

Translated from German by Allison Brown.

1. The following are the responses of Germans who were asked questions about contact with different groups:

"Do not want too much to do with Turks" *(34%, N = 721)*

with asylum seekers	66%
with Arabs	64%
with Blacks	50%
with Jews	25%

"Do not want too much to do with asylum seekers" *(33%, N = 700)*

with Arabs	67%
with Blacks	50%
with Turks	32%
with Jews	25%

"Do not want too much to do with Jews" *(13%, N = 273)*

with Turks	88%
with Arabs	84%
with Blacks	80%
with asylum seekers	80%

"Do not want too much to do with Blacks" *(21%, N = 443)*

with Turks	85%
with Arabs	76%
with asylum seekers	75%
with Jews	38%

Bergmann and Erb 1991a, data from Institut für Demoskopie 1987.

2. Cluster analysis of a 19-item scale with two points per item in the 1986 Institut für Demoskopie (IfD) poll (N = 2,254) revealed the following respondent distribution of the extent of anti-Jewish sentiment:

29–33 points	Strong positive attitudes	42.1%
27 points	Somewhat positive attitudes	13.1%
21–22 points	Somewhat negative attitudes	29.5%
11 points	Strong antisemitic attitudes	15.3%

The 1987 IfD follow-up study (N = 2,102) resulted in similar respondent patterns, although respondents who agreed with at least half of the 19 antisemitic statements were defined as strongly antisemitic.

The 1989 Emnid-Institut survey (N = 2,272) with seven anti-Jewish questions and a 27-point scale obtained results comparable to those of the IfD survey about the distribution of attitudes toward Jews:

0–5 points	Not antisemitic	46%
6–13 points	Somewhat antisemitic	40%
14–19 points	Strongly antisemitic	10%
20–27 points	Extremely antisemitic	4%

3. Respondents with 6 or more critical or anti-Jewish answers out of a total of 16 questions were labeled antisemites (Emnid-Institut 1992).

4. A survey of eastern and western college students in the summer of 1992 showed that both groups rated Jews with the same level of antipathy (East, 5.5%; West, 5.2%). However, their opinions toward Israelis differed greatly: 18.5% of western German students did not like Israelis, whereas 30.1% of eastern students did not (see Brusten 1995).

5. The fact that eastern Germans more often than western Germans hold only those

persons guilty of the persecution of Jews who were active participants in the Holocaust and who personally knew what happened provides evidence of this assumption. Eastern Germans also interpret the degree of awareness about the Holocaust in a stricter fashion. A portion of western Germans, on the other hand, tends to blame the Holocaust on the entire population of Germany at the time (during the Third Reich), or Germans in general *(Spiegel 1992)*.

6. A survey in December 1991 of ninth- to twelfth-grade high school students in Jena also found that young people, more often than the total population, expressed the opinion that they "would not like to have too much to do with Jews" (13% vs. 8% among the total population) and that they "would not like to have too much to do with Israelis" (26% vs. 16% among the total population) (see Wittenberg, Prosch, and Abraham 1995).

7. Starting in the 1960s, the GDR employed a relatively small number of foreign workers (1989, 95,000) on the basis of bilateral government agreements. Legally, their social status was equal to that of GDR citizens, but outside the workplace they had almost no contact with Germans. Despite the propagation of international friendship, GDR policy toward foreign workers was highly restrictive; there was no right to asylum and the GDR had not ratified the 1951 Geneva Convention on Refugees. At the same time, however, all xenophobic or antisemitic activities were suppressed and severely punished.

8. As early as 1990, a majority in both western and eastern Germany supported restrictive legislation with respect to asylum (60% in the West and 53% in the East). The respective figures for 1991 were 69% (West) and 64% (East). By the end of 1992, figures for the West and East were almost equal: 72% (West) and 70% (East) (see IfD 1992a).

9. Chancellor Helmut Kohl spoke of a "national state of emergency," expressing a feeling that was widespread at the time, though his remarks also served to intensify the situation even further.

10. The different age distribution in eastern and western Germany is conspicuous. The General Population Survey (Allgemeine Bevölkerungsumfrage [Allbus]) of June 1992 found that rejection of asylum seekers in the West was most pronounced among the older generations; in the East, on the other hand, it was greatest among the younger generations.

11. Paul B. Hill assumes that this disparity is due to the political experiences of East German citizens. They had lived in a totalitarian regime, and their only opportunity to leave their country was as refugees—a situation similar to that of the asylum seekers (Hill 1993: 42).

12. In 1992, in the new eastern states, 24% were opposed to any further immigration of foreigners from EC countries (in the western states, 9%). Thirty-six% in the East were against non-EC guest workers (in the western states, 28%). In 1991, opposition to immigration was slightly greater (see Hill 1993: 40 ff).

13. Expression of "dislike" for particular immigrant groups, as reported in the Emnid-Institut surveys of 1989 and 1991:

	1989	*1991*	*Difference*
Turks	30%	19%	11%
Asylum Seekers from Eastern Europe	40%	31%	9%
Asylum Seekers from Africa	49%	38%	11%
Ethnic Germans from Eastern Europe	27%	21%	6%
N	2,272	1,875	

14. Based on interviews in May 1990 with eastern German youth aged 15–18, Lederer and others (1991) also came to the conclusion that eastern respondents were slightly more authoritarian than their western German counterparts but that the differences were surpris-

ingly small when one takes into account the extremely different educational and ideological systems to which the respondents were exposed. The only major difference was found in levels of xenophobia and ethnocentrism. Many more eastern German young people supported ethnocentrist statements such as, "Germans as a whole are better than Turks, Poles, Israelis, or Congolese." Sixty-five percent of East German respondents agreed that "Germans are better than . . . Turks" (West, 22%); "better than . . . Poles" (East, 67%; West, 19%); "better than . . . Israelis" (East, 65%; West, 14%); "better than . . . Congolese" (East, 55%; West, 17%); "better than . . . French" (East, 8%; West, 9%). (See Lederer et al. 1991: 591, 593).

15. Frequencies in the different age groups are as follows: age below 25 (East, 12%; West, 8%); age 25–34 (East, 16%; West, 2%); age 35–49 (East, 9%; West, 6%); age 50–64 (East, 8%; West, 11%); above age 65 (East, 16%; West, 20%). (See Stöss 1993a: table 15.)

16. Today 90% of the public supports prosecution of antisemitic offenses and only 6% are opposed. Opposition to violence against foreigners is significantly lower: in December 1991, 27% of western Germans and 13% of eastern Germans expressed understanding for right-wing extremist actions; these figures dropped to 16% in eastern and western Germany in the aftermath of the pogrom in Rostock (*Spiegel* 1992, IfD 1992a). A large majority of German respondents (80%) also supported the banning of antisemitic groups in 1990; only 12% were opposed to such a ban. The opposition was even lower among 18- to 29-year-olds (7%). (See Jodice 1991: table 6b.)

17. The Federal Office for the Protection of the Constitution (Verfassungsschutz) distinguishes among violations of law with proven or suspected extremist right-wing background between violent acts (manslaughter, bomb and arson attack, breach of the public peace, bodily harm, considerable damage to property) and other offenses (threatening/coercion, hate propaganda, public incitement, slander, etc.). In addition, extremist violations of law are divided into xenophobic, antisemitic, and political violations, among others. With the exception of antisemitic hate propaganda and public incitement, the number of offenses has continuously decreased from its peak in 1993. Violent acts have already started to decrease since 1993 after their apex in 1992, whereas lesser offenses have declined since 1994 (Bundesministerium des Innern 1993, 1994).

18. According to the Verfassungsschutz, the strong increase in the category of "other offenses" can be explained by "the disproportional 130 percent increase of hate propaganda and public incitement to racial hatred." In contrast to 1993, in 1994 many hate pamphlets have been mailed out several times. For example, 35 pamphlets under the pseudonym "Hugenberg" and 15 under "Hermann-Wahnfried Eichmann" were discovered. Some of them were addressed to police headquarters and the public prosecutor's office. The statistic contains about 190 cases where preliminary proceedings were instituted based on multiple charges of the same offense. Also, slander and property damage without considerable violence were on the rise (9.5 times increase) (Bundesministerium des Innern 1995: 88).

19. In case of the Lübeck synagogue arson attack in March 25, 1994, the young attackers believed the synagogue was not occupied. Nevertheless, they accepted the possibility that the life of Jewish residents might also be threatened.

3

HERMANN KURTHEN

Antisemitism and Xenophobia in United Germany

How the Burden of the Past Affects the Present

When in the early 1990s ugly pictures of xenophobic violence, swastika graffiti, and vandalism replaced the joyful and peaceful pictures of German unification, some observers speculated that the horrific past of Germany would surface again (Sana 1990, Mead 1990). The fear that again an army of industrious and obedient *Volksgenossen* (members of the German national collective) would mobilize and overrun Europe was not stifled by reports of millions of marchers who protested the violence by candlelight. Continued antisemitic and xenophobic resentment in a nation that was responsible for the Holocaust has been viewed as an indication that postwar Germany's policy of dealing with the past has failed.[1] Events such as the so-called historians' debate about the uniqueness of the Holocaust in the mid-1980s were seen as an attempt to whitewash German responsibility for the Holocaust. Some were equally worried by the "tendency to pass over the terror and misery of the Third Reich and to focus instead on the normality and continuity of everyday life before, during, and after the Hitler years" (Kushner 1991: 23). Similarly, it was feared that once the iron curtain was removed a formidable antisemitism would reappear in the former socialist German Democratic Republic (GDR) nurtured by decades of anti-Zionist and anti-Israeli propaganda. Such fears and reservations led observers to ask whether postwar Germans in the East and West had drawn sufficient lessons from the failures of their past. It raised other questions such as: What do postwar Germans in the East and West know about the Holocaust and Nazism? What impact had socialist anti-Zionism on East German attitudes toward Jews and Israel? Was suppression of Holocaust remembrance a central cleavage for the political culture and self-perception of postwar Germany (see Bergmann and Erb 1991a)? Was antisemitism only disguised under a thin layer of philosemitic official statements (see Safran 1986: 278, Weil 1990: 136, Wisse 1994: 26), or was it merely replaced by a new scapegoat—xenophobia against immigrants (Eric Hobsbawm, cited in Fein 1987: 365)? Before I shed some light on these questions by comparing poll data from German and international surveys, I shall first describe the context in which one should consider anti-semitism and anti-Israel resentment, xenophobia, and Holocaust knowledge—that is, Germany's relationship with its Nazi past.

Remembrance in Germany: The Context

The question of how to deal appropriately with the past has plagued the Federal Republic of Germany (FRG) since its foundation 50 years ago. Politicians, academics, teachers, journalists, and ordinary citizens have developed different arguments and strategies for remembrance and coming to terms with the past. The political culture, intellectual debate, and public discourse in Germany have never been able to escape the memories of the past because—in comparison with other countries—Germany's recent history invites many uneasy questions. In fact, such events as commemorations, war crime trials, political scandals, incidents of anti-foreigner violence, and debates in postwar and post-Wall Germany indicate the sensitive nature of issues pertaining to how Germany should deal with its past. Since the foundation of the FRG, Germans have walked a fine line between suppression and remembrance, between the desire to distance themselves from deeds of the past and acceptance of collective guilt, shame, and responsibility. For some the awkward past has been a reason for defiant ignorance, revisionism, and amnesia. For others it is a source of constant embarrassment and moral conflict, leading to a serious examination of conscience.

The retention of memories of the Holocaust and World War II has been termed coming to terms with the past *(Vergangenheitsbewältigung)* or better, confrontation of the past *(Vergangenheitsaufarbeitung)*.[2] This term describes different pedagogic, political, and cultural strategies that have been employed to describe, explain, interpret, reshape, and give meaning to events that led to Nazism, the Holocaust, and their aftermath in Germany and Austria. One can distinguish between a more legalistic way of coping with the past in Austria, a political approach in the former GDR, and a moral-political-pedagogic strategy in West Germany. Rainer Lepsius has developed a handy formula to characterize major differences in these three countries. Austria, he claimed, externalized the past as a German problem; Communist East Germany universalized Nazi fascism as part of a global class struggle; and West Germany normatively internalized, (i.e., officially accepted) moral and material liability for Nazi crimes (Lepsius 1989: 250 ff.; see for empirical substantiation, Bergmann, Erb and Lichtblau 1995).

The historical rupture of unification, the end of the Cold War, and the subsequent removal of communication taboos have invited attempts to historicize West Germany's dealings with the past. Roughly three phases have been distinguished: (1) a phase of suppression during the first years after World War II (1945–58), (2) a period of transition and growing awareness (1959–78), and (3) a period of prominent consideration of the past with attempts to normalize and put the past into perspective (1970 to the present). Werner Bergmann in his analysis of the framing of the past subdivides these phases further, distinguishing diachronic and synchronic events (Bergmann 1994a; see appendix, table 3.1). Others like Jeffrey K. Olick—using the concept of collective memory (Halbwachs 1992)—divide the postwar formation of West German society into periods according to how the West Germans dealt culturally, psychologically, and politically with the past (Olick 1994).

In contrast, a history of East Germany's ways of coping with the past has yet to be written. East Germans paid huge reparations to the Soviet Union until the end of the 1950s. However, East Germans did not make large reparations for the sufferings of Jews, and it was not until the 1980s that a debate started in some circles about Jewish life before and after World War II. Synagogues were repaired, books and movies were made public, and cautious political steps were undertaken toward a rapprochement with world Jewry and Israel. But the East German response to the Jewish Holocaust never had West German dimensions. Nevertheless, postunification surveys found common ground among East and West Germans in their assessment of the tragedy of the Holocaust, the rejection of National Socialism, dictatorship, militarism, and war, though for current West Germans coming to terms with the past has had a stronger impact on their postwar identity and political culture (see Lutz 1993: 158 ff.).

Academic literature in Germany normally identifies four methods of coping with the past: (1) legal proceedings against former Nazis, (2) financial restitution to victims of the Holocaust and World War II, (3) postwar political and constitutional conclusions and actions, and (4) the moral, psychological, pedagogical, and historical ways to deal with the legacy of the Holocaust and its impact on the national and cultural West German identity. Whereas the first three dimensions are less controversial, the fourth dimension is more disputed and contested, as suggested by academic and popular literature on the subject (Dudek 1992).

The question of success or failure of remembrance is of importance because it is perceived as a cornerstone of West Germany's reintegration into the West after the war. If confrontation of the past had little or no effect on German attitudes and political culture, a repetition of past mistakes seems more likely. From that perspective, unification and any strengthening of Germany economically, politically, or militarily could bear the potential of future disaster.

Two schools of thought about Germany's coping with the past can be distinguished depending on (1) standards of judgment used for making historical comparisons; (2) defining moral principles of responsibility, guilt, and punishment; and (3) assessing the virulence of antisemitism, the interpretation of antisemitic incidents, and the reaction of the political establishment. Optimists claim remembrance was a success because its intentions have been largely fulfilled (Meier 1990, Groll 1990, Jesse 1991, Wolffsohn 1993, R. M. Müller 1994). Pessimists criticize the foundation of *Vergangenheitsbewältigung* in West Germany and its intentions and practice, pointing, for example, to present levels of antisemitism and xenophobia as proof of its failure (Henningsen 1989, Zipes 1991, Giordano 1992, Buruma 1994). I shall outline some of the arguments on both sides of the academic and public debate.

Pessimists accuse the majority of Germans of having ignored the crimes of

Nazism and of failing to seriously acknowledge their guilt and responsibility. The terms *second guilt* (Giordano 1987) and *third guilt* (Hennig 1988: 26 ff.) have been coined to characterize silencing, relativization, minimization, and historical revisionism supposedly transferred from the war to postwar generations. Hans Magnus Enzensberger charged those Germans who claimed they could not feel remorse for crimes they did not commit personally of a lie of life *(Lebenslüge)*. Such judgments rest on the assumption of collective responsibility or guilt, a failure to choose resistance during the war, and on the existence of collective methods to confess crimes and deal with the burden of the past. In fact, the nature and size of Nazi crimes makes it difficult to distinguish individual crimes from the collective political, cultural, and social context in which they were committed. It poses questions that have not yet been sufficiently resolved. Where did guilt start and where does it end? Was a bystander, a voter, or a member of the NSDAP (National-Sozialistische Deutsche Arbeiter Partei) as guilty as a camp guard or person directly involved in killings? How many Germans had knowledge of and willingly supported the Holocaust? How much were the Nazis able to hide their genocidal policy? Have those Germans who paid for their belonging to the National Socialist collective with life, health, property, loss of homeland, and family members been punished sufficiently? How should the postwar generations who can experience the past only in the abstract, intellectually and historically (Martin Broszat, in Baldwin 1990: 105), deal with the legacies of the past? How far-reaching is their moral, material, and political responsibility toward the victims and their descendants (Trautmann 1991: 9, citing Meier 1990)?

Other pessimists acknowledge that Germans have developed a sense of shame and guilt but are incapable of truly mourning. Their continuing struggle with contradictory feelings of secret guilt and resentment makes acceptance of the past and healing impossible (Mitscherlich and Mitscherlich 1975). Applying the Freudian concept of individually displaced aggression, anger, and guilt to group consciousness, this view maintains that the psychic dispositions of many Germans have not changed because the past has been collectively suppressed and silenced. If prejudice and ideological debris of the past is still embedded in personalities, emotions, and attitudes of contemporaries, is it not likely that history will repeat itself, they ask. Why do antisemitic attitudes exist in a country with only a tiny minority of Jews, even now, 50 years after the Holocaust?[3] Is the attempt to reevaluate Hitler's dictatorship by putting it into a comparative historical context, that is, the historians' debate *(Historikerstreit)* an example of hidden revisionist trends in West German society (Eckhard Jesse, in Gauly 1988: 37)? To what extent does the official—often declamatory and ritualized—atonement of German leaders represent the feelings and attitudes of the population? How deeply has the past been engraved in the Germans' collective memory?

Researchers like Bergmann and Erb have tried to give some answers to these questions and coined the term *communication latency* (Bergmann and Erb 1986; 1991a: 276). It describes an environment where antisemitism is a public taboo and socially undesirable but nevertheless coexists in private communications. Other approaches go further and refer to the notion of *dormancy* (Chanes 1994: 36) or claim a hidden refinement of antisemitism disguised as philosemitism.[4] Such assumptions, however, raise new questions. Can large groups of people hide their true opinions from the public? Under what circumstances is such hidden resentment transformed into open prejudice and active participation in violent acts? How does one distinguish honest positive feelings toward Jews and Israel from excessive admiration and uncritical sentiments based on compulsory needs to reconcile feelings of shame, anger, and guilt? Because notions of dormancy, hidden hate, and philosemitism are hard to prove, some have recommended abandoning such terminology because it demonstrates a lack of knowledge or investigation (Smith 1991).

Optimists reject the harsh judgments and assumptions of pessimists about an alleged German failure to deal with the Nazi past. This school of thought does not share the postulate of resilient and strong antisemitism in Germany, the notion of collective guilt, or the speculations about hidden hate and anti-Jewish philosemitism. Authors such as Kielmannsegg (1989), Grosser (1990), J. Herz (1990: 23), Dudek (1992: 49), Kittel (1993), Merkl (1994), and R. M. Müller (1994) point out that criticism is often based on unrealistic expectations of how most people react to their own guilt feelings. Germans should not be judged by rules of conduct from which other peoples are exempted. They argue that in this century no other nation has instigated, with similar intensity over a time span of almost 50 years, the prosecution of crimes that have been committed by their own people on orders of their own government. Few countries with totalitarian periods in their history— it is argued—have ever been as persistent in their efforts to deal with their past, to compensate victims, to overcome and eradicate prejudice, and to establish a firm democratic order in such a short historical time.

Optimists argue further that comparatively low levels of anti-Jewish prejudice are proof that postwar reeducation, denazification, and restitution *(Wiedergutmachung)* have been successful. Germany, they argue, did not have a very strong liberal democratic political tradition before 1945, and the rabid antisemitic ideology of the Nazis ended less than two generations ago. For decades, East Germans were confronted with socialist anti-Zionist, pro-Arab, and anti-Israel propaganda. But the FRG officially accepted material and moral responsibility for the acts of the Nazi Reich. West Germany continuously undertook symbolic acts of collective penitence, publicly apologized to persecuted Jews, and actively supported the state of Israel financially and politically since its foundation. And Germany has refrained from any acts that could be seen as a repetition of the past, that is, power politics, (nuclear) military armament, and imperialist conquest for a "place in the sun."

Against the accusation of a lenient coping of the past in the 1950s and 1960s, optimists argue that only a "silent mastery of the past" (Rabinbach 1990: 45 ff.) or "latency" (Lübbe 1983: 334) avoided a cultural and social "civil war" in postwar Germany. It is argued that the integration of former supporters and bystanders *(Mitläufer)* of the regime combined with an official discrediting of Nazism and its ideology provided the groundwork for the creation of a stable democracy, itself a precondition to overcoming the evils of the past. According to optimists, the political conditions under which the FRG started to cope with Germany's past were much less ideal than they now appear. Many Germans had suffered heavy personal losses, were preoccupied with survival and reconstruction, and were still dealing with the shock of defeat, destruction, expulsion, loss of national sovereignty, and military rule of Allied occupation forces until 1950. Then the Cold War took over and building a reliable bulwark against communism took precedence over thorough democratization, denazification, and settling accounts of the past. For the ordinary German the outcome of the war resulted in self-pity and the perception that they were more like victims than perpetrators. (Lüdtke 1993: 548 f, 561).

Besides questioning the simplistic categorizing of the average German as a murderous Nazi perpetrator and willing executioner, optimists also criticize rigid standards of "correct" remembrance and the degree of personal and collective guilt and moral responsibility. Should survivors who lived through that time be held collectively guilty, even if some either "opposed the Nazi government, have been painfully denazified, or have seriously repented their loyalty to an infamous regime"(Merkl 1989: 12)? Optimists also ask if guilt can be inherited or morally transferred to later generations (see Pauley 1992: 331).[5] What kind of remembrance and what institutions and norms of conduct may allow postwar-born Jews and Germans to overcome the past that stands between them?

The fact is that contemporary Jews and Germans and their respective intellectual and political establishments concentrate on different aspects of German-Jewish relations and have developed distinct narratives (Watson 1992). Although dialectically intertwined, they draw moral, historical, and political lessons from the Holocaust that are not identical in every aspect (Wolffsohn 1993). According to Charles S. Maier, the Holocaust and its remembrance is central for the legitimization of Israeli nationhood and the Aliah (the return to Israel for religious Jews, see Maier 1988: 163 ff.).[6] In contrast, Germans have a tendency to avoid identifying their national history only with the Holocaust guilt.[7] According to human capability and collective interests of remembrance and mourning, both countries and peoples put, and use, the Holocaust in a different historical, political, and moral context.

Many Germans—deluged by a flood of books, newspaper stories, and TV programs on the Hitler era and the Holocaust—want to dispense with or distance themselves from that dark part of their history because it impedes the individual and collective self-image and pride of a people who believe they belong to Western civilization and culture. Some are tempted to offset Nazi crimes by comparing them with genocidal policies of other times and others nations *(Aufrechnung);* some criticize sterile ritualized remembrance and official politics of history *(Geschichtspolitik;* see Wolffsohn 1993) or the notion of collective responsibility, the continuation of reparation demands, and alleged widespread self-hatred (Mohler 1980, Zitelmann 1993b). Bergmann and Erb use the term *secondary resentment* to describe the mind-set of persons who—as a result of the burden of guilt—resent the continuation of remembrance, moral responsibility, and material reparation (Bergmann and Erb 1990: 121 f. and 1991a: 231 ff.). Several hypotheses have been brought forward to explain the dynamics of dealing with the past. Some observers see the emergence of a new, "modernized" antisemitism (Abella 1994: 54) replacing the stereotype of the "coward Jew" with the "unforgiving," "revengeful," and "oversensitive Jew" (Kushner 1991: 26 ff.). Jews are resented not despite but because of Auschwitz (Leggewie 1994: 335). Others point at the exploitation of Israel's unpopular policy toward the Palestinians, particularly in East Germany, where pro-Arab and anti-Israel propaganda became "a mask for antisemitism, or an extension or sublimated version of it" (Brown 1994: 8). Pessi-mists speculated that such resentment—linked with xenophobia—had become the foundation of a popular right-wing movement of organized political antisemitism in united Germany.

Based on recent international and German opinion polls, I shall—from a socio-logical point of view—try to shed more light on Germany's coping with its past. I shall concentrate on what some (Frank Stern 1994, Chanes 1994: 34 f.) have called an attitude syndrome toward foreigners and Jews (including the Holocaust, its remembrance, and Israel). I hypothesize that opinion polls comparing these issues over time are expressions of identity formation and reflect political cultures and attitudinal dispositions. They are more than just situational reflections of cur-rent events (Trautmann 1991: 14). I agree with Gavin Langmuir that survey analy-sis over time allows us to make inferences about prevailing cultural (conformist) norms in the expression of attitudes (Langmuir 1990: 323). They also give us hints about processes of collective learning and collective memory configurations.

In the following discussion, the strength and distribution of attitudes in Ger-many in comparison with other countries will be analyzed. What are the Germans' attitudes toward remembrance? Are large numbers of East and West Germans de-nying the past and the truth of the Holocaust? How much do they know about the Holocaust? Is antisemitism linked with other forms of resentment, such as xeno-phobia? And had anti-Zionist education in the former GDR a measurable effect?

The Data

International and German representative opinion polls conducted after 1989–90 were evaluated by descriptive methods common in social science research. Most of the polls analyzed were sponsored by the American Jewish Committee (AJC). Of the three German polls, two were arranged by the AJC: one was undertaken in October 1990 with 995 West and 826 East Germans (Jodice 1991) and one in January 1994 with 992 West Germans and 442 East Germans (Golub 1994).[8] The third German poll was financed by the German weekly magazine *Der Spiegel* (1992) and undertaken between November 30 and December 17, 1991, with 1,875 West German and 947 East German respondents.[9] In addition, published findings from other polls sponsored by the AJC after 1989–90 in Western and Eastern Europe, Russia, the United States, and Argentina were used for comparative pur-poses (see appendix: table 3.2).

Empirical Findings: East and West Germany in International Comparison

In a descriptive analysis, questions from three postunification German surveys were compared with findings from ten international polls undertaken after 1989. Response ratios of dichotomized answers were used to compare response patterns.

High ratios indicated little anti-Jewish prejudice, little social distance from Jews, much Holocaust knowledge, and much concern about antisemitism.

To put the findings in a nutshell: the international comparison indicates that absolute or relative majorities of respondents in Western and Eastern Europe, Russia, the United States, and Argentina are more sympathetic than hostile toward Jews. They show social acceptance of Jews, display Holocaust knowledge, reject Holocaust denial, support remembrance, but do not perceive antisemitism as a serious problem now or in the future (see appendix, table 3.3).

Contrary to often-repeated rumors, attitudes toward Jews in the former Soviet Union and former socialist Eastern European countries do not indicate the existence of widespread and strong antisemitic resentment or a significant impact of pro-Arab, anti-Israel and anti-Zionist propaganda of the past.[10] Support for the equation of "Zionism is racism" was only somewhat stronger in East European countries (Hungary, Poland, Slovakia) than in East and West Germany (1990), and Austria (1991). Gudkov and Levinson found for the former Soviet Union, after its breakup called the Commonwealth of Independent States (CIS), and Cohen and Golub found for Poland, Hungary, and the former Czechoslovak Socialist Republic (CSR), that anti-Zionist attitudes were concomitant with positive attitudes toward Israel (Gudkov and Levinson 1994, Cohen and Golub 1991: 1 f., 6). In other words, the impact of Cold War division, isolation, and socialist anti-Zionism seems to have left only a limited mark in Eastern Europe and Russia. Variations in attitudes toward Jews do not reflect significant geographic patterns that resemble a West-East tilt of antisemitism or anti-Jewish social distance. Rather, differences in outcomes have to be explained by specific national conditions and cohort effects, as earlier European and North American studies indicate (Bergmann and Erb 1991a, Smith 1991, 1994). But further research and more in-depth analysis is needed to confirm the trend of changes in social distance, emotional rejection, and discrimination against Jews in Eastern Europe and the former Soviet Union.[11]

For Western democracies, including Germany, the international comparison reveals that the Holocaust has been accepted as a central event in modern history that should not be forgotten. In Germany, the United States, France, and Britain more than half of all respondents believe the Holocaust is relevant today, "although it happened almost 50 years ago." Majorities also believe it is important "to know about and understand the Holocaust." The number of those responding "not important" was below 7% in all countries. The international survey comparison also contradicts the earlier-mentioned pessimistic notion of a strong suppression of the past, rampant ignorance, revisionism, and denial of facts in Germany. Attitudes in West and East Germany do not differ from general trends in Western Europe and the United States. Rather, the findings indicate a relative success of West German postwar reeducation and reform of its political culture. West Germans and particularly East Germans have a good knowledge of the Holocaust unmatched by British, American, or French respondents. The revisionist (but, in its double negative wording, confusing) question about the possibility "that the Holocaust never happened" has no mass support.[12] The German response ratios indicate comparatively little antisemitic prejudice or social distance toward Jews but strong concern and awareness about antisemitism.[13] The results suggest that pessimism and international concern about widespread and rising antisemitism in postunification Germany are not justified. Rather, such concerns seem to reflect prevailing memories and historical narratives of Germany's Nazi past (see similar results in Bergmann 1990a: 151; see also appendix, table 3.5).

In the case of East Germany, Western observers feared the impact of the indoctrination of the population with pro-Arab and anti-Israel propaganda; which depicted Zionism as a dangerous nationalist ideology that threatened stability in the Near East. Observers also expected the isolation of East Germans from the Western discourse about the past would be reflected in widespread and strong antidemocratic, racist, and antisemitic attitudes (see, for example, Andrei S. Markovits, cited in Merkl 1994: 292). Until 1989 the official state ideology of the socialist rulers proclaimed East Germany an inheritor of German antifascism which represented a clear break with the past of National Socialism (F. P. Lutz 1993: 160). The government provided the population with a consistent interpretation of the past, but prevented an unrestricted debate about Germany's guilt and responsibility. With Soviet support the socialist GDR also refused to pay reparations to Israel or world Jewry, and it failed to recognize Israel as a legitimate state.[14]

Surprisingly, postunification surveys discredit fears of strong anti-Jewish resentment in East Germany. On the contrary, on almost all items East Germans reveal less antisemitic resentment, less social distance, and a greater knowledge of the Holocaust than West Germans, Austrians, Americans, French, British, or East European respondents (see appendix, table 3.3, questions 1–5, 8–12, and table 3.5). Poll figures regarding the equation of Zionism with racism are similar for East and West Germany. In other words, stringent antifascist education seems to have had rather a suppressing effect on anti-Jewish resentment in East Germany (similarly P. P. Lutz 1991: 354).[15]

Although East and West Germans have in international comparison a relatively good ranking on most items, particularly West Germans deviate on two issues (see appendix, table 3.5). They resent Jewish influence in society more frequently and they display comparatively low levels of support for remembrance of the Nazi past, although they have good knowledge about the Holocaust and do not support revisionist claims. A correlation analysis reveals that opposition to remembrance and antisemitic (and xenophobic) attitudes increase with little knowledge and low education. But among a sizable group of German respondents, rejection of remembrance also accompanies good Holocaust knowledge. In a 1994 poll (Golub 1994), 27% of those with very good knowledge of the Holocaust in the East and 53% in the West also believed at the same time in the decreasing importance of the Holocaust for the present.

It remains unclear why Holocaust knowledge is unrelated to support for continuing strong remembrance and commemoration of Nazi crimes among a considerable group of Germans. Is this a sign of hidden anti-Jewish resentment as the pessimistic view suggests? Or has the taboo against antisemitism—popularized in the German media and in political education—and the official rhetoric in favor of remembrance pushed resentment into the niches of private communication (communicative latency), possibly giving rise to a new secondary resentment (Bergmann and Erb 1991a)? To answer these and related questions, German poll data have been subjected to bivariate, factor, and regression analyses, using attitude scales and response typologies. Although such an empirical approach is not free from limitations and cannot, for example, answer questions about the transformation of attitudes into behavior or the impact of single historical events on mass attitudes, the analysis sheds some verifiable light on the relationship between antisemitism, xenophobia, and remembrance.[16]

Antisemitism and Remembrance in Germany

When discussing the issue of antisemitism and xenophobia, it is necessary to keep in mind the broader cultural and social framework, as well as historical developments. Hatred and hostility against Jews has been a constant of Western civilization for more than 2,000 years. This animosity does not mean that attitudes and behavior have not changed over time. In fact, "modern" anti-Jewish stereotypes are an amalgam of Christian religious "beliefs" and nineteenth-century philosophical and ideological ideas that later were embellished and transformed into various subdiscourses that molded political resentment with biological or anthropological racism, anticommunism, anticapitalism, and anti-Zionism (Bauer 1994). Researchers, therefore, have distinguished premodern, mostly religious and mythological antisemitism from modern, mostly politically, ideologically, and racially motivated antisemitism. In addition, anti-Jewish resentment also may be related to guilt feelings and national pride, group conflict, competition about scarce resources, and ethnocultural distance (Weil 1990: 131, Langmuir 1990).

Earlier research about the transformation of antisemitic prejudice in postwar West Germany suggests that antisemitism motivated by religion, nationalism, race, and economics is on the retreat. Social distance, emotional rejection, and the readiness to discriminate against Jews have changed significantly (Weil 1987: 175 ff., 1990: 137 f., Bergmann and Erb 1991a, Silbermann and Sallen 1992, Merritt 1993, Noelle-Neumann and Köcher 1993). In a comprehensive overview about empirical research in Germany between 1946 and 1989, Bergmann and Erb (1991a) have used various survey instruments (e.g., antisemitism indexes, sympathy, and trait scales) to measure prejudice. They found that between 10% and 15% of German respondents have antisemitic attitudes, among them about 5% exhibit very strong prejudice in contrast to about 20% who are apparently unprejudiced respondents. Bergmann reported that a 1974 study found "racial antisemitism" among 8% of the population, "political antisemitism" among 5%, and "economic antisemitism" among 13% (Bergmann 1990b: 119). "Religious antisemitism," focusing on the alleged "Jewish deicide" of Jesus, was found to exist only in small pockets among older, poorly educated respondents in rural and Catholic regions.

Evaluation of three postunification German polls confirm these findings. For example, in the 1991 poll by *Der Spiegel* (1992), about 1.9% of all German respondents in the East and 4.5% in the West supported the statement that "Jews have some responsibility for the death of Jesus, as the Bible says." These and other responses suggest that at present, consistent and strong religious, political, or economic antisemitism has neither an ideological basis nor institutional, official, or popular support in East or West Germany. And the existing levels of resentment are in no way comparable to the organized political antisemitism of the first part of the century or found during the regime of National Socialism.

Not only antisemitic attitudes but also antisemitic actions are unpopular. In an 1987 poll, 82% of all West German respondents favored punishment for any anti-Jewish activities, 89% favored punishment for the desecration of cemeteries, and 71% rejected anti-Jewish proclamations by politicians (Bergmann 1990b: 116). In the 1990 Jodice poll, four out of five respondents in the East and a relative majority in the West were in favor of continuing the prosecution of Nazi war criminals after unification. About 85% in the East and 70% in the West thought the German government should continue, "after the unification of the two German states, [to] teach about the Nazi period in history lessons in the schools." Almost four out of five respondents in the East and West agreed that the German government should continue to ban antisemitic groups. Majorities in the East (75%) and West (59%) also considered a Jewish candidate for president of united Germany acceptable (Golub 1994).

On the other hand only about 30% in the West and 40% in the East agreed with the statement, "Because of the events during the Third Reich, we have a special obligation toward Jews and also toward Israel. We cannot treat Israel like any other country on earth." But more than two out of five respondents in the West and one out of five in the East in 1990 and 1994 agreed somewhat or strongly with the statement, "Jews are exploiting the National Socialist Holocaust for their own purposes" (Jodice 1991, Golub 1994).[17] In the 1991 poll undertaken by *Der Spiegel* (1992), 75% in the West and 57% in the East rejected Jewish and Israeli demands for reparation payments to compensate in the aftermath for the lack of reparation payments by the former socialist East Germany.[18] And in the 1994 Golub survey, 56% in the West and 36% in the East agreed somewhat or strongly with the statement, "Today, in the aftermath of German unification, we should not talk so much about the Holocaust, but should rather draw a line under the past" (Golub 1994, table 20).[19]

Could the dynamics of suppression, anger, shame, guilt, responsibility, and reparation become the source of a new secondary antisemitism as the pessimists have suggested? How can it be explained that respondents who do not deny the Holocaust, who have good knowledge about the past, who are concerned about antisemitism, and who support the continuation of Nazi prosecution at the same time wish to "draw a line," and reject additional reparation payments to Jews and Israel by a united Germany—in lieu of the former East Germany's refusal to do so?

An explanation for this ambivalent attitude, particularly in West Germany, points at the increasing historical distance between the events of the Nazi era and the present. Postwar generations, now representing more than four out of five Germans, have no personal experience and only a second hand knowledge of the past. To be held collectively responsible for the sins of prior generations seems to most an abstract and purely moral concept (Jarausch 1988: 286). Some may fear that keeping alive negative war memories artificially reopens old wounds and even hatreds that besmirch "their" postwar democratic and economic miracle and efforts to overcome shadows of the past by normalizing neighborly relations. Polls and observers agree that throughout the life of the Bonn Republic, West Germans displayed comparatively low levels of national chauvinism and pride. With memories and witnesses of the past slowly fading away, postwar Germans are in search of a positive social identity that restores feelings of pride and integrity, an identity that is less stained with the human horrors, painful events, and moral descent of the Holocaust, as well as the events of World War II with the resulting total defeat, mass expulsion from Germany's former eastern provinces and areas of settlement in Eastern Europe, and Cold War division?

Some evidence exists that many of the war generation reacted to information about the Holocaust with guilt, shame, anger, fear, confessions, and prayers for forgiveness, whereas others responded with silence, defiance, and comparison of Nazi crimes with other genocidal acts in world history. Germans born after the war may be tempted to defend their personal distance from the past and their newly won identification with and pride in the national collective. Among both war and postwar generations, some may find comfort in the simple but ignorant formula of "drawing a line" or of considering the past closed *(einen Schlußstrich ziehen)*. In fact, Bergmann found that support for such an attitude fluctuated (following public and media events) but rose in the West from 34% in 1958 to 67% in 1969, 62% in 1978, 67% in 1987, and 56% in 1994 (Bergmann 1990b: 122 f.). An analysis of the 1994 Golub poll indicates that younger West Germans tend to be more open toward remembrance. In the East, however, the findings were not so definite and the factors that influenced respondents' answers have to be more thoroughly investigated in the future.

But are the wish to avoid a confrontation with the past and the fact that many respondents do not exhibit an overwhelming rejection of single statements such as "Jewish World influence" or "Jews are exploiting the . . . Holocaust" (see also chapter 2, tables 2.3–2.5) proof of strong antisemitism, as pessimists suggest (e.g., Jodice 1991: 10)? According to attitudinal research such a conclusion is only validated if support for such statements is embedded in a coherent and rigid ideological framework. An antisemitic syndrome may exist if support for the "exploitation" question is linked with other traditional stereotypes about the "powerful" and "revengeful" Jew (Kushner 1991), who supposedly stirs up old memories of hatred instead of facilitating reconciliation and peace. In fact, far-right extremists try to instrumentalize and manipulate Holocaust shame, fear, and guilt, using the "Jewish exploitation" cliché. As Anson Rabinbach has observed, they claim to be victims of a presumptuous "Jewish monopoly on the moral capital of suffering which holds the present hostage to the past" (Rabinbach 1990: 60). Hard-core antisemites also look for opportunities to defend their attitudes by legitimating negative views about Jews. Many are eager to document evidence of Jewish or Israeli wrongdoing, whether accurate or not. Those who set off German misdeeds with Jewish ones or use the "exploitation" phrase tend to overlook that they themselves manipulate and exploit history and remembrance by defensively projecting their own national guilt on others. The existence of such right-wing thought patterns, however, does not necessarily imply that large segments of the population share them.

One method to avoid an overgeneralization of single statements and to measure the distribution of rigid and coherent attitudes is the use of scales.[20]

Scales Measuring Antisemitism, Remembrance, Xenophobia, and Holocaust Knowledge Based on Three German Attitude Polls

Three German postunification surveys (Jodice 1991, Spiegel 1992, and Golub 1994) were used to investigate the distribution of coherent attitudinal patterns on antisemitism, remembrance, xenophobia, and Holocaust knowledge. To measure antisemitic resentment, the author recoded and dichotomized poll questions concerning "too much Jewish power," the view that Jews "provoke hostilities," or the belief that "Jews are responsible for the hate against them." Responses to these statements with strong commonalities within similar topic groups were selected with principal-component factor analysis (orthogonal varimax rotation). This resulted in scales containing between 3 and 6 questions to measure antisemitism, remembrance, Holocaust knowledge, xenophobia, foreigner resentment, and foreigner antipathy. Scales are not identical for all three opinion polls because of differences in questions used for scale construction (see appendix, table 3.6). Differences in response patterns are most likely explained by differences in wording, questionnaire construction, sample size, and other contextual effects.[21]

Response Types in East and West Germany

To more closely investigate prejudiced and nonprejudiced respondents and their characteristics, a response typology was developed based on the combination of scales (see appendix, tables 3.8–3.10). Because the used scales differ for each of the three German polls and because of the different timing of the surveys, the percentages vary. Nevertheless, a scale comparison supports the notion of attitudinal coherence and confirms significant differences in attitudes between East and West Germans (see appendix, table 3.11). A correlation analysis also informs about the strength of links between scale items, although the data do not allow for inferences about causality and directions of relationships (see appendix, table 3.12). One important finding is a strong positive relationship between xenophobia, antiforeigner resentment, and antisemitism. The pessimistic assumption that xenophobia also can be explained by an assumed failure of remembrance (i.e., "a culture of suppression") or that lower levels of foreigner hostility and social distance in the East (see appendix, table 3.6) are only a result of the quarantine of East Germany from Western influences cannot be empirically confirmed by the data.[22] Rather, xenophobia and hostility toward foreigners can be explained as a function of ethnocultural intergroup conflict and economic competition (Kuechler 1994, Saalfeld 1994, Kurthen and Minkenberg 1995). Given the much higher number of foreigners in the West (7 million) compared with the East (250,000 in 1994), lower levels of antiforeigner hostility in the East are not surprising.[23] Xenophobia rose in the East after 1989 and led in some communities to an outburst of hostility

only after the post-Wall influx of asylum seekers and undocumented illegal workers, the unexpected economic strains of unification, the insensitive political instrumentalization of the migration and asylum issue, and irresponsible media attention
(see Kurthen 1995).

A somewhat unexpected finding is the different strength of relationships of Holocaust knowledge in the East and West (see appendix, table 3.12).[24] Although
data are only available from the *Spiegel* (1992) survey, the assumption that little
Holocaust knowledge is strongly related to antisemitism, xenophobia, and opposition to remembrance is not confirmed for West Germany, but it is for East Germany. In other words, Holocaust knowledge in the West is not a very reliable
variable to predict attitudes toward Jews, xenophobia, or disagreement with remembrance. Knowledge of the Holocaust may exist parallel with anti-Jewish resentment and vice versa. This finding confirms the more complex and ambivalent
attitude of many West Germans toward the past. It also illustrates differences between West and East Germany as reported earlier in the international comparison.

The comparison of poll findings from 1990, 1991, and 1994 (see appendix, table
3.11) reveals a continuing postunification trend toward more tolerance of and less
prejudice against Jews and a greater willingness to come to terms with the past
(remembrance). This finding contradicts the pessimistic expectations and alarm
signals of observers in and outside Germany. But significant differences exist between West and East Germany. Unprejudiced responses (scale type 4) are found
significantly more frequently in East Germany (between 50% in 1991 and 70% in
1994 of all responses) than in West Germany (30% in 1990/91 to 48% in 1994).
Respondents agreeing with stereotypes about Jews and opposing remembrance
(scale type 1) represent about 20% in 1994 to 32% in 1990 of all answers in West
Germany and 6% in 1994 to 9% in 1991 in East Germany. Between one and two
out of five respondents in the East and West oppose remembrance although they
show no visible evidence of antisemitic prejudice (scale type 3). Prejudiced respondents in favor of Holocaust remembrance (scale type 2) are only a small and
almost negligible group in East and West Germany. In other words, there is a
significant group of ambivalent respondents in both parts of Germany. Second,
East Germans, in contradiction to popular narratives, are surprisingly less prejudiced and more open confronting the past than many in the West—blinded by
anticommunism—have predicted or have been willing to concede. These findings
have to be interpreted in light of the differing histories of confrontation of the past
in East and West Germany.

As Rainer Lepsius stated, the more coherent and ideologically loaded socialist
antifascism helped East Germans abandon antisemitic ideological debris and develop a distant, selective view of German national history (Lepsius 1989: 247 ff.).
The East German regime suppressed Nazi antisemitism and substituted it relatively
successfully with an amalgam of officially decreed antifascist internationalism and
elements of *obrigkeitsstaatlich* (authoritarian) traditions. What was left of antisemitic and racist attitudes after the war was contained by the regime and slowly
fell into oblivion. In contrast, West Germans have much stronger opinions about
Germany's moral, legal, and financial responsibilities for the Nazi past. In the

West, remembrance was more controversial, less ideologically coherent, and more ambivalent. It underwent various cycles and periods (as mentioned earlier). Opposition to remembrance in the West is more a function of the interpretation of the recent past and the wish to identify with an untainted national history and collective identity. The official public taboo against antisemitism helped to silence and contain the revival of antisemitism in the Konrad Adenauer era until a democratic political culture had developed. According to the pessimistic view, antisemitic prejudice was never wholly overcome; instead, it underwent changes and became latent (Bergmann and Erb 1990). Can this explain why ambivalent attitudes toward remembrance are more widespread in the West? Cross-tabulation (not shown) confirms for the *Spiegel* (1992) survey that support for latency questions[25] was moderately (but not significantly) correlated with ambivalent responses (see appendix, table 3.9, scale type 3aS and 3bS, and table 3.10, scale type 3aG). Can we conclude that all nonantisemitic respondents who—at the same time—oppose remembrance, are hiding their true opinions about Jews out of sheer opportunism? Such an answer ignores that ambivalence toward remembrance and continuing reparations hides a variety of motives not evaluated by preset poll questions. Some respondents may not want to cope with unrelenting guilt, shame, and feelings of anger. Others may feel their patriotic sentiments threatened, and still others may have seriously contemplated the past and may want to bring such considerations to a conclusion. Perhaps some think that Germany has paid for its crimes. Postwar-born respondents may also believe that they should not be held responsible any longer because the Nazi crimes were an event of the past (for a range of motives, see Curtis 1986: 10, Safran 1986: 277 f., Wodak et al. 1990: 29, 147 ff., 216 f., 352 ff., Sniderman and Piazza 1993: 168).

Is it possible that some respondents hide the full extent of their prejudices by refusing to answer sensitive questions? Latency correlates in the *Spiegel* (1992) survey with a high nonresponse ratio among antisemitic persons, but only in the case of East Germany (see appendix, table 3.9, scale type 1bS). As for ambivalent responses, however, refusal to answer or undecided answers may not only indicate evasion—as Selznick and Steinberg explain in their antisemitism study (1969: 31 f.). They are often indicative of misunderstanding or unfamiliarity with questionnaires, the aggressive wording of a question, lack of knowledge, distrust in the confidentiality of the interviewer, time constraints, and other factors (Smith 1993: 384). Karmasin (1992: 40), for example, asked nonrespondents about their reasons for refusing to answer a question about Austria's Nazi involvement. Forty-three percent said they declined to answer because they found *both* assumptions of the original question true, and 35% felt incompetent or had never thought about the question (the latter group were typically elderly respondents with lower education). Twenty-three percent refused to answer (42% of this group had a university education). Some of the well-informed and well-educated respondents seemed to have declined answers because they disagreed with stereotypical questions that trapped desired answers as proof of the poll sponsor's or researchers' stereotypical attitudes about respondents' prejudices.[26] Further investigations into the dynamics of latency and ambivalence toward remembrance and reparations should take a closer look at the methodological limitations of standardized questionnaires (e.g., multiple meaning of wording) and evaluate more thoroughly response motives and the desirability effects of answers, that is, the adaptation of the expression of attitudes to cultural norms (Langmuir 1990: 323).

Demographic Characteristics of Respondents

With scales we are able to assess not only the distribution of certain response sets but also the demographic and individual characteristics of respondent types. Who are those who resent Jews and remembrance (scale type 1) in comparison to those who express resentment but support Holocoust remembrance (scale type 2)? How do nonantisemitic respondents in support of "drawing a line" (scale type 3) differ from those who support remembrance of the Holocaust (scale type 4)? Do those with antisemitic opinions have characteristics in common with a person described as having an "authoritarian personality" (see Adorno et al. 1973)? What relationship exists between certain attitudes and demographic characteristics such as education, age, religion, place of residence, political identification, and personality traits.[27]

Using standard evaluation techniques and independent variables common in attitudinal research, a demographic analysis of response types and attitude scales was undertaken. Logistic regression with weighted variables is a tool to control independent variables against each other in case the dependent variable is skewed and dichotomous. Log-likelihood ratios and levels of correct model predictions give a clue about how much each independent variable contributes to a dependent variable's variance. Significance levels show if a variable is important for explaining a given attitude syndrome measured by a response type or attitude scale.

The finding can be best illustrated using the *Spiegel* (1992) survey. This poll has the advantage of having a comparatively large (and reliable) sample size and a particularly sophisticated questionnaire. In a nutshell, logistic regression confirms (1) East-West German differences and commonalties and (2) a significant impact of variables such as social class (education/occupation/income), political orientation, authoritarian disposition, age, and residence on attitudes about Jews, foreigners, and remembrance.

A brief description of significant outcomes follows (see appendix, table 3.13). Persons who score above average on antisemitism, foreigner resentment, and antiremembrance share three characteristics in both the East and the West: low education/blue-collar occupation, intention to vote for the populist right-wing "Republikaner" Party,[28] and support for the authoritarian question of disciplining youth. Besides these commonalities, differences also exist. Persons in the East with strong resentment against foreigners and opposing remembrance more likely live in rural areas and cities with populations of fewer than 50,000. In West Germany, antisemitic and antiforeigner respondents are more likely to live in areas with a higher degree of urbanization. Also, the age factor is more explicit in the West, that is, older persons tend to be more resentful toward Jews and foreigners or tend to oppose remembrance. In the East, the age factor is only significant for persons resentful of foreigners. Gender, religious affiliation, north-south region, and economic situation (with the exception of antiforeigner hostility) are variables that are not very strongly affiliated with the antisemitism, antiforeigner, and remembrance scales.

Respondents with high scores on the antiforeigner scale are unsatisfied with their economic situation in both the East and the West. This finding seems to confirm the assumption that suspiciousness of and distance from foreigners is partially a function of ethnocultural intergroup conflict and economic competition among lower-class members who are threatened by economic and social changes. In the West such persons also express little interest in political affairs, intend to abstain from voting or support the far right-wing "Republikaner" Party, and attend churches infrequently. In other words, they may have few social and community ties and show signs of status deprivation and political disillusion, blaming others for personal and societal shortcomings. Persons in the West who oppose continuing remembrance of Nazi crimes have similar characteristics as those who are hostile and suspicious toward foreigners.

An analysis of respondent types (prejudiced and antiremembrance, nonprejudiced and proremembrance, and nonprejudiced and antiremembrance) confirms characteristic differences between respondent types.[29] In East and West Germany, prejudiced respondents differ significantly from nonprejudiced along lines of social class, Left-Right party alignment, and support for discipline. In the West, additionally, age, gender, political participation (party vote), economic satisfaction, and political interest are attributes where scale type 1 and 4 respondents differ.[30] In East Germany, characteristics like urbanization, region, and gender are of importance.

The differences between scale type 1 and 4 respondents in the West very much reflect what has been called the conflict between the old and the new political agenda that emerged during the transformation processes of postindustrial societies (Inglehart and Rabier 1986). The New Politics cleavage is characterized by a polarization between low-prejudiced, postmaterialist, younger and better educated voters with sympathies for the Green Party or the Social Democrats on the Left versus materialistic and less-educated voters with working- and middle-class backgrounds with traditionally CDU/CSU (Christlich-Demokratische Union/Christlich Soziale Union) and SPD (Sozial Demokratische Partei Deutschlands) sympathies on the Right. At the extreme end are populist New Right parties (e.g., the "Republikaner Party" that capitalize on those parts of the old middle and working classes who perceive their status as particularly threatened by the ongoing social and cultural change, and who feel not sufficiently represented by the traditional majority parties.[31] In the last decade such contested issues were the protection of the environment, immigration and its consequences (multiculturalism, ethnic diversity), and identity questions (national pride, rejection of supranational institutions such as the European Union [EU], the United Nations [UN], and the North Atlantic Treaty Organization [NATO]), and coping with the past.

How do ambivalent nonantisemitic but remembrance-critical and foreigner-hostile respondents fit into that picture? According to the data they have some commonalties with prejudiced respondents, such as low education, prodiscipline-authoritarianism, and (blue-collar) lower-class affiliation. The similarity of ambivalent with prejudiced respondents suggests that many respondents conform to opinion trends in society and their reference group. Some may even hide their hostile opinions toward Jews and could be counted under the latency category.

In contrast, respondents of the nonantisemitic and nonantiforeigner type who op-pose Holocaust remembrance are characteristically authoritarian males who do not belong to the blue-collar group (East) or have a significantly higher education (West). These respondents are not in favor of voting for either the "Republikaner" Party, Green Party, or the Partei des Demokratischen Sozialismus (PDS) in either the East or (less clear) the West. It is not unrealistic to suppose that an unknown percentage of these respondents (well-educated, feeling not threatened by foreigners, and aware of the current taboo against antisemitism) use the less stigmatizing remembrance issue to express their desire to move beyond the past and develop a new sense of national pride. Ambivalent respondents obviously represent a heterogeneous group of people whose response motives and attitudes need to be investigated further with more so-phisticated methods (see also Bergmann and Erb 1991a: 240).

It is of interest that many of the properties of prejudiced respondents fall under the label of "working-class authoritarianism" (Lipset 1960). Their characteristics also resemble the conception of the inflexible or rigid, prejudiced personality as developed in *The Authoritarian Personality* (Adorno et al. 1973) and related stud-ies about the psychopathology of prejudice.[32] Recently Sniderman and Piazza (1993: 87) have reported similar relationships between racial stereotyping and sup-port for authoritarian values in the United States. A survey in the Netherlands (Scheepers, Felling, and Peters 1990) suggests that authoritarianism is an often-overlooked predictor of ethnocentrism and prejudice that is itself related to educa-tion, age, social class, church involvement, and status anxiety.

More investigation of the socioeconomic conditions, political demands, and cul-tural values that accompany ongoing social change and the reorganization of the political system in Germany may help to uncover some of the questions about future trends in antisemitism, xenophobia, and remembrance, including the growth of postmaterialist and postnational pacifist Western and authoritarian materialistic political cultures, particularly in the East. Thus future studies should concentrate in particular on (1) how distinct political cultures and personality "types" react to socioeconomic changes that trigger ethnocultural pluralism via immigration (which covers issues such as xenophobia and antiforeigner attitudes), and (2) how these cultures and personalities respond to the search for a revived or new under-standing of the national collective via a redefinition of national identity and history (the latter is clearly related to Holocaust and war remembrance). My research indicates that antisemitism is related to both dimensions: xenophobia and national identity. Its dynamism might result from its bridging function. An increase in xe-nophobia will affect antisemitic resentment just as the frustrated search for a us-able and untainted national past may lead to an increase in secondary anti-Jewish resentment.

German Attitudes toward Israel

Some observers have speculated that antisemitic attitudes, distance from ethnic and cultural groups, and opposition to remembrance are linked to negative attitudes toward Israel. The analysis of the *Spiegel* (1992) poll confirms for West German respondents a relationship between antisemitism, ascription of "typical" negative Jewish traits (from a trait scale with 22 characteristics), and a relatively strong sympathy with the Arab cause. Other opinions about the peace process between Israel and its neighbors are only moderately correlated with antisemitism, a finding that is supported by prior surveys (Bergmann and Erb 1991a).[33] In fact, Lily G. Feldman and Michael Wolffsohn attest for Germany and Smith for the United States that the opinion about Israel is shaped by the political context of Middle East politics, independent of the ratings of Jews (Feldman 1984, Wolffsohn 1993: 108 ff., 99 f., Smith 1991: 16).[34] Until 1967 the German public expressed more sympathy for Israel than its Arab neighbors. Since then the percentage of those preferring neither Israel nor the Arabs has increased, similar to U.S. and West European opinions. In the *Spiegel* poll, undertaken in December 1991, shortly before the American-led UN attack on Iraqi forces in Kuwait, unprejudiced German respondents were more pessimistic about a continuing peace in the Middle East. They displayed distance toward both conflicting parties and expected the Israeli government to take the first steps toward peace. Indicative of this shift is that persons rating low on antisemitism (i.e., younger, more educated and Left respondents) were, in contrast to prior decades, also more critical toward Israel's policy in the Middle East. The sufferings of Holocaust victims and World War II generations are no longer seen as excuses for a harsh Israeli policy toward the Palestinians and Arabs. In other words, a skeptical view prevails that should not be confounded with ideological anti-Zionism or antisemitism. The majority of German respondents did not support the equation that "Zionism is racism." In fact, Left or Right anti-Zionism never attracted a measurable population segment nor was it influential in West German intellectual circles.[35]

Low-level resentment against Jews and Israel in East Germany fit into the hypothesis of the role of socialist antifascism described earlier. Nevertheless, this finding is somewhat surprising if one considers decades of East German pro–Palestine Liberation Organization (PLO) propaganda and anti-Israel politics. Also remarkable is the fact that in comparison with the West the average East German is more optimistic about the peace process and does not prefer Arabs over Israelis. Overall Germans in the East and West have a comparatively positive image of Israelis. On a sympathy scale of −5 to +5, 34% of all Germans—regardless of age—perceive Israeli Jews very sympathetically, 12% view them sympathetically, 38% were neutral, 10% view them unsympathetically, and 2% view them very unsympathetically. East Germans (mean: +1.14) had a somewhat more positive attitude than West Germans (mean 0.95). Compared with other nations and ethnic groups, Germans rank the Israelis close to Austrians, French, and Americans and ahead of, for example, Turks, Gypsies, or Palestinians. The latter are perceived by German respondents as culturally more distant.

Although most respondents in the East and West want to treat the State of Israel like any other state, a majority of respondents in the *Spiegel* (1992) poll realizes that the Holocaust still puts a heavy strain on Israelis' opinions about Germany. They also correctly assume that a large group of Israeli Jews is not yet open for reconciliation. A parallel survey in Israel sponsored by *Der Spiegel* in December

1991 confirms that the positive feelings of Germans toward Israeli Jews are not reciprocated.[36] For example, in 1991, a majority of Israeli respondents strongly identified united Germany and the Germans with their Nazi past.[37] Israelis expressed pessimistic and negative attitudes about German unification and the strength of democratic traditions in Germany. They also were concerned about German xenophobia and antisemitism (Wolffsohn 1991). For most Israelis the Nazi and Holocaust image of Germany still is an obstacle to more friendly relations in the present and future. Many Israelis also include postwar-born Germans in their anti-German resentments.[38]

Summary

Many arguments may be brought forward about how East and West Germans come to terms with the Nazi and Holocaust legacy. The gloomy portrait drawn by pessimists that West Germans have clearly failed to heed the lesson of the past, the alarmist cries of a rising tide of neo-Nazi antisemitism,[39] and the notion that anti-Zionism in East Germany masked popular anti-Israeli and anti-Jewish resentment are not supported by the findings of public opinion polls undertaken after unification (see also Marrus 1986: 177). In international comparison, Germany has a rather positive record regarding Holocaust knowledge, antisemitism, social distance, and concern about Jewish prejudice. In addition, many indicators—not only surveys—testify that the public in Germany in the last pre-Wall decades and after unification has rather intensified its efforts to cope with the past. From that viewpoint, it seems paradoxical that allegations of a failure to seriously confront the past have continued (see C. Hoffmann 1990).

From the end of World War II to 1995, a period that spans at least three generations, the Holocaust and World War II had an impact on the identity formation of Germans. Although confronted with, exposed to, and to some extent socialized by this past, generations of Germans born after the war (representing now over 85% of the German population) are rarely involved in personal interactions with Jews. But fictional and nonfictional books, movies, schooling, media reports, Nazi trials, public scandals, political speeches, memorials, and exhibitions have educated the Germans to such an extent that cognitively the memory of Nazism, the war, and the Holocaust cannot be easily suppressed. Shame, anger, and guilt are deeply felt in a large segment of the German population. Among the better educated postwar generations, the Holocaust has become a central focus of the recollection of the recent past (Weil 1990: 140, 157).[40] For the majority of contemporary Germans, the past is present; knowledge about the Holocaust exists and is available—often unavoidable—and they are not inclined to deny the truth of the Holocaust. Even those who want to overcome the guilt burden, those who are tired of self-incrimination or who consider themselves not personally responsible, are not necessarily identical with small groups of deniers and revisionists. Not everyone who supports the notion of "drawing a line," naively trying to remove the "Nazi stain" (Jarausch 1988), is a staunch antisemite with a coherent ideological view about National Socialism, Jews, and Israel. Many, tired of the guilt burden, have a rather conservative and patriotic worldview but support democracy (see F. P. Lutz 1993: 164 ff.).

Based on the *Spiegel* (1992) survey and using conservative estimates, three groups of people with different attitudes toward Jews, foreigners, and remembrance were found in East and West Germany, varying according to occupation, education, political affiliation, age, residence, and political interest: (1) an unprejudiced group of urban, younger, and better educated respondents who are willing to confront the past (West, 18%; East, 30%); (2) an ambivalent and less clearly definable response group who want to consider the Nazi past closed but are not (openly and expressively) prejudiced against Jews, although they are often resentful of foreigners (West, 30%; East, 28%); and (3) those who do not feel responsibility for the past, identify Jews in a negative way with remembrance, and have resentment against foreigners (West, 19%; East, 7%). The latter group represent attitudes that could be exploited by far right-wing ideologues and organizations. However, it is important to acknowledge that persons who share attitudes of the third group are *not* identical with a few hard-core old and neo-Nazis. Besides, transforming the third group's resentment into political action is not easy to accomplish if all other conditions are hostile. These findings are similar to other poll evaluations (see chapter 2). Particularly in the western part of Germany, the characteristics of type (1) and (3) respondents fit into the anti-authoritarian post-materialist–authoritarian materialist pattern, which is related to what has been defined as the New and Old Politics dimension that cuts across the older Left and Right cleavages based on social class, education, party alignment, urbanization, and political participation (see Kurthen and Minkenberg 1995).

In comparison with the more pervasive xenophobia against East European and non-European immigrants and asylum seekers, anti-Jewish feelings are not predominant in German society, and Jews are not the main targets of hostility and bigotry. If one considers opinions toward Israel, the Holocaust, and Jews as proof of antisemitism, German respondents display comparatively little prejudice. Although there might be a small but noisy extreme Right, the poll data indicate that there is a large group of Germans in the East and the West who reject antisemitism, accept the Jewish community, sympathize with Israel, and are opposed to attempts of the right-wing extremists to stir up anti-Jewish resentment and reject Holocaust remembrance. Some evidence exists that the nature and level of "traditional" antisemitism have changed into what has been called secondary resentment (Bergmann and Erb 1991a), but it is also true that anti-Jewish attitudes have continuously decreased over the last 40 years. Given generational changes and a stable liberal and democratic political culture it will most likely continue to decline further.

Distrust and antipathy toward foreigners is more widespread and differs significantly from anti-Jewish resentment. Whereas the latter contains elements of traditional political envy and conspiracy combined with resentment resulting from guilt, national pride, and reparation, attitudes toward foreigners differ by ethno-cultural distance, skin color, and immigration type. They contain strong elements of social competition, welfare chauvinism, and scapegoating of immigrant minorities. In 1991 45% of the population in the West and 40% in the East disliked foreigners. In 1994 this hostility seemed to be somewhat lessened, with 23% of the respondents perceiving foreigners as hostile in the West and 17% in the East (see appendix, table 3.6).

My analysis also confirms a relationship between antiforeigner resentment and antisemitism. In particular, in West Germany a correlation exists between foreigner scapegoating and resentment against Jews, though somewhat different scales were used. In 1994 the relationship between projected hostility of foreigners and antisemitism had become stronger in the East (see appendix, table 3.12). This may indicate an attitudinal right-wing hardening among prejudiced respondents in the East. In fact, respondents with a consistent antisemitic view are also most likely to be hostile toward foreigners, oppose remembrance, have authoritarian tendencies, and support antidemocratic attitudes.[41]

What conclusions can be drawn from these findings?

1. Xenophobia and antisemitism have to be seen in both historical and international comparative perspective, otherwise there is a danger of either exaggerating or downplaying their significance. Antisemitic attitudes and behavior, more than hostility against foreigners, are officially a public taboo and institutionally illegal in Germany. Public awareness about antisemitism is high, and anti-Jewish resentment is neither politically nor intellectually respectable, nor is it officially embedded in the political culture. In comparison with xenophobia there are no social forces or influential political advocates that could lead to a significant growth of antisemitism at the present. And there is no indication that after unification antisemitic incidents have significantly increased as the result of a popular, elite-supported political movement similar to that during the last years of the Weimar Republic. Comparatively small and fragmented fringe groups that promote prejudice and hatred against immigrant minorities and Jews are lacking support, leadership, an attractive ideology, and other means to sustain a political movement. Even within right-wing subcultures rabid antisemites are isolated (Bergmann 1990a: 152), whereas ambivalent feelings toward foreigners are more widespread.

2. These facts do not mean, however, that xenophobia, nationalist arrogance, and hatred of all sorts, including antisemitism, are unimportant, do not contain dangerous political potential, could not be revived, or may experience only a short-lived upsurge. In the case of anti-Jewish resentment, new sources and expressions have to be recognized, resulting from the burden of the past (collective guilt, remembrance, and reparation) and the unrealizable search for an untainted national identity. Xenophobia is fed by the failure to recognize that Germany has become an immigrant country and by the inexperience of the country with ethnocultural diversity. But on the whole the conditions for a simple renewal or repetition of the Nazi past in united Germany are unfavorable, and it would take a cataclysmic event such as a supranational upheaval and unprecedented domestic and international changes for such a change to occur (Feingold 1985: 323).

3. Remembrance of the past and historical consciousness about Nazi crimes should not be relativized, apologetically whitewashed, or offset against genocidal acts committed by other nations. Nor should the historically unique course of responsibility and restitution taken by the German government be cast into the marketplace of moral, political, and financial claims and counterclaims as if these

voluntary obligations were—in the words of Jürgen Habermas—some sort of natural and granted insurance for damages (*Schadensabwicklung*) (see Merkl 1989:
495). Awareness of the sufferings of other groups and nations allows the German
people also to recognize their betrayal by a Nazi leadership, who led them merci-
lessly "into the slaughter of the Second World War" (Wolffsohn 1993: 208), ending with division, expulsion, and loss of homelands in the East. Recollection of
the past sharpens the conscience against all sorts of present-day racism and xenophobia, demagogy, and political adventurism.

4. Unfortunately, even with the best pedagogical intentions, increasing chrono-
logical distance makes it harder and harder to revive or even to imagine the sufferings of millions. But coping with the past should not become a compulsive, rou-
tinely performed national act of self-accusation that is not free from self-
righteousness. Any attempt to moralize and ritualize remembrance or to condemn
those who do not respond polictically correctly will probably not result in the
desired outcome.[42] Compulsory exercises in philosemitism, ritualistic breast-
beating, or alarmist anti-antisemitism will not be of much help either (Jesse 1990:
560). One cannot transfer guilt feelings or impose collective or individual mourning, sensitivity, compassion, and responsibility. The "first step of moral development" (Wisse 1994: 27) could be the growth of a feeling of responsibility for
one's individual acts without blaming others or using other means of self-
exculpation. Such an honest learning process could result in a nonhypocritical,
moral sensibility toward the multifaceted side of national histories, pride in the
overcoming of narrow nationalism and ethnocentrism, and a critical attitude toward collective ideologies and generalizations.

APPENDIX

TABLE 3.1. History of Vergangenheitsaufarbeitung in West Germany, 1945–1995

Frame	1945–1952	1953–1958	1959–1966	1967–1978	1979–1989	1990–1995
Central events	Nuremberg trials, "deviance" of Jewish displaced persons, antisemitic scandals, compensation agreements, and German Jewish-Israeli reparation agreement	Diary of Anne Frank, second German compensation law, establishment of German-Israeli diplomatic relations	Antisemitic scandals, graffiti and cemetery desecrations, movies, plays, Eichmann and Auschwitz trials, compensation payments by businesses	Debate about juridical limitation (*Verjährungs-debatte*), "68" generation revolt against fathers, Fassbinder affair	*Holocaust* TV series, Nachmann scandal, Bitburg, historians' debate, Weizsäcker and Jenninger speeches, no legal limitations of Nazi genocide, compensation funds for enforced laborers (Poland, Russia)	German unification, Gulf War, German military aid for Israel, German payments to compensate for East Germany, Rostock council scandal, postunification xenophobia, arson of Lübeck synagogue and Sachsenhausen camp barrack, *Schindler's List*, 50th anniversary of allied WWII victory
Official explanations of Nazism and its victims	Dictatorship, National Socialism as "catastrophe," Germans as victims too, National Mourning Day (Volkstrauertag)		Moral dramatization of guilt and reparation, Jews victims of racial oppression		Focal point on Holocaust and Jews but other victim groups are also remembered, Germany accepts moral responsibility and lessons (vigilance, awareness), ambivalence in remembering 1945: defeat versus liberation narrative	
Public memory of Holocaust	Suppressed or offset by postwar expulsions and war crimes against Germans		Slow change	Constant public information	Guilt and shame but wish to draw a line and stop dwelling on the past	
Official framing of antisemitism	Unacceptable and extremist, punishable by law		Distancing through taboos and rituals	Refinement of taboos and rituals	Totally unacceptable, antisocial, and antinational	
Official treatment of former Nazis	1945–1949: Denazification, reeducation; since 1950: reintegration of bystanders into society, war crime trials		Early retirement schemes, expulsion from public service of activists	Diverse individual and camp trials	Criticism of lenient postwar treatment, search, extradition, and punishment of war criminals continues	

Public attitudes toward Jews/German Jews	Distance and antipathy	Indifference	Rising acceptance	Rising acceptance, positive traits		Acceptance of special relationship and responsibility
Public attitude toward Israel/Israeli Jews	Indifference	Pro-Israeli, anti-Arab		Pro-Arab, anti-Israeli		Sympathy but ambivalence toward Israel's Arab policy, wish for normalization, fear of instrumentalization of Holocaust
Degree of antisemitism according to polls	Strong and rising antisemitism, often under mask of philosemitism	Slow decrease	Reduction	Slow reduction		Little antisemitism among educated and cohorts born after 1935, growing "guilt burden" resentment
Public reaction to antisemitism	Indifference, avoidance of issue	Rising opposition and awareness	Public protests	Latent pressure to assimilate to norms		Strong public protests and sensitivity, government intervention to avoid domestic and international criticism
Institutions fighting antisemitism	Media, democratic parties, churches, constitution	Media, democratic parties, churches, literati, historical research	Schools, media, parties, churches, literati, historical research, cultural institutions, universities, Bundes- und Landeszentralen für politische Bildung			Media, school education, elites, unions, political and cultural institutions, camp memorials and exhibitions, movies, public commemorations and speeches
Public memory of 1933–1945	Prewar years: more positive; war years: more negative	Prewar years: more positive; war years: more negative	Slow change			Prewar and war years more negative, Holocaust memory predominant
Factors determining adult cohort views on the past	Personal experience	Personal experience, schools, media	Reports from (grand-) parents, teachers, media, institutions, etc.			School, media, and personal reports
Right-wing parties and membership	Increasing membership after foundation of FRG in 1949	Decreasing membership after ban and during "economic miracle"	National Democratic Party	National Democratic Party	Rise of Republican Party	Increasing right-wing organization membership after unification
Political reaction to right-wing extremism	Marginalization, ban of extremist parties	Marginalization	Ban of Deutsche Reichs Partei	Marginalization	Ban of Auschwitz lie	Legal bans of neo-Nazi and skinhead groups and music groups, German pressure for prevention on international level

Source: Bergmann 1994.

65

TABLE 3.2. Overview of German and International Attitude Survey Data

Survey	Number of Respondents	Sample	Date	Pollster	Sponsor
What Do Americans Think about Jews? (Smith 1991)				Various U.S. public opinion polls	
United Germany and Jewish Concerns: Attitudes toward Jews, Israel, and the Holocaust (Jodice 1991)	995 West Germans, 826 East Germans	Representative age 18+	1990 (Oct. 1–15)	Emnid-Institut	AJC
Attitudes toward Jews in the Soviet Union: Public Opinion in Ten Republics (Gudkov and Levinson 1992)	4,206	Representative	1990 (Sept. 21–Nov. 12)	Soviet Center for Public Opinion and Market Research	AJC
Attitudes toward Jews in Poland, Hungary, and Czechoslovakia: A Comparative Survey (Cohen and Golub 1991)	1,200 Poles, 1,201 Hungarians, 1,132 Czechoslovaks	Representative age 18+	1991 (Jan. 7–21)	Penn + Schoen Assoc., Demoskop Res. Agency (Poland), Median (Hungary), and Assoc. f. Indep. Social Analysis (Czechoslovakia)	AJC
Austrian Attitudes toward Jews, Israel, and the Holocaust (Karmasin 1992)	2,000	Representative age 14+	1991 (June 24–Aug. 21)	Gallup Austria	AJC
Juden und Deutsche (Spiegel 1992)	1,875 West Germans, 947 East Germans	Representative age 18+	1991 (Nov. 30–Dec. 17)	Emnid-Institut	Spiegel Verlag
Juden und Deutsche (Spiegel 1992)	820 Israeli Jews, 180 non-Jewish Israelis	Representative age 18+	1991 (Dec.)	Gallup Israel	Spiegel Verlag

Study	Sample	Population	Date	Organization	Sponsor
Attitudes toward Jews in the Commonwealth of Independent States (Gudkov and Levinson 1994)	3,965	Representative	1991 (Mar. 4– Apr. 26)	Russian Center for Public Opinion and Market Research	AJC
What Do the Americans Know about the Holocaust? (Golub and Cohen 1993)	506	Representative 10th–12th grade students	1992 (Oct. 19–30)	Roper	AJC
What Do the Americans Know about the Holocaust? (Golub and Cohen 1993)	992	Representative age 18+	1992 (Nov. 14–21)	Roper	AJC
What Do the British Know about the Holocaust? (Golub and Cohen 1993)	1,025	Representative age 16+	1993 (May 5–10)	Gallup Great Britain	AJC
British Attitudes toward Jews and Other Minorities (Golub 1993)	959	Representative age 16+	1993 (Sept. 2–7)	Gallup Great Britain	AJC
What Do the French Know about the Holocaust? (Golub and Cohen 1994)	1,046	Representative age 15+	1993 (Oct. 8, 9, 11)	Louis Harris France	AJC
Current German Attitudes toward Jews and Other Minorities (Golub 1994)	992 West Germans, 442 East Germans	Representative age 18+	1994 (Jan. 12–31)	Emnid-Institut	AJC
Holocaust Denial: What the Survey Data Reveal (Smith 1995)	991	Representative age 18+	1994 (April)	Roper USA	AJC

TABLE 3.3. International Country Comparison of Dichotomized Questions and Response Ratios

Question	Germany							U.S.A.	
	West Leaders 1990	East Leaders 1990	West 1990	East 1990	West 1994	East 1994	Adults 1989/90	Adults 1992	Students 1992
1 Zionism is racism: Disagree somewhat or strongly/agree	62%/30%	55%/37%	41%/33%	38%/33%					
Response ratio (question 3)	*2.1*	*1.5*	*1.2*	*1.2*					
2 Jewish president: Wouldn't matter or like to have/prefer not					72/22	75/21	91/5		
Response ratio (question 5)					*3.3*	*3.6*	*18*		
3 Jews provoke hostility: No/yes					69/8	75/6			
Response ratio (question 2)					*8.6*	*13*			
4 Jewish societal influence: Right amount or too little/too much					40/24	36/8	68/21		
Response ratio (question 1)					*1.7*	*4.5*	*3.2*		
5 Jews as neighbors: Approve or makes no difference/disapprove					59/30	75/20	87/11		
Response ratio (question 4)					*2*	*3.8*	*7.9*		
6 Antisemitism: Very serious or somewhat a problem/not at all	46/52	93/6	60/26	83/7	72/19	77/14			
Response ratio (question 6)	*0.9*	*16*	*2.3*	*12*	*3.8*	*5.5*			
7 Future of antisemitism: Will increase somewhat or greatly/decrease or remain the same	22/72	38/59	32/53	58/28	45/40	55/37			
Response ratio (question 7)	*0.3*	*0.6*	*0.6*	*2.1*	*1.1*	*1.5*			
8 Holocaust definition: Extermination, murder, persecution of Jews, etc./other responses or DK/NA					91/9	73/27		61/38	48/53
Response ratio (question 8)					*10*	*2.7*		*1.6*	*0.9*

TABLE 3.3. (continued)

		Argentina 1992	UK 1993	France 1993	Austria 1991	Hungary 1991	Czech Rep. 1991	Slovakia 1991	Poland 1991	Lithuania 1992
1	Zionism is racism: Disagree somewhat or strongly/agree				35%/25%	21%/25%	17%/52%	21%/42%	19%/39%	
	Response ratio (question 3)				1.4	0.5	0.3	0.5	0.5	
2	Jewish president: Wouldn't matter or like to have/prefer not	91/8	85/12		61/31	81/17	71/20	57/32	54/40	51/40
	Response ratio (question 5)	11	7.1		2	4.8	3.6	1.8	1.4	1.3
3	Jews provoke hostility: No/yes	76/5		79/8	46/14	90/6	70/2	51/14	65/19	
	Response ratio (question 2)	5.1		9.9	3.3	15	35	3.6	3.4	
4	Jewish societal influence: Right amount or too little/too much		49/8		55/8	64/17	51/5	41/25	32/26	47/11
	Response ratio (question 1)		6.1		2	3.8	10	1.6	1.2	4.3
5	Jews as neighbors: Approve or makes no difference/disapprove	52/41								29/70
	Response ratio (question 4)	1.3								0.4
6	Antisemitism: Very serious or somewhat a problem/not at all		38/48		45/30	51/34	28/72	34/66	39/44	
	Response ratio (question 6)		0.8		1.5	1.5	0.4	0.5	0.9	
7	Future of antisemitism: Will increase somewhat or greatly/decrease or remain the same		25/56		24/45	25/53	13/58	26/44	17/51	
	Response ratio (question 7)		0.5		0.5	0.5	0.2	0.6	0.3	
8	Holocaust definition: Extermination, murder, persecution of Jews, etc./other responses or DK/NA		56/44	68/32						
	Response ratio (question 8)		1.3	2.1						

TABLE 3.3. *(continued)*

Question	Latvia 1992	Estonia 1992	Belorus 1992	Moldavia 1992	Ukraine 1992	Russia 1992	Azerbaijan 1992	Kazakstan 1992	Uzbekistan 1992
1 Zionism is racism: Disagree somewhat or strongly/agree									
Response ratio (question 3)									
2 Jewish president: Wouldn't matter or like to have/prefer not	53/28	62/22	64/20	79/5	65/23	61/24	64/16	70/21	38/39
Response ratio (question 5)	1.9	2.8	3.2	16	2.8	2.5	4	3.3	1
3 Jews provoke hostility: No/yes						69/3			
Response ratio (question 2)						23			
4 Jewish societal influence: Right amount or too little/too much	18/8	30/2	55/15	27/1	49/9	33/11	32/11	55/13	40/5
Response ratio (question 1)	2.3	15	3.7	27	5.4	3	2.9	4.2	8
5 Jews as neighbors: Approve or makes no difference/disapprove	37/63	39/61	33/67	53/47	48/53	42/57	24/77	31/70	24/76
Response ratio (question 4)	0.6	0.6	0.5	1.1	0.9	0.7	0.3	0.4	0.3
6 Antisemitism: Very serious or somewhat a problem/not at all									
Response ratio (question 6)									
7 Future of antisemitism: Will increase somewhat or greatly/decrease or remain the same									
Response ratio (question 7)									
8 Holocaust definition: Extermination, murder, persecution of Jews, etc./other responses or DK/NA									
Response ratio (question 8)									

TABLE 3.3 *(continued)*

Question	Germany West 1994	Germany East 1994	U.S.A. Adults 1989/90	U.S.A. Adults 1992	U.S.A. Students 1992	U.S.A. Adults 1994	U.K. 1993	France 1993
9 Recognition of Nazi label for Jews: Yellow star, Star of David/other responses or DK/NA	91/9	98/2		42/58	42/58	42/58	47/53	88/12
Response ratio (question 9)	*10*	*49*		*0.7*	*0.7*	*0.7*	*0.9*	*7.3*
10 Camp recognition: Concentration camps/other or DK/NA	91/9	95/5		62/38	48/52	67/33	76/24	90/10
Response ratio (question 10)	*10*	*19*		*1.6*	*0.9*	*2.0*	*3.2*	*9*
11 Estimate of killed Jews: 6 mil./other number or DK/NA	36/64	36/64		35/65	28/72	41/59	41/59	45/55
Response ratio (question 12)	*0.6*	*0.6*		*0.5*	*0.4*	*0.7*	*0.7*	*0.8*
12 Knowledge of other persecuted groups: Sum of correct answers/incorrect or DK/NA	202/21	240/16		102/42	71/55	100/45	179/29	146/15
Response ratio (question 11)	*9.6*	*15*		*2.4*	*1.3*	*2.2*	*6.2*	*9.7*
13 No relevance of Holocaust today: Strongly or mostly disagree/agree	49/40	68/22		63/21	54/26	65/21	73/18	79/20
Response ratio (question 13)	*2.2*	*3.1*		*3*	*2.5*	*3.1*	*4.1*	*4*
14 Know and understand Holocaust now: Essential or very important/somewhat or not important	65/27	75/20		72/15	64/21	76/14	72/24	88/12
Response ratio (question 14)	*2.4*	*3.8*		*4.8*	*3.1*	*5.4*	*3*	*7.3*
15 Revisionist claim: Heard this claim/not heard	62/29	56/34		38/54	21/66	49/47	50/46	67/33
Response ratio (question 16)	*2.1*	*1.7*		*0.7*	*0.3*	*1.0*	*1.1*	*2*
16 Holocaust never happened: It seems impossible/possible	79/7	82/10		65/22	63/20	84/7	84/7	94/5
Response ratio (question 15)	*11*	*8.2*		*3*	*3.2*		*12*	*19*

Note: High response ratios indicate little antisemitic resentment, little social distance, strong concern about antisemitism, good Holocaust knowledge, support for Holocaust remembrance, and rejection of revisionism. Response ratios represent the division of positive by negative item responses.

TABLE 3.4. International and German Poll Questions

1:	"The view that 'Zionism is racism' has gained currency on the contemporary scene. Do you agree strongly, agree somewhat, disagree somewhat, or disagree strongly with this statement?"
Hungary, Poland, Czechoslovakia:	"Several years ago, the United Nations passed a resolution saying that Zionism is racism. Do you agree or disagree with this resolution?"
2:	"If a party nominated a Jew as its candidate for president of [nation], would you approve, disapprove, or would the candidate's Jewishness make no difference to you?"
Germany:	"If a party nominated a Jew as its candidate for president of Germany, would you approve, disapprove, or would the candidate's Jewishness make no difference to you" (in percents).
U.S.A:	"I'm going to read a few attributes that might be found in a candidate for president. Tell me if each would make you more likely to vote for that candidate for president, or less likely to vote for that candidate, or if it wouldn't matter."
Argentina:	"Would you or would you not vote for a presidential candidate who was Jewish?"
CIS:	"What would be your attitude if a Jew became president of your republic?: I have nothing against it, I wouldn't like it, can't say definitely."
3:	"Do any of the following groups [group] behave in a manner which provokes hostility toward them in our country?" (only answers listed for Jews).
4:	"Do you feel that the following groups [group] have too much influence, too little influence, or the right amount of influence in our society?" (only answers listed for Jews).
CIS:	"How much influence do the following groups [Jews] have in our society: too much, too little, a reasonable amount?"
Argentina:	"Do any of the following groups [Jews] have too much power and influence in Argentina?"
5:	"How do you feel about having [group] in your neighborhood? Would you like to have some [group] neighbors, wouldn't it make any difference to you, or would you prefer not to have any [group] neighbors?" (only answers listed for Jews).
Argentina:	"How would you feel about having members of the following group [Jews] as neighbors? Would you like it, would you be indifferent, or would you dislike it?"
CIS:	"How would you feel if your neighbors belonged to the following ethnic groups? I would like to have them as neighbors, it does not matter to me, I would rather not have them as neighbors?"
6:	"Do you think antisemitism in our country is a very serious problem, somewhat of a problem, or not a problem at all?"
7:	"Looking ahead over the next several years, do you think that antisemitism in [country] will increase greatly, increase somewhat, remain the same, decrease somewhat, or decrease greatly?"
8:	"As far as you know, what does the term 'the Holocaust' refer to?"

TABLE 3.4. *(continued)*

9:	"Many Jews in Europe were forced to wear a symbol on their clothes during the Second World War. What was it?" (open-ended).
10:	"From what you know or have heard, what were Auschwitz, Dachau, and Treblinka?" (open-ended).
11:	"Approximately how many Jews were killed in the Holocaust?" (open-ended with codes).
12:	"In addition to the Jews, which of the following groups, if any, were persecuted by the Nazis?"
13:	"Please tell me whether you strongly agree, mostly agree, mostly disagree, or strongly disagree: 'The Holocaust is not relevant today because it happened almost 50 years ago.' "
14:	"In your view, how important is it for [nationality] to know about and understand the Holocaust: is it essential, very important, only somewhat important, or not important?"
15:	"Some people claim that the Nazi extermination of the Jews never happened. Have you ever heard this claim, or not?"
16:	"Does it seem possible or does it seem impossible to you that the Nazi extermination of the Jews never happened?"

TABLE 3.5. Ranking of East and West Germany's Response Ratios in International Comparison

Topic	Question #	Attitude Question	West Germany	East Germany
Resentment	1	Zionism is racism (disagree)	2 of 7	2 of 7
	2	Jewish president (approve)	9 of 20	7 of 20
	3	Jews provoke hostility (no)	6 of 10	4 of 10
	4	Jewish influence society (no)	17 of 19	7 of 19
Social distance	5	Jews in neighborhood (approve)	3 of 14	2 of 14
Concern	6	Antisemitism is a problem in society (yes)	4 of 10	1 of 10
	7	Future of antisemitism in society (increase)	4 of 10	1 of 10
Knowledge	8	Knowledge of term "Holocaust" (yes)	1 of 6	2 of 6
	9	Recognition of yellow star/Star of David (yes)	2 of 7	1 of 7
	10	Recognition of concentration camp names (yes)	2 of 7	1 of 7
	11	Knowledge of estimate of killed Jews in Holocaust (yes)	3 of 7	3 of 7
	12	Knowledge of persecuted victim groups (yes)	3 of 7	1 of 7
Remembrance	13	Relevance of Holocaust today (agree)	7 of 7	3 of 7
	14	Need to understand and know Holocaust (yes)	7 of 7	4 of 7
Revisionism	15	Heard claim that Holocaust never happened (yes)	1 of 7	3 of 7
	16	Possible that extermination never happened (no)	3 of 6	4 of 6

Note: Response ratios represent dichotomized answer patterns to the same or similar question in comparison with other Western and European countries (see appendix, tables 3.3 and 3.4). For example, the West Germans' ranking position of 1 indicates that they display the best knowledge in understanding the meaning of the term "Holocaust" in comparison with six other countries polled. Elite opinion leaders' responses in East and West Germany are not included.

TABLE 3.6. Scales Used for Evaluation of Three German Attitudinal Surveys

Jodice Poll 1990	Antisemitism Scale	Antiremembrance Scale		
	Cronbach's alpha = .76 Jews exploit Holocaust (Q26) Too much Jewish world influence (Q27)	Cronbach's alpha = .67 Put Holocaust behind us (Q20) Against payment of reparations after unification (Q21A) For normal relationship with state Israel (Q22)		
Dichotomized coding	0 = Weak antisemitism (0, 1) 1 = Strong antisemitism (2)	0 = Support remembrance (0, 1) 1 = Oppose remembrance (2, 3)		
West	Weak 63.8%, Strong: 36.2% N = 915	Support: 30.8%, Oppose: 69.2% N = 1,020		
East	Weak: 86%, Strong: 14% N = 732	Support: 59.7%, Oppose: 40.3% N = 845		
Spiegel Poll 1992	Antisemitism Scale	Antiremembrance Scale	Antiforeigner Scale	Foreigner Antipathy Scale
	Cronbach's alpha = .73 Jews exploit Holocaust (V21) Jews partly responsible for hate (V23) Too much Jewish world influence (V55) Not liking Jews in Germany (V630) Not liking Jews in Israel (V650)	Cronbach's alpha = .59 Feel no shame for German crimes (V22) Draw a line and consider past closed because crimes of others similar (V105) Guilt talks is jealousy of others (V106)	Cronbach's alpha = .73 Foreigners intensify unemployment (V92) Foreigners abuse welfare (V93) Politicians privilege foreigners (V94)	Cronbach's alpha = .73 Dislike Turks in Germany (V610) Dislike asylants from Eastern Europe (V690) Dislike asylants from Africa (V730) Dislike accepted asylants (V810)

	Antisemitism Scale	Antiremembrance Scale	Low Holocaust Knowledge Scale	Xenophobia Scale
Dichotomized coding	0 = Weak antisemitism (0–2) 1 = Strong antisemitism (3–5)	0 = Support remembrance (0,1) 1 = Oppose remembrance (2, 3)	0 = Weak resentment (2, 3) 1 = Strong resentment (0, 1)	0 = Like groups (0, 1) 1 = Dislike groups (2–4)
West	Weak: 71.7%, Strong: 27.3% N = 1904	Support: 35.8%, Oppose: 64.2% N = 1703	Weak: 34.1%, Strong: 65.9% N = 1,897	Like: 54.6%, Dislike: 45.4% N = 1,889
East	Weak: 87.5%, Strong: 12.5% N = 988	Support: 50.9%, Oppose: 49.1% N = 993	Weak: 43.8%, Strong: 56.2% N = 987	Like: 59.6%, Dislike: 40.4% N = 972
Golub Poll 1994	Antisemitism Scale	Antiremembrance Scale	Low Holocaust Knowledge Scale	Xenophobia Scale
	Cronbach's alpha = .80 Resent Jewish neighbor (F110_8) Jews provoke hostility (F111_8) Too much Jewish societal influence (F113_8) Disapprove Jewish presidential candidate (F116) Too much Jewish world influence (F117) Jews exploit Holocaust (F128)	Cronbach's alpha = .68 Holocaust not relevant today (F125) Knowledge and understanding of Holocaust unimportant (F127) Draw a line and consider past closed (F129)	Cronbach's alpha = .55 Little knowledge of term Holocaust (F118) Little knowledge camps (F119) Little knowledge of yellow star (F124)	Cronbach's alpha = .79 Gypsies provoke hostility (F111_2) Arabs provoke hostility (F111_3) Vietnamese provoke hostility (F111_4) Turks provoke hostility (F111_5) Poles provoke hostility (F111_6) Africans provoke hostility (F111_7)
Dichotomized coding	0 = Weak antisemitism (0–2) 1 = Strong antisemitism (3–6)	0 = Support remembrance (0–1) 1 = Oppose remembrance (2–3)	0 = Much knowledge (0–1) 1 = Little knowledge (2–3)	0 = Weak xenophobia (0–2) 1 = Strong xenophobia (3–6)
West	Weak: 72.1%, Strong: 27.9% N = 1160	Support: 56.5%, Oppose: 43.5% N = 1129	Much: 81.4%, Little: 18.6% N = 1167	Weak: 77.4%, Strong: 22.6% N = 1055
East	Weak: 86.1%, Strong: 13.9%, N = 301	Support: 75.9%, Oppose: 24.1% N = 292	Much: 69.6%, Little: 30.4% N = 302	Weak: 83.3%, Strong:16.7% N = 269

TABLE 3.7. German Attitudinal Survey Questions

Golub Poll 1994

F110__8: "How do you feel about having Jews in your neighborhood?" Answer: "Would you like to have some Jewish neighbors?" (1), "Wouldn't it make any difference to you?" (2), "Would you prefer not to have any Jewish neighbors?" (3).

F111__2: "Do Gypsies behave in a manner which provokes hostility toward them in our country?" Answer: "Yes" (1), "No" (0).

F111__3: "Do Arabs behave in a manner which provokes hostility toward them in our country?" Answer: "Yes" (1), "No" (0).

F111__4: "Do Vietnamese behave in a manner which provokes hostility toward them in our country?" Answer: "Yes" (1), "No" (0).

F111__5: "Do Turks behave in a manner which provokes hostility toward them in our country?" Answer: "Yes" (1), "No" (0).

F111__6: "Do Poles behave in a manner which provokes hostility toward them in our country?" Answer: "Yes" (1), "No" (0).

F111__7: "Do Africans behave in a manner which provokes hostility toward them in our country?" Answer: "Yes" (1), "No" (0).

F111__8: "Do Jews behave in a manner which provokes hostility toward them in our country?" Answer: "Yes" (1), "No" (0).

F113__8: "Have Jews too much influence in our society?" Answer: "Too much" (1), "Too little" (2), "The right amount" (3).

F116: "If a party nominated a Jew as its candidate for president of Germany, would you approve (1), disapprove (2), or would the candidate's Jewishness make no difference to you?" (3).

F117: "Now, as in the past, Jews exert too much influence on world events." Answer: "Agree strongly" (1), "Agree somewhat" (2), "Disagree somewhat" (3), "Disagree strongly" (4).

F118: "As far as you know, what does the term 'the Holocaust' refer to?" Answer open-ended with codes: "Extermination etc. of Jews by Hitler/Nazis/Germans" (1), "Extermination etc. of Jews" (2), "Other relevant responses" (3), "Others" (4).

F119: "From what you know or have heard, what were Auschwitz, Dachau, and Treblinka?" Answer open-ended: "Concentration camps" (1), "Other responses" (2).

F124: "Many Jews in Europe were forced to wear a symbol on their clothes during the Second World War. What was it?" Answer open-ended: "Yellow star/Jewish star/Star of David" (1), "Other responses" (2).

F125: "The Holocaust is not relevant today because it happened almost 50 years ago." Answer: "Agree strongly" (1), "Agree somewhat" (2), "Disagree somewhat" (3), "Disagree strongly" (4).

F127: "In your view, how important is it for Germans to know about and understand the Holocaust?" Answer: "Essential" (1), "Very important" (2), "Only somewhat important" (3), "Not important" (4).

F128: "Jews are exploiting the National Socialist Holocaust for their own purposes." Answer: "Agree strongly" (1), "Agree somewhat" (2), "Disagree somewhat" (3), "Disagree strongly" (4).

TABLE 3.7. *(continued)*

F129__: "Recently someone said: 'Today, in the aftermath of German unification, we should not talk so much about the Holocaust, but should rather draw a line and consider the past closed [*Schlußstrich ziehen*].' Would you say this is correct (1) or incorrect?" (2).

Jodice Poll 1990

Q20: "With the opening of a new chapter in German history, 45 years after the end of the Second World War, it is time to put the memory of the Holocaust behind us?" Answer: "Agree strongly" (1), "Agree somewhat" (2), "Disagree somewhat" (3), "Disagree strongly" (4).

Q21a: "Do you think that the German government should, after unification of the two German states, pay reparations to Jews?" Answer: "Agree strongly" (1), "Agree somewhat" (2), "Disagree somewhat" (3), "Disagree strongly" (4).

Q22: "As far as our relationship to Israel is concerned, we should not let ourselves be burdened by the past and the events during the Third Reich. Israel is a state like any other" (1), "Because of the events during the Third Reich, we have a special obligation toward Jews and also toward Israel. We cannot treat Israel like any other country on earth" (2).

Q26: "Jews are exploiting the National Socialist Holocaust for their own purposes." Answer: "Agree strongly" (1), "Agree somewhat" (2), "Disagree somewhat" (3), "Disagree strongly" (4).

Q27: "Now as in the past, Jews exert too much influence on world events." Answer: "Agree strongly" (1), "Agree somewhat" (2), "Disagree somewhat" (3), "Disagree strongly" (4).

Spiegel Poll 1992

V21: "If somebody would tell you, "Many Jews try to take advantage of the Third Reich and make the Germans pay for it,' how would you answer?" Answer: "That's correct" (1), "There's some truth" (2), "That's incorrect" (3), "It is impossible to answer" (4).

V22: "I am ashamed that Germans have committed so many crimes against Jews." Answer: Scale of 6 possible answers ranging from "Strongly agree" (1) to "Strongly disagree" (6).

V23: "Jews are partly to blame for the persecution and hate against them." Answer: Scale of 6 possible answers ranging from "Is entirely true" (1) to "Is entirely untrue" (6).

V55: "Jews have too much influence in the world." Answer: "True" (1), "Not true" (2), "Undecided" (3).

V92: "Foreigners coming now to Germany aggravate the unemployment of Germans." Answer: "Yes" (1), "Fairly certainly" (2), "Less certainly" (3), "No" (4).

V93: "Foreigners coming now to Germany abuse the services of our welfare system." Answer: "Yes" (1), "Fairly certainly" (2), "Less certainly" (3), "No" (4).

V95: "Most German politicians are too concerned about foreigners coming now to Germany and not concerned enough about Germans." Answer: "Yes" (1), "Fairly certainly" (2), "Less certainly" (3), "No" (4).

V105: "We should draw a line and consider the past closed [*Schlußstrich ziehen*]. Other people have done just as bad things as we have." Answer: Scale of 6 possible answers ranging from "Disagree very strongly" (1) to "Agree very strongly" (6).

TABLE 3.7. *(continued)*

V106: "The permanent talk about the guilt of the Germans in other countries often indicates envy about German efficiency and affluence." Answer: Scale of 6 possible answers ranging from "Disagree very strongly" (1) to "Agree very strongly" (6).

V610: "Please judge some people according to your sympathy for them. How sympathetic are you to the Turks living in Germany?" Answer: Scale of 11 possible answers ranging from "Very unsympathetic" (−5) to "Very sympathetic" (+5).

V630: "How sympathetic are you to the Jews living in Germany?" Answer: Scale of 11 possible answers ranging from "Very unsympathetic" (−5) to "Very sympathetic" (+5).

V650: "How sympathetic are you to the Jews living in Israel?" Answer: Scale of 11 possible answers ranging from "Very unsympathetic" (−5) to "Very sympathetic" (+5).

V690: "Please judge some people according to your sympathy for them. How sympathetic are you to the asylum seekers from Eastern Europe?" Answer: Scale of 11 possible answers ranging from "Very unsympathetic" (−5) to "Very sympathetic" (+5).

V730: "Please judge some people according to your sympathy for them. How sympathetic are you to the asylum seekers from Africa?" Answer: Scale of 11 possible answers ranging from "Very unsympathetic" (−5) to "Very sympathetic" (+5).

V810: "Please judge some people according to your sympathy for them. How sympathetic are you to the foreigners in Germany accepted as legal political refugees?" Answer: Scale of 11 possible answers ranging from "Very unsympathetic" (−5) to "Very sympathetic" (+5).

TABLE 3.8. Response Typology Based on Attitude Scales (Jodice Poll 1990)

Scale Type	Response Characteristics		West Germany 1990 N=940	East Germany 1990 N=800
	Antisemitism	Remembrance		
1J (N = 366)	Strong	Oppose	32.0%	8.1%
2J (N = 68)	Strong	Support	3.3	4.6
3J (N = 548)	Weak	Oppose	34.4	28.1
4J (N = 758)	Weak	Support	30.3	59.1

TABLE 3.9. Response Typology Based on Attitude Scales (*Spiegel* Poll 1992)

Scale Type	Response Characteristics			West Germany 1991 N = 1,894	East Germany 1991 N = 980
	Antisemitism	Remembrance	Antiforeigner		
1aS (N = 434)	Strong	Oppose	Strong	19.1%	7.3%
1bS (N = 58)	Strong	Oppose	Weak	2.0	2.1
2aS (N = 125)	Strong	Support	Strong	5.5	2.1
2bS (N = 17)	Strong	Support	Weak	0.7	0.4
3aS (N = 846)	Weak	Oppose	Strong	30	28.3
3bS (N = 362)	Weak	Oppose	Weak	13.1	11.5
4aS (N = 397)	Weak	Support	Strong	11.4	19.6
4bS (N = 635)	Weak	Support	Weak	18.2	29.6

TABLE 3.10. Response Typology Based on Attitude Scales (Golub Poll 1994)

Scale Type	Response Characteristics			West Germany 1994 N = 1,127	East Germany 1994 N = 291
	Antisemitism	Remembrance	Holocaust Knowledge		
1aG (N = 44)	Strong	Oppose	Little	3.5%	1.7%
1bG (N = 198)	Strong	Oppose	Much	16.5	4.0
2aG (N = 35)	Strong	Support	Little	2.1	3.9
2bG (N = 78)	Strong	Support	Much	6.4	2.0
3aG (N = 100)	Weak	Oppose	Little	6.1	10.8
3bG (N = 219)	Weak	Oppose	Much	17.4	7.7
4aG (N = 100)	Weak	Support	Little	5.4	13.4
4bG (N = 644)	Weak	Support	Much	42.5	56.4

TABLE 3.11. Distribution of Response Types Based on Dichotomized Attitude Scales from Three Consecutive German Polls in 1990, 1991, and 1994

Scale Type	Response Characteristics		West Germany			East Germany		
	Antisemitism	Remembrance	1990 N=940	1991 N=1,894	1994 N=1,127	1990 N=800	1991 N=981	1994 N=291
1	Strong	Oppose	32.0%	21.1%	20.0%	8.1%	9.4%	5.7%
2	Strong	Support	3.3	6.2	8.5	4.6	2.5	5.9
3	Weak	Oppose	34.4	43.1	23.5	28.1	39.8	18.5
4	Weak	Support	30.3	29.6	47.9	59.1	49.2	69.8

Note: Typology percentages differ in each category because scales from the three surveys are based on different questions (see appendix, tables 3.6 and 3.7).

TABLE 3.12. Strength of Attitudinal Pearson's *r* and Gamma *γ* (in parentheses) Correlations of West and East German Respondents Polled in Three Consecutive German Polls in 1990, 1991, and 1994 Based on Dichotomized Scales

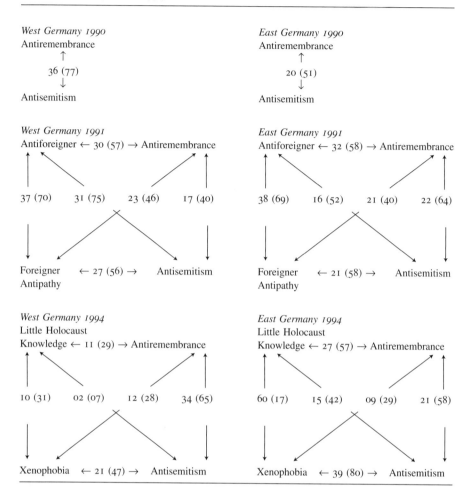

West Germany 1990
Antiremembrance
↑
36 (77)
↓
Antisemitism

East Germany 1990
Antiremembrance
↑
20 (51)
↓
Antisemitism

West Germany 1991
Antiforeigner ← 30 (57) → Antiremembrance

37 (70)   31 (75)   23 (46)   17 (40)

Foreigner   ← 27 (56) →   Antisemitism
Antipathy

East Germany 1991
Antiforeigner ← 32 (58) → Antiremembrance

38 (69)   16 (52)   21 (40)   22 (64)

Foreigner   ← 21 (58) →   Antisemitism
Antipathy

West Germany 1994
Little Holocaust
Knowledge ← 11 (29) → Antiremembrance

10 (31)   02 (07)   12 (28)   34 (65)

Xenophobia   ← 21 (47) →   Antisemitism

East Germany 1994
Little Holocaust
Knowledge ← 27 (57) → Antiremembrance

60 (17)   15 (42)   09 (29)   21 (58)

Xenophobia   ← 39 (80) →   Antisemitism

TABLE 3.13. Summary of Logistic Regression Coefficients for Attitude Scales and Response Typologies in East and West Germany (*Spiegel* Poll 1991)

Dependent Variable	Antisemitism Scale 1991		Antiforeigner Scale 1991		Antiremembrance Scale 1991	
	East	West	East	West	East	West
Age (years)	-.00	.01*	.01*	.01***	.01	.01***
Sex (male)	-.33	.15	-.02	-.07	.13	.12
Education (high)	-1.37***	-.08	-.50*	-.85***	-.79***	-.25
Occupation (non−blue collar)	-.03	-.32**	-.62***	-.33**	-.44**	-.27*
North-South (South)	.41	.60***	.23	.16	.20	-.33*
City size (over 50,000)	-.32	-.53***	-.86***	.41**	-.57***	-.24
Catholic (yes)	X	.20	X	.94***	X	-.12
Protestant (yes)	-.04	.25	.12	.73***	.11	-.38
Atheist (yes)	-.18	.11	.16	.43	.41	-.87***
Church attendance (often)	.29	-.03	-.42	-.54***	.33	-.28*
Green−PDS voter (yes)	-1.38*	.11	-.46	-.26	-.42	-.66*
CDU/CSU voter (yes)	-.13	.30**	.13	.31**	.28	.13
"Republikaner" voter (yes)	3.60***	1.35***	2.70*	2.31***	.76	1.42***
No vote (yes)	-.46	.14	.35	.42*	.35	.60***
Political interest (no)	.09	.16	-.05	.69***	-.06	.49***
Pro-youth discipline (yes)	.92***	.49***	.60***	.72***	1.52***	.85***
Economic situation (unsatisfactory)	-.20	.07	.41**	.36***	.01	-.04
Constant	-1.87***	-2.49***	-.19	-1.11***	-1.01**	.30
N	938	1,831	941	1,830	943	1,834
−2 Log Likelihood	593.8	2068.7	1134.6	2077.6	1087.8	2168.1
Degrees of freedom	16	17	16	17	16	17
Correctly placed	89%	72%	67%	72%	70%	70%

*p < .05. **p < .01. ***p < .001. − = negative correlation. X = variables excluded from regression because cell contents are too small or data is missing.

TABLE 3.13. (continued)

Dependent Variable	Scale Type 1aS (1991): Antisemitic/ Antiforeigner/ Antiremembrance		Scale Type 3aS (1991): Weak Antisemitic/ Antiforeigner/ Antiremembrance		Scale Type 3bS (1991): Weak Antisemitic/ Foreigner Neutral/ Antiremembrance		Scale Type 4bS (1991): Weak Antisemitic/ Foreigner Neutral/ Proremembrance	
	East	West	East	West	East	West	East	West
Age (years)	.00	.01	.01*	.00	-.01	.01	-.00	-.02***
Sex (male)	.32	.17	-.10	-.14	.56**	.29*	-.06	-.14
Education (high)	-1.85***	-.13	-.57**	-.95***	.04	.63***	.61***	.47***
Occupation (non–blue collar)	.08	-.40***	-.72***	-.03	.57*	.07	.61***	.53***
North-South (South)	.25	.16	-.12	-.23	.27	-.30	-.55***	.18
City size (over 50,000)	-.56	-.03	-.73***	-.16	.35	-.09	.79***	-.48**
Catholic (yes)	X	.70*	X	.44	X	-.88***	X	.06
Protestant (yes)	-.22	.66*	-.06	.18	.21	-.88***	-.37	.30
Atheist (yes)	-.07	.42	.21	-.14	.22	-1.03***	-.43	.75*
Church attendance (often)	.30	-.35*	-.21	-.36**	.24	.42*	.09	.30
Green–PDS voter (yes)	-.72	-.07	.07	-.38	-.65	-.70	.77***	.65*
CDU/CSU voter (yes)	-.27	.29*	.13	-.08	.46	.12	-.66***	-.52***
Republikaner voter (yes)	2.70***	1.60***	-1.21	.16	-2.03	-1.33	-2.39	-5.45
No vote (yes)	-.36	.23	.78***	.23	-.44	.22	-.19	-1.03***
Political interest (no)	-.21	.32*	-.21	.34**	.20	-.26	-.23	-.97***
Pro-youth discipline (yes)	1.04***	1.04***	.93***	.31***	.74***	-.26	-1.36***	-.79***
Economic situation (unsatisfactory)	-.15	-.01	.27	.03	-.13	-.00	-.31	-.34**
Constant	-2.99***	-3.01***	-1.55***	-1.03***	-3.26***	-1.46***	.02	-.29
N	943	1,834	943	1,834	943	1,834	943	1,834
–2 Log Likelihood	433.6	1667.5	987.4	2140.3	636.6	1365.4	901.0	1472.3
Degrees of freedom	16	17	16	17	16	17	16	17
Correctly placed	93%	80%	75%	69%	88%	87%	76%	83%

*p < .05. **p < .01. ***p < .001. - = negative correlation ; X = variables excluded from regression because cell contents are too small or data is missing.

TABLE 3.14. Variables Used for Logistic Regression of Attitude Scales
(*Spiegel* Poll 1992)

Age of respondent (interval)
Sex of respondent (o = female/1 = male)
Education (o = primary-secondary/1 = secondary+)
Occupation (o = blue collar/1 = other than blue collar)
Employment (o = employed or in training/1 = not or not employed any more)
Union membership (o = no/1 = yes)
Region (o = North/1 = South)
City size (o = under 50,000/1 = over 50,000)
Religious affiliation Catholic (1 = Catholic/o = other)
Religious affiliation Protestant (1 = Protestant/o = other)
Religious affiliation atheist (1 = atheist/o = other)
Respondent's church attendance (1 = often/o = seldom)
Sunday vote, i.e., respondent's vote if there would be a national election next Sunday (1 = Green
    Party-PDS/ o= Other)
Sunday vote (1 = Christian Democratic Union/Christian Social Union/o = other)
Sunday vote (1 = "Republikaner" Party/o = other)
Sunday vote (1 = nonvoter/o = other)
Respondent's political interest (o = yes/1 = no)
"The youth should be much stronger disciplined" (Man sollte die Jugendlichen härter anfassen)
    (1 = agree/o = disagree)
Judgment of own economic (wirtschaftliche) situation (1 = unsatisfactory/o = satisfactory)

NOTES

The author is grateful for helpful comments on earlier drafts by Kay Losey, Konrad Jarausch, Siegfried Mews, Henry Landsberger, Stefan Immerfall, and Heike Trappe.

1. In this chapter the term *antisemitism* will be used "broadly to cover less favorable or lower ratings and evaluations of Jews" (Smith 1991: 1), thereby not limiting the term to extreme anti-Jewish hostility (Allport 1954: 9). Such a broad definition reflects the increasing difficulty to define and compare present-day antisemitism in Western countries in the terms of "classical" racial antisemitism during the first half of this century (Bauer 1994: 12). The term *xenophobia* signifies unduly fearful, hostile, or contemptuous attitudes toward strangers or foreigners, particularly in the cultural and political realm. The terms *remembrance* and *confrontation* of the past *(Vergangenheitsaufarbeitung)* will be used to depict an attitude that accepts Germany's shame or guilt, takes responsibility and makes reparations for the Nazi crimes, keeps uncomfortable memories alive, and agrees that knowledge and understanding of the Holocaust are important for future generations to avoid a repetition.

2. Because a past cannot be overcome nor undone, Andrei S. Markovits suggests the less euphoric terms *confrontation* and *coping with the past (Vergangenheitsaufarbeitung),* which I also prefer *(Markovits* 1990: 273).

3. Jews in united Germany (the huge majority living in the West) currently represent about 60,000 persons or 0.08 percent of the population. Their number has strongly risen since unification because of the influx of Jewish immigrants and refugees from the former Soviet Union.

4. Philosemitism became a "German therapy for German pain. The Jew became the enemy who now had to be loved" (Frank Stern 1994: 86).

5. Like Michael R. Marrus, they argue that "most people alive in North America and Europe were born considerably after World War II; for them, the notion of some sort of personal or inherited responsibility for what happened to Jews forty years ago seems inherently absurd. . . . For most the Holocaust occurred further back in their sense of time than many of us like to imagine. It was not their parents who were making decisions during the war years, but their grandparents or even their great-grandparents" (Marrus 1986: 177).

6. "Jews are as bound to Germany as Germany is to Jews. . . . mainly latter-generation Germans, want to break out of these unavoidable links. The other, Jewish side cannot allow the Germans to escape this historical bind without endangering their own Jewish identity" (Wolffsohn 1993: 66 f.).

7. "It is a matter of human weakness for the memories of the relatives of those who harmed others to be less developed and long-term than the memories of those who were harmed. This also applies to the relations between peoples and countries" (Yitzhak Ben Ari, former Israeli ambassador to Germany, cited in Levkov 1987: 289).

8. The 1990 and 1994 AJC data were made available by David Jodice (D3 Systems) and the Zentralarchiv für Sozialforschung in Cologne, Germany. The author is indebted to Dr. David Singer, Research Director of the AJC in New York for support in data acquisition. The 1990 poll included interviews with 101 East and West German political and economic leaders, a majority of whom display significantly lower prejudice and resentment than the average German respondent. Elite responses are included in the sample and not separately evaluated.

9. The *Spiegel* data presented are based on a raw data evaluation of extracted item marginals with some cross-tabulation results the author received from the *Der Spiegel* magazine. Additional evaluations are based on data analyses undertaken at Technical University of Berlin, Center for Research on Antisemitism.

10. Nevertheless, the results have to be interpreted cautiously because the relatively high nonresponse ratio and the wording of the "Zionism" and other questions raise some doubt about the reliability to measure antisemitism and prejudice with the questionnaire used. See the critical discussion of poll instruments and methods to measure antisemitism by Feingold (1985: 320), Curtis (1986: 8), Glazer (1986: 155 ff.), Marrus (1986: 172 ff.), Raab (1986: 288 f.), Segre (1986: 145 ff.), Weil (1987: 183), (1990: 138), Smith (1991: 22 ff.), Bauer (1994: 20), Brown (1994: 8), and Smith (1994: 5 ff.).

11. Studies about antisemitism in Eastern Europe after 1990 have focused on the ultranationalist, xenophobic, and revisionist political fringe (e.g., Braham 1994). Few studies have attempted to assess the distribution of antisemitism in comparative perspective by using mass opinion poll data.

12. The appearance of the revisionist historian David Irving, for example, resulted in a public demonstration of 10,000 "anti-facists" in Berlin in May 1992, a number hardly matched anywhere else (Merkl 1994: 447).

13. In comparison with the average respondents the economic and political leaders in East and West Germany polled in 1990 (Jodice 1991) display significantly lower anti-Jewish resentment, are more supportive of remembrance and reparations, and feel more content that antisemitism is not threatening German society. Only East German leaders displayed—shortly after unification—more insecurity about the extent and future of antisemitism.

14. According to Jack Zipes, the Communist Party rationalized its decision as follows: "After all, why should the victims of fascism, namely the communists, pay other victims for crimes that they, the communists, did not commit? Recognition of Israel was likened to recognition of guilt" (Zipes 1991: 12). In contrast, West Germany accepted responsibility, recognized Israel, returned property to Jewish exiles, and has paid since 1951 about $57

billion to Jewish agencies, individuals, and the State of Israel. West Germany agreed to compensate Holocaust survivors for the rest of their lives. The last payments are estimated to last until 2025. The *Wiedergutmachung* is estimated at a total of at least about $80 billion dollars (Herbst and Göschler 1989, German Information Center 1994).

15. Polls also indicate that liberal Western values and attitudes are relatively strongly embedded in East German mass opinion. The question remains, how could East Germans after 13 years of Nazism and 40 years of socialist indoctrination maintain, develop, or acquire this quickly a democratic political culture that resembles very much those in the West? See chapter 5.

16. The use of mathematical-statistical models and standardized poll answers necessarily implies a loss of information and generalizations. A particular disadvantage is the lack of knowledge about individual response motivations and legitimations that can be gained sufficiently only by qualitative in-depth studies.

17. Comparative data for this statement are only available for Austria. A 1991 poll found that 32% of polled Austrians agree strongly or somewhat with the "exploitation" question, 37% disagree strongly or somewhat, and 32% did not answer. Those who disagree are younger, better educated, less religious, more urban, Green party voters. In contrast, 50% of voters in the Freiheitliche Partei Österreichs (FPÖ) a populist right-wing party, agree with the statement. Also, weekly churchgoers and older men living in rural areas are more suspicious (Karmasin 1992). Resentment in Austria is lower than in West Germany because until the Walheim affair in 1986 neither domestic nor external moral and political pressures existed in Austria comparable to those in the FRG, nor has Austria paid reparations to the same degree as West Germany (Pauley 1992).

18. Though not very popular, united Germany paid several hundred million dollars to Jewish organizations inside and outside Germany in the wake of unification and ensured compensation of prewar and wartime-related Jewish property claims in East Germany. The $880 million in German humanitarian aid and military assistance to Israel during the Gulf War also was related to Germany's special obligations toward Israel's security and well-being resulting from the past.

19. But 35% of this group supporting "drawing a line" also thought the Holocaust is still "relevant today," 57% believed it important "to know about and understand the Holocaust," and 75% were concerned about antisemitism in Germany. Similarly, among respondents of the 1990 Jodice survey who wanted to "put the memory of the Holocaust behind" them, 56% believed that prosecution of "Nazi war criminals" should continue, 81% agreed to "ban antisemitic groups," and 83% wanted the German government to continue to "teach about the Nazi period in history lessons in the schools. However, only 19% of respondents thought that Germany should, after unification, continue to "pay reparations to Jews."

20. The author is aware of the methodological problems of poll data evaluation, such as scale reliability, questionnaire construction, nonresponse, questionnaire wording, index building, recoding, and so on. (Smith 1991). Because of the absence of other reliable alternatives measuring mass opinions, a cautious use of scales is legitimate.

21. For example, increased German-Jewish/Israeli tensions during the Gulf War in December 1991, seem to have influenced response patterns in the *Spiegel* (1992) survey compared to the polls of 1990 and 1994. Questions that show atypical variations over time were "Jewish world influence," "drawing a line," "reparation payments to Israel," "Jewish exploitation of the Holocaust," the German-Israeli relationship, Arab-Israeli relations, and questions about the Middle East peace process.

22. See B. Rommelspacher, cited by Bergmann and Erb (1991a: 295, n. 7).

23. In interpreting survey data, it is important to distinguish between widely reported violent incidents against mainly asylum seekers, Gypsies, Arabs, Turks, and non-White

foreigners—often undertaken by small groups of apolitical youth gangs, local skinheads, and drunks—and mass opinion analyzed here (see Farin and Seidel-Pielen 1993).

24. Pearson's product moment correlation coefficient r is a dimensionless index that ranges from a value of -1 (a perfect negative) to $+1$ (a perfect positive linear relationship between two data sets). A value of 0 indicates no linear relationship. Gamma γ is a measure of association between two ordinal-level variables. Gamma γ is symmetric and ranges from 0 (no relationship) to 1 (perfect relationship).

25. The latency questions are: "Many do not dare to give their true opinion about Jews" and "For me the whole Jewish topic is somewhat unpleasant." Unfortunately these questions were only available for the Spiegel 1992 poll.

26. Questions with wording that provoked strong sentiments and biased judgment were more often refused and more often categorized under the nonresponse group. Questions with high percentages of undecided respondents in the *Spiegel* 1992 poll were those about "drawing a line" [*Schlußstrich*], "Jewish Holocaust exploitation," "collective responsibility of Germans," "Jewish world influence," "reparation for East Germany," "truth of Holocaust reports," "superiority of Germans," and the alleged "Jewish deicide." The fact that many respondents refused to give answers to simplistic or stereotypically worded questions may, as Karmasin (1992) has demonstrated for Austria, reveal awareness about the prejudicial character of a question or issue and indicate that such preset answers do not capture the complexity and variation of respondent motives.

27. See Selznick and Steinberg (1969), Clark and Martire (1982), Weil (1990: 140, 157), Bergmann and Erb (1991a), Smith (1991), Sniderman and Piazza (1993), and Smith (1994).

28. The "Republikaner" offer simple solutions for various national and social problems: statism, ethnocentrism, rewriting of German history, fixation on traditional family structures and gender roles, hypernationalism, and so on (Jaschke 1990).

29. Scale type 2 respondents display similarities with scale type 1 persons. Therefore and because of their relatively small size, they were excluded from further analysis.

30. The characteristics of the contrast groups are similar to findings of a qualitative study among 2,000 West Germans in January 1991 about historical awareness (see F. P. Lutz 1993: 157 ff.).

31. See Minkenberg (1992: 59–70, 1994: 174 ff.), Kowalsky and Schroeder (1994), and Kurthen and Minkenberg (1995: 188 f.).

32. See, for example, Ackerman and Jahoda (1950), Allport (1954), Bettelheim and Janowitz (1964), Simpson and Yinger (1972).

33. The questions were, "Do you believe in an enduring peace in a time not too far?" and "Who should be more conciliatory after the first peace negotiations in Madrid in November 1991—Israelis or Palestinians?"

34. During Israel's involvement in the Lebanon War of the 1980s, U.S. ratings of Israel declined parallel to an increasing political rift between the United States and Israel. In contrast, the threat to Israel during the Gulf War and the recent peace initiatives of the Israeli Rabin-Peres government have increased sympathy toward Israel.

35. During the Gulf War, the Green Party was blamed for Left antisemitism and anti-Zionism. However, the party has developed a self-critical and open dialogue, particularly during and after the Gulf War (Martin W. Kloke, cited in Strauss, Bergmann and Hoffman 1990: 152). Simplistic and antagonistic views on the Middle East conflict and the Israeli-Arab peace process have been more critically debated in this party than in any other. Post-unification polls verify that Green Party supporters are the least antisemitic and least xenophobic group.

36. Fifty-nine percent of Israeli Jews have a negative and 17% a neutral view (mean -1.6 on a scale from -2 to $+2$). Israelis perceive Germans as negative as they do Pales-

tinians. Only a minority of Israeli Jews are willing to distinguish between Nazi Germany and Germany today. Twenty percent of Israeli Jews perceive Germans sympathetically and 4% "very sympathetically," in contrast to those who see Germans unsympathetically (25%) or very unsympathetically (34%).

37. A preliminary evaluation of the Israeli survey using scales found that about 38% of Israeli respondents displayed strong anti-German resentment; among them were 25% who expressed negative attitudes about Germans in connection with strong memories about the Holocaust. Another 26% were proremembrance but had no coherent negative view about Germany. Thirty-five percent of all respondents had neither strong memories about the Holocaust nor were they anti-German. This group was typically Israeli-born males with weak ties to Orthodox Judaism or the political Right and with low interest in German affairs. The strongly anti-German group represented in particular highly educated females with strong attachment to religion and a strong interest in German affairs.

38. The sympathy gap between Israeli Jews and Germans also shows up in mutual trait scales. Measuring 22 traits on a scale from 1 (positive trait) to 7 (negative trait), German respondents judged Israeli Jews more positively (mean: 3.22). In contrast, Israelis' judgment about Germans (mean: 4.15) was more negative. When asked, many respondents in both countries chose sterotypical traits about the other group. However, respondents in both countries gave each other surprisingly similar evaluations regarding traits such as independence, decisiveness, creativeness, self-consciousness, conscientiousness, cosmopolitanism, trustfulness, and tolerance. This may indicate a shift to a more realistic and reciprocal perception in which Germans and Israelis discover commonalities that may create a bridge from the past to the future.

39. "A world of difference exists between a wave of antisemitism and a wave of articles and television programs about antisemitism" (Cesarani 1991: 14).

40. See a similar effect for Israel (Smith 1991: 24, n. 15) and M. Zimmermann (1992).

41. See also F. P. Lutz (1993: 170) and scale type 4 respondent characteristics.

42. One has to avoid trying to "build a mandatory guilt feeling into a conscience, be it individual or national, [because it would create] . . . a situation that demands release—release from the tensions of always being guilty, of being irredeemable. Ultimately it leads to denial, because denying the past is easier than bearing the guilt" (John G. Gagliardo, cited in Levkov 1987: 461).

4

MANFRED BRUSTEN

Knowledge, Feelings, and Attitudes of German University Students toward the Holocaust

Immediately after German unification, social scientists had a historic chance to conduct "binational" comparative research on the Federal Republic of Germany (FRG) and the German Democratic Republic (GDR). Until then the states had been two separate, independent political entities with different and partially antagonistic political and economic structures. Social science got the chance not only to study the peaceful process of unification, transformation, and integration of two societies but also to conduct research that had not been possible for decades because of the tense and hostile political atmosphere between West and East. Thus, for instance, it suddenly became possible to do comparative research within these two societies on the effects of the very distinct process of political socialization and its impact on knowledge, emotions, and attitudes. The question was: What are the most striking typical differences in knowledge, emotions, and attitudes of young West Germans and East Germans as a result of the two antagonistic sociopolitical systems?

My own research about East and West German students' knowledge and attitudes concerning the Third Reich and the Holocaust conducted in 1992 is unique in that respect.[1] It concentrated on two fields:[2] (1) the investigation of differences and similarities in knowledge, emotions, and attitudes related to the Holocaust among students in West and East Germany;[3] (2) the exploration of the political background of knowledge, emotions, and attitudes related to the Holocaust.

Research Design and Sample

Our research was conducted in the early summer of 1992 in Wuppertal, Halle, Magdeburg, and East Berlin. In all, 1,342 students of different academic fields in five universities, teacher academies, and technical colleges participated in the survey. The sample consisted of 699 West German students, born and educated in the FRG and 643 students born and brought up in the former socialist GDR.

The extensive questionnaire covered mainly questions related to German history, in particular the Third Reich and the Holocaust, but also more recent issues, such as resentment toward foreigners, nationalism, and German unification. To prevent a possible bias and to improve sample representativity, the survey was conducted in about eighty smaller graduate classes *(Seminare)* in various faculties. Nevertheless, because of financial and organizational limits of the research, as well as demographic differences in the student population in West and East Germany, the two samples showed some significant structural differences: the average age of West German students was 24.4 years; the average age of participants in the East was only 21.7 years. There were also notable differences with regard to sex (West, 63% males /38% females; East, 38% males/62% females) and with regard to academic fields (in the West more student participants were in engineering and economics; in the East more were in mathematics/computer science and education). However, a closer analysis of the findings indicated no impact of these demographic sample differences on overall response patterns.

As mentioned, the main goal of this research was to acquire a basic knowledge of what students in West Germany and East Germany know about the Holocaust, how they feel about it, and what they think about it.

Knowledge

In order to get to a valid and reliable measurement for the students' knowledge about the Holocaust, *knowledge* was interpreted as knowledge of facts. To measure such knowledge, we administered to the students a multiple-choice test with questions on six central dimensions of the Holocaust. For each question, five choices were offered, of which only one was correct. The six central dimensions of Holocaust knowledge were:

- The Nazi program euphemistically known as the "Final Solution of the Jewish Question"
- The Treblinka extermination camp in Poland
- The November 1938 pogroms, called the "Reichskristallnacht"
- The anti-Jewish Nuremberg Laws of 1935
- The "euthanasia" program, or the extermination of mentally ill persons after the fall of 1939
- The Wannsee Conference in January 1942, which marked the beginning of the implementation of the Jewish Holocaust in Europe.

Since the response pattern on all questions was similar, only one question will be used as an example: knowledge about the Nuremberg Laws (see table 4.1). According to the distribution of answers, this question was the most difficult one: less than two out of five students (in West and East) gave a correct answer. Most of those who failed confused the Nuremberg Laws of 1935 with the decrees governing the Nuremberg Trials in 1945 (West, 28.8%; East, 35.5%). Many others

TABLE 4.1. Knowledge concerning the Nuremberg Laws

"The Nuremberg Laws were . . ." (multiple-choice)	West German Students	East German Students
1. Decrees of the victorious powers (Allies) of 1945 regulating the Nuremberg Trials against the Nazi perpetrators	28.8%	35.5%
2. Laws put into effect by the Nazi government in 1935 to establish restrictions on Jews and other minorities	39.8	36.2
3. Laws after Hitler's assumption of power in 1933 to step up the German economy after inflation	1.6	1.4
4. Laws which were enforced in Nuremberg after the beginning of the Second World War in 1939	2.1	3.7
5. Laws from 1949 aiming at denazification in the Federal Republic of Germany	19.3	12.0
6. No answer/do not know	8.4	11.2
N	699	643

seemed to believe that the Nuremberg Laws referred to the laws regulating the denazification after the founding of the FRG in 1949 (West, 19.3%; East, 12.0%). These results prove that the knowledge of the Nuremberg Laws is fairly low. Among the more than 60% who did not give a correct answer in the East and West, only 8.4% (West) and 11.2% (East) openly admitted that they did not know what was meant by the Nuremberg Laws. Nine out of ten respondents who did not give the right answer had no knowledge or just randomly chose one of the five multiple-choice alternatives. The latter assumption, however, also casts some doubt on the correct answers. Did some respondents randomly choose the right answer?

The results presented in table 4.2 show that the knowledge of facts about the Holocaust was, even within the student population, not as good as one would have expected from a highly educated sample,[4] considering that the multiple-choice questions were comparatively easy to answer and that some respondents give correct answers only by chance. In addition, not only the Nuremberg Laws question caused difficulties. Even in the case of the well-known-term "Final Solution," 24% of the West German students and 30% of the East German students gave wrong answers or did not know what the term meant. About 15% in each sample erroneously believed that the "Final Solution" referred to Hitler's ideas about the persecution of Jews in his book *Mein Kampf*.

Knowledge about Treblinka, one of the largest and best-known extermination camps in Poland, was even worse: 43% in the West and 30% in the East were ignorant of the camps. The better results in the East probably can be explained by the fact that antifascist GDR school education included not only visits to camps but also relatively comprehensive information about the most notorious concentration camps.

Fifty-four percent in the West and 57% in the East gave wrong answers about the Wannsee Conference; 28% in the West and 18% in the East confused the conference with the Potsdam Conference of the victorious allied powers at the end of World War II, from July 17 to August 2, 1945, in Potsdam—geographically very close to Berlin-Wannsee.

TABLE 4.2. Knowledge of Facts about the Holocaust

Holocaust Topic and Its Correct Definition (multiple-choice)	West German Students	East German Students
1. The Kristallnacht is the name for: the night of the pogroms against Jews all over Germany in November 1938	91.0%	91.2%
2. The Euthanasia program of the Nazis: means the planning and execution of a specific extermination program for the mentally ill	80.4	77.8
3. The Final Solution was: the name of the program for the direct and total extermination of Jews from 1941 onward	75.8	69.5
4. Treblinka was: an extermination camp for Jews from Warsaw and other ghettos where more than 800,000 people were exterminated	57.2	69.5
5. The Wannsee Conference was: the conference preparing the Final Solution to solve the "Jewish question" in Germany and Europe in January 1942	46.1	42.6
6. The Nuremberg Laws were: laws put into effect by the Nazi government in 1935 to establish the restrictions put on Jews and other minorities	39.8	36.2
N	699	643

To generalize the findings from single multiple-choice questions, we developed a measure to indicate the general knowledge level, using a scale comprising response patterns to all questions within one topic (table 4.3). According to this scale, 19% of both student samples were considered to have a low knowledge of facts (having between 0 and 2 correct answers) in contrast to about 38% who had a high knowledge, having answered 5 or all 6 questions correctly.

Emotional Reactions

Public and private discussions about the Holocaust are generally not just about knowledge of facts but often contain a specific emotional and moral element, such as feelings of guilt and shame or, in some cases, even denial of facts. Therefore, it seemed reasonable and necessary to measure emotional reactions of students discussing the Holocaust or, to be precise, the emotional reactions students admit or claim to have.[5]

TABLE 4.3. Categories of Students according to Their Knowledge of Facts about the Holocaust

Category	West German Students	East German Students
Students with low knowledge (0–2 correct answers)	18.6%	19.0%
Students with medium knowledge (3–4 correct answers)	42.2	43.8
Students with high knowledge (5–6 correct answers)	39.2	37.2
N	699	643

TABLE 4.4. Emotional Reaction to the Holocaust

Emotional Reaction	West German Students		East German Students	
	%	N	%	N
I feel guilt	28.8	680	26.9	607
I feel paralyzed	31.5	669	28.6	574
I feel shame	40.3	660	40.7	570
I feel anger	71.8	670	65.7	580
I feel fear	73.6	688	70.3	603
I feel shocked	86.0	681	88.8	588

Scale: Emotional Reaction to the Holocaust

West German Students				East German Students			
Low	Medium	High	N	Low	Medium	High	N
15.4%	30.6%	54.0%	635	14.8%	30.7%	54.5%	528
	Cronbach's alpha .6893				Cronbach's alpha .6946		

Confronted with choices, as shown in table 4.4, most students described themselves as shocked. A majority also admitted fear and anger, and a considerable
minority felt guilt and shame.[6] These findings are surprising because most students
were born in the 1960s and, therefore, were certainly not personally involved in
the Holocaust, World War II, or the difficult times of the early postwar years. It is
also remarkable that the emotional reactions of students born and raised in the
former GDR do not differ from their fellow students in the West, neither in rank
order nor in percentages. This striking similarity in the two student samples is
unexpected when one considers that the two samples experienced a very different
political socialization before German unification in 1989.

Again we were not only interested in the distribution of answers to single questions but also in categorizing levels of emotional attachment. Therefore, an
emotional-concern scale was constructed on the basis of responses to all items.
According to this scale only 15% of the students in West Germany and East Germany display low emotional concern, 31% medium emotional concern and 54%
high emotional concern.

Attitudes

Beside knowledge of facts and emotional reactions, we analyzed verbalized attitudes related to the Holocaust. We hoped that this would give us insight into how
the German postwar third generation copes with the 13 years of Nazism and the
Holocaust in the historical past, a past of which they have no personal experience.

In order to measure these attitudes, a long catalogue of statements was compiled
to cover a range of topics. For this purpose we used Likert scales with seven
scores ranging from strong agreement to strong disagreement. Electronic data processing and the use of scales and factor analysis allowed us to construct the following three subscales:[7]

1. Personal interest in the Holocaust
2. Relevance of the Holocaust for today
3. Demands to "draw a line" through the Nazi past *(einen Schlußstrich ziehen).*

However, one must keep in mind that the measurement of attitudes on sensitive issues with strong moral implications and emotional impact (see chapter 3) may also reflect "desirability effects."[8] Nevertheless, our findings are quite revealing.

Personal Interest

A desirability effect most clearly shows up in the distribution to the question about a respondent's personal interest in the Holocaust (table 4.5).[9] Only a very small minority of the students (8.6% in the West and 7.3% in the East) admit their lack of interest in the Holocaust item and consequently agree with the statement, "Who today is still interested in the Holocaust—certainly not me." In comparison with the findings about knowledge and other responses it appears that this answer distribution underestimates ignorance and disinterest. On the other hand one might argue that, at least in the interview situation, such a confession carries no sanctions or moral obligation and, therefore, correctly reflects the degree of interest.

But the desirability effect put aside, the responses indicate an unexpectedly strong personal interest in the issue. For example, between 46.2% (West) and 49.0% (East) of all students disagree with the statement, "I can spend my time on more meaningful things than the Holocaust." A neutral observer might come to

TABLE 4.5. Personal Interest in Dealing with the Holocaust

Statement	West German Students				East German Students			
	Disagree	Undecided	Agree	N	Disagree	Undecided	Agree	N
1. I can spend my time on more meaningful things than the Holocaust	46.2%	22.4%	31.4%	678	49.0%	23.4%	27.6%	623
2. I am actually really fed up with the Third Reich and the Holocaust now	59.5	14.8	25.7	690	72.4	15.5	12.1	626
3. Who today is still interested in the Holocaust—certainly not me	81.9	9.5	8.6	694	83.5	9.2	7.3	630

Scale: Personal Interest in the Holocaust

West German Students				East German Students			
Low	Medium	High	N	Low	Medium	High	N
15.4%	20.3%	64.3%	674	9.8%	20.7%	69.5%	610
	Cronbach's alpha .8326				Cronbach's alpha .8361		

the conclusion that, given the preoccupation of most people with the present, it would not be absolutely unreasonable to expect a larger percentage of students in agreement with that statement. Another statement measuring interest in the Holocaust refers to a response one can hear among young people in Germany today concerning lectures in schools, movies, and television reports on this dark side of Germany's most recent history: "I am actually really fed up with the Third Reich and the Holocaust now." Only 12.1% in the East agree with this statement, whereas this percentage is more than double in the West (25.7%). Either socialist antifascist education in the East has had some impact or the plethora of commemorations and diversity of information available to students in the East after unification is seen as enriching and important. In the West, however, the abundance and sometimes overly moralistic information and righteous teaching about the Nazi past may be responsible for the relatively high dissatisfaction among respondents.

But overall, the Holocaust interest scale shows that only a minority of students in the West (15.4%) and East (9.8%) can be considered as hard core "ignorants." In contrast, about two-thirds of the students (West, 64.3%; East, 69.5%) are highly interested or pretend to be interested.

The Importance of the Holocaust for Today

Another scale measuring attitudes toward the Holocaust combines four statements that refer to the importance of the Holocaust for the present (table 4.6). Again, only a comparatively small group of students (West, 10.8%; East, 8.3%) claim that the Holocaust has no importance for them today, in contrast to 72.3% (West) and 77.3% (East) who are convinced that the past is present and that a lesson should be drawn from it.

A similar distribution can be found with regard to the statements, "What happened during the Holocaust has no importance any more for me" and "What I know about the Holocaust influences my behavior and my philosophy of life even today." Interestingly, a majority of the postwar-born students in the West and East accept responsibility for German-Jewish reconciliation "as a German," although they are "personally not responsible for the Holocaust at all." [10]

A clear majority of the students accept the historical burden of the past as some kind of guideline for their current behavior, indicating a successful reorientation and reeducation of postwar Germans. This supports an optimistic view of how both East and West Germans cope with the past *(Vergangenheitsbewältigung)*, though from very different ideological and political perspectives (see chapter 3). Interestingly, many students display critical mistrust about their fellow countrymen's awareness. A majority believes somewhat righteously that "many Germans underestimate the importance of the Holocaust for today" (West, 69%; East, 77%). Without doubt, educated university students have a better Holocaust knowledge and higher awareness than the "average" German respondent. This is confirmed by other more representative surveys. [11] But that does not imply that awareness and knowledge have not increased at all among the general public. In fact, it

TABLE 4.6. Importance of the Holocaust for Today

Statement	West German Students				East German Students			
	Disagree	Undecided	Agree	N	Disagree	Undecided	Agree	N
1. What happened during the Holocaust has no importance any more for me	84.0%	7.6%	8.4%	693	82.1%	8.1%	9.8%	632
2. What I know about the Holocaust influences my behavior and my philosophy of life even today	17.7	11.2	71.1	694	2.9	17.6	59.5	629
3. Although I am not personally responsible for the Holocaust at all, I am as a German nevertheless called upon to strive for a reconciliation between Jews and Germans	8.1	19.4	63.5	685	16.6	22.6	60.8	619
4. Many Germans underestimate the importance of the Holocaust for today	12.1	19.4	68.5	698	12.2	14.1	77.3	606

Scale: Importance of the Holocaust for Today

West German Students				East German Students			
Low	Medium	High	N	Low	Medium	High	N
10.8%	16.9%	72.3%	675	8.3%	14.4%	77.3%	606
	Cronbach's alpha .7600				Cronbach's alpha .7653		

would be surprising if the educated classes were less informed and less concerned about such issues as the Holocaust and Germany's Nazi past.

Demands to Draw a Line

A third scale measures attitudes about popular demands that the debate on the Third Reich and the Holocaust be ended (table 4.7). Twelve percent in the West and 8.6% in the East are in favor of "drawing a line," but a significant majority of students (West, 73.4%; East, 78.3%) without doubt advocate the continuation of remembrance.

In the West 10.6% and 8.3% in the East feel that the "continuing discussion of the Holocaust is of no use to anybody today." Another typical response is to avoid playing down and relativizing German responsibility for the Holocaust by comparing Nazi crimes with those committed by other nations. Although about 80% of all students (West and East) reject this sort of justification or setting off *(Aufrechnung)*, at least 11 to 12% of all respondents agree that after it became "evident that other nations have committed mass murders as well, we should stop continually discussing the killing of Jews during the Third Reich."

Another argument refers to the importance of more acute problems today and implies an end of the continuous remembrance of the Holocaust. A great majority of students reject this reasoning. About 77% in the West and even 83% in the East believe that "although there are . . . many other acute and big problems [in the world today], one should, nevertheless deal also with the Holocaust [of] more than 45 years ago." Whereas only 12.6% in the West and 7.7% in the East disagree with such a time/distance argument, nearly twice as many agree as far as the Nazi past is concerned. In the West 22.4% and in East Germany 16% feel that now, "more than 45 years after the end of World War II, we should not talk so much about the Nazi past any more."

Compared with nationwide representative opinion research by the Emnid Institute our findings about German university students are very positive (see *Der Spiegel* 1992: 68). According to *Der Spiegel's* (1992) opinion poll, 62% of the German population support the idea that "forty-six years after the end of the war we should no longer talk so much about the persecution of the Jews but put an end to the debate." [12] As in our research, the percentage of people polled by *Der Spiegel* who want to end the debate is notably higher in West Germany (66%) than in East Germany (46%) and higher among older respondents (70% of those aged 60 and over) than among younger ones (53% of those aged 18–29); it is also higher among those with lower education (70%) than among those with higher education (48%). [13] Because university students are younger and highly educated, we can expect that our sample was less inclined to ask for an end to the debate about the Holocaust.

Political Consequences

Besides investigating knowledge, emotional reactions, and verbalized attitudes toward the Holocaust, our research sought to answer the important question about

TABLE 4.7. Demands to Put an End to the Debate over the Third Reich and the Holocaust (*Schlußstrich*)

Statement	West German Students				East German Students			
	Disagree	Undecided	Agree	N	Disagree	Undecided	Agree	N
1. The continuing discussion of the Holocaust is of no use to anybody today	82.6%	6.8%	10.6%	695	83.0%	8.7%	8.3%	630
2. Because it has become evident that other nations committed mass murders as well, we should stop continually discussing the killing of Jews during the Third Reich	80.6	7.2	12.2	690	80.4	8.6	11.0	629
3. Although there are indeed many other acute and big problems, one should, nevertheless, deal also with the Holocaust more than 45 years ago	12.6	10.9	76.5	696	7.7	9.3	83.0	622
4. Today, more than 45 years after the end of the Second World War, we should not talk so much about the Nazi past any more, but put an end to it	65.0	12.6	22.4	692	73.3	10.4	16.3	625

Scale: Demands to Put an End to the Debate over the Past

West German Students				East German Students			
Low	Medium	High	N	Low	Medium	High	N
73.4%	14.5%	12.1%	684	78.3%	13.1%	8.6%	609
	Cronbach's alpha .8877				Cronbach's alpha .8731		

whether students are consciously willing to derive certain consequences or lessons from the Holocaust. Factor analysis confirmed that 6 of the survey's chosen statements formed a quite satisfactory scale for measuring the readiness to elicit the political consequences that resulted from the Third Reich and the Holocaust. Table 4.8 shows that only a very few students declined to derive any political consequences from the Nazi past (West, about 2%; East, about 4%). Thirteen percent in both samples were categorized as somewhat ambivalent about whether they should and could derive political consequences from the legacy of the Third Reich.

Overall the findings confirm that students are unanimous in their support of democracy and pluralism in order to prevent the reappearance of events like those during the Third Reich. In their concern about national minorities in all parts of the world, many consider it necessary to become politically active. Only two statements deviate from that pattern: those about whether strong national feelings should exist (29.7% in the West and 40.8% in the East disagreed) and the question about avoidance of too much political involvement (88.1% in the West and 76.9% in the East agreed).[14]

The Intercorrelation between Knowledge, Emotions, and Attitudes concerning the Holocaust

Although we have treated knowledge, emotions, and attitueds so far as separate, in fact, they are very much interrelated. We tested this by comparing various scales. Table 4.9 gives an overview about Pearson's correlation coefficients.[15]

Assuming that only those who know the facts about the Holocaust can have the appropriate emotional response and, consequently, develop an emotional concern about the Holocaust, the data in table 4.9 show that such a hypothesis is rather weak and is only significant—if at all—for the West (Pearson's $r = .1517$). A stronger correlation, however, was found in the West and East between knowledge and attitudes. In other words, the greater the knowledge of facts, the more positive are the attitudes related to the Holocaust, that is, personal interest, importance for today, and remembrance. Most significantly related are emotional concern and attitudes as table 4.9 demonstrates. A very significant relationship was also found between attitudes related to the Holocaust and the readiness to derive political consequences. Respondents who reject an end of Holocaust remembrance are clearly willing to derive political lessons from the past, such as support for democratic and pluralistic attitudes, concern about national minorities, and reservations about strong national feelings.

Basic Political Orientation as an Influencing Factor

One of the most remarkable findings of our 1989 research was the importance that basic political orientation has on the knowledge of facts, emotional reactions, and,

TABLE 4.8. Readiness to Derive Political Consequences from the Third Reich and the Holocaust

Statement	West German Students				East German Students			
	Disagree	Undecided	Agree	N	Disagree	Undecided	Agree	N
1. To make sure that events like those during the Third Reich do not reappear, I support democratic and pluralistic attitudes and behavior in our society	1.9%	6.2%	91.9%	693	3.8%	13.6%	82.6%	627
2. The Third Reich has demonstrated that one should not get involved too much in political activities	88.1	4.8	7.1	688	76.9	13.0	10.1	624
3. To prevent something like the Holocaust happening again, one should become politically active	4.6	10.7	84.7	692	6.1	13.2	80.7	621
4. An important lesson for me to be drawn from the Holocaust is: strong national feelings should not exist anywhere any more	29.7	13.3	34.8	688	40.8	20.7	38.4	622
5. After what happened during the Holocaust, we should be concerned particularly about national minorities in all parts of the world	7.1	10.7	82.2	693	10.2	13.1	76.7	627
6. If some of my friends make jokes about Jews or Turks, I feel that this is nothing to be concerned about	70.2	16.2	13.6	691	37.3	22.3	20.2	614

Scale: Readiness to Derive Political Consequences from the Third Reich and the Holocaust

West German Students				East German Students			
Low	Medium	High	N	Low	Medium	High	N
2.2%	13.5%	84.3%	674	4.2%	12.6%	83.1%	593
	Cronbach's alpha .6800				Cronbach's alpha .6794		

TABLE 4.9. Intercorrelations (Pearson's *r*) between Knowledge of Facts, Emotional Reaction, and Attitudes Related to the Holocaust

Scale	West German Students					East German Students				
	(2)	(3)	(4)	(5)	(6)	(2)	(3)	(4)	(5)	(6)
(1) Knowledge of facts	.1517	.2867	.2506	−.2987	.2544	.0599	.2427	.2098	−.2769	.2505
(2) Emotional reaction		.5412	.5724	−.5253	.4582		.5397	.5889	−.5418	.4947
(3) Personal interest			.7302	−.8252	.5719			.7241	−.7841	.615●
(4) Importance				−.7801	.6404				.7609	.692●
(5) Demands to end debate					−.6599					−.692●
(6) Political consequences										

in particular, attitudes concerning the Holocaust. Therefore, in 1992 we again asked the students about their basic political orientation. A commonly used question that measures this is, "If we had federal elections next Sunday, which political party would you vote for?" A comparison with other indicators of political orientation shows that party preference is worthy of somewhat closer investigation.[16] However, this does not solve the question whether party preference is a factor that influences attitudes toward the Third Reich and the Holocaust or whether given attitudes toward the Third Reich and the Holocaust influence political preferences based on a party's political standing on specific issues.[17]

Because unification had a considerable influence on the political party system in Germany, particularly in East Germany, a look at the voting behavior of students may be important. Table 4.10 clearly indicates that—compared to the voting behavior of the general public—students in West and East Germany have strong preferences for the Green Party (West, 35.5%; East, 39.0%).[18] Second, students in the East were still much less in favor of the traditional democratic parties CDU, FDP, and SPD than their peers in the West in 1992. East German students support to a considerable extent the PDS (21.3%), a modernized socialist party built on

TABLE 4.10. Party Preference of Students in West and East Germany

"If we had federal elections next Sunday, which political party would you vote for?"	West German Students		East German Students	
	N	%	N	%
REP (right-wing)	9	1.5	10	2.0
CDU (conservative)	108	18.1	38	7.5
FDP (liberal)	66	11.1	41	8.1
SPD (Social Democrat)	193	32.2	113	22.2
Bündnis 90/Green party	212	35.5	198	39.0
PDS (Socialist)	9	1.5	108	21.3
Total	597	100.0	508	100.0
No answer/no vote	102		135	

the rubble of the former Socialist–Communist Party in East Germany, which in the West receives only little attention and support.[19]

We asked another crucial question to find out if the rank order of the political parties as shown in table 4.10 corresponded with the general political orientation of a person along the Left–Right axis. The student respondents were asked to mark their own political position on a 10-point self-assessment scale ranging from the extreme Right to the extreme Left. The extremely high correlation between party preference and political self-assessment on the Left-Right axis (Pearson's *r* is .6482 in the West and .6304 in the East) justifies the decision to keep party preference as a single and significant indicator of more deeply rooted basic political orientations of a respondent.[20]

Political Orientation and Holocaust Knowledge

To better understand the political background of attitudes concerning the Holocaust, we cross-tabulated Holocaust knowledge, emotions, and attitudes with party preference. Table 4.11 shows that—at least for the West—there is no significant difference in Holocaust knowledge and party preference. It is true that students who prefer right-wing parties in general know less about the facts of the Holocaust than those who prefer left-wing parties, but the correlation is not strong (in the East it is even lower).[21]

Political Orientation and Emotional Concern

With respect to emotional reactions toward the Holocaust, however, the differences according to party preference are quite striking (see table 4.12). Students preferring political parties of the Right show much less emotional concern with respect to the Holocaust than those preferring political parties of the Left—in West Germany and East Germany as well.

TABLE 4.11. Scale: Knowledge of Facts about the Holocaust according to Political Orientation

Party reference	West German Students				East German Students			
	Low	Medium	High	N	Low	Medium	High	N
EP	33.3%	33.3%	33.3%	9	20.0%	60.0%	20.0%	10
DU	24.1	43.5	32.4	108	21.2	36.8	42.1	38
OP	22.7	43.3	31.8	66	9.8	33.7	36.6	41
PD	19.7	39.4	40.9	193	23.9	38.1	38.1	113
90/Green	10.4	44.8	44.8	212	16.7	48.0	33.4	198
OS	22.3	33.3	44.4	9	13.0	39.8	57.2	108
	104	256	237	597 (100%)	88	223	197	508 (100%)
	17.4	42.9	39.7		17.3	43.9	38.8	
Missing				102				135
Pearson's *r*		.1596				.0602		
Significance		.0000				.1754		

TABLE 4.12. Scale: Emotional Concern regarding the Holocaust according to Political Orientation

Party Preference	West German Students				East German Students			
	Low	Medium	High	N	Low	Medium	High	N
REP	75.0%	25.0%	—	8	100.0%	—	—	8
CDU	29.6	33.7	36.7	98	26.7	46.7	26.7	30
FDP	21.3	49.2	29.5	61	24.2	51.5	24.2	33
SPD	20.5	29.0	50.6	176	24.1	37.3	38.6	83
B90/Green	13.9	24.1	62.0	187	16.2	27.2	56.6	173
PDS	28.6	42.9	28.6	7	16.5	29.4	54.1	85
N	112	164	261	537 (100%)	86	134	192	412 (100%)
%	20.9	30.5	48.6		20.9	32.5	46.6	
Missing				162				231
Pearson's r		.2645				.2775		
Significance		.0000				.0000		

Political Orientation, "Drawing a Line," and the Readiness to Derive Political Consequences

Even more remarkable were differences between various Holocaust attitudes and party preference. All scales used reveal the same pattern: attitudes toward the Holocaust are strongly linked with the basic political background of a person, ranging from the political Right to the political Left. High sympathy with right-wing parties is correlated with lower interest in the Holocaust,[22] with lower belief in the Holocaust's importance for today,[23] and with a stronger demand for putting an end to the debate about the past (table 4.13).

With respect to the demand "to draw a line" through the past, two statements were found to be very indicative. Respondents in favor of right-wing politics ex-

TABLE 4.13. Demand to Put an End to the Debate on the Past (*Schlußstrich*) according to Political Orientation

Party Preference	West German Students				East German Students			
	Low	Medium	High	N	Low	Medium	High	
REP	11.1%	11.1%	77.8%	9	30.0%	—	70.0%	I
CDU	48.1	26.4	23.3	106	38.2	35.3	26.5	3
FDP	8.7	22.2	19.0	63	68.3	24.4	7.3	4
SPD	81.8	10.4	7.8	192	77.1	13.8	9.2	10
B90/Green	90.8	4.3	4.8	207	88.0	7.7	4.4	18
PDS	88.9	11.1	—	9	86.7	8.6	4.8	10
N	442	73	71	386 (100%)	380	60	42	482 (100%
%	75.4	12.3	12.1		78.8	12.4	8.7	
Missing				113				16
Pearson's r		−.4272				−.3993		
Significance		.0000				.0000		

press much more often and emphatically that "today, more than 45 years after the end of the World War II, we should not talk so much about the Nazi past but put an end to the discussion." Although only minorities of students in West Germany (22.4%) and East Germany (16.3%) agree with this statement, respondents who prefer the conservative CDU are much more in favor of ending remembrance than students who prefer to vote, for example, for the SPD or for the Green Party respectively, Bündnis 90 in the East.

Differences according to political orientation in relation to Holocaust attitudes have also been found in other studies and surveys. In a nationwide representative survey in the FRG before unification, 78% of those respondents who preferred the CDU were in favor of the statement: "Today, 40 years after the end of World War II, we shouldn't talk so much about the persecution of Jews, but draw a line through the past." In the same poll, 61% of SPD supporters and 41% of Green Party supporters held the same opinion (see Bergmann and Erb 1991a: 241).[24]

But party preference seems not only to have an influence on attitudes and opinions related to the Holocaust but also has a strong influence on the readiness of a person to derive appropriate political consequences from the Third Reich and the Holocaust (see table 4.14). The more students in West and East Germany prefer Right political parties, the less they are inclined to derive political lessons from the past, such as support for democratic and pluralistic attitudes, concern about national minorities, and reservations against strong national feelings. The more respondents are in favor of the Left, the more they are willing to derive such political consequences.[25]

If one considers the common understanding of the dynamics of Left-Right attitudes and its implications for a respondent's ideological disposition, one might argue that these findings are not that surprising and were even predictable. However, the findings about the relationship between party preference and Holocaust attitudes are remarkable insofar as German universities and students today are not

TABLE 4.14. Readiness to Derive Political Consequences from the Third Reich and the Holocaust according to Political Orientation

Party Preference	West German Students				East German Students			
	Low	Medium	High	N	Low	Medium	High	N
REP	22.2	66.7	11.1	9	70.0	10.0	10.0	10
CDU	0.9	19.6	79.4	107	20.6	23.5	35.9	34
FDP	—	12.7	87.3	63	—	27.5	72.5	40
SPD	0.5	7.4	92.0	188	4.7	14.2	81.1	106
B90/Green	—	4.0	96.0	199	—	10.6	89.4	179
PDS	—	—	100.0	8	2.8	6.5	90.7	107
N	4	57	313	574 (100%)	22	61	393	476 (100%)
%	0.7	9.9	89.4		4.6	12.8	82.6	
Missing				125				167
Pearson's r		.4138				.3884		
Significance		.0000				.0000		

at all politically mobilized or organized along party lines. Moreover, the similarity of findings in the East and West are striking because the political system and political socialization in both parts of Germany were up to 1989 (two years before this investigation) very different and even partially antagonistic and hostile to each other.

Party Preference and Attitudes toward the Holocaust

So far this study has taken party preference as an indicator of the basic political orientation of a person—ranging from the political Right to the Left. Although this is a common way to analyze the political background of knowledge, emotional reactions, attitudes, and political consequences related to the Holocaust, it is nevertheless fairly unclear what the political associations and implications of party preference are.

To investigate party preference and thus the political context of attitudes related to the Holocaust in more detail, we have developed additional scales that measure:

- National identity and nationalism
- Authoritarian and antidemocratic mentalities
- Reservations concerning foreigners.[26]

Table 4.15 gives all of the necessary information on the intercorrelations between party preference and its associated scales. The data show that party preference for the Right highly correlates with nationalism, antidemocratic attitudes, and xenophobia.[27] Party preference therefore is an indicator that is useful to determine not only voting intentions but also general political attitudes and patterns of prejudice. One may deduce from this finding that the political milieu is important in forming attitudes that are correlated with party preference, in this study the emotional reaction, attitudes, and knowledge about the Holocaust.

Summary

One of the primary goals of our research was to shed some light on what German university students in the East and West know and feel about the Holocaust two years after unification. Related to earlier binational research conducted in 1989 (using a similar research design, sample, and questionnaire), we found that stu-

TABLE 4.15. Intercorrelations (Pearson's r) between Party Preference and Its Associations

Scale	West German Students			East German Students		
	(2)	(3)	(4)	(2)	(3)	(4)
(1) Party preference (Right to Left)	−.5356	−.4908	−.5227	−.5012	−.3022	−.4430
(2) Nationalism		.6114	−.6660		.5242	−.6609
(3) Antidemocratic mentality			−.6491			−.6116
(4) Antiforeigner						

dents in the East and West have striking response similarities although they were socialized in antagonistic political systems. Knowledge, emotional reactions, and attitudes about the Holocaust differed most significantly along a Right-Left pattern for which we used party preference as an indicator. Respondents in favor of the political Left have a somewhat higher knowledge and display significantly more concern about the Holocaust, its legacy, and its lessons for today than do their peers who prefer the political Right.

The results of this research indicate that didactic efforts in the schools, the universities, and the general public to increase knowledge and empathy about the darkest years in modern Germany's history through increased education and information about the Holocaust and Nazi Germany were more successful than critics are willing to concede, although re-education in both Germany's had different political intentions and antagonistic ideological foundations. However, our findings also point at weak spots and the need to continue these efforts of providing information and education to reduce prejudice and resentment and to create emotional, moral, and political awareness of Germany's responsibilities and accomplishments.[28]

Further, it would be wrong and unwise to disregard these findings as unimportant because the results are not representative of the German population in general. Without doubt, as an educated population segment the students' responses are more positive than one can expect from the general public. But students are not just one group among others. They are the ones who will sooner or later occupy the ranks of the political, social, economic, educational, and cultural elite in the FRG. Therefore, their clout will be much larger than their numbers suggest. In 1990, Germany's university student population totaled about 1.7 million persons or about 25% of the 19–26 age group.

From that perspective, our postunification research not only provides clues about prevailing Holocaust attitudes and their intercorrelations but also casts some light on what might become public opinion in united Germany in a not too distant future.

NOTES

The author is very much indebted to Hermann Kurthen for generous help with translation, proofreading, and critical comments.

1. Originally, my 1992 research was planned as a follow-up study of research conducted in 1989. The purpose was to study changes in attitudes after unification, but the East-West comparison became more promising. Nevertheless, I shall refer occasionally to the earlier survey, although its theoretical approach and the questions asked were quite different. The focus was on how the process of working through the Holocaust influenced attitudes about current issues. The 1989 research was planned as the first step of a three-year binational (German-Israeli) comparative research project conducted in close cooperation with colleagues at Wuppertal's partner-university in Beersheba, Israel. In particular, Dan Bar-On initiated the research and the development of a specific theoretical framework. The 1989 project was purely quantitative and used a questionnaire handed out to pupils and students

in Germany and Israel (in Germany 610 pupils aged 13–18 and 321 students aged 19–25 participated). In 1990, qualitative research followed using personal interviews and a kind of "action research" (exchange of students between Israel and Germany). For more information about the first step in Germany in 1989, see Brusten and Winkelmann (1992), Brusten (1992), and Brusten and Winkelmann (1993). With respect to the theoretical perspectives and the original research design see Bar-On, Beiner, and Brusten (1988). For a comparison of findings from Israel and Germany, see Bar-On et al. (1993).

The three-year project from 1989 to 1991 was financed by the German-Israeli Foundation (GIF). In contrast, the 1992 Holocaust attitude survey was supported by German students personally interested in the issue and participating in a research seminar in social sciences at the University of Wuppertal. In addition, without the support, advice, and help of about seventy colleagues in West and East Germany who opened their seminars for this research, the survey would not have been possible.

2. For international comparative purposes, one might relate the findings to results from other recent surveys in other countries, for example, the surveys conducted for the American Jewish Committee (AJC) in the United States, Great Britain, and France by Golub and Cohen (1993a, 1993b, 1994). It was decided not to undertake this quite useful comparison because of reasons of limited space and methodological and sample incompatibilities. Besides, it is often overlooked that, in doing this kind of research, the historical and sociopolitical context is of great importance. Therefore, the distribution of answers to the same or similar questions in different countries has to be interpreted extremely carefully.

3. Although the present research compared respondents in two formerly politically separated parts of one nation (West Germany and East Germany), several pretests very clearly showed the need to adapt the questionnaire to two different political cultures. East German students had manifold difficulties with questionnaires developed in West Germany regarding the misunderstanding or lack of knowledge of certain terms. For example, westerners were very familiar with the meaning of the term *Holocaust* but had problems with the term *antifascist resistance (antifaschistischer Widerstand),* which was common to East Germans. Some terms are well known in both parts of Germany but carry very different ideological meanings and political connotations, such as *social stratum (Soziale Schicht)* and *social class (Soziale Klasse).* Other misunderstandings resulted from differences in experience and historical perspective. The term *foreigner* represented different images and social status in the two parts of Germany. Also, the perceived distance from National Socialism or the Third Reich was more distinctly expressed in the East. Such differences made it difficult to formulate questions that invoked the same associations among our respondent sample in the East and West.

4. An exact comparison of the 1992 and 1989 findings is not possible because of differences in measurement, that is, a different selection of questions and revisions in the phrasing of the same or similar questions and answers. However, the answer distribution in both surveys was similar for correct answers (N = 521 in 1989) regarding, for example, questions about the Reichskristallnacht (97.3%), the so-called Final Solution (73.0%), the euthanasia program (72.2%), the Treblinka concentration camp (71.1%), and the Nuremberg Laws (52.2%).

The 1989 reasearch also confirms our assumption that some respondents guessed the right answer. The knowledge level in 1989 differs from question to question. Ninety-two percent of those who gave the correct answer to the Reichskristallnacht question confidently knew the right answer. This confidence percentage was much lower for questions about the Final Solution (53%), the euthanasia program (48%), Treblinka (36%), and the Nuremberg Laws (39%). Thus, of the 52.2% of students who gave a correct answer to the last question about the Nuremberg Laws, only 39% were sure that their answer was correct; this represents only 20% of the total student population on the survey (see Brusten and Winkelmann 1992: 9 f.).

5. With respect to individual emotional reactions, students could express their feelings on a Likert scale with seven scores ranging from -3 (extreme disagreement) to $+3$ (extreme agreement). Table 4.4 presents only the positive agreements ($+1$ to $+3$). In the case of the emotional-concern scale, however, all individual reactions were computed. For purposes of easier presentation, disagreements ranging from -1 to -3 were defined as low and agreements ranging from $+1$ to $+3$ were defined as high.

6. A similar measurement in the 1989 research produced comparable results. Asked about their emotional reactions to the Holocaust, 92% of West German students admitted they felt shocked, 57% fear, 51% anger, 44% shame, and 18% guilt (see Brusten and Winkelmann 1993: 191).

7. According to factor analysis, the statements of all three subscales represent one single attitudinal dimension. Therefore, the subscales (themselves based on single scale–analysis) can be considered as three different aspects measuring the importance of the Holocaust for German students today.

8. Very positive attitudes raise the question how these attitudes can he interpreted. Are they (1) an honest expression of interest; (2) an attempt to meet public expectations; (3) unwillingness to admit not being interested; or (4) an expression of philosemitism hiding antisemitism? See Frank Stern 1992: 341 ff.

9. In tables 4.5–4.8, the term *disagree* covers the full range of disagreement (from -3 to -1), and the term *agree* represents agreement from $+1$ to $+3$ on the Likert scale. Corresponding scales define low as representing scores from -3 to -1, and high scores ranging from $+1$ to $+3$.

10. In distinguishing between Jews and Germans, one has to keep in mind that this was done only for pragmatic reasons. Interestingly, before Hitler such a distinction was not officially in use.

11. According to a recent nationwide survey (see Golub 1994: 34) 11% of all German respondents agree strongly and 26% mostly with the statement that "the Holocaust is not relevant today because it happened almost 50 years ago," whereas 33% disagree mostly and 20% strongly. This hides considerable differences between the East (5% vs. 17% agree; 37% vs. 31% disagree) and the West (12% vs 28% agree; 32% vs 17% disagree) and between education level of respondents (41% with low education agree, 47% disagree; 33% with higher education agree, 59% disagree). Differences by age, sex, and religion are only of minor relevance.

12. The 1992 *Spiegel-Spezial* no. 2, Juden und Deutsche, report was based on a survey by the Emnid-Institut (Bielefeld) from November 30 to December 17, 1991. Results were also published in the weekly *Der Spiegel* magazine, January 13, 1992, pp. 52–66; January 20, 1992, pp. 41–50.

13. Similar results were found in the most recent nationwide German survey conducted by Emnid for the AJC (see Golub 1994: 38). The statement, "Recently someone said: 'Today, in the aftermath of German unification, we should not talk so much about the Holocaust, but should rather draw a line under the past.' Would you say this is correct or incorrect?" was supported by 56% and opposed by 29% of West German respondents (of East German respondents, 36% were in favor and 54% were opposed). Age also played a significant role in determining the response to the question. Older respondents were more likely in favor "drawing a line" than younger ones (46% aged 18–29, 51% at aged 30–49, 56% 50 and over). Fifty-nine percent of respondents with low education were in favor, compared to 45% of respondents with higher education.

14. The political involvement statement obviously caused some confusion. It was not

absolutely clear whether it meant a warning against a political involvement in Nazi politics or whether it was indicative of a more general attitude for abstention from politics.

15. As mentioned in note 7, the three subscales regarding personal interest in the Holocaust, importance of the Holocaust for today, and the demand to end the debate on the Third Reich and the Holocaust represent only different dimensions of a scale that measures general attitudes toward the Holocaust. The subscales have the following intercorrelations (Pearson's *r*):

Scale	West German Students			East German Students		
	(2)	*(3)*	*(4)*	*(2)*	*(3)*	*(4)*
(1) Knowledge of facts	.1317	.2992	.2544	.0599	.2479	.2505
(2) Emotional reactions		.6077	.4582		.3939	.4947
(3) General "attitude" scale			.7222			.6723
(4) Political consequences						

16. A considerable proportion of the students (West, 14.6%; East, 21.0%) refused to name a political party listed in table 4.10 because they would not vote at all or preferred splinter parties not listed in the questionnaire. An analysis of this refusal group shows that such respondents are not sympathetic to radical protest groups or to parties on the extreme Right or the extreme Left but represent "average" respondents.

17. According to research in West Germany, preference for certain political parties may result from the influence of sociodemographic, traditional, economic, and regional factors (see Falter, Rattinger, Troitzsch 1989).

18. Here it may be useful to characterize the political parties cited in this chapter: REP (Republikaner Partei) = right wing; CDU/CSU (Christlich Demokratische Union/Christlich Soziale Union) = conservatives; FDP (Freie Demokratische Partei) = liberals; SPD (Sozialdemokratische Partei Deutschlands) = Social Democrats; Green Party (Grüne/Bündnis 90) = Left environmentalists; PDS (Partei des Demokratischen Sozialismus) = democratic successor of the former (Sozialistische Einheitspartei Deutschlands [SED]), the dominant Marxist-Leninist party in the former GDR.

19. The voting behavior of West German respondents in 1992 was similar to that found in the 1989 survey. No comparable figures exist for East Germany. Of the 82% of students who responded by giving their party preference in the hypothetical case of an upcoming election, 0.9% supported the REP, 20.2% the CDU, 7.9% the FDP, 36.7% the SPD, and 34.3% the Green Party. This compares with voting behavior of the Wuppertal population during the actual federal elections on December 2, 1990: 32.8% for the CDU, 44.3% for the SPD, 8.5% for the FDP, 8.4% for the Green Party, and 3.9% for other parties.

20. Multiple regression analysis of student respondents' party preference explains 41% of the variation of Left-Right political self-assessment in the West and 33 percent in the East. Other variables account for less than 1% of the variation.

21. Correlations between party preference and knowledge about the Holocaust are insignificant for male respondents but highly significant for females.

22. The correlation between party preference and personal interest in the Holocaust for West and East German students is highly significant: Pearson's *r* is .3559 in the West, .3310 in the East. Whereas only 48.1% of West German students who prefer the CDU claim to be personally interested in the Holocaust, the corresponding percentages of students is 72.5% for social democratic supporters and 76.7% for Green Party supporters. The comparative figures for East German students are 51.4% for CDU supporters, 61.6% for SPD supporters, 79.1% for Green Party supporters, and 80% for PDS supporters.

23. The correlation between party preference and the statement that the "importance of the Holocaust for today" is high: Pearson's *r* is .3351 for West German students, .4060 for

East German students. Whereas 60% of the students in the West who preferred the CDU assume that the Holocaust is of high importance today, 84.0% of the students who preferred the SPD and 89.7% of the students who favored the Green Party support that notion. The corresponding figures for East German students are 48.6% for CDU supporters, 70.4% for SPD supporters, 81.6% for Green Party supporters, and 89.4% for PDS supporters. These findings compare with a representative nationwide survey in 1994 (N = 1,434; see Golub 1994: 34), in which 15% of respondents who said they would vote for the CDU agreed strongly and 31% mostly with the statement, "The Holocaust is not relevant today because it happened almost 50 years ago" (46% disagreed). Eleven percent of potential SPD voters strongly agreed and 22% mostly agreed, whereas 56% disagreed.

24. Party preference in the most recent nationwide German survey conducted for the AJC (Golub 1994: 38) had a similar effect (see n. 13). Fifty-nine percent of those voting for the CDU/CSU and 51% of those voting for the SPD felt that "a line should be drawn," whereas 29% of CDU/CSU supporters and 35% of FDP supporters felt that this was incorrect.

25. Further correlations of the 1992 research between party preference (and its political associations) and the perception of certain "ethnic minorities" and in particular "Jews" are found in Brusten (1995). Although the correlations are not as high, students in West and East Germany in favor of the political right wing have considerably less sympathy for Jews (and even less for Jewish immigrants from Eastern European countries) than do students who prefer the political Left. See also Bergmann and Erb 1991a: 261 ff.

26. For similar scales used in the 1989 research, see Brusten and Winkelmann (1992). In both West and East there is a strong relationship between attitude toward the Holocaust and sympathy for Jews. The more strongly respondents express emotional concern regarding the Holocaust (Pearson's r is .2828 in the West, .3467 in the East), the greater their personal interest in the Holocaust (West, .2676; East, .3568) and the perception that the Holocaust is of importance for today (West, .3041; East, .3824). Low support for "drawing a line" (West, .2367; East,.3859) correlated with greater sympathy for Jews (see Brusten 1995).

27. The correlations between party preference and its political associations are considerably lower for East German students, as shown in table 4.16. The main reason for this difference, according to our analysis (not shown here), is the fact that political attitudes of PDS supporters are more nationalist and authoritarian anti-democratic than one would expect from the ranking of this socialist party on the far left side of the Right-Left scale. Supporters of the PDS also display greater reservations concerning the acceptance of foreigners than, for example, "Green Party" supporters, who are located on the Right-Left scale between the PDS and the SPD.

28. Prior research about a popular television series *(Holocaust)* and movies *(Schindler's List)* indicates that media can have a significant impact on Holocaust awareness. On the other hand some indications suggest that an inflated use of Holocaust rhetoric for partisan interest may have counterproductive effects that could be exploited by antisemitic right-wing organizations (Ginzel 1991). Each nation has to be confronted anew with the lessons of its past, but the way this is done depends on current domestic and world events as well as on the predominant national media and communication culture.

5

FREDERICK D. WEIL

Ethnic Intolerance, Extremism, and Democratic Attitudes in Germany since Unification

As often happens, press and scholarly accounts diverge in describing developments in Germany since reunification. The press and media tend to focus on signs of popular discontent with democracy, political extremism, xenophobia, and antisemitism, especially in eastern Germany. Scholars present a more varied view. Although they find plenty of indications of discontent with the economic burdens of reunification, little evidence has emerged that Germans have veered sharply toward antidemocratic, extremist, or bigoted attitudes. On the contrary, West German attitudes on these fundamental issues have not deteriorated much since the Berlin Wall came down, and surprisingly, East Germans often express even more democratic or tolerant views. In this chapter, I shall examine trends in antisemitism and xenophobia since reunification against the backdrop of attitudes toward democracy and political extremism.

Protest, Legitimation, and Extremism in Germany since 1989

The main outlines of the period are well known. For the first two years after the Berlin Wall fell in the autumn of 1989, reunification seemed to progress with unexpected ease. In July 1990, East Germans were permitted to convert their currency to Western deutsche marks (DM) on generous terms. Legal reunification occurred in October 1990, much sooner than anyone had thought possible. Federal elections were held in a unified Germany in December 1990, and with Chancellor Helmut Kohl promising better times ahead, even the East voted for his Christian Democratic/Free Democratic (Christlich Demokratische Union [CDU]/Freie Demokratische Partei [FDP]) coalition parties (Gibowski and Kaase 1991). And surveys from early 1990 to late 1991 (described later) showed that despite 40 years under very different regimes, East Germans were remarkably similar to West Germans on a wide variety of basic values—including attitudes on democracy. Virtually none of this was predicted prior to 1989.

Then, in late 1991, two years after the Wall fell, things began to go badly. In September, right-wing extremists attacked a refugee residence in the eastern town of Hoyerswerda with Molotov cocktails, bottles, and steel balls, and a mob of ordinary citizens cheered them on. This was only the beginning, for 1992 marked the onset of a recession with growing economic distress in the East; economic anxiety in the West; a crippling public-sector strike; a further rise of neo-Nazi activity; right-wing rioting and attacks on foreigners and minorities; substantial extreme-right voting; and government paralysis on the question of immigration and political asylum. But at the same time, massive prodemocratic demonstrations took place to protest extremism. Even the normally sanguine *Economist* predicted in the spring of 1992 that although Germany's long-term prospects were good, the short and medium term would be difficult.

Political extremism resurfaced in this context. Since the early or mid-1980s, western Germany has experienced its third wave of right-wing extremism since World War II (Beyme 1988, Stöss 1993b, Zimmermann and Saalfeld 1993). Legal offenses, including acts of violence, membership in extreme and far-right organizations, and voting for right-wing parties all increased after that. The far-right "Republikaner" Party (REP), so far, mainly a post-West phenomenon, received 7.1% of the nationwide (i.e., western) vote in the 1989 elections for the European parliament and 10.9% of the vote in the 1992 Baden-Württemberg state elections. Extreme rightism subsided in the euphoria that immediately followed unification: support for the REP dropped to 2.3% in the West in the 1990 federal elections. It then increased during the controversy over immigration and asylum rights but declined after the constitutional revision of the right to asylum in early 1993. Western support in monthly Allensbach polls rose to a high of 8.5% in the second quarter of 1992, then fell to between 3% and 4% in the first months of 1994. By the 1994 elections in the West, the REP received only 3.9% of the June vote for the European Parliament and a mere 2% in the October national elections (1% in the East). Right-wing violence also declined from high levels in 1992 (per capita violence was higher in the East) in the face of renewed police enforcement and vigorous prosecution and sentencing of offenders (*New York Times,* December 10, 1993). Yet it remains to be seen whether this spells the end of the third wave of right extremism.

Likewise, neocommunism may not have reached the dead end in East Germany that numerous studies predicted, despite their descriptions of a shrinking, aging, and marginalized voter base (Bortfeldt and Thompson 1993, Falter and Klein 1994, Krisch 1993, Moreau 1994, Moreau and Neu 1994, Minnerup 1994, Phillips 1994). East German support for the successor communist party, the Party of Democratic Socialism (Partei des Demokratischen Sozialismus [PDS]), fell from 16.4% in the first free elections for the East German parliament (Volkskammer) in March 1990 to 11.1% in the December 1990 federal elections, and then to a nadir of 6.5% in an Infas poll in June 1991 (Bortfeldt 1991: 525). However, PDS support has climbed steadily since that low point: in Allensbach surveys, it reached 22% in December 1993 and held steady in the 17% to 19% range during the first months of 1994. The PDS received 21% of the vote in the December 1993 communal elections in Brandenburg, 19% of the East German vote in the June 1994 elections to the European Parliament, and 20% of the East German vote in the October 1994 national elections. Again, it may be too early to write off neocommunism in eastern Germany.

Yet the changing fortunes of extremism do not necessarily indicate changes in political confidence and democratic legitimization: the picture is more varied (see Weil 1993, 1994a, Noelle-Neumann 1992, 1994).[1] Allensbach surveys through the end of 1991 reveal quite high levels of political confidence and support for democracy in western Germany and, surprisingly, almost as high levels in eastern Germany. On many indicators, political support in East Germany was closer to West German levels than to East European levels (Plasser and Ulram 1993, Weil 1993). Postunification eastern Germany appears to have been born strongly democratic. East and West Germans alike overwhelmingly rejected a one-party system, a single strong ruler, historical Nazism, and the curtailing of liberties to reduce disorder; they supported a variety of democratic rights; and they defined democracy in much the same way. Naturally, there were also differences, especially concerning the goals of the old East German regime (as against its practices) and the difficulties of the transition. Compared to their western German compatriots, eastern Germans were still more attracted to the ideals of communism; they were more skeptical that democracy could solve their problems; they were more in favor of grand coalitions; they valued rights and liberties less, especially when set against economic needs; they had less political and interpersonal trust; and they were less tolerant of ethnic minorities. However, contrary to a variety of theoretical expectations, easterners exhibited even more political affect, or attachment to the nation, and somewhat more acceptance or understanding of limited political conflict (a liberal norm) than westerners. Thus, a year or two after the fall of the Berlin Wall, eastern Germans expressed levels of democratic support not reached in the West until 30 years or more after Hitler and not reached yet by many East European countries.

By 1992, conditions greatly worsened in Germany, but a December survey reflected these problems only in certain respects. On the one hand respondents were very worried about asylum seekers and immigrants, the economy, crime, and general conditions in Germany. And they did not believe that anyone was doing enough about these problems: they were increasingly disappointed in and alienated from politicians, the major parties, parliament, and the state. Political confidence declined. On the other hand basic democratic values remained very strong in both parts of Germany, and respondents overwhelmingly believed that people who attack foreigners should be punished. Despite growing problems, eastern and western Germans actually strengthened their view that democracy is the best form of state and that it is able to handle the problems that have arisen in Germany.

From early 1993 through the October 1994 election, a constitutional amendment restricting asylum rights permitted authorities to reduce radically the influx of foreigners; the severest recession since World War II bottomed out and a recovery began; but unemployment continued at very high rates, especially in the East. Surveys showed that, at the bottom of the recession, record numbers of eastern and western respondents found conditions in Germany disturbing (above 80 percent, compared to highs in the 40% to 50% range through the 1980s) and were disappointed by the major parties. Yet in the course of 1994, optimism began to rise again, disaffection (including frustration about parties or *Parteienverdrossenheit*) fell, and the governing coalition was returned to office in the October election (Jung and Roth 1994, Köcher 1994). In the East, opinions of a market economy continued to slide, whereas nostalgia for the idea of socialism—already much stronger than in the West—rose strongly again. Yet in both parts of Germany, there was little weakening in democratic values on some indicators (whether democracy is the best form of state) and only a modest slide—and possible recovery—on other indicators (whether one person or several should rule). Thus, worsening social and economic conditions were accompanied by a rise in support for extremist parties and a decline in political confidence; but support for democracy did not weaken substantially. Indeed, democratic values were surprisingly strong, even in eastern Germany after a 40-year experience of communism and a dozen years of Nazism. At least at the aggregate level, then, extremism could be interpreted as a reaction to poor conditions and low confidence in political authorities—in short, a protest—not an expression of declining support for democracy.

An analysis of individual opinions in a December 1992 survey is consistent with this interpretation (see Weil 1994b for a fuller analysis). Respondents' worries about the asylum problem, the economy, and other problems lowered their confidence in government and increased their propensity to support extremist parties; but they did not lead them to withdraw their support for democracy. Yet even during this difficult period, social and economic distress was not the major cause of distrust, extremism, and opposition to democracy. Partisan and ideological factors proved more important for protest, and nothing strongly reduced the widespread democratic attitudes. Partisanship and lack of political efficacy led to political distrust. Political distrust and mainly partisanship, ideology, and xenophobia led to right-wing extremism; partisanship and ideology alone led to left-wing extremism. And political distrust, xenophobia, and right-wing extremism were connected to antidemocratic attitudes, but the connection was much weaker. Thus, partisanship and ideology rather than distress generated a nexus of protest, whereas support for democracy was relatively shielded from this nexus. It remains to be seen exactly how ethnic intolerance fits into this picture.

Recent Trends in Antisemitism and Xenophobia

Press accounts have often suggested that a new wave of antisemitism and xenophobia has erupted in Germany since reunification, especially in the East, where it had previously been suppressed by the Communist authorities. However, opinion surveys again indicate that these accounts may be misleading. Instead, the data show little rise of intolerance in the West since the Berlin Wall fell—except when West Germans follow Europe-wide trends—and, again surprisingly, generally

TABLE 5.1. "Do you feel that the following groups have too much influence, too little influence, or the right amount of influence in our society?" (Jews)

| Response | West | | | | | | | | | | East |
	1959	1965	1967	1969	1970	1971	1975	1981	1984	1994	1994
Too much influence	23%	18%	19%	17%	15%	14%	14%	20%	16%	24%	8%
Too little influence	26	20	16	17	18	22	18	34	34	8	12
The right amount	39	26	25	30	22	28	36	43	46	32	24
Undecided	12	36	40	36	45	35	31	3	3	36	56

Source: Emnid-Informationen 1984, no. 11/12, pp. 9–10; Golub 1994, pp. 21–22.

higher levels of tolerance in the East. The data are fairly consistent across a wide variety of questions. Classical indicators of political antisemitism show these patterns clearly. The view that Jews have too much power and influence did not rise appreciably in the West after reunification, and easterners were more tolerant than westerners. However, fewer easterners had an opinion about domestic Jewish power than westerners, perhaps because even fewer Jews live in the East than in the West, although their numbers are small there as well.

Similarly, there was no significant worsening in West Germany in the opinion that Jews should be expelled from the country or sent to Israel. Rather, after declining in the 1950s, this opinion has been fairly stable since the 1960s; and easterners did not differ substantially from westerners.

Another important indicator of political antisemitism is willingness to vote for a Jew of one's own party. Previous studies (Weil 1987, 1990) have shown that this form of antisemitism was stronger in West Germany and France than in the United States in the 1960s and 1970s. American antisemitism has fallen to under 10% since the 1960s on most surveys, and as table 5.4 shows, West German antisemitism has also fallen since that time, but not as dramatically. Yet again, East Germans are more tolerant by 10 percentage points.

Social distance questions are not ideal indicators of intolerance, but they are often used as such. One of the most widespread questions is objections to living near certain groups. When Jews are included in a list of groups, they are generally

TABLE 5.2. "Jews have too much influence in the world. Would you say that's true or not?"

| Response | West | | East |
	1987	1992	1992
True	33%	36%	21%
Not true	43	38	50
Undecided	24	26	29

Source: Allensbach Surveys, 4094 (1987), 5064 (1992).

TABLE 5.3. "Would you say it is better for Germany to have no Jews in the Country?" (1987–1992: "If somebody said, it would be better for us Germans if all the Jews went to Israel, would you agree or not agree?")

Response	West								East
	1952	1956	1958	1963	1965	1983	1987	1992	1992
Better	37%	29%	22%	18%	19%	9%	13%	18%	15%
Not better	20	35	38	40	34	43	67	54	56
Undecided	43	36	40	42	47	48	20	28	29

Source: Noelle and Neumann 1967, p. 96; Allensbach Surveys, 4094 (1987), 5064 (1992).

found to be among the least objectionable in most Western societies. In surveys since reunification, East and West Germans object much more strenuously to Gypsies (63–68%), political extremists (54–79%), homosexuals (24–35%), and Muslims (17–29%) than to Jews (6–12%). This form of antisemitism has remained steady or declined somewhat in the West since the mid-1970s and is virtually identical in the East and West.

International comparisons show that although Germans generally know more about the Holocaust than do people in other countries, they express less support for remembrance (Golub 1994: 12–14). However, studies also show that West Germans have become more willing in recent decades to see war crimes prosecuted further, rather than "to draw a line" and move beyond the past (Bergmann and Erb 1991a: 233–246; see also chapter 3). Table 5.6 parallels these findings. West Germans have become somewhat more willing since reunification to talk about the Holocaust or the persecution of the Jews, but East Germans are much more willing to do so. There is probably a simple explanation for this East-West difference. Following World War II, East and West Germany interpreted the parti-

TABLE 5.4. "Assuming your party—the one you like best—proposes as federal chancellor a very capable man who is a Jew. Would you agree to a Jew becoming federal chancellor?" (1994: "If a party nominated a Jew as its candidate for president of Germany, would you approve, disapprove, or would the candidate's Jewishness make no difference to you?")

Response	West		East
	1960	1994	1994
Approve	31%	9%	12%
Disapprove	45	30	20
Makes no difference	—	50	63
Don't know	24	12	5

Sources: IfD 1960; Golub 1994.

TABLE 5.5. "On this list are various groups of people. Could you please sort out any that you would not like to have as neighbors?" (Jews)

Response	West						East	
	1975	1981	1986	1987	1991	1992	1991	1992
Jews	16%	14%	22%	11%	12%	7%	11%	6%

Source: IfD.

tion of Germany differently. Westerners claimed that they had inherited the true lineage of the German state and nation, where as easterners claimed that they had purged themselves of Nazi remnants and accused the West of being the successor state to the Nazi regime. Thus, both easterners and westerners probably believe (for different reasons) that further talk of old Nazi crimes concerns mainly westerners. It is naturally easier for East Germans (and citizens of other countries) to blame West Germans than for West Germans to blame themselves.

However, when East or West Germans are asked about crimes against Jews (or in this case, gravestones in Jewish cemeteries) in present-day Germany, there is no such ambivalence. All respondents, before and after reunification, East and West, massively believe that these crimes should be taken seriously and favor punishing the perpetrators.

Interestingly, the picture changes when respondents are asked, not about their *opinions* of Jews, but about their *perceptions* of antisemitism in their part of the country. As tables 5.8–5.11 show, East Germans believe more readily than West Germans that lots of their compatriots are prejudiced against Jews, that antisemitism is a serious problem in Germany, that antisemitism is on the rise, and that antisemitic groups probably have a big following among young people. And this time, West German perceptions of antisemitism have grown somewhat since reunification. These perceptions are clearly at odds with the findings on opinions. Al-

TABLE 5.6. "Recently someone said, 'Today, 40 years after the end of the war, we should stop talking so much about the persecution of the Jews, but rather draw a line under the past.' Would you say this person was right or not right?" (1994: "Recently someone said, 'Today, in the aftermath of German unification, we should not talk so much about the Holocaust, but should rather draw a line under the past.' Would you say this is right or not right?")

Response	West			East
	1986	1987	1994	1994
Right	66%	67%	56%	36%
Not right	24	21	29	54
Undecided	10	12	15	10

Sources: IfD 1986; Golub 1994.

TABLE 5.7. "Gravestones in old Jewish cemeteries here have sometimes been damaged or covered with graffiti. Do you think that people who do such things should be punished, or do you think it shouldn't be taken so seriously?"

| Response | West | | East |
	1986	1994	1994
Punish	89%	93%	95%
Not so serious	6	3	3
Undecided	5	4	2

Source: IfD.

though easterners are generally less antisemitic than westerners according to their answers in surveys, they *believe* that they are worse. And although westerners have generally become less antisemitic since reunification, they *believe* that they have become worse. What accounts for this disparity? One possible answer is that stated opinions simply reflect officially sanctioned ideology but that perceptions reveal latent or hidden antisemitism which respondents see around them but are unwilling to express openly or acknowledge in themselves (Bergmann and Erb 1986, 1991a). Although this theory seems persuasive, a survey of American studies of antisemitism failed to find much empirical support for it (Smith 1994: 19–22). Another related theory holds that perceptions may simply reflect what people read in the press and hear in the media and that press reports reflect the preconceptions of reporters (Noelle-Neumann 1984). Considering that press reports have focused so strongly on antisemitic incidents in the East and on emerging extremism in both parts of Germany since reunification, it is hardly surprising that easterners think that things are worse there or that westerners think that things have deteriorated since reunification. A third possibility is that antisemitic incidents and public opinion are not rigidly connected. Perhaps a small number of extreme antisemites has in fact become more active—and their activities are accurately reported in the

TABLE 5.8. "Do you think that lots of people are prejudiced against Jews, or not so many, or very few?"

| Response | West | | East |
	1987	1994	1994
Lots of people	20%	23%	27%
Not so many	37	32	27
Very few	29	31	35
Impossible to say	14	14	11

Source: IfD.

TABLE 5.9. "Do you think that antisemitism in Germany is currently a very serious problem, somewhat of a problem, or not a problem at all?"

Response	West		East	
	1990	1994	1990	1994
Very serious problem	9%	25%	32%	29%
Somewhat a problem	51	47	51	48
Not a problem at all	26	19	7	14
Don't know	14	8	10	9

Source: Jodice 1991; Golub 1994.

press—but at the same time, antisemitism has not become more widespread among the bulk of the population. The public and the press accurately perceive the extremist incidents but mistakenly take them as an indicator of public opinion, which they are not. Of course, any or all of these three theories may be correct—each one fits the data—but they cannot be proven here.

Just as racism overshadows antisemitism as a form of prejudice in the United States, intolerance of foreigners and immigrants has become the major problem of bigotry in Europe in recent years. A good deal of the media coverage has focused on Germany. Indeed, Germany received vastly more immigrants per capita than any other country in the world in the late 1980s and early 1990s until it changed its extremely liberal constitutional asylum provisions in 1993. However, despite the large number of foreigners in Germany, analysts have shown that antiforeigner bigotry is not substantially worse there than in other European countries—although it became worse throughout Europe in the 1980s and 1990s (Kuechler 1994). Tables 5.12–5.14 show some increase in intolerance in West Germany since reunification, but this increase simply parallels trends throughout Europe. Therefore, it does not appear that reunification uniquely increased xenophobia in Germany. As far as intra-German differences are concerned, the media have again stressed bigotry in the East more than in the West. Yet the survey data are mixed

TABLE 5.10. "Looking ahead over the next several years, do you think that antisemitism in Germany will increase greatly, increase somewhat, remain the same, decrease somewhat, or decrease greatly?"

Response	West		East	
	1990	1994	1990	1994
Increase	32%	45%	58%	55%
Remain the same	43	32	20	31
Decrease	10	8	8	6
Don't know	16	15	13	9

Source: Jodice 1991; Golub 1994.

TABLE 5.11. "Sometimes one hears that there are groups
of young people who are against Jews, for example,
who paint anti-Jewish graffiti on house walls, and so on.
Do you think that these groups have a big following
among young people, or do you think that these are
just little groups, and most young people don't agree
with them at all?"

Response	West 1986	West 1994	East 1994
Have a big following	7%	26%	36%
Most don't agree	76	58	46
Impossible to say	17	16	18

Source: IfD.

on this question. As tables 5.12–5.15 show, East and West Germans exhibit different levels of intolerance on different questions. On the two questions whether
there are too many foreigners in Germany, East Germans express more bigotry in
one formulation and less bigotry in the other formulation. West Germans are more
often disturbed by people of other nationality, race, or religion than are East Germans. And East Germans favor giving Germans preferential treatment for jobs
much more often than do West Germans. This last question probably reflects the
extremely high levels of unemployment in East Germany. Aside from this, the
inconsistent East-West differences are rarely large (not more than 13%) and probably should not be overinterpreted. Thus, economic hardship aside, East and West
Germans do not differ clearly in ethnic intolerance.

Causes of Antisemitism and Xenophobia

The survey results summarized in the previous section are surprising in light of
the press reports. Contrary to impressions created by the press, antisemitism and
xenophobia did *not* increase greatly in Germany with reunification—or at least to

TABLE 5.12. "If somebody said, 'I basically have nothing against foreigners [1970:
'foreign workers'], but there really are too many of them in our country,' would you agree
with this opinion or not?"

Response	Belgium 1970	France 1970	Italy 1970	Netherlands 1970	West Germany 1970	West Germany 1991	West Germany 1992	East Germany 1991	East Germany 1992
Agree	62%	59%	17%	61%	54%	66%	67%	65%	77%
Disagree	23	32	63	32	38	21	21	21	13
Undecided	15	9	21	7	8	13	12	14	10

Source: Eurobarometer, IfD.

TABLE 5.13. "Generally speaking, how do you feel about the number of people of another nationality living in our country [1991–1992: . . . people living in [our country] who are not nationals of the European Community countries]: are there too many, a lot but not too many, or not many?"

Respondents	"Too Many"			
	1988	1991	1992	1993
West Germany	45%	58%	57%	60%
East Germany	—	45	48	57
European average	39	53	53	53

Source: Eurobarometer.

the extent that they did, they appear to be part of a general European pattern. And antisemitism and xenophobia are *not* appreciably stronger in East Germany than West Germany—rather, it is often the reverse. Now I shall investigate some of the factors that are thought to cause ethnic intolerance.

Data

Most of the data discussed earlier in this chapter either stem from surveys that I did not have on hand for analysis or did not contain enough of the causal factors that I wanted to investigate. Instead, I analyze a survey that was conducted by the IfD Allensbach in December 1992 in eastern and western Germany, primarily to measure democratic attitudes.[2] The institutes carried out 1,081 face-to-face interviews in western Germany, and 1,131 interviews in eastern Germany, to create representative samples of the population over age 16 in each region. Late 1992 is an appropriate time point at which to investigate ethnic intolerance under the toughest possible conditions. The economy was at a nadir, the asylum problem

TABLE 5.14. "Some people are disturbed by the opinions, customs, and way of life of people different from themselves. Do you personally, in your daily life, find the presence of people of another nationality disturbing? . . . people of another race? . . . people of another religion?"

Respondents	"Disturbed"								
	Nationality			Race			Religion		
	1988	1991	1993	1988	1991	1993	1988	1991	1993
West Germany	15%	18%	13%	18%	20%	15%	13%	18%	13%
East Germany	—	11	13	—	14	15	—	9	9
European average	12	15	15	15	18	17	13	18	17

Source: Eurobarometer.

TABLE 5.15. "Somebody recently said to us, 'When jobs are scarce, employers should give priority to German people over foreigners.' Would you agree or not agree?"

	West		East	
Response	1991	1992	1991	1992
Agree	61%	51%	78%	70%
Disagree	26	31	12	17
Undecided	13	18	10	13

Source: IfD.

was still unresolved, and political dissatisfaction and support for extremist parties were rising.

Hypotheses and Variables

The December 1992 survey contains a wide array of possible causal factors and a large number of questions on tolerance of foreigners, democratic attitudes, and support for extremist parties but, unfortunately, just one question on antisemitism (and not the best one at that: acceptance of a Jewish neighbor).[3] The questions on the survey are mostly replications or adaptations of questions used and tested in comparable situations. Most questions come from West German surveys, some come from American or other European surveys, and a few were tested earlier on East German surveys (see Weil 1993 and 1994b for fuller descriptions of the development of the questionnaire). The texts of the questions used here are listed in the appendix to this chapter. This appendix also shows how the questions are combined in scales and gives short descriptions of the sources of the scales in previous research literature. Figure 5.1 gives an overview of the hypotheses.

The dependent variables are (1) tolerance of foreigners and (2) tolerance of Jewish neighbors. Tolerance of foreigners is a factor that combines two of the questions raised earlier—whether there are too many foreigners in the country and whether there is discrimination against foreigners for scarce jobs—as well as questions about changing the asylum law, violence against foreigners, and acceptance of ethnic minorities as neighbors. These questions all load strongly on a single factor and therefore constitute a robust single-dimensional scale of ethnic (in)tolerance. Tolerance of Jewish neighbors is a single yes-no question from a list of possible neighbors. It is less than ideal as a measure of antisemitism for two reasons: (1) social distance is not the best indicator of antisemitism, and (2) the variable is a single indicator, dichotomous, and skewed, with only 6 or 7% not wanting a Jewish neighbor. By contrast, the antiforeigner scale is made up of many components, has many gradations, and has a normal statistical distribution.

The causal (independent) variables can be divided into several groups.

1. Social structure variables include age, sex, education level, income class, economic situation, unemployment, and church attendance. Prior research has

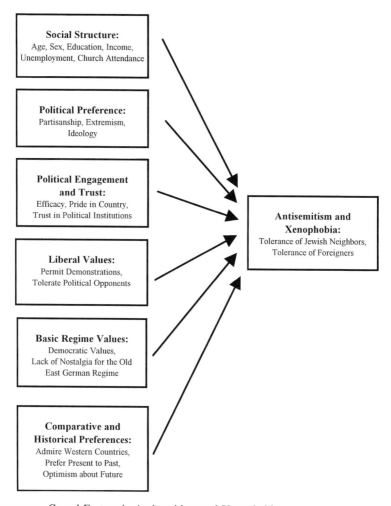

FIGURE 5.1. Causal Factors in Antisemitism and Xenophobia

shown that youth and higher education most consistently promote ethnic tolerance and that the other variables only sometimes exert an influence.

2. Political preference variables include major-party partisanship, support for extremist parties, and ideology. Support for the Christian Democrats (CDU/CSU) or Social Democrats (SPD) is usually not related to ethnic tolerance once Left-Right ideology is controlled for, as is done here. Otherwise, left-center parties (SPD) are usually more tolerant than are right-center parties (CDU/CSU)—and people on the Left are more tolerant than people on the Right. By contrast, sympathy for extremist parties (the post-Communist PDS and the far-right REP) may affect ethnic tolerance over and above Left-Right self-placement. The REP virtually define themselves by their xenophobia, whereas the socialist PDS (and the Communist Party from which they emerged) have historically given strong lip

service to ethnic tolerance, even if they were less than tolerant in practice. Although the far Left has often taken strong anti-Israel and anti-Zionist positions, it has generally espoused tolerance of Jews in a domestic context—at least when it was out of power.

3. Political engagement and trust variables are often found to promote ethnic tolerance. These variables include political efficacy, whether one can trust most people, whether one can speak freely, and interest in politics. Pride in being German may reduce ethnic tolerance because nationalism is generally related to ethnocentrism and disregard for other peoples. This effect may be less pronounced in the contemporary United States, where nationalism or patriotism is decreasingly defined in ethnic terms; but most Europeans still define the nation in ethnic terms, as many Americans also did historically (Lipset and Raab 1978). Political trust or confidence is not clearly related to ethnic tolerance. Since political confidence is influenced by whether one's favorite party is in office or not, controlling for party preference and ideology should remove the partisan and ideological elements, which might affect bigotry. Also, because political confidence is related to political engagement, controlling for the latter should remove the effects of efficacy and other forms of political self-confidence that reduce bigotry.

4. Political liberal values, however, generally promote ethnic tolerance. The variables tested here include tolerance of demonstrations, tolerance of free speech, and acceptance of political extremists.

5. Basic regime values may influence ethnic tolerance in different ways. Support for democratic values should strongly promote ethnic tolerance. To be sure, some forms of democracy, defined as narrow majority rule or as a variant of nationalism, have historically reduced ethnic tolerance. However, the variable used here is defined more broadly as is done in most Western countries and includes support for minority rights and civil liberties. Opposition to the old East German regime is measured by opposition to the ideals of socialism or communism and (lack of) nostalgia for the old regime. It is unclear that this variable is related to ethnic tolerance.

6. Comparative and historical preferences. Comparative preference for a democratic regime is measured by admiration for Western countries. Historical preference for the present democratic regime as against the prior nondemocratic regime is measured by evaluation of the general situation now as against the past; optimism about the future is also measured. It is not obvious how these indicators should be related to ethnic tolerance. In West Germany, they should behave similarly to democratic values. But in East Germany, previous research has identified a certain triumphalism that combines admiration for Western countries with opposition to the old regime. This triumphalism sometimes leads to various kinds of intolerance (Weil 1994b). However, these effects are not strong in either East or West Germany and are likely to be wiped out when other variables are controlled for.

Analyses and Interpretation

Bivariate correlations and multivariate regressions[4] were computed for the two measures of ethnic tolerance. The high levels of explained variance and correctly placed cases show that the regression models fit the data well, that is, they do a good job of explaining why people answered the questions as they did. The most impressive result of these analyses is how similar the patterns are in East and West Germany and on both forms of ethnic tolerance. Thus, the similarities we saw in the trend data in the earlier discussion were not just superficial but were based on many of the same underlying factors. Other studies have shown the same parallels in the political culture of East and West Germany since reunification (Gibowski and Jung 1993, Klingemann and Hofferbert 1994, Veen 1993, Weil 1993, 1994b). The East–West differences are important and will be noted, but considering that the two parts of the country were separated and ruled by very different types of regime for 40 years, the similarities are striking and surprising.

Table 5.16 shows that the causes of tolerance of foreigners are broadly similar in eastern and western Germany, but with certain significant differences. Ideology and identity politics are the strongest predictors. In particular, sympathizers of the right-wing REP, self-professed conservatives, and those who are proud to be German are much less tolerant of foreigners in both the East and the West. Mainstream partisanship played a somewhat lesser role but in the same ideological direction. Supporters of the CDU/CSU are less tolerant and SPD supporters are more tolerant, but the SPD effect was washed out in the multivariate model. These results reflect the policy positions of the parties on restricting asylum rights: the CDU/CSU favored major restrictions; the SPD did not. Bivariate correlations (not shown) also indicated that Liberal Party (FDP) voters were not significantly more tolerant, but that Green Party voters were a good deal more tolerant. These results make more sense for Green than for FDP voters, because both parties advocated a more liberal asylum policy, although the Greens did so more strongly. Sympathizers of the post-Communist PDS are also more tolerant of foreigners.

People who are politically engaged are also more tolerant of foreigners. In particular, political efficacy and trust in people promote ethnic tolerance. And those who are interested in politics are also more tolerant, but the effect is stronger in the West. However, the feeling that one can speak freely is not stably related to tolerance (and the effects are wiped out in the regression models).

Trust in government or politicians produced inconsistent results. This may be due to the inclusion of certain items in the trust scales. Thus, the trust-politicians scale includes an item on worries about the flood of asylum seekers. And the trust-government scale implicitly includes support for the CDU/CSU, which wanted to restrict the influx of foreigners. Although the scales were intended to be general, these topical items may have skewed their effect on tolerance of foreigners.

Democratic attitudes promote ethnic tolerance in both parts of Germany. Other forms of support for a regime affect tolerance differently in the East than they do in the West. Thus, in West Germany, opponents of the old eastern Communist regime and those who see past and future improvement are more tolerant. By contrast, these same people are *less* tolerant in East Germany. This may be a sign of the eastern German triumphalism noted earlier, except that the effects are weak and disappear when other factors are taken into account.

Political liberalism also promotes ethnic tolerance, but rather weakly and inconsistently. Those who support the right to demonstrate are more tolerant, though the effect is weakened or disappears in the multivariate model. And easterners—but

TABLE 5.16. Tolerance of Foreigners in East and West Germany (December 1992), Correlation Coefficients and Standardized Regression Coefficients (Betas)

Variables	Correlations		Regressions	
	West	East	West	East
Social Structure				
Age	−.15**	.01	—	—
Sex (male)	.03	.01	.06†	−.02
Education level	.32**	.13**	.12**	.04
Income class	.11**	.02	—	—
Economic situation good	.23**	.06*	.07*	.10**
No experience/fear unemployment	−.05	−.06	—	—
Church attendance	−.02	−.01	.04	.09**
Political Preference				
Preference ranking of SPD	.17**	.10**	—	—
Preference ranking of CDU	−.18**	−.31**	−.08*	−.14**
Sympathy for REP	−.42**	−.30**	−.28**	−.13**
Sympathy for PDS	.14**	.24**	.09**	.02
Left-Right self-placement (Right)	−.34**	−.39**	−.08*	−.21**
Political Engagement and Trust				
Political efficacy	.31**	.13**	.13**	.08*
Can trust most people	.24**	.14**	.13**	.07*
Can speak freely	.12**	−.14**	—	—
Interest in politics	.23**	.13**	.10**	.00
Proud to be German	−.31**	−.36**	−.14**	−.22**
Trust government institutions	.01	−.06*	−.13**	.08
Trust politicians	.15**	−.03	.10**	.00
Liberal Values				
Support demonstrations	.22**	.14**	.07*	.03
Tolerance of free speech	−.07*	−.12**	—	—
Accept political extremists	−.03	.14**	.05	.14**
Basic Regime Values				
Democratic values	.26**	.16**	.06*	.10**
Against old East German regime	.12**	−.13**	—	—
Comparative and Historical Preferences				
Admire Western countries	−.02	−.01	—	—
Situation better now versus past	.23**	−.12**	.11**	−.03
Predict future situation	.13**	−.09**	—	—
View next 12 months with hope	.14**	−.07*	—	—
N; Adjusted R^2	1,081	1,131	.42	.30

Source: Own calculations based on IfD 1992.
*p < .05.   **p < .01.   †p < .10.   — = not significant.

not westerners—who are tolerant of extremist neighbors are more tolerant of foreigners. Strangely, those who tolerate the speaking rights of extremists are more xenophobic, though this effect is wiped out in the multivariate model. This result is probably an artifact of the scale construction, because tolerance here means allowing both a revolutionary and a racist to speak. The scale probably correlates with xenophobia because it also taps racist attitudes.

Finally, with a few exceptions, social structural factors do not have large or consistent effects, but when they do have an effect, their influence seems to be more crystallized in the West. Thus, better educated people are more tolerant in the West; but in the East, the effect becomes insignificant in the multivariate model. This finding has precedent. Previous studies have shown that education does not always promote tolerance in newer democracies, only after democracy has been in place long enough to socialize new generations (Weil 1982, 1985, 1991, 1994a). Young and well-to-do people are also somewhat more tolerant in the West, but not in the East (these effects disappear in the multivariate model). By contrast, churchgoers are more tolerant in the East, but not in the West. And people who feel that the economy is good are more tolerant in both parts of Germany. Yet contrary to press reports, the experience of unemployment has no significant effect on xenophobia; nor are men generally more intolerant than women.

Thus, the strongest and most consistent predictors of xenophobia in both parts of Germany are political: sympathy for the REP, nationalistic pride, rightist ideology or support for conservative parties, and weak adherence to democratic values. Economic distress also promotes xenophobia in both parts of Germany. Ethnic tolerance is also more crystallized in the West, as befits a more established democratic political culture (the explained variance is higher). Westerners who are better educated, optimistic, and politically engaged and critical are more tolerant of foreigners. The same factors play a role in the East, but more weakly: the causal structure is not as strongly crystallized there.

As table 5.17 shows, the same factors that promote Tolerance of foreigners also promote Tolerance of Jews, but their effects are weaker for the latter. As we have seen, there are two probable reasons for this weakness. First, the indicator of antisemitism is less than satisfactory: it measures social distance rather than prejudice, and the variable is dichotomous and skewed. Second, foreigners probably overshadow Jews as an object of intolerance in present-day Germany: there is more public awareness and public debate about foreigners, and antisemitism is more officially frowned upon than xenophobia.

As was the case with xenophobia, ideology and identity politics are strong predictors of antisemitism. Sympathizers of the right-wing populist "Republikaner" Party, supporters of the CDU/CSU, those who are proud to be German, and self-professed conservatives are less tolerant of Jewish neighbors in both the East and the West. (However, Left-Right self-placement and—in the West—CDU/CSU support are washed out when the other factors are taken into account.) SPD supporters and—in the East—PDS sympathizers are more tolerant in the bivariate correlations but not in the multivariate models. The only other strong and consistent predictor of tolerance of Jewish neighbors is democratic attitudes. No other measure of regime support has any effect on antisemitism in eastern or western Germany. Trust in government and trust in politicians also have no effect.

TABLE 5.17. Tolerance of Jewish Neighbors in East and West Germany (December 1992), Correlation Coefficients and Logistic Regression Coefficients

Variables	Correlations		Regressions	
	West	East	West	East
Social Structure				
Age	−.07*	.02	—	—
Sex (male)	.04	−.01	—	—
Education level	.11**	.08**	.17	.09
Income class	.09**	.04	—	—
Economic situation good	.07*	.02	—	—
No experience/fear unemployment	−.05	−.03	—	—
Church attendance	−.02	.01	—	—
Political Preference				
Preference ranking of SPD	.10**	.12**	—	—
Preference ranking of CDU	−.08*	−.10**	−.20	−.14*
Sympathy for REP	−.23**	−.21**	−.51**	−.25*
Sympathy for PDS	.00	.11**	—	—
Left-Right self-placement (Right)	−.16**	−.15**	—	—
Political Engagement and Trust				
Political efficacy	.07*	.04	—	—
Can trust most people	.07*	.08*	—	—
Can speak freely	.09**	−.04	—	—
Interest in politics	.05	.15**	.17	.77**
Proud to be German	−.17**	−.20**	−.61**	−.83**
Trust government institutions	.03	.04	—	—
Trust politicians	.04	.00	—	—
Liberal Values				
Support demonstrations	.07*	.00	—	—
Tolerance of free speech	−.07*	−.16**	−.04	−.35**
Accept political extremists	.00	−.02	.28*	.16
Basic Regime Values				
Democratic values	.19**	.18**	.40**	.45**
Against old East German regime	.04	−.05	—	—
Comparative and Historical Preferences				
Admire Western countries	.03	.03	—	—
Situation better now versus past	.07*	.00	—	—
Predict future situation	.06	.00	—	—
View next 12 months with hope	.03	−.02	—	—
N; constant	1,081	1,131	4.37**	3,84**
−2 Log Likelihood			464.8	411.2
Degrees of freedom			8	8
Correctly placed			93%	94%

Source: Own calculations based on IfD 1992.
*p < .05.   **p < .01.   — = not significant.

People who are politically engaged are generally more tolerant of Jewish neigh-bors, but the only effect that survives in the multivariate models is interest in politics in the East. Political liberalism also reduces antisemitism in some cases, but its effects are even spottier than they were for xenophobia. Tolerance of dem-onstrations and of extremist neighbors promote tolerance of Jewish neighbors in two out of eight coefficients. And, as before, those who tolerate the speaking rights of extremists are more antisemitic. (Recall that this result is probably an artifact of the scale construction because tolerance means allowing both a revolutionary and a racist to speak.)

Finally, social structural factors again have few effects on antisemitism. The effects that do emerge are more crystallized in the West, but they are all wiped out in the multivariate models. Better educated people are more tolerant in both parts of Germany, but these effects become insignificant in the multivariate model. Young, well-to-do, and economically satisfied people are also somewhat more tol-erant in the West, but not in the East and not when other factors are controlled. No other social structural factors have any effect.

Thus, the strongest and most consistent predictors of antisemitism in both parts of Germany are again political: sympathy for the far-right REP, nationalistic pride, weak adherence to democratic values, and—less consistently—support for conser-vative parties or rightist ideology. However, this time antisemitism is not so clearly crystallized in the West because so few additional factors remain significant once these strong political factors are taken into account. In the East, interest in politics and tolerance of the speaking rights of radicals and racists are significantly related to antisemitism. In the West, acceptance of extremist neighbors is related to antise-mitism. Nothing else survives in the multivariate models.

Summary

Press and media reports from reunified Germany have often been alarming. In the years following 1989, Germany survived its steepest recession since World War II. The burdens of rebuilding the East have weighed heavily on westerners; east-erners have been resentful of the continuing economic disparities, which show little sign of being overcome for decades. Reunified Germany has experienced the largest influx in the world of foreigners seeking asylum or citizenship, many of them ethnically different from the Germans. In this context, right-wing and big-oted extremism grew, and far-right parties did well in a number of elections. Many horrible xenophobic, racist, and antisemitic incidents have been reported in the press. In the East, against predictions, the post-Communist PDS refused to disap-pear but grew instead and now regularly garners about 20% of the vote in eastern elections.

However, paradoxically, opinion surveys give little cause for alarm about Ger-mans' commitment to basic democratic values and ethnic tolerance—in the East as well as in the West. East Germans emerged from some 56 years of Nazi and Communist dictatorship with nearly as strong a commitment to democracy as the citizens of most long-established democracies. Nor did West Germans' commitment to democracy fade. To be sure, under the hardships of the conversion to a market economy, many East Germans expressed nostalgia for the security of the old regime and doubted that the German democracy they had joined was the best form of state. But few actually wanted to turn back the clock or adopt a nondemocratic form of government. In the West, Germans became more intolerant of foreigners after reunification, but this simply paralleled a Europe-wide trend. West Germans did not become appreciably more antisemitic, and they do not differ radically from other Europeans in this regard. And again, East Germans did not differ much from West Germans in ethnic tolerance after reunification—indeed, they were often even more tolerant—even though press reports suggested that long-suppressed ethnic hatreds were now free to boil over.

The structure of ethnic tolerance might also be expected to differ in the East and the West, yet it is broadly similar. Many past studies of German antisemitism have concentrated on factors like age, education, and social isolation, which also have a strong influence in the United States. And other studies have suggested that the effects of social structure on tolerance are weaker in new democracies. Yet in the present study, adherence to democratic values and the distance or closeness to political extremism strongly overshadow social structural factors in explaining antisemitism and xenophobia in both parts of Germany. Perhaps this is why East Germans are somewhat more tolerant of Jews and foreigners than West Germans, even though their commitment to democratic values is slightly weaker. Support for the far Right REP is the best predictor of bigotry, and the REP are stronger in the West.

Ethnic intolerance appears to be heavily politicized in reunified Germany. When ethnocentric parties are weak, bigotry remains delegitimated and is prevented from growing. In the wake of the 1994 national elections, the third wave of extreme rightism seems to have receded in the West and to have never yet swelled in the East. Perhaps East German tolerance—which is near the European average—is more a legacy of the Communist regime's suppression of the extreme Right than its less heartfelt suppression of bigotry. Prior to Hitler's seizure of power, Germans were not considered especially antisemitic, but after the German electorate rejected democratic parties and voted in the extreme Right in 1932–33, the Nazi state committed the worst crimes against Jews and ethnic minorities that the world has seen. And Germans today are not more antisemitic or xenophobic than other Europeans. Perhaps the continuing strength of democracy and weakness of the extreme Right still provide the best bulwark against ethnic intolerance in reunified Germany, just as they seem to do in other countries around the world.

Yet we would be wrong to believe that extremism derives its strength primarily from ethnic intolerance or antidemocratic sentiments in the general population. Extremism in the population is primarily an ideological and partisan phenomenon, a product of disaffection with the political mainstream. The broad population does not support extremism primarily because it hates minorities or opposes democracy, but because it is indifferent to their fate. Yet because the leaders of extremist parties do often hate them, minorities and democracy are generally the first victims when extremists come to power.

APPENDIX: QUESTION TEXTS AND SCALE CONSTRUCTION

This appendix shows the survey question texts used to construct variables for the analyses. Question texts are grouped according to variables and scales used in the analyses. They are listed in the order in which they appear in the tables. Variables and scales are always based on the finest-grain categorizations available in the survey. Unless otherwise indicated, scales are factors from principal components factor analysis. Eigenvalues for western/eastern Germany are given in the scale title, and factor loadings for western/eastern Germany are given following each item. In cases where a factor includes a subsidiary factor among its items, Eigenvalues are given for the subsidiary factor, and loadings are given for the subsidiary items.

Some of the following variables are taken straightforwardly from the questionnaire. These include the basic demographic, behavioral, and political questions: age (A), sex, education level (B), income class (C), experience or fear of unemployment (E), church attendance (F), and preference ranking of the SPD and CDU/CSU (G). In the cases of unemployment (E) and party preference (G), different operationalizations were tried—each supported by its own theoretical justification. The different operationalizations produced very similar results, and the strongest ones were used.[5] Several further indicators are standard opinion questions replicated from the literature or previous surveys or are straightforward measurements of basic concepts: left-right self-placement (I), the feeling that one can trust most people (K), the feeling that one can express one's political opinions freely (L), interest in politics (M), and national pride (N).

Variables used in the analyses such as tolerance of foreigners (1), economic situation (D), unemployment (E), party sympathy (H), political efficacy (J), and those ranging from support demonstrations (O) to admire Western countries (V) are scales constructed from the survey questions. Some of these scales are established in the literature, and some of them are new. Most of the scales used were computed with factor analysis, and impressively, the factor structures were almost identical in eastern and western Germany, even though marginal frequencies often differed between samples.

The *dependent variables* are:

(1) Tolerate foreigners (Eigenvalues = 2.22/1.99) is a factor that combines several standard questions about ethnic minorities from the European Values Study (EVS) and the Eurobarometer with more recent questions about immigration, asylum, and violence against foreigners in Germany today.

1. Somebody recently said to us, "When jobs are scarce, employers should give priority to German people over foreigners." Would you agree or not agree? [Disagree] (.77/.70)

2. If somebody said, "I basically have nothing against foreigners, but there really are too many of them in our country," would you agree with this opinion or not? [Disagree] (.82/.75)

3. Are you personally for a change of the right-to-asylum law so that fewer refugees will enter the country, or are you against a change so that those who are politically persecuted won't be turned away? [Against a change] (.73/.72)

4. Here are two people talking about the recent acts of violence against foreigners in Germany. Which of them do you agree with? (a) I'm not in favor of violence, but obviously,

one has to shake things up a little before anything happens. (b) Of course something has to be done, but I'm against violence in all cases because it represents a danger for democracy. [Agree with b] (.46/.44)

5. On this list are various groups of people. Could you please sort out any that you would not like to have as neighbors? (.46/.47) [Don't mind as neighbors; Factor (Eigenvalue = 4.42/3.72) including:]

(a) People of a different race. (.76/.63)

(b) Immigrants/foreign workers. (.67/.55)

(c) Muslims. (.69/.72)

(d) Jews. (.76/.73)

(e) Hindus. (.71/.78)

(2) Accept Jewish neighbors.

1. On this list are various groups of people. Could you please sort out any that you would not like to have as neighbors? [Jews]

The *independent variables* are:

(A) Age and sex. Age is coded 16–17, 18–20, thereafter in 5–year intervals up to age 79, and 80 and older. Sex is coded (1) for males and (0) for females.

(B) Education is coded in 9 levels of certification that differ somewhat in western and eastern Germany.

(C) Income of the head of the household is coded in 11 levels in western Germany, and household income is coded in 5 categories in eastern Germany.

(D) Economic situation (Eigenvalues = 1.55/1.56) is a combination of evaluations of the general national economy, the respondent's personal economic situation, and a factor of economic worries. Despite distinctions in the literature between sociotropic and personal economic evaluations (Kinder and Kiewiet 1981), the indicators are interrelated and in most cases predict outcomes similarly.

1. Generally speaking, what do you think of the present economic situation in Germany? [Very good, good, so-so, bad, very bad] (.71/.38)

2. And what do you think of your own present economic situation? [Very good or good] (.80/.67)

3. We're trying to find out what people worry about. Could you please lay out these cards on this strip according to the way you feel about them. When you can't decide about a card, simply lay it on the side. [I'm very worried about it at the moment; I worry about it quite often; I sometimes worry about it; I'm not at all worried about it] (.62/.62) [Factor (Eigenvalue = 1.34/1.27) including:]

(a) Unemployment. (.74/.71)

(b) That my economic situation will get worse, that I'll have to cut back on everything. (.70/.73)

(c) That the housing shortage will keep getting worse. (.69/.57)

(E) Experience or fear of unemployment (simple count of positive responses).

1. Have you been unemployed in the last two years or in earlier times? (western Germany). Are you unemployed at present? (eastern Germany).

2. Are you afraid you could become/remain unemployed in the next half year?

3. Has anyone else in your household been unemployed in the last two years, or is anyone unemployed now?

4. Are you afraid anyone in your household could become/remain unemployed in the next half year?

(F) Church attendance. [Every Sunday, almost every Sunday, now and then, seldom, never, not member of a church]

(G) Preference ranking of SPD and CDU/CSU.

1. On these cards are the names of the parties that have political importance in the Federal Republic. Certainly, you don't like all these parties equally. Could you please sort these cards according to how much you like these parties? It goes like this: you put the party you like best on top. Under that, you put the one you like second best, and so on. And the last one is the party you like least. [Parties that are ranked: CDU/CSU, SPD, FDP, the Greens/Bündnis 90, the "Republikaner," PDS (former Communists in eastern Germany only). Variable is rank number, coded so that high preference is scored high.]

(H) Sympathy for PDS (former Communists)/"Republikaner" (right radicals) (Eigenvalues = 2.04/2.86; 3.13/2.73) measures extremism. Voting for the extreme Right or Left has generally been quite low in western Germany since the early 1950s, and vote intentions were so low in the present survey that they would have produced skewed variables. Thus, the present factors include additional questions that permit lesser expressions of sympathy for the post-Communist PDS and far-right "Republikaner." Still, substantial percentages of respondents in both the East and West refused to express any sympathy for extremist parties whatsoever. [Note: Parallel questions asked about each; Eigenvalues and loadings given for "Communists West/East; Republikaner West/East," respectively]

1. People disagree whether it is possible for the PDS/"Republikaner" to work with the other parties. Do you think that in the long run, normal cooperation with the PDS/"Republikaner" will be possible, or not? [Cooperation possible] (.87/.77; .83/.82)

2. Are you in favor or against cooperation of the PDS/"Republikaner" with other parties? [For cooperation] (.89/.84; .86/.82)

3. And if somebody said, "It wouldn't be so bad if the PDS/"Republikaner"got more support," would you agree or don't you see it that way? [Welcome more support] (.69/.81; .74/.72)

4. If there were an election for the Bundestag next Sunday, which party would you vote for—could you tell me which party on this list that is? You only have to mention the appropriate number. [PDS/"Republikaner"] (.09/.55; .66/.55)

5. On these cards are listed the names of the parties that have political importance in the Federal Republic. I'm sure you don't like all of these parties equally. Could you please lay out these cards in the order in which you like the parties? It works like this: you put the card of the party you like best on top. Next you put your second favorite party, and so on, and you put the party you like least on the bottom. [Rank of PDS/"Republikaner"; PDS choice not given in West] (—/.62; .85/.75)

(I) Left-right self-placement.

1. Parties are sometimes divided up according to whether they are left, middle, or right. I have a paper that has a ruler drawn on it. How would you describe your own political position, where on this ruler would you place yourself? [100–point scale]

(J) Political efficacy (Eigenvalues = 1.67/1.60) is a standard set of efficacy questions from the University of Michigan National Election Studies (see, e.g., Abramson 1983). Although these items are sometimes found to be multidimensional, in the present case, the four items form a single factor.

1. "Voting is the only way that people like me can have any say about how the government runs things." [Disagree] (.35/.31)

2. "I don't think that public officials care much about what people like me think." [Disagree] (.38/.45)

3. "Sometimes politics and government seem so complicated that a person like me can't really understand what's going on." [Disagree] (.33/.21)

4. "People like me don't have any say about what the government does." [Disagree] (.61./63)

(K) Can trust most people.

1. Do you think one can trust most people? [Can trust]

(L) Can express political opinions freely.

1. Do you feel that one can express his political opinions freely in Germany today, or is it better to be careful? [Can speak freely]

(M) Interest in politics.

1. Generally speaking, are you interested in politics? [Yes]

(N) Proud to be German.

1. How proud are you to be a German? [5–point scale: proud]

The following two indicators measure political confidence:

(O) Trust governmental institutions (Eigenvalues = 1.95/1.96) is a factor that combines two of the standard University of Michigan confidence indicators with a confidence factor derived from the EVS. The EVS factor measures trust in various state institutions and is distinct from another factor (not shown here) that measures trust in several institutions of civil society. In order to validate that trust in governmental institutions is distinct from democratic values, indicators for both concepts were entered into a single factor analysis. A scree test indicated that two factors must be extracted that correspond to the theoretical distinction. (For a scree test, one charts the Eigenvalues [which reflect explained variance] of the factors and looks for an "elbow" in the curve. One stops extracting factors when the curve levels out and additional factors no longer add as much to the explained variance.) These factors correlate at .20 and .17 (West and East) in an oblique rotation; and when the factors are calculated separately, as is done here, they correlate at .27 and .30 (West and East). These tests further confirm that political confidence and democratic values are distinct but moderately related. The factor for democratic values (T) is described later.

1. How much of the time do you think you can trust the government in Bonn to do what is right—just about always, most of the time, only some of the time, or none of the time? [Always/most of time] (.83/.84)

2. Would you say the government is pretty much run by a few big interests looking out for themselves or that it is run for the benefit of all people? [All people] (.78/.78)

3. Please look at this card and tell me, for each item listed, how much confidence you have in it. Is it a great deal, quite a lot, not very much, or none at all? [A great deal or quite a lot] (.81/.80) [Factor (Eigenvalue = 2.67/2.44) including:]

(a) Parliament. (.78/.77)

(b) Courts. (.70/.64)

(c) Police. (.71/.62)

(d) Civil Service. (.71/.59)

(e) Army. (.58/.67)

(P) Trust politicians (Eigenvalues = 2.67/2.56) is a factor that includes questions about politicians and political parties. These are mostly standard Allensbach questions, although some are new. This factor is similar to the trust in governmental institutions factor (O) and correlates strongly with it (.64 and .68 in the West and East). It was not combined with trust in governmental institutions (or with democratic attitudes) because many scholars of political support (e.g., Lipset and Schneider 1983) argue that one must distinguish between institutions and incumbents. There was a second reason for not combining the two factors. The trust in government factor (O) closely approximates indicators most often used in the literature, and for the sake of comparability, items on parties and politicians were kept separate.

1. Do you believe that the representatives in Bonn first and foremost represent the interests of the populace or do they have other interests which are more important to them? [Interests of people] (.72/.75)

2. Do you believe that one must have great abilities to be a member of parliament in Bonn? [Yes] (.51/.58)

3. Are you disappointed in the three parties—CDU/CSU, SPD, and FDP—or wouldn't you say that? [Wouldn't say that] (.67/.66)

4. When you think about our politicians, what do politicians see as most important: power and privilege or the welfare of our country? [Welfare of our country] (.75/.74)

5. Here are two people talking about politicians. Which of them says more closely what you also think—the top one or the bottom one? [Top one:] I cannot understand it. Politicians know very well what the majority of the people want, but they simply cannot agree. The politicians talk and debate a lot, but in the end they seldom come to a clear decision. [Bottom one:] With difficult problems it is not simple to achieve a decision. Therefore it is important that the politicians allow themselves time and ample debate to work out a solution to problems. [Bottom one] (.62/.59)

6. We're trying to find out what people worry about. Could you please lay out these cards on this strip according to the way you feel about them. When you can't decide about a card, simply lay it on the side. [I'm very worried about it at the moment; I worry about it quite often; I sometimes worry about it; I'm not at all worried about it—not worried] (.71/.57) [Factor (Eigenvalue = 5.18/4.85) including:]

(a) That one can trust politicians less and less. (.76/.70)

(b) That hardly any clear political decisions will be made, only lousy compromises. (.75/.71)

(c) That the administration is too weak. (.71/.69)

(d) That the politicians can't agree, that they're always fighting. (.67/.68)

(e) That the politicians have too little courage to make tough decisions. (.66/.58)

(f) That our politicians aren't capable of solving the tough problems here. (.66/.70)

(g) That simply nothing is being done to stop the flood of asylum seekers. (.46/.36)

Liberal attitudes in the next three scales are measured by indicators of acceptance of public contestation and political tolerance.

(Q) Support demonstrations (Eigenvalues = 1.32/1.23) combines an Allensbach question from the 1950s with a factor from a battery of items developed in 1968 by Rudolf Wildenmann and Max Kaase (see Kaase 1971).

1. Some people say that the German people are too patient and are always putting up with much too much from their government. What do you think: should people demonstrate against the government much more often than in the past, or don't you think much of that? [More often] (.72/.75)

2. On these cards, we have put together a series of commonly heard opinions about people's behavior. We would like to find out what people really think. Please sort out the cards on this scale according to how much you agree or disagree with each statement. (.80/.68) [Factor (Eigenvalue = 2.06/1.68) including:]

(a) Every citizen has the right to go to the streets for his convictions if necessary. [Agree] (.68/.44)

(b) Everyone should have the right to stand up for his opinion, even if the majority disagrees. [Agree] (.52/.65)

(R) Tolerance of free speech (Eigenvalues = 2.18/2.03) is a factor that combines willingness to allow a revolutionary and also a racist to speak publicly. Tolerance has been defined as putting up with what you do not like (Crick 1971, King 1971, 1976). The present questions are combined so that tolerance is measured as putting up with both ends of a political spectrum. If one does not measure what the respondent dislikes (see Sullivan, Piereson, and Marcus 1982), at least one might assume that the respondent does not like both ends of the same spectrum. The items in this scale (tolerating a revolutionary and a racist speaker) are taken from the International Social Survey Project, connected to the General Social Survey, and are adaptations of Stouffer's (1955) tolerance questions.

1. There are some people whose views are considered extreme by the majority. First consider people who want to overthrow the government by revolution. Do you think that such people should be allowed to hold public meetings to express their views? [Allow] (.74/.66)

2. Now consider people who believe that whites are racially superior to all other races. Do you think that such people should be allowed to hold public meetings to express their views? [Allow] (.89/.88)

3. (Allow both speakers: .92/.91)

(S) Accept political extremists (Eigenvalues = 1.18/1.17) is also a factor that combines willingness to have a left-wing and a right-wing extremist as a neighbor. It is derived from the EVS and is one factor among several taken from a list of groups (another factor is included in the dependent variable tolerance of foreigners [1])

1. On this list are various groups of people. Could you please sort out any that you would not like to have as neighbors? [Don't mind as neighbors; factor including:]

(a) Left-wing extremists. (.76/.71)

(b) Right-wing extremists. (.85/.68)

The following two indicators measure regime values:

(T) Democratic values (Eigenvalues = 1.72/1.64) is a factor that includes support for democratic institutions and practices, opposition to National Socialism, a definition of democracy consistent with representative Western regimes, the belief that German democracy is the best form of state, and the opinion that democracy can solve Germany's problems. Two of these items are factors from subsidiary factor analyses. The representative definition of democracy contrasts with participatory or economic definitions of democracy. And a democratic norms factor contrasts with factors measuring understanding of conflict, support for free expression, and opposition to the use of force.[6] The items in the democratic values factor are taken from previous Allensbach surveys, Wildenmann and Kaase's battery of questions, and surveys conducted by the post-Franco Spanish government.

1. Two men are discussing how a country should be governed. One says: "I like it best when the people place the best politician at the top and give him complete governing power. He can then clearly and quickly decide with a few chosen experts. Not much talking is done and something really happens!" The other says: "I prefer that a number of people have to determine something in the country. They do sometimes go round and round until something is done, but it is not so easy for abuse of power to occur." Which of these two opinions is closest to your own view—the first or the second? [Second] (.66/.37)

2. A question about Hitler and National Socialism: Some say that if you disregard the war and the persecution of the Jews, the Third Reich was not so bad. Others say that the Third Reich was a bad thing no matter what. What is your opinion? [Nazism was a bad thing] (.47/.45)

3. In your opinion, what is most important about democracy? Which things on this list are absolutely necessary for one to be able to say of a country, this is a democracy? (.66/.52) [Factor (Eigenvalue = 1.02/1.83) including:]

(a) Freedom of the press and opinion, that everyone can freely express their political opinions. (.59/.66)

(b) That one can choose from several parties to vote for. (.60/.69)

(c) That free elections with secret ballots are held regularly. (.63/.68)

(d) A strong opposition that keeps the government in check. (.43/.38)

(e) That everyone can freely practice their religion. (.38/.51)

(f) Independent courts that judge only according to the law. (.63/.41)

4. On these cards, we have put together a series of commonly heard opinions about people's behavior. We would like to find out what people really think. Please sort out the cards on this scale according to how much you agree or disagree with each statement. (.33/.56) [Agree; factor (Eigenvalue = 1.04/1.19) including:]

(a) A living democracy is inconceivable without a political opposition. (.26/.58)

(b) Every democratic party should have the right in principle to enter government. (.47/.32)

(c) The interests of the whole people should always have priority over the special interests of individuals. (.29/.24)

5. Do you believe that the democracy that we have in Germany is the best form of state or is there another form of state which is better? [Best form of state] (.53/.59)

6. If someone says, "We can solve the problems we have in the Federal Republic with democracy," would you agree or not? [Agree] (.64/.61)

(U) Against old East German regime (Eigenvalues $= 1.27/1.55$) was intended to complement the democratic values factor (T). Whereas the democratic values factor was meant (among other things) to contrast current democracy with fascism, opposition to the DDR was meant to contrast current democracy with communism. However, the present factor does not tap basic attitudes on democracy well: democratic attitudes do not correlate strongly or consistently with attitudes toward communism or socialism. Of course, some would argue that although fascism is diametrically opposed to democracy, socialism is not necessarily related to democracy, positively or negatively. There have been democratic socialist regimes and theories (Sweden and social democracy), as well as antidemocratic socialist regimes and theories (the Soviet Union and Leninism). Although most Communist regimes have claimed to be democratic, their practice may have put doubt into the minds of many observers—enough, at least, to reduce the correlation in an opinion survey. Thus, the opposition to the DDR factor simply measures support and nostalgia for the ideals and practices of the old Communist regime: whether communism or socialism were good ideas badly carried out, and whether the respondent is glad the East German regime ended and was reunified with the democratic West. But this factor does not measure negative attitudes toward Western-style liberal democracy.

1. Do you consider communism [half sample: socialism] to be a good idea that was badly carried out? [No] (.38/.64)

2. Is the German reunification more an occasion for joy or concern for you? [Joy] (.68/.78)

3. When you look back to the last years in the DDR [in western Germany: for the people there], were conditions really quite bearable or would you say that there absolutely had to be a change? [Absolutely had to change] (.64/.67)

4. Sometimes one wishes that he could turn back the Wheel of History. How do you feel? Have you ever thought that it would have been better if the two Germanys had not reunited, that it would have been better to have kept the original DDR, or have you never thought about that? [Would not be in favor of returning to before reunification] (.49/.28)

The next four indicators measure comparative or historical preferences for a democratic form of government. Such indicators are especially relevant in post-transition countries like eastern Germany, where comparisons are made to the pretransition, nondemocratic state (see Linz and Stepan 1989, Rose and Mishler 1993, Weil 1993, 1994a).

(V) Admire Western countries (Eigenvalues $= 1.13/1.08$) is a factor composed of a preference for working closely with America, together with a subsidiary factor measuring admiration for the United States, Great Britain, and France. This subsidiary factor was one of several that emerged from an analysis of a longer list of countries.

1. A very general question about German foreign policy: How important will it be for us in the future to work closely with America, that is, the U.S.A.? [Very important or important] (.75/.73)

2. Different countries have different forms of government and follow their own political paths. If you think about the countries on this list, which of them are admirable countries for you? For which of these countries do you especially like the political life? (.75/.73) [Factor (Eigenvalue = 2.65/1.41) including: U.S.A. (.75/.74), England (.74/.73), France (.72/.54)]

(W) Evaluation of the general situation now as against the past is a factor meant to evaluate the respondent's impression of improvement or deterioration since unification. It is based on questions asking for a rating from 0 to 10 of the general situation in the respondent's part of the country. The rating for the past is subtracted from the rating for the present.

1. If you think back to the time when Germany was still divided, what do you generally think of the situation at that time? Tell me according to this ladder: 0 would mean that the situation in our part of Germany was very bad, and 10 would mean that the situation here was very good. Which number best expresses what the situation here was like back then? What is the situation like at the present time? Which number best expresses the present situation in our part of Germany? [Present rating minus past rating]

(X) Outlook for future situation is based on the same series of questions as in the previous item, but with respect to the future.[7]

1. If you look into the future, how will our part the country develop; how good or bad will the situation here be? Tell me again according to this ladder. [0–10 ladder]

(Y) View next 12 months

1. A question about next year. Do you look forward to 1993 with hopes or fears?

NOTES

The research for this study was conducted with the support of a grant from the Alexander von Humboldt Foundation (awarded to Elisabeth Noelle-Neumann and the author) and a grant from the National Science Foundation (grant number SES-9023331) and a fellowship from the German Marshall Fund of the United States (both awarded to the author). I would like to thank Elisabeth Noelle-Neumann, director of the Institut für Demoskopie Allensbach; Max Kaase and Franz Urban Pappi of the University of Mannheim; and Mary Gautier of Louisiana State University for their collaboration, help, and support.

1. The rest of this section summarizes ongoing collaborative research by the author and Elisabeth Noelle-Neumann. This research is based on special surveys on democratic values and monthly omnibus surveys conducted by Allensbach in East and West Germany since March 1990 (and in West Germany since the late 1940s). For studies of similar themes based on different data see, for example, Feist (1991), Gabriel (1993), Gibowski and Jung (1993), Klingemann and Hofferbert (1994), Kuechler (1992, 1994), Minkenberg (1993), and Veen (1993).

2. The survey was funded by the Alexander von Humboldt Foundation for the research project, "The Development of Democratic Attitudes in Eastern Germany: A Comparison of Eastern with Western Germany," with principal investigators Frederick D. Weil and Elisabeth Noelle-Neumann.

3. At the time we designed the survey, we decided we did not have sufficient funds to do a full investigation of antisemitism and therefore focused on other issues. The question about Jewish neighbors is part of a more general tolerance scale.

4. For tolerance of foreigners, ordinary least squares regressions were used because the dependent variable is continuous and normally distributed. For tolerance of Jewish neighbors, logistical regression was used because the dependent variable is dichotomous and skewed. It would have been desirable to use comparable types of regression, but this was not possible with the available data.

5. A major-party sympathy rating and a vote intention were also tested for party preference. For unemployment, experience alone and fear alone were tested. In both cases, these alternative operationalizations produced weaker results, and since there were no overwhelming theoretical reasons for preferring them, they were not used.

6. The loadings on this subsidiary factor are lower than on many others. However, the factor analysis showed roughly the same structure in German surveys in 1968, 1979, 1991, and 1992—the latter two surveys in both East and West Germany. This temporal consistency is unusually strong and suggests that the analysis taps some underlying dimensions, even if there has been some decay in its clarity in the most recent survey.

7. An index was also computed comparing the future to the present, but its variance was so small that the index proved unstable in analyses. Most respondents did not predict much change from the present to the future.

II

MOVEMENTS, GROUPS, AND ORGANIZATIONS PROPAGATING ANTISEMITISM AND XENOPHOBIA IN UNITED GERMANY

6

WILFRIED SCHUBARTH

Xenophobia among East German Youth

The collapse of the socialist regimes and the end of confrontation between the two antagonistic political blocs triggered deep-seated transformations and shocks in Germany and throughout Europe. These developments have been accompanied by a growth in nationalism, xenophobia, antisemitism, and violence (Butterwegge and Jäger 1992, Otto and Merten 1993, Förster et al. 1993). In Germany, too, the end of East Germany and eastern Germany's accession to the Federal Republic of Germany (FRG) were linked with an increase in nationalism and xenophobia related to changes in the political culture. Although excessive extremist right-wing violent activities in Germany after the period of 1990–93 appear to have decreased, a range of factors indicating a right-wing trend within the society makes continued attention to nationalism, right-wing extremism, and xenophobia advisable. This is the case for both eastern and western Germany; right-wing extremism and xenophobia are problems affecting all of Germany, not specifically the East. Nevertheless, developments in eastern Germany lead one to ask how hatred of foreigners and xenophobia could escalate to such an extent in a socialist state that considered itself a "stronghold of antifascism," and spoke constantly of "friendship among the peoples" and "proletarian internationalism." Was something merely surfacing for which the stage was already set in the authoritarian East German system, or was extremist violence and hatred only a byproduct of the collapse of the socialist system and unification?

Since the prominent violent attacks on foreigners and asylum seekers in Hoyerswerda, Rostock, Mölln, and Solingen in the early 1990s, increasing efforts have been made to study the causes of growing susceptibility to right-wing extremism and xenophobic violence. Most academic attempts to explain these events start with the social transformation in people's lives caused by the process of social individualization,[1] which—according to Wilhelm Heitmeyer—under certain circumstances may support the development of right-wing extremist, xenophobic attitudes (Heitmeyer et al. 1992, 1995). Other explanations refer to the theories of the authoritarian personality by Theodor W. Adorno and others (1973) or are derived from individual psychology, group sociology, and extremism theory (e.g., Pfahl-Traughber 1993, Wahl 1993, Lillig 1994, Willems 1993). Some make changes in the political culture in the Federal Republic responsible for growing right-wing extremism (see Butterwegge 1994b, 1994a, Heitmeyer 1994b). Finally, questions are raised as to the differences and similarities of extremism and violence in eastern and western Germany.

This chapter examines causes, origins, and dynamics of right-wing extremism and xenophobia among young people in the eastern German states. My analysis is based on three basic assumptions: First, xenophobia has taken on a new qualitative dimension in eastern Germany in recent years. It has become a central keystone of right-wing extremism. Second, right-wing authoritarianism is a means of dealing with radical social change, assisted by changes in the political culture and the overall social climate. Third, xenophobia and anti-immigrant violence differ in the East and the West not in principle but in degree and single causes.

I shall develop in more detail my theses in eight questions based on socialization theory (Hurrelmann and Ulich 1991) and recent findings of empirical youth research (see Melzer 1992, Deutsches Jugendinstitut 1992, Schubarth and Stenke 1992, Förster et al. 1993, Hoffmann-Lange 1995b).

What connection exists between xenophobia, antisemitism, right-wing extremism, and violence?

Empirical studies of eastern German young people have confirmed the basic assumption that right-wing extremism combines ideologies of ethnocultural and racial difference with intolerance and a greater readiness to use violence (see Förster et al. 1993: 103 ff.). Xenophobic attitudes, along with ultranationalist, antisemitic, and anti-Communist orientations, form the heart of the right-wing extremist syndrome. The more strongly xenophobic and ultraright-wing attitudes are held, the more probable is intolerance or use of violence. This becomes particularly apparent among right-wing-oriented groups, such as skinheads, where strong xenophobia is generally paired with hatred of Jews and a strong potential for violence.

What trends can be observed among eastern German young people with regard to xenophobia and violence?

In former socialist East Germany, foreigners and xenophobia were not really an issue of everyday life. Officially, "socialist friendship among peoples" and "internationalist" education were propagated. In fact, isolation from the outside world and restrictive policies toward immigrants and resident aliens from socialist "brother countries" contained, until the fall of 1990, the existence of a relatively monocultural society. The comparatively few foreign nationals in East Germany were largely isolated from the East German population. Only about 160,000 non-

Germans lived in East Germany, primarily citizens of Vietnam, Mozambique, Cuba, and Poland, representing only 1% of the population (excluding the members of the Soviet force). Xenophobic manifestations in the so-called socialist German Democratic Republic (GDR) were played down or treated as taboo. Especially in the 1980s, as the gap between reality and the socialist regime's political propaganda became progressively larger, thus undermining the credibility of the "real existing socialism," one could observe an increasing distance in the public opinion toward the former "friendly socialist countries" and growing sympathy for former "imperialist enemies." This indicated a fundamental shift in political attitudes (see, e.g., Friedrich 1990, Förster et al. 1993).

In the course of the collapse of East Germany and subsequent German unity, the relationship in eastern Germany toward foreigners changed significantly, although the low percentage of resident foreigners remained almost unchanged. Some of East Germany's foreign contract workers returned to their countries of origin, and growing numbers of asylum seekers were assigned to hostels in the eastern German states based on a federal quota system. This distribution of refugees, often insensitive to local conditions, triggered openly expressed hatred and violent attacks on asylum seekers by gangs of young people—in the early stages often applauded by adult spectators. Numerous studies confirm the development of resentment against asylum seekers, Gypsies, and other foreigners from Eastern Europe, Asia, and Africa (see Melzer 1992, Förster et al. 1993). According to our survey in 1992, among about 2,000 youngsters (for more detail, see Förster et al. 1993: 138), approximately one in two eastern German adolescents reject foreigners and demand a reduction in the proportion of foreign nationals living in the country, although they represent only 1% of the eastern German population in comparison with about 10% in the western part of Germany. Approximately three-quarters of all young people neither know foreigners personally nor do they have non-German friends. Not even half of them would be willing to invite a foreigner into their homes, which suggests strong social distance. Young people with antiforeigner attitudes generally overestimate the foreigners' share of the population. One in three assumes that foreign nationals make up over 10% of the population of East Germany although they represent, in fact, less than 1.5%. This is a typical example for the correlation between affective rejection of a scapegoat or "enemy" and fearful overestimation of its size—and often also its power, threat, and (in the case of asylum seekers) its costs to taxpayers. Rejection and fear of foreigners can often be attributed to an overactive imagination and irrationality.

A comparison of xenophobia among young people in eastern and western Germany shows that it is among eastern Germans up to 15% higher (see Melzer 1992, Deutsches Jugendinstitut 1992). East and West Germans clearly rank foreigners differently: U.S.-Americans and the French, for example, are ranking high in sympathy, whereas Poles, Turks, and especially Gypsies (Sinti and Romany) are disliked. These ethnonational prejudices are not only held by young people but also apply to the older generations, particularly those over age 60. According to surveys conducted (Melzer 1992, Förster et al. 1993, and Hoffmann-Lange 1995b) central determinants of attitudes toward foreigners are political orientation, gender, educational level, and family background. The stronger the identification with right-wing political positions, the stronger are xenophobic attitudes. Almost all right-wing extremists are hostile to foreigners, though not everyone who dislikes foreigners is also rightwing. Attitudes of young females are 10–15% more favorable to foreigners than those of young men of the same age group. The influence of education and family background is also noticeable; young people with better education, (e.g., college and college preparatory high school [Gymnasium] students) have more positive views of foreigners than young people with lower levels of education. This is also true for young people whose parents have college degrees.

Panel studies from the early 1990s lead us to conclude that trends toward radicalization are present among some adolescents too, parallel to the polarization between right-wing- and left-wing-oriented youths (Förster et al. 1993). Approximately one in three male high school students and apprentices is not opposed to physical violence against other people. Four percent of male apprentices and 1–2% of high school students have already participated in violent actions against foreigners, and an additional 10–15% would be willing to do so, verifying a potential for right-wing radicalization. About 5% of males in both eastern and western Germany show sympathy with right-wing skinheads, as comparative youth studies indicate (e.g., Hoffmann-Lange 1995b: 292, Neunter Jugendbericht 1994: 191). Regarding antisemitic attitudes, empirical findings contradict each other. Although studies in 1991 (Wittenberg, Prosch, and Abraham 1991, Melzer 1992) claim that antisemitism was much less widespread among eastern than western German young people, more recent studies indicate an increase in antisemitism among eastern German young people (Förster et al. 1993: 125).

What typical attitude patterns toward foreigners exist among eastern German young people?

With the help of nonrepresentative essay analyses and qualitative interviews with about 100 young East German male and female pupils (eighth graders) in 1991, greater insight was gained into fundamental thought and argumentation patterns with regard to foreigners. Four typical argumentation patterns were found (for more detail, see Schubarth and Stenke 1992).

1. Universalists: "It's a human rights issue." About a tenth of the more than a hundred essays by schoolchildren belong to the universalist category. This group of respondents oppose judging people according to skin color, religion, nationality, or ethnic background. They refer explicitly to human rights and universal values and see no hierarchy between Germans and foreigners. Respondents firmly oppose violence and demand consistent prosecution of violent offenders. A central pattern in their argumentation is the call for understanding of and empathy with the situation of foreigners in Germany. They appeal for greater tolerance and express a desire to learn from other people. They also hope to break down prejudices and nationalist arrogance in Germany:

> There are no superior races or peoples; those who believe this come close to supporting fascist views.

I thoroughly condemn attacks on hostels for foreigners.

In addition, one must fight the causes of right-wing radicalism that lie within the social system; they're not simply marginal phenomena.

Prejudice against foreigners should be broken down, and you can't make generalizations.

As a rich country, Germany must contribute to solving the problems in the countries involved.

People have to learn to share.

2. Proforeigners: "Foreigners are nothing but perfectly normal people." Such ideas were expressed in one-third of the essays. The proforeigners emphasize basically positive views. Foreigners are perceived as "normal" people, though it is also acknowledged that they are different in certain ways (skin color, language, culture, religion). But such diversity should be tolerated as long as it remains within the realm of the "normal." In justifying their position, respondents typically do not use nationalist rhetoric, economic, or welfare-abuse arguments against foreigners. But they assume the existence of an abstract benchmark of normality, which is, in fact, based on the culture they live in. However, this is generally not reflected more closely. Proforeigners expect that Germans and foreigners should adapt to each other in order to be able to live together. Foreign cultures are seen as an enrichment, but the limits of tolerance are reached when on the part of the "others" (e.g., among Sinti and Romany) no willingness is seen to adapt. Some typical statements are:

> I think foreigners are basically just people like us. They can't help it if they're Black, for example. Personally I haven't had any experience with foreigners yet. But I think everyone should have something to do with foreigners some time, get to know their problems and culture, and only then really make up their minds.

> I think it's nice when different people live together in one country. But I don't think it's all right that most foreigners don't know how to behave in another country.

> I don't have anything against foreigners. I like to eat foreign foods and I like foreign clothes. But I have something against foreigners who come to Germany, collect money, and don't work.

> Foreigners and Germans can live well together. We can learn a lot from their nationality, their customs and traditions.

3. Ethnocentrics: "We have enough problems of our own. This response type was found among two-fifths of the essays analyzed. The respondents reveal a rigid dichotomous view of foreigners. Distinctions are made between "real" political refugees, and so-called "pseudo" asylum seekers and economic refugees. Such categorization seems almost natural and is not accompanied by further reflection. The same dichotomous thought patterns were found with regard to group identity. The main point of reference—having a strong influence on judgments—is the certainty of being German. However, this collective identification is used in various ways of argumentation (e.g., national identity influences priorities of polit-

ical action). Young respondents demand that politicians should concentrate first on solving the problems of (eastern) Germans. Problems of other people should be dealt with only after eastern Germans have achieved prosperity and are ensured their rights. Foreigners are welcome if they contribute to the lives, prosperity, and well-being of Germans. Guest workers are seen primarily in their economic function. They seem to have no independent significance of their own, a view that could be called ethnocentric. In addition, respondents insist that foreigners should not disturb German law and order. Otherwise, their presence should not be guaranteed. If they do not adapt to the rules of the host country, it is considered the foreigners' own fault if their security is threatened and if they are attacked. But respondents emphasize at the same time that violence against foreigners serves no purpose—it does not solve any problems. Though some essays indicate understanding for the causes of violent acts, they call for a rapid political solution of the "foreigner" problem. Only if politicians fail, people must take the initiative themselves. Some representative statements are:

> Basically I have nothing against foreigners. They don't bother me in their countries or as tourists. But I don't like the fact that a lot of the foreigners in Germany apply for asylum when they aren't even politically persecuted. These "pseudo" asylum seekers get more money than our own retired people who have worked their whole lives.

> Especially in the eastern German states, there are enough problems building up the economy, we don't need any additional problems. My mother might lose her job. What if a foreigner gets her job?

> Our people were supposed to have no problems after the political changes; that's what Kohl promised. But now a lot are unemployed, the price of electricity has tripled, rents and public transportation have gone up sixfold. How are our people supposed to deal with that?

> All of this annoys us a lot, so it's perfectly natural that we don't understand why politicians spend so much money on foreigners instead of helping their own compatriots.

> I don't think attacks on foreigners' hostels are good, they don't solve anything, but we've been abandoned by our politicians. That's why people have taken things into their own hands.

4. Antiforeigners: "I'm at war with foreigners." About one-tenth of the essays were counted to belong to this attitude group, which is dominated by a negative and strongly stereotypical image of foreigners; they are perceived above all as criminals, swindlers, drug dealers, and violent offenders. Foreigners appear as an all-powerful threat, irrespective of personal experience. Elements of ethnocentric justification are supplemented by arguments motivated by racism and xenophobia. The pupils perceive themselves as extremely underprivileged in comparison with foreigners. This perception of relative deprivation is the defense mechanism to legitimate the rejection of resident aliens and asylum seekers. But can we assume that, if prejudiced respondents were better-off, they would tolerate foreigners? I suspect xenophobic hostility has deeper attitudinal and psychological roots, regardless of economic deprivation.

What are the main characteristics of xenophobic respondents? Most express "understanding" of youth violence, although a willingness to participate in such violence was not clearly spelled out in the essays. Respondents also have no desire to have any contacts with foreigners, nor is it seen as beneficial and positive to have them as neighbors. On the contrary, social distance is expressed through support for statements like: "All foreigners should leave the country." Some other citations from the essays are:

I'm at war with foreigners because foreigners take our jobs and homes.

I hate all foreigners who do illegal things here in Germany, like drugs, cigarette trade, prostitution, etc.

It will get to the point that they bring lots of children into the world here in our country and reproduce like weeds. I mean, to them we're foreigners too, but we're a little different.

I can't imagine a future with foreigners since there will always be different interests. It starts with the culture and religion. It's not right that Arab music blares at me from the window of a student dormitory every morning on my way to school.

I can understand the attacks on the hostels, because a lot of anger has built up among Nazis, skinheads, and other people. When you realize that every third person you meet is a foreigner, it can make you really sick.

In the future I wish for a foreigner-free country.

To summarize, the qualitative analysis of one hundred student essays leads me to the conclusion that about half of all essays examined expressed a more or less strongly negative attitude toward foreigners. Their views of the issues surrounding foreigners are dominated by an assessment of their own deprived situation as overwhelmingly precarious and insecure. Thus the focus of perceptions compares the situation of foreigners in light of the students' own problems. These findings are identical to other quantitative surveys. Förster and others (1993) found that young people justify their opposition to the presence of foreigners by arguing that they supposedly "worsen the housing shortage" (74%), "live at German expense" (58%), "take away jobs from Germans" (55%), and "tend toward crime and violence" (38%). Poll questions do not reveal very clearly the structure of arguments, which, as I have shown, is based on an underlying ethnocentric orientation. However, the support of 30% of all young respondents to the poll statement, "Only German customs and traditions should be permitted in Germany; foreigners should adapt completely," can be interpreted as a confirmation of these assumptions. Another 20% of interviewed youngsters were "indifferent," from which I conclude that half of all young people express a wish to live in a predominantly German culture.

The question arises whether the patterns of perception and argumentation found among eastern German students differ from those of western German young people. A comparison with existing studies highlights both similarities and differences. The demand for adaptation to German culture is also common in the West, as are the perception of foreigners as competitors and the view that they often live at German welfare and taxpayers' expense (although surprisingly enough, eastern Germans are also perceived as foreign by western Germans in this sense). Even demands for forced deportation were raised (see Jäger 1992a, 1992b). The East-West differences in attitudes seem to be that western Germans distinguish more clearly between guest workers and asylum seekers, though in both parts of Germany Sinti and Romany are similarly disliked. The somewhat lower antiforeigner resentment in the West can be explained with the western Germans' much longer experience and increasing societal integration of a large group of labor migrants and their offspring on the job, in schools, as neighbors, and in the public.

What effect did social transformation have on the lives of eastern German young people?

The social changes that started in the fall of 1989 changed the lives of eastern German citizens dramatically. For young people the changes were a significant experience, requiring the mobilization of all of their abilities and energy. Nearly every area of life was greatly affected. The most significant change was the loss of familiar rules, values, and traditions as reference points and a large-scale devaluation of behavioral patterns in public life that had formerly ensured success in the socialist society. Behavioral orientations adequate for the new system could only be formed in the course of a longer-term learning and socialization process. In addition, "significant institutional support and important authorities for adolescent development . . . lost their validity in a fashion that was probably traumatic for young people in East Germany" (Mayer 1991: 96).

Typical of such a period of change is that it is less a natural transition from one political and economic system to another than the transposition of a social system onto completely different conditions—that is, a systemic transformation. The high speed and radical societal changes intensified human problems. Many GDR citizens who found themselves in situations of previously unknown proportions of socioeconomic insecurity have been overwhelmed, and their psychosocial stress-bearing capacity have not been able to cope with the unexpected changes. The development of fundamentally new attitudes became necessary, such as attitudes required for planning for the personal future. A largely predictable life or "normal" (state-controlled) future was replaced by a nearly incalculable individual life course; certainty was replaced by many uncertainties, requiring a different way of thinking and greater flexibility than East German young people had been able to acquire. The need for a rapid transition from a passive and responsive way of life to a more active and determined one can be typically demonstrated by young people who now faced unseen challenges in the labor market after having been accustomed to secure apprenticeships and jobs under the former regime.

Social relationships changed just as drastically. Classmates and coworkers became competitors for training and jobs, solidarity rapidly broke down, and the role of money in daily life (and communication) was greatly enhanced. Many parents' own existential worries and the increased pressure for mobility and flexibility left their mark on children and adolescents, many of whom complained that their parents no longer had as much time for them. The role of money in how young people spent their free time also became more pronounced than it had been previously. The new, varied consumer offerings, which at first overwhelmed many young people, often contrasted with their limited financial ability; in addition, many formerly state-sponsored and low-cost youth clubs, sports associations, meeting places, and the like were closed.

Changes in the political realm also have been breathtaking. Previously, only one officially legitimate "truth" existed; now pluralism prevailed, and it was difficult for many people to deal with it. Many young people were not accustomed to forming their own opinions and expressing them argumentatively. The loss of the hypertrophied politicization practiced in East Germany was greeted with relief by young people; yet political decision-making processes in the new society seemed just as difficult for the individual to understand and to influence. At the same time, young people's negative experiences with opportunistically "transformed" young people or adults increased their cynicism, skepticism, and fears. This clearly shows what a deep rift the transformation of the system made in the lives of young eastern Germans. Socialized in a system that no longer exists, they must now quickly and radically adapt to a completely different society, one into which their western German peers were born and socialized. Among eastern Germans, the incompatibility of the two social systems has led to manifestations of anomie, as well as disorientation and isolation. But the social networks and support systems (family, neighbors, community, mass organizations, etc.) that might help to cope with the changes have been broken down in the course of the changes or are in the process of dissolution. A dilemma has become apparent: the social changes not only created greater anomie and isolation but also destroyed helpful support systems before new ones had been developed. The manifestations of anomie, disorientation, and isolation that increased immensely with the social transformations are thus fertile ground for ideologies that offer orientation, support, a sense of belonging, and clarity.

These transformations in eastern Germany must be viewed in light of the background of modernization processes that have been present for some time in Western industrialized democracies, as discussed in connection with the concept of the risk society (see Beck 1986, Beck and Beck-Gernsheim 1994). The present transitions in eastern Germany and Eastern Europe are moving in the same direction, accompanied by similar costs and benefits. Negative outcomes seem to be more painful in eastern Germany because they occur in direct comparison with and under the influence of West Germany. Suddenly things disappear that have been taken for granted, hopes are disappointed, and disillusion sets in. The ambivalence of this push for modernization is obvious: progressive changes and new chances to develop one's individuality are coupled with risks, losses, new burdens, and dangers.

Where do right-wing authoritarian patterns for dealing with these problems come from? What role did the legacy of the authoritarian socialist state play?

The problems described herein need not automatically lead to right-wing extremism. It depends, rather, on the way problems are subjectively and collectively interpreted and what mechanisms or strategies are utilized. Coping strategies de-pend primarily on the patterns of interpretation and the mechanisms for conflict resolution acquired during early socialization, as well as the stock of norms, knowledge, and ideology present in a society (Hurrelmann and Ulich 1991). The legacies of both Nazism and socialism weigh heavily in this regard. In particular, East Germany's prescribed Stalinist antifascism could not effectively combat the passing down of fascist, undemocratic ideological fragments from one generation to the next (Schubarth, Pschierer, and Schmidt 1991). On the contrary, experience with an authoritarian state with undemocratic social structures, intolerance, intimi-dation, repression, and violence served to preserve authoritarian, undemocratic thought and behavioral patterns (for a critical view, see Friedrich 1993, Oester-reich 1993). Conditions and structures promoting extremism were brought about by the absolutist control of everyday life by Communist Party ideology and propa-ganda, which permanently reproduced dualist generalizations of friend-and-foe, black-and-white schemes. Other factors were undemocratic decision making in politics and daily life from above *for* instead of *by* the people; the contradictions between an "official" public political culture and a private, informal culture; an absence of freedom of opinion, which impeded the formation of opinions without fear and the development of an ability to engage in an open and honest discourse; the lack of tolerance and encouragement of xenophobic prejudices and ethnocen-tric arrogance against other people (e.g., toward Poles); the preservation of a monocultural society in which contact with "alien" cultures was only allowed to a limited extent; the tendency of the socialist state to resolve social conflicts, eco-nomic problems, and ideological contradictions by repression, ostracism, igno-rance, silencing, and other means of oppression.

Socialization under these social conditions left a significant mark on the mind-set and development of social "traits" of eastern Germans. Thus, there was a ten-dency to encourage the formation of orientation and behavioral patterns, such as the willingness to tolerate or support authoritarian, paternalistic behavior on the part of the authorities; an instrumental assessment of political performance and legitimacy of the political leadership based on the criteria concerning whether the government ensured adequate material prosperity; fear of accepting responsibility and a tendency to delegate it to those at the top; an insufficiently developed ability to reflect on political issues; the willingness to accept censorship; a lack of analyti-cal capacities to distinguish propaganda from facts and to recognize overgeneral-izations and simplifications; the persistence of dualist (dialectical) perceptions and thought patterns; insufficient self-confidence; weak egos; lack of civil courage; insufficient tolerance (especially tolerance of dissent); and the lack of a stable universalist and intercultural orientation.

Given such deficiencies of socialization, the references to underclass authoritari-anism and subaltern–petty bourgeois political and cultural habitus *(Unterta-nengeist)* are not unjustified, at least for some segments of the eastern German population. Parallels with the Nazi regime and the imperial period come to mind, particularly with regard to authoritarian expectations and intolerance of foreigners and "deviant" opinions. The East German political culture retained without doubt certain Prussian elements. Authoritarian and antidemocratic patterns could easily be integrated into Stalinist and later bureaucratic socialism and thus linked to Prussia's traditional etatism and paternalism (Greiffenhagen 1991). The paternalist relationship between the East German socialist welfare state and its citizens fostered the development of psychological dependency coupled with the sacrifice of civil liberties. Consequences were diffuse anxieties and a fear of freedom after the socialist patronage disintegrated. These socialization effects, which have to be differentiated according to social milieu, educational level, and gender strongly influenced coping strategies in the transition period. How can one otherwise explain, for example, the frantic search for simple answers, new certainties, and scapegoats or the great degree of uncertainty, anomie, and exaggerated demands on the state's responsibility for welfare? Acquired patterns of perception and interpretation act as a filter in peoples' minds when they assess current political processes and respond to the overwhelming diversity of information suddenly available in the media and public. In other words, thought and behavioral patterns, many of them similar to traditional right-wing authoritarianism, existed long before the dissolution of East Germany. In fact, the socialist state and society played a considerable role in (re)producing them, as evidenced by the existence of a right-wing youth scene, as well as suppressed xenophobia and nationalism in the private opinions of East Germans before unification.

To what extent did unification policies foster the development of xenophobia and right-wing extremism among young people?

Many billions of marks have flowed into building up eastern Germany. However, little effort has been made to understand the psychological consequences of the changes. Instead, eastern Germans frequently experienced false promises, exploitation of their inexperience, naïveté, feelings of helplessness, and isolation. Eastern Germans hoped for, and politicians had promised, an economic upswing and individual prosperity. Dissatisfaction has been created primarily by the fact that promises are taking longer to achieve and that the unification process developed differently than expected. At the beginning of the 1990s, three-quarters of young respondents in the East judged the overall economic situation in eastern Germany to be bad or very bad (Veen et al. 1994). Studies confirm that an overwhelming majority of eastern Germans see themselves as second-class citizens (Neunter Jugendbericht 1994: 89). Many young people perceive a move to western Germany as the only solution to a hopeless situation. In addition to disappointments about the loss of job security and the failure of material prosperity to appear immediately, many feel disappointed about the lack of direct democracy they experience. There is a widespread feeling that important decisions are made far above the heads of ordinary people. The perception of having been cheated, formerly linked with the old system, now frequently includes the post-1989 period. Youth studies (Förster et al. 1993, Neunter Jugendbericht 1994) have found that only a minority of respondents are satisfied with the new political system, which suggests problems with political legitimacy. It is no surprise that interest and involvement in politics, too, have reached a nadir, after the enthusiasm in the fall of 1989. Only about half of all eastern German young people eligible to vote participated in the all-German parliamentary elections in 1990 and 1994. Young people who want to be heard find nobody paying attention. Therefore some feel a need to turn to more radical means. "Do I have to become radical first?" was the provocative question raised by youngsters at a round-table discussion on violence, in the face of an absence of opportunities. Youth officials of democratic parties admit to having somehow lost the support of young people since 1989. Detailed strategies and programs to help young people are rare. Instead, public places and opportunities to spend leisure time are disappearing or sacrificed for commercial interests. Abandoned by politicians, some youngsters feel anger, frustration, and envy. They compensate for their emotions by aggressively falling prey to simplistic solutions, the search for scapegoats, ethnocentrism, ultranationalism, and xenophobia; they complain that the state worries less about Germans than about foreigners.

Distance and alienation from politics, the feeling of being abandoned, and the perception of being unable to accomplish anything are among the main causes of growing radical tendencies among young people. Disillusionment with socialism has been followed by disillusionment with the social market economy and Western democracy. Following learned patterns of thought many people still expect, even after the changes in eastern Germany, that their loyalty toward government will be rewarded by comprehensive welfare and job programs. Disappointment of such expectations can lead to withdrawal into the private sphere, disillusionment with politics, a struggle for individualist survival, or a search for collective security outside existing democratic structures.

The modalities of German unification emancipated political subjects only to a limited extent, and it also reinforced elements of the traditional political culture. "Reckless recapitalization of the disintegrated GDR was not followed by thorough democratization, demilitarization and 'civilization' of the society" (Butterwegge 1990: 29). Worse, instead of publicly articulating the problems of social modernization and the consequences of German unity, Germans projected their fears, ambiguities, and confusion onto asylum seekers and foreigners. Unification policies thus played a significant part in shifting the focus of the problem among certain segments of the population toward the wrong target.

What changes in political culture and society contributed to the growth of xenophobia?

Even if one takes into account problems and outcomes of unification, they do not sufficiently explain the new quality of right-wing extremism and the escalation of violence against asylum seekers and foreigners between 1991 and 1993. Recent changes in the political culture contributed to the growth of resentment. In the former East Germany, not only democratic but also extremist right-wing parties and Nazi ideologies were officially prohibited and publicly attacked. But nationalism and xenophobia remained under the surface, extending beyond a few skinheads and lunatics. But without democratic and public political discourse and because foreigners and Jews were almost invisible, prejudices, fears, and hate had no public place for expression. Following unification, the heated West German public debate about the real or alleged abuse of the very liberal German asylum law and the influx of asylum seekers and postunification carpetbaggers stirred up feelings of envy, hate, and powerlessness. In addition, the conflict among democratic political parties about these issues removed further taboos about expressing resentment and thus served to encourage right-wing radicals. The polarization triggered by the so-called asylum debate gave ostensible legitimacy to extremist opinions. This may even have contributed to the encouragement of xenophobic violence because it led to a closing of ranks between political violence, active fellow traveling, and right-wing populist policies. A minority of extremist young people to some extent perceived themselves as popular vanguards, fighting for the interests of a larger segment of the population. Government reactions to violence— such as the relocation of refugee hostels and the proposed constitutional amendments to the asylum law (article 16 of the FRG's Basic Law)—were considered as successes by right-wing radicals. They seemed to confirm that politically motivated violent behavior paid off, encouraging emulation of xenophobic attacks by others. The resulting spiral tended to normalize and legitimize xenophobic behavior and violence and break down existing normative barriers. Hesitant or insufficient responses by politicians and police thus proved to have serious consequences. This failure of the political culture to respond is another reason why right-wing extremism emerged in eastern Germany (Bergmann and Erb 1994a).

The role of some of the media was also detrimental to efforts to quell the rising resentment and violence. In some instances, they insensitively ignited and reproduced the young people's xenophobic thought and argumentation patterns (Schubarth and Stenke 1992). The influence of the media and of public discourse can be observed in the language used by young people, for example, in the terms *"pseudo" asylum seekers, economic refugees,* and *flooding* of Germany. The catastrophic mood spread by some of the media confirmed existing feelings of insecurity and fear, pointing at foreigners and asylum seekers as scapegoats. In addition, if we take into account that most eastern German young people had absolutely no contact with foreigners in their immediate neighborhoods, it becomes clear to what extent their ideas on these issues were determined by outside information. The Darwinist mood that set in after unification was also important. It led to a social climate of social coldness, loss of solidarity, atomization, and a distance from the weak that called into question common bonds among humans and thus endangered the foundations of social democracy.

How did the causes of xenophobia differ in the East and the West?

As mentioned earlier, xenophobic attitudes seem to be more prevalent among eastern German young people than among those in the West. It cannot be determined with absolute certainty whether this is a result of different conditions of socialization or whether it can be attributed to divergent lifestyles, different degrees of social and economic security, and anomie. Recent studies indicate that motives and manifestations of right-wing extremism and xenophobia differ between eastern and western German young people (for more detail, see Melzer and Schubarth 1993), whereas the causes are similar. Because socioeconomic and cultural marginalization are more widespread in the East, nationalism and xenophobia among eastern German young people is stronger.

I share the widespread belief among youth researchers and social scientists (see

Heitmeyer et al. 1992, 1995) that right-wing extremism is linked to young people's everyday experiences, such as feelings of insecurity, helplessness, and isolation *(Vereinzelung)*. Experiences of modernization in eastern Germany are more radical and rapid than in the West, increasing internal conflict and tensions. The greater degree of actual or anticipated insecurity and anomie is probably the main reason for the greater susceptibility toward right-wing extremism among eastern German adolescents, in combination with the authoritarian socialization they acquired in the socialist system. However, remaining effects of authoritarian structures should not be underestimated even in Western countries, though they are less pronounced and more subtle (Claussen 1989).

The particular way of dealing with Germany's Nazi past in the East and West is another cause considered to be important in explaining the postunification wave of xenophobia and right-wing extremism. Perhaps the official and prescribed anti-fascism in East Germany more strongly inhibited individual efforts to come to terms with this period than was the case in West Germany. As a result of cultural and political changes in the late 1960s, opportunities arose in the West enabling citizens to deal with the legacy of Nazism in a more open and honest manner without the fear of taboos. But in both parts of Germany, minorities remained who continued to believe in prejudices and undemocratic ways of thinking, which extremists tried to exploit in times of crisis and insecurity.

In addition, alienation from democratic politics and lack of trust in social institutions—also a factor favoring right-wing extremism—have affected both parts of the FRG. The population in the East, however, is more cynical and frustrated than that in the West. Whether this is a legacy of state socialism or based on recent experience after unification is still an open question.

Ultimately, right-wing extremism and xenophobic violence after unification should be seen in conjunction with transformations in the political culture after 1989 and the socioeconomic difficulties of adjustment throughout Germany that followed. Immigration and the unprecedented influx of huge numbers of ethnic Germans, asylum seekers, and others altered the climate of hospitality toward foreign nationals. The fact that right-wing extremism in eastern Germany was more uncivilized and enjoyed in some cases the sympathies of lower- and middle-class population segments cannot hide the fact that right-wing extremism and xenophobia are not just East German problems but are problems that have national and international dimensions. When anti-immigrant and antirefugee prejudice and violence became an embarrassing dimension in the course of German unification, it became an all-German problem that can only be combated through joint efforts throughout German society as a whole.

Summary

For more than 5 years, Germany has been a gigantic "social laboratory," as unification has been labeled (Giesen and Leggewie 1991). However, observers in Germany are not only witnesses of a live experiment involving millions of people but also actors—though East and West are affected differently by the ongoing changes.

Social scientists are challenged to observe, reflect, and participate in the process of systemic transformation and the joining of two formerly distinct entities. From a sociological viewpoint, the forced speed of the transformation resembles a video-tape on fast-forward in which the eastern part of Germany is overwhelmed by the choices and risks of postindustrial modernization. Xenophobia, violence, fear, insecurity, reorientation difficulties, and identification problems seem to be concomitant symptoms of a society in transition.

Five years after Germany's unity was reestablished, eastern Germany finally has reached the point where a sense of normalization has set in. This normality is reflected in the decrease of hostile acts and resentment against foreigners. All available data confirm a change in trends of violence and resentment between 1993 and 1995 (see Bundesministerium des Innern 1995, Förster and Friedrich 1995). Young eastern Germans now have a significantly more positive attitude toward foreigners, and the wave of violence has subsided to some degree. However, tensions and resentment have not died out completely. According to a survey among 2,000 East German youth in 1992, about 40% of respondents had emotional aversions toward foreigners, whereas a follow-up study at the end of 1994 still found 25% with negative attitudes (Förster and Friedrich 1995). Between 1992 and 1994, the percentage of those with positive dispositions rose from 17 to 28%. Also, the number of persons with amicable personal relationships with foreigners almost doubled from 20 to 38% between 1992 and 1994. Similarly, resentment toward Jews, which increased during unification and the Gulf War, has abated and been replaced by more positive sentiments since 1993–94 (Förster and Friedrich 1995).

Reasons for these shifts are manifold. At least four causes may have contributed to the decrease in xenophobia and violence. First, significant changes took place in the political culture of united Germany. The reform of the asylum law ended for the time being the polarizing and agonizing debate about the abuse of asylum and immigration. The bold opposition by a broad coalition of concerned citizens, politicians, democratic parties, churches, unions, media, artists, and grassroots organizations to antiforeigner violence and displays of neo-Nazi rhetoric, music, and symbols, led to further silencing, isolation, and drained resources for the noisy extremist fringe and their passive bystanders.

Second, the clear signals given to violent offenders by police and judiciary have increased the legitimacy and authority of state agencies and have led to a certain consolidation of laws and normative standards of civilized behavior among disaffected youth. The direct and straightforward prosecution of criminal offenses has had a deterring effect, particularly among right-wing extremists.

Third, specific activities, especially the promotion of social and youth work on local, regional, state, and federal levels, have contributed to the decline in xenophobic attitudes and activities. For example, the Federal Campaign Program against Aggression and Violence (Aktionsprogramm der Bundesregierung gegen Aggression und Gewalt) deliberately promoted beneficial activities of eastern German youth and, as a result, has successfully intervened and prevented violence.

Fourth one should not underestimate the learning process that has taken place among East Germans. They are becoming accustomed to new societal circumstances, particularly living in a risk society. In fact, the population has accomplished immense adjustments and adaptations and developed new abilities and capacities to deal with the latest challenges.

At the moment it is difficult to predict the further course of xenophobia and violence in eastern Germany. Much will depend on the ability of people to become integrated into the new society, particularly the youth. The question is whether they can find a productive individual and social place in society or whether larger groups will become isolated and marginalized. In other words, the challenges for an active and up-to-date approach toward youth, education, and social policy are still enormous.

NOTE

Translated from German by Belinda Cooper and Hermann Kurthen.

1. Social individualization is defined as the process whereby individuals are given the opportunity to make more choices and thus increase their decision-making capabilities, which results in expanded life-chances but also entails risks.

7

JULIANE WETZEL

Antisemitism among Right-Wing Extremist Groups, Organizations, and Parties in Postunification Germany

At the heart of the inflammatory rhetoric of far-right groups and organizations in Germany lies xenophobia, targeted mainly at foreigners (see chapter 1). In such circles, German Jews are considered "aliens" too, and antisemitism has always been a core element in right-wing extremist ideology and propaganda. In recent years, a new type of antisemitism has taken center stage as a result of opposition to current remembrance of the Holocaust past and its culmination in Auschwitz. This so-called secondary antisemitism does not rely on classic sources of prejudice arising, for example, from religious stereotypes or intergroup conflicts over equal rights, social integration, and political power such as those found in primary antisemitism. Instead, it is related to collective memories of a discredited past; thus it is causally connected with German guilt, shame, and responsibility toward Jews.

One way of dealing with the Nazi period is the attitude of "drawing a line" *(einen Schlußstrich ziehen)* or moving beyond the continuous focus of historical remembrance on the Third Reich and the Holocaust. This opinion is widespread in the German population, most of whom were born after 1945. In an Emnid survey conducted in early 1994, more than half of all respondents (52%) supported the notion of ending the discussion of the painful Nazi past (Golub 1994: 38). The same poll asked if "Jews are exploiting the National Socialist Holocaust for their own purposes." Fifteen percent of the poll respondents strongly agreed and 24% somewhat agreed. Earlier surveys also confirm that many Germans support the statement that "the permanent talk about the guilt of the Germans in other countries often indicates envy about German efficiency and affluence" *(Der Spiegel* 1992).

Right-wing extremists try to profit from such tiredness of and distancing from the past for their own purposes. The fact that the agonizing Nazi chapter in German history cannot be easily closed is interpreted by extremists as promoting the interests of Jews and foreign countries *(Ausland)*. The resentment that results from such perceptions is exploited by members of the far Right. They accuse Jews and Israel of keeping alive memories of Nazi crimes for the sake of moral and ultimately financial gain. Extremists also charge Jews with conspiracy and with brainwashing the German population. For example, they claim that a "media dictatorship" and "forces behind the scenes"—referring to a supposedly Jewish press monopoly—produce "horror stories," which are propaganda designed to "reeducate" and blackmail the German people (*Unabhängige Nachrichten*, July 1994). Such distortions of reality and history are typical of extreme-right publications.

I shall describe the specifically antisemitic ideological mind-set and goals of the far-Right extremist subculture, the neo-Nazi fringe, and the right-wing parties by analyzing their publications and other print media (see the appendix to this chapter).

Rhetoric of Antisemitic Propaganda in Right-Wing Extremist Publications

The program of the neo-Nazi German Nationalists (Deutsche Nationalisten),[1] founded in Mainz in July 1993, contains such terms as *usury (Wucher)* and *money lending (Zinswirtschaft),* which are well-known code words for antisemitic concepts. Such terms are often used in conjunction with statements like, "Since the end of World War II, large parts of Germany have been managed by foreign powers," and demands that "reparations payments to foreign powers cease" (*blick nach rechts,* October 5, 1993).

Threats of punishment and actual prosecutions have led right-wing extremist organizations to be more cautious in their tactics. A tendency to use veiled insinuations can be observed throughout the extremist spectrum. Concepts such as "foreigners" or "foreign powers" conceal conspiracy theories that frequently aim to falsify or deny the intentional extermination of European Jews in the Holocaust. Such concealed rhetoric has become more common since the judicial organs of the Federal Republic of Germany (FRG) have begun keeping a closer watch on right-wing extremist agitators, taking preventive measures, and severely punishing offenders. Thus public, openly antisemitic tirades are rarely encountered. This does not mean, however, that antisemitism has lost its significance as a point of coalescence for right-wing extremists—nationally and internationally. Communication occurs by way of coded language or ambiguous texts that convey clearly decipherable messages. Readers or listeners are called upon to interpret vague, ambiguous texts and read between the lines of printed or spoken words to reach the actual meaning. This is easier for right-wing indoctrinated recipients than for people without exact knowledge of the message being conveyed. In addition, the most up-to-date technical support systems are used, including videos and computer networks. They easily serve the purposes of anonymous authors and are difficult for the authorities to monitor.

Besides these strategies, propagandists of the far Right like to use another tactic that is difficult to attack legally: playing down events by making relativizing comparisons. For example, in February 1994 the *Deutsche Rundschau*, published by the German League for Nation and Homeland, called the Allied indiscriminate aerial bombing attack on Dresden "the greatest and perhaps most obscene act of genocide in the history of humanity in terms of time, area covered, and suffering." It also criticized the Cologne-based and government-funded Deutschlandfunk radio station for commemorating "turn-of-the-century" antisemitism rather than the German victims of the Dresden attack who perished in an Allied-created urban "extermination oven." Right-wing extremist ideology requires such transposition of terms to make it possible—after a comparative historical offsetting of all the negative aspects of the Nazi state—to retain an ultimately innocuous or even positive image of Nazism that could serve as a model for a new version of old ways of thinking. Extremists do all they can to place the period of the Nazi dictatorship in a better light to allow "pride in the German Fatherland" and preserve an unbroken history and tradition. But the recourse to popular denial mechanisms that can be found in German society are not the final objective sought by right-wing extremists; they long for an untainted Nazi ideology as a foundation, providing them with a solid base for their beliefs. Leaders of the far Right are perfectly aware that the use of a rhetoric of denial and historical falsification allows them to recruit new supporters to be further brainwashed with hard-core Nazi ideology.

Holocaust Denial and the Theory of War Guilt

For some time, Holocaust denial was not a central theme of far Right publications aimed mainly at young people. Since the fall of the Berlin Wall, however, denial is experiencing a boom, and revisionism has become an important link connecting the entire far Right subculture. In these publications, not only the Holocaust is a target of vitriol. Asylum seekers, Turks, and other minority groups are also verbally threatened. Often the roles of perpetrator and victim are completely reversed, as in an article in the *Remer-Depesche* of July 1993 entitled "The Substitute Holocaust." The article stated: "Because no one gets upset anymore over burning asylum seekers' hostels, some of which incidentally are set on fire by the asylum seekers themselves, other buildings had to burn. . . . And what will happen when no one gets upset anymore about burning Turkish buildings? Then the Israeli secret service, the Mossad, will begin burning Jews and blaming Germans. If the old one no longer works, that would really be a new, a substitute Holocaust!"

A similar popular right-wing extremist accusation claims that the Jews themselves were to blame for their persecution and for antisemitism. A survey by the Emnid pollster between November 30 and December 17, 1991, commissioned by the weekly German magazine *Der Spiegel* (1992) revealed that 5% of all respondents thought it entirely true and 8% somewhat true that "Jews are partly to blame for the persecution and hate against them."[2] As flimsy evidence, far-Right agitators point to a letter from Chaim Weizmann, then-president of the Jewish Agency, to British Prime Minister Neville Chamberlain on September 2, 1939. In this letter, Weizmann assured Chamberlain that Jews all over the world were on England's side in the war against Hitler. Using the academic authority of a few historians who deviate from the mainstream such as Ernst Nolte (1987), a deceased professor emeritus of history at the Free University of Berlin, right-wing apologists have interpreted Weizmann's remarks as a declaration of war on Germany. Right circles also repeatedly cite even earlier evidence of an alleged Jewish declaration of war against the Reich printed in the January 1979 issue of the magazine *Mut* (which has repented that printing and excluded from circulation the "Holocaust International" issue). *Mut* quoted excerpts from an article in the British newspaper *Daily Express* of March 24, 1933, entitled "Judea Declares War on Germany." *Mut* commented: "This Jewish declaration of war and the disastrous German reaction in the subsequent months and years were fateful for Germany and Europe." The doubtful theory of a Jewish declaration of war appeared again in January 1994 in the *Remer-Depesche* in connection with Ernst Nolte's book *Points of Conflict (Streitpunkte)*. For the apologists of the past, the question of the authenticity of Nolte's interview—that is, whether it actually took place, was compiled from statements in Nolte's book, or was clipped from other interviews—was beside the point. In any case, stereotypes such as the belief that Jews wielded anti-German financial and world power are used to justify the Nazi response to the "declaration of war by the World Jewish Congress," thus indirectly calling into question the victim status of Jews in the Holocaust. Consequently, the *Remer-Depesche* called its article, "If the Holocaust Is a Lie, Anti-Judaism Is a Duty!"

Numerous other anti-Jewish allegations charge, for example, that Jews extort reparations with the help of the "Auschwitz lie" and an alleged Jewish-inspired reeducation campaign, thus financially exploiting German feelings of guilt. A similar form of argumentation was used by the former head of the Nazi-German Labor Service (Reichsarbeitsdienst [RAD]), Erwin Schönborn,[3] an antisemite active in far-Right circles. He claimed in a flyer that Anne Frank's diary was a fabrication, libeling it as "a product of Jewish, anti-German horror propaganda designed to support the lie of 6 million gassed Jews and to finance the State of Israel" (Klein 1984: 103, Drahtzieher 1992: 14).

Israel as a Substitute for Agitation

Hate propaganda targeting Israel has become for some extremists a substitute for the lack of a sizable group of German-Jewish scapegoats because the Jewish community in Germany is relatively small (estimated at about 40,000 in 1994). This shift has surfaced among right-wing extremists (though, incidentally, among others as well) since the 1970s as an entirely new aspect of antisemitic and anti-Zionist agitation. Criticism of the Jewish state provides a welcome podium for relatively unchecked, open airing of antisemitic prejudice. There is little danger of violating existing German laws using this method, within certain limits. Therefore, repeated emphasis on the parallel between the genocide of the Jews and the fate of the Palestinians is a standard element in antisemitic rhetoric involving setting off and downplaying Nazi crimes.

In an article entitled "The Right, Antisemitism, and Xenophobia" in the magazine *Europa vorn,* Hans Rustemeyer wrote: "We, the New Right, have difficulty not with the Jews, but with the multiculturalists. [Ignatz] Bubis [head of the Central Council of Jews in Germany], in any case, seems to advocate this multicultural idea." The supposed dissociation from antisemitic prejudice is immediately negated by the next sentence, which clearly aims to discredit Ignatz Bubis as the representative of Jews in Germany. The illustrations that introduce the article reveal its true character. The caption of two photographs placed opposite one another reads: "Jews as victims (left, in Berlin 1941); Jews as perpetrators (right, on the Gaza Strip in 1993 with Palestinians herded together)" (*Europa vorn* 47, 1993: 6).

Public statements by Jewish representatives about the firebombing of the Lübeck synagogue on the night of March 25, 1994, led the *Deutsche Wochen-Zeitung* to write, "And remarkably enough, none of the Jewish speakers mentioned the million times more horrible deed at Hebron, where Israeli bandits earlier carried out a mass murder on praying Arabs in the Ibrahim Mosque, the maliciousness of which is almost unbelievable" (April 8, 1994). This accusation against German-Jewish leaders and the responsibility forced upon them for any injustice occurring in Israel implies an equation of Jews with Israelis (which is, in fact, not unique to right-wing extremists). The *Deutsche National-Zeitung* wrote in a similar vein when it asked Michel Friedman, a member of the Central Council of Jews in Germany "who was born in Paris and whose parents come from Cracow," why "national masochism, self-flagellation, and obsession with guilt should be considered so healthy and salutary only for the German people? . . . Where and when does Israel commemorate the expulsion of hundreds of thousands of Palestinians?" (May 20, 1994). Friedman was also the recipient of a letter written in the spring of 1994 by Günther Deckert, chairman of the National Democratic Party (Nationaldemokratische Partei [NPD]). Once again, it used the abstruse equation of Jews and Israelis as an insult: "For decades, the land of the Jews has been Israel, not Germany! So what are you still doing in our country?" (*blick nach rechts,* July 19, 1994; *taz,* January 20, 1995).

The *Remer-Depesche,* primarily an organ of Holocaust denial ("Auschwitz—It's Over for the Gas Chambers," "There Were No Gas Chambers. There Was No Genocide of the Jews" [cited by report of Bundesministerium des Innern 1991: 104]), came up with a similar rhetorical phrase as the *Deutsche National-Zeitung.* An "open letter" sent to former German president Richard von Weizsäcker included the following remark: "For years, you kowtowed to certain specific Jewish liars, which made many decent Germans sick. . . . What do you care about the thousands of Palestinians bestially slaughtered in their own land by the Israeli occupiers?" (cited by report of Bundesministerium des Innern 1991: 104).

Older Antisemitic Topoi

Right-wing extremists never tire of passing off the same old antisemitic topoi as new discoveries. These include the medieval antisemitic motif of the "Jewish swine" ("Judensau"). On July 20, 1992, shortly after the death of Heinz Galinski, head of the Central Council of Jews in Germany, was cheered in the right-wing press, the neo-Nazi Thomas Dienel and three skinheads threw a pig's head cut in half into the front yard of the Jewish community center in Erfurt. Dienel had been a member of the East German Communist Party, a functionary of the Communist youth league (Freie Deutsche Jugend [FDJ]), and later the founder of the neo-Nazi German National Party (DNP). A note attached to the pig's head said: "That swine Galinski is finally dead. More Jews should be" (cited by Innenminister des Staates Thüringen 1992: 35). In October 1993 the memorial at the Grunewald train station in Berlin, one of the departure points for Nazi deportations of Jews, was desecrated with two pigs' heads. Investigators suspected right-wing extremist motives (*Berliner Morgenpost,* October 21, 1993).

Statements from the so-called *Protocols of the Learned Elders of Zion* (1978) have also been disseminated (see *Die Bauernschaft,* September 1993: 24), along with the so-called Jewish declaration of war against Germany, accusations of forgery leveled at the diary of Anne Frank,[4] and the brochure *Germany Must Perish!* (1979) by Theodore N. Kaufman. The *Remer-Depesche* reported in January 1993 that President Franklin Roosevelt, to whom it claimed Kaufman was an adviser, had considered the Kaufman plan to exterminate Germans interesting. The Freedom for Germany Circle (Freundeskreis Freiheit für Deutschland [FFD]) also distributed a flyer entitled *Anti-German Weapons of Extermination,* which stated: "In the Second World War, Nathan Kaufman, adviser to the American president, proposed that the German people be exterminated after the war through sterilization. All German men and women were to be operated on and made infertile. The necessary procedure was described in detail and disseminated throughout the world in the brochure *Germany Must Perish.* This plan was not carried out following the armistice. However, plans to exterminate the German people still exist."[5] In a publication in 1941, the Reich Ministry of Propaganda had also tried to convince people that the "Jew Kaufman" was not acting on his own and that his "abstruse ideas" were shared by the American public. None of this was true (Benz 1992b: 88). Nevertheless, the abstruse ideas of a Nathan Kaufman were developed further by the far Right. It claimed that, now that Kaufman's extermination plans had failed, international Jewry was trying to overrun Germany with foreigners through mass immigration (asylum) and a multicultural society, and thus gradually exterminate Germans.

As with the declaration-of-war theory, the now-banned militant racist FFD attempts to portray the Holocaust as the consequence of wrongful Jewish behavior— that is, a sort of logical defense mechanism. The circle, which maintains contacts with all sorts of right-wing extremist groups, stirs up feelings of hatred against Jews and foreigners, primarily through flyers. It is among the antisemitic groups that constantly bring up the misunderstood biblical concept of "chosenness," at the same time demonstrating their xenophobia: "The people demand an END TO FOREIGNERS! The Jews Gerhard Baum and Burkhard Hirsch (Free Democratic Party) are concerned. . . . Juda is boiling! After all, infiltration by foreigners is one of the most important cornerstones of the Chosen People's strategy to eliminate Aryan existence."[6]

Subcultural Media

Although skinhead music is certainly not solely an expression of right-wing views, and its glorification of violence cannot be ascribed to any one political tendency, the statements of many skinhead bands place them within the far-Right spectrum. Their nationalistic, racist lyrics incite persecution of foreigners and Jews, not even stopping short of calls for murder; thus they convey ideas that facilitate neo-Nazi recruiting. In its song "Doitschlandlied," for example, the band Brutal Sharks (Brutale Haie) encourages the struggle against foreigners: "Foreigners snuck in. . . . You don't need to live here; move to your Kanakenland [loosely: nigger country]" (cited from report of Bundesministerium des Innern 1993: 96). Along with antiforeigner lyrics, the repertoire of the group Sound Interference (Tonstörung) from Mannheim includes unmistakably hate-filled antisemitic songs: "Whet your knife on the sidewalk, slide the knife into a Jewish body. Blood must flow like a river, and we don't give a shit about the freedom of this Jew republic! A black pig hangs in the synagogue. . . . Smear the guillotine with Jewish fat."[7]

Among right-wing extremist computer games, the "Anti-Turk Test" rivals the "Aryan Test." Far-Right ideology—the cult of the Führer, racism, and Nazi symbols—addresses mainly schoolchildren in this monitoring-resistant propaganda medium. The judicial organs of the FRG are faced with the currently unsolvable problem of finding the unknown makers of these games. Only speculations exist about the authors. In most cases, investigations have been closed, as neither the producers nor the distributors can be located; they hide behind labels such as Association of German Anti-Niggers, Adolf Hitler Software Ltd., or Men at Work Crew.

Unlike computer games, extremist publications have difficulty avoiding oversight by organs of the state. Writers of far-Right fanzines with racist and antisemitic contents—about one-third of all publications of the skinhead subculture—have greatly moderated their tone because of intensified investigation by the police, the Bundesminister des Innern (Ministry of the Interior), and the Federal Office for the Protection of the Constitution (Amt für Verfassungsschutz), as well as numerous trials.[8] Now they use harmless-sounding innuendoes, the actual racist and antisemitic meanings of which are easy for members of the subculture to decipher. However, the fanzine *Brown Broom (Brauner Besen)*, which appeared for the first time in mid-1993, is not as reserved. It combines racist and antisemitic propaganda: "*The Brown Broom* is dedicated to any political activity that is suppressed and persecuted by this damn Jewish state!" (cited by report of Bundesministerium des Innern 1993: 99).

Fanzines are one of the areas of activity where networking between skinheads and neo-Nazi groups is manifested. Members of the Free German Workers' Party (Freie Arbeiter Partei [FAP]) influence the subculture through their publications. *Head-On (Frontal)* appeared in Essen from 1991 to 1993 and has now been replaced by *Modern Times (Moderne Zeiten); Prussia's Glory (Proissens Gloria)* was founded in 1991 in Berlin (Fromm 1993: 83). These fanzines bring together Ku Klux Klan symbolism, xenophobia, antisemitism, and racism. Yet they also agitate against "Kühni the gay king"—neo-Nazi leader Michael Kühnen, who died of AIDS in 1991 (Fromm and Kernbach 1994b: 74).

Neo-Nazi Organizations

The FAP not only has a decisive influence on fanzines but also in recent years has become more and more of a catchall for the far-Right subculture, serving as a militant cover organization for various right-wing extremist groups that have continued their activities underground after being banned. This infiltration has also brought militant antisemitism into the party. An extreme antisemitic wing of the party operated under the leadership of Jürgen Mosler, former member of the NPD and its youth wing, the Young National Democrats (Junge Nationaldemokraten [JN]) and the Viking Youth; the Mosler group left the FAP in 1990 (Fromm 1993: 81). Nevertheless, the antisemitic connection continues through close contacts with Gary Rex Lauck's NSDAP Organization Abroad (National-Sozialistische Deutsche Arbeiter Partei-Aufbau Organisation [NSDAP-AO]), whose headquarters are in Lincoln, Nebraska. This group spreads the vilest antisemitism through its publications and pamphlets, broadcasting slogans such as "Fight the Jewish parties KPD, SPD, CDU, CSU, FDP" (Fromm 1992: 79), and through adhesive labels, and other propaganda materials. It is quite likely that many members of the FAP are simultaneously active in the NSDAP-AO.

The NSDAP-AO maintains intensive connections with the cadre organization, Covenant of the New Front (Gesinnungsgemeinschaft der Neuen Front [GdNF]), a catchall for Nazi activists. The antisemitism of this organization of former Kühnen supporters is indicated by the fact that the GdNF shows the Nazi propaganda film *The Eternally Wandering Jew (Der ewige Jude)* to young sympathizers for training purposes. The American distributor, Gary Lauck of the NSDAP-AO, "likes the film because it shows the truth. . . . In fact, it's much too tame." When asked whether the comparison between Jews and rats was not hateful, Lauck answered, "I agree that it's unfair to the rats to be compared to Jews, and I apologize to the rats. But rats are considered dirty, undesirable elements, and that is an exact description of what Jews are" (*Drahtzieher* 1992: 45).

Today, the GdNF, which became less and less important following Kühnen's death, is little more than the editorial board of the "fighting organ of the National Socialist movement in Germany," the *Neue Front,* which is now distributed anonymously through a contact address in The Netherlands. It contains racist and antisemitic caricatures, promotes the view that the diary of Anne Frank is a forgery, and glorifies Saddam Hussein as an Arab hero (Lange 1993: 90). The Anti-Zionist Action (AZA), an organization within the orbit of the FAP that uses the *Neue Front* as a publication medium, also glorifies the Iraqi president. The logical consequence is the accusation that Zionism desires world domination, so that "without a solution to the Jewish question, no salvation for humanity" is possible (Drahtzieher 1992: 60). Expressions of support for Iraq are frequent. During the Gulf War, in particular, Iraqi flags appeared at neo-Nazi marches and demonstrations. This link was even observable in cemetery desecrations. In January 1991, graffiti in southern Germany stated: "Ciao Jewish pig, Iraq fight!" and "PLO better than Adolf SS." The use of green paint was further evidence of an unmistakable reference to the PLO and the Intifada (*blick nach rechts,* February 12, 1991). During the Gulf War, old Nazis, as well as younger representatives of right-wing extremist organizations, took the opportunity to publicize their antisemitism openly along with their anti-Americanism. In its pamphlet, the German Citizens' Initiative denounced "American-Jewish world domination, the creation of which is the actual goal of the Judeo-Anglo-Americans and the actual reason for the Gulf War" (Bundesministerium des Innern 1991: 103).

A caricature making the rounds in the right-wing milieu shows the following meshing of antisemitism and anti-Americanism. A grotesque man identified as a Jew by his earlocks and beard, with the stereotypically "Jewish" attributes of large ears and a broad hooked nose, bears the inscription "USA" on his forehead (Drahtzieher 1992: 60). A similarly grotesque face stares up from the pages of the magazine *Die Bauernschaft.* An illustration of a man with all the usual "Jewish" attributes reaches to grab something, suggesting that he is in the process of taking over the United States, the outline of which is wrapped in a chain with dollar signs hanging from it (*Die Bauernschaft,* September 1991: 80). The *Berlin-Brandenburger-Zeitung* published by the Nationals also made use of this combination of antisemitic and anti-American propaganda. Under the headline, "Truman Memorial Center: Memorial to Mass Murder Established," it reported in detail: "Truman, a member of the 33rd degree of Freemasons (actually Samuel Truman), held talks with his successor Eisenhower (also of Jewish extraction), among others, in the House on Griebnitz Lake (in Potsdam), built in 1891." Of course, neither Harry Truman nor Dwight D. Eisenhower was of Jewish extraction, and whether or not they were Jewish is immaterial in every respect, but this technique becomes important in connection with another article in the same newspaper. The article, probably fearing possible legal consequences, did not mention Ignatz Bubis, chairman of the Central Council of Jews in Germany, by name but instead referred to that "Frankfurt real estate speculator whose background is alien to the race [volksfremder Abstammung], and who reminds us daily with a grim face of our dark past" (*Berlin-Brandenburger-Zeitung,* July/August 1994).

Leading Jewish representatives, above all the members of the Central Council of Jews in Germany, are constantly the focus of antisemitic agitation. The militant antisemitic magazine *Die Bauernschaft,* run by longtime Nazi Thies Christophersen, calls Ignatz Bubis "Leader of the Jews" or "Chief of the Jews" (*Die Bauernschaft,* March 1994: 31). In the *Deutschland-Report* (Germany Report), produced by the circle around longtime Nazi and Auschwitz denier Otto Ernst Remer and published until recently in Brighton (England), Ignatz Bubis is always given the epithet "Leader of the Jews" (*Deutschland-Report 1993–94).* Under the headline, "Bubis as German President?," the *Deutsche National-Zeitung* felt compelled to reveal his "true background" (November 26, 1993). In August 1994, an anonymous group called Headwind *(Gegenwind)* sent out flyers with a photo of Ignatz Bubis and the words, "With 'friends' like these, who needs enemies!"[9]

Right-Wing Extremist Parties

While neo-Nazi fringe groups still operate to a great extent with antisemitic propaganda, far-Right parties like the NPD, the German People's Union (DVU), and the "Republikaner" Party address prominently racist, xenophobic, nationalist, and ethnocentric resentment. They are more reserved in their antisemitic statements. One of their standard slogans is the demand for an end to discussing the dark sides of the Nazi period, packaged in as legally harmless a form as possible. For a long time, public stigmatization of antisemitism made parties like the "Republikaner" cautious about making obviously anti-Jewish statements. Caution was advisable not only because of the danger of being classified as an organization hostile to constitutional principles but also in order to give the impression of being a populist, right-wing conservative party. It seemed opportune for the "Republikaner" Party to unmistakably distance itself from openly antisemitic groups. Despite all of their public reservations, antisemitism in the form of innuendo is part of standard "Republikaner" practice. Longtime chairman Franz Schönhuber repeatedly spoke out publicly against anti-Jewish prejudices but betrayed his statements with "yes but" arguments:

> The Republikaner will not forget what Germany owes to Jewish scientists. But experience teaches us that prescribed, even forced love leads to its opposite, that is, to rejection, and in extreme cases to hatred. And that is why we refuse to have to like every single Jewish functionary. And we believe some would be well advised to give up their constant attempts to humiliate our people, so that they do not become pacemakers of an antisemitism that we Republikaner are doing everything we can to prevent.[10]

In May 1994, Schönhuber once again insisted, "We are not anti-Semites," and added, in a strange echo of Nazi descriptions of the Jews, "but neither are we subhuman." In the same breath, the former REP leader complained that the media was afraid to go head-to-head with him in public; instead, "that snotty, arrogant Friedman [Michel Friedman, member of the Central Council of Jews in Germany] appears on television every three days." But "we won't grovel" (*Tagesspiegel*, May 22–23, 1994).

After Franz Schönhuber had pointed out more than once that he "did not have to like Galinski," he called on the (since-deceased) head of the Central Council of Jews in Germany, on the occasion of the "Republikaner" Party convention on January 13 and 14, 1990, to stop defaming "German patriots." "Shalom, Mr. Galinski, leave us alone already, stop your jabbering. . . . We will no longer allow ourselves to be humiliated. . . . Mr. Galinski, it will be your fault if there should be despicable antisemitism in this country again" (Elsässer 1992: 131). At the party convention in Berlin a year later, on March 15–16, 1991, the Central Council of Jews in Germany was called the "Fifth Internal Army of Occupation" (Elsässer 1992: 138).

The latest variation in the REP's attacks suggests a break in the caution exercised up to now. This time, Schönhuber responded directly to an event by reversing accusations of hate propaganda. On March 26, 1994, at the "Republikaner" state convention in Erding, Bavaria, one day after the firebombing of the Lübeck synagogue, Franz Schönhuber accused Ignatz Bubis of hate propaganda because the previous day Bubis had spoken of "intellectual arsonists" as the perpetrators of the deed. "The person who ensures antisemitism in Germany," said Schönhuber at a press conference, "is Mr. Bubis" (*taz,* March 28, 1994). These statements were harshly criticized by the public and examined by prosecutors for possible violations of the law. Nevertheless, Schönhuber repeated these statements a number of times; for example, at an election rally on August 28, 1994, near Dachau, he said, "If a Mr. Bubis turns Republikaner supporters into arsonists, then I say today and tomorrow and until the end of my days, Mr. Bubis, that is hate propaganda" (*Frankfurter Allgemeine Zeitung,* August 29, 1994). In a press statement on April 18, 1994, Schönhuber had taken the same position: "There must be an end to Mr. Bubis's renewed defamatory and empty words that Republikaner are intellectual arsonists. . . . Mr. Bubis, is your moral and business conscience so clear that you can afford such a superior verdict?" (*Der Republikaner,* May 1994). The constant repetition of the same accusations solidifies the suspicion that Schönhuber was acting quite consciously, attempting to exploit latent feelings. Such insults might have assured him of the approbation of right-wing extremists and anti-semites, but the hoped-for support of a broad section of the electorate has not materialized.

A February 1993 survey showed the importance of antisemitic statements in "Republikaner" circles, not only at the leadership level but also among party voters. Between 50 and 70% of regular "Republikaner" voters responded positively to antisemitic stereotypes and those targeted at Israel (Allensbach, IfD Survey, February 1993). A year later, Emnid found that 32% of potential right-wing "Republikaner" Party voters strongly agreed and 24% agreed somewhat with the statement, "Now, as in the past, Jews exert too much influence on world events." Forty-three percent of right-wing voters believed that "Jews behave in a manner which provokes hostility toward them in our country" (see Falter 1994: 149, and Golub 1994). Probably the most important finding of this survey was that potential voters of the "Republikaner" and of the DVU (2.5% out of a total of 1,414 respondents), even if merely protest voters, seemed to have a relatively coherent right-wing extremist worldview (Falter 1994: 156).

This was also shown by an antisemitic incident within the ranks of the "Republikaner" in September 1994. Opposition to Alexander Hausmann's bid to replace the resigning Franz Schönhuber as national party chairman was aroused with the suggestion that a "half-Jew" could not be considered for the post. In a letter to Schönhuber, Josef Brunner of Lower Bavaria warned, "I can only give you my personal opinion of your wish that Alexander Hausmann become national chairman. I cannot imagine that a half-Jew would have a chance to lead our party; I know the grass roots too well for that" (*Süddeutsche Zeitung,* September 22, 1994). These statements led to inner-party debates but had no serious consequences. However, Alexander Hausmann played a strange role at the party convention in Sindelfingen in December 1994, at which Rolf Schlierer was elected Franz Schönhuber's successor. In a speech praising Schönhuber's contributions to the party, Hausmann took up these antisemitic attacks and identified himself with them, stating that he shared Schönhuber's criticism of Jews "with no ifs, ands, or buts" (*Süddeutsche Zeitung,* December 19, 1994).

Antisemitism plays a far more significant role in the DVU and NPD than in the "Republikaner" Party. Publications of the press empire of DVU's chair, Gerhard Frey, especially the weekly *Deutsche National-Zeitung,* insinuate racist and antisemitic attitudes, manifested above all in such descriptive adjectives as "impudent" Poles, "blackmailing" Jews, and "criminal" foreigners. Jewish and Israeli subjects are intertwined and placed in negative contexts. Trivializing the Holocaust is of central importance too. Thus there are close contacts with the British revisionist historian David Irving. Gerhard Frey also engages in an active exchange of ideas and visits with the Russian demagogue Vladimir Zhirinovsky, known for his antisemitic and abstruse tirades.[11]

The "decriminalization" and purging of history demanded by parties like the DVU, NPD, and REP are not limited to publications and verbal statements. Verbal attacks on memorials and commemorative sites are attempts to whitewash German history and eliminate recollection of the past—that is, to give practical effect to what far right-wing parties and the spectrum's publications regularly discuss. Thus the "Republikaner" youth group of the Berlin regional headquarters demanded in a flyer: "No more school trips to 'memorials,' for these mass methods of dealing with the past are a crime against the souls of schoolchildren! No false view of history should be forced on them!" (Bredehöft and Januschek 1994: 27).

Summary

The passage of time since the experience of Nazism and its crimes has influenced attitudes toward Jews in many ways; this influence is most apparent in the manner in which far-Right extremist subcultural circles, neo-Nazi organizations, and far right-wing parties express anti-Jewish and antisemitic opinions. This secondary antisemitism is related to the question of Germany's dealing with its Nazi past. In one segment of the German population, uneasiness with the burden of recent history has increased the call to end the prominent and continuous commemoration of crimes committed in the name of Germany and to "draw a line" and move beyond dwelling on the Nazi past. Right-wing extremists interpret such distress as a gradual breakdown of a public taboo—that is, a broad condemnation of antisemitism. Therefore extremists have increased their antisemitic rhetoric, hate propaganda, and distortions of history in the belief that they can count on broad social support and exploit resentment and frustration among a segment of the population. However, incidents such as the arson attack on the synagogue in Lübeck and the strong public reaction against such attacks indicate that although antisemitic resentment may still exist and build upon latent emotions, violent attacks meet with broad disapproval in united Germany.

The span of 50 years since the end of the war has led right-wing extremist circles to increasingly dilute historical facts, ultimately trivializing and in the most extreme cases even denying the murder of the Jews. The fact that the "Auschwitz lie" and other revisionist claims have increasingly spread among far-Right circles since the late 1980s, and have even become a unifying factor among a divided extremist fringe, is due not only to the length of time since World War II and the lack of personal memory and experience of the postwar-born generations but also to the extremists' need to decriminalize the period from 1933 to 1945. The extremists realize that widespread knowledge of the Holocaust and memories of the war and its aftermath in Germany and abroad stain the name of National Socialism and the ideology and policies it stands for. For example, in polls from April 1995 and earlier only a very tiny faction of respondents (less than 2 percent) expressed the opinion that looking back "National Socialism as a whole had more positive (than negative) sides."[12] Therefore extremists attempt to whitewash the past. In addition, the various aspects of the "burden of the past" have gained a crucial function because of the numerous opportunities it offers to play on anti-Jewish and anti-Israeli prejudices. It can be used by extremists to defame Jews living in Germany and throughout the world, to criticize reparation payments, and to blame Israel. Jews are accused of blackmailing Germany and the world with the fate they "supposedly suffered."

Only a continuous and clear rejection of right-wing extremist and neo-Nazi ideas by the public can make a difference. This approach would include the continuing utilization of all legal means to combat prejudice and stereotypes against Jews, immigrants, and minorities. As the years after 1993 have shown, such deterrence at least leads to a reduction of violent right-wing extremist incidents and a delegitimization of far-Right parties and organizations in the German public.[13]

APPENDIX: STATISTICS ON RIGHT-WING EXTREMIST GROUPS AND PERIODICALS

TABLE 7.1. Membership of Various Right-wing Extremist Groups

	1991	1992	1993	1994	1995
Militant right-wing extremists	4,200	6,400	5,600	5,400	6,200
Neo-Nazi organizations	2,100	2,200	2,450	3,740	2,480
German People's Union (DVU) (according to the party's own figures)	24,000	26,000	26,000	20,000	15,000
German National Democratic Party (NPD)	6,700	5,000	5,000	4,500	4,000
Die Republikaner (REP)	—	—	23,000	20,000	16,000

Newspapers and Periodicals

In all cases, circulation figures are based on publishers' own statistics and cannot be verified; smaller skinhead and neo-Nazi newsletters have not been included here since they are generally photocopied or hectographed single sheets with very small circulations.

Die Bauernschaft
Circulation: 5,000 quarterly; founded in 1968; published until 1994 by Thies Christophersen, who lives in Denmark, author of the pamphlet *Die Auschwitz-Lüge (Auschwitz*

Lie), which denies Nazi genocide. Since the December 1994 issue (vol. 24), Ernst Zündel of Toronto, a German-Canadian and leading representative of revisionism and the "Auschwitz lie," has taken over as publisher of the magazine. Since that time, *Die Bauernschaft* has been printed and mailed only once from Antwerp, Belgium.

Deutsche National-Zeitung
Circulation: 130,000 weekly, the highest circulation among right-wing extremist publications; published by Gerhard Frey (since 1959), leader of the German People's Union (DVU); aggressive style with shrewd wording to avoid criminal prosecution.

Deutsche Rundschau
Circulation figures not available but rather insignificant. Organ of the German League for People and Homeland (Deutsche Liga für Volk und Heimat), which emerged as a catchall organization for disillusioned former "Republikaner" Party members.

Deutsche Wochen-Zeitung
Circulation: 25,000 weekly; published by Gerhard Frey; many sections are identical to the *Deutsche National-Zeitung.*

Europa vorn
Circulation: 15,000; published quarterly until 1989; starting in 1991 monthly, currently biweekly. The magazine is based on the pseudoscientific racist ideology of the Nouvelle Droite of Alain de Benoist. Through his periodical (*Elemente, Elements, Elementi,* etc.), which is published in a variety of languages in many countries, Benoist tries to bring together representatives of the New Right on an intellectual level.

Remer-Depesche
Circulation figures not available; irregular publication (1992, seven issues); published by Otto Ernst Remer, the former Hitler Youth leader, retired brigadier general, and commander of the Berlin guard battalion who participated in the suppression of the July 20, 1944, assassination attempt on Hitler; militantly antisemitic; main propaganda organ of Auschwitz denial; printed in Barcelona out of fear of legal repercussions (similar to *Deutschland-Report,* which has since ceased publication).

Der Republikaner
Circulation: 85,000 monthly; founded in 1983 as the organ of the "Republikaner" Party; published by Franz Schönhuber, longtime party leader.

Unabhängige Nachrichten
Circulation: 8,000 monthly; published by Friends of Independent News (Freundeskreis unabhängige Nachrichten); includes articles from the entire right-wing extremist spectrum, in particular old Nazis.

NOTES

Translations by Belinda Cooper and Hermann Kurthen.

1. According to a report in *Der Spiegel* magazine, a ban is being considered on the German Nationalists (see *blick nach rechts,* December 20, 1994).

2. On a scale of six possible answers ranging from "Is entirely true" (1) to "Is entirely untrue" (6), 31% of the 2,851 German respondents chose value (6), 22% value (5), 16% value (4), 17% value (3), and 8% value (2).

3. Schönborn was acquitted of public incitement to racial hatred in early 1979. The judgment was based on his right to free expression.

4. On March 28, 1990, neo-Nazi Edgar Geiss was fined of 6,000 DM for calling Anne Frank's diary a forgery. (See Königseder 1994: 288; *blick nach rechts,* May 7, 1990).

5. The pamphlet is reproduced in Fromm (1993: 87).

6. Flyer no. 56, cited in the report of the Office for the Protection of the Constitution of the Federal Ministry of Interior (Bundesminister des Innern 1992: 123). Baum and Hirsch, both members of Parliament, are non-Jews but are very much engaged in German-Jewish relations and human rights questions

7. Demo tape "Doitsche Musik," 1992, cited in Bundesminister des Innern (1992: 84), supplemented by Erb (1994: 40).

8. At the beginning of September 1994, the federal government announced that in the first three months of that year, 4,163 investigations into right-wing extremist or xenophobic offenses had been initiated. Half of the investigations involved dissemination of propaganda for organizations considered hostile to constitutional principles. In 730 cases, the charge was incitement to racial hatred; 529 defendants had already been convicted (*Süddeutsche Zeitung,* September 7, 1994).

The 1995 report of the Verfassungsschutz counted 7,592 violations of law with proven or suspected extremist right-wing background in 1994, among them 1,489 violent and 6,463 other acts; 3,491 cases were directed against foreigners and 1,366 against Jews (Bundesministerium des Innern 1995).

9. Flyer in the archives of the Center for Research on Antisemitism, Berlin.

10. Excerpts from the lead article, "Wen sollen wir wählen?," by Franz Schönhuber in *Republikaner* 12 (1986), reproduced in Funke (1989: 41).

11. Zhirinovsky spoke at a DVU meeting in Mühlhausen, Thuringia, on April 16, 1992 (Bundesminister des Innern 1992: 58).

12. Unfortunately the poll question did not specify the respondent's interpretation of "positive" or "negative" sides.

13. According to the Federal Office for the Protection of the Constitution (Verfassungsschutz), the number of violent acts of Right extremists declined from 2,639 in 1992 and 2,232 in 1993 to 1,489 in 1994.

8

BRIGITTE BAILER-GALANDA

"Revisionism" in Germany and Austria
The Evolution of a Doctrine

History of "Revisionism"

Most people understand so-called revisionism[1] as just another word for the movement of Holocaust denial (Benz 1994, Lipstadt 1993, Shapiro 1990). Therefore it
has been suggested that the word "negationism" be used instead. However, it is
the author's point of view that "revisionism" covers topics other than denial of the
National Socialist mass murders. In Germany and Austria especially, some people
have tried to minimize or apologize for other issues of National Socialist politics
after 1945. These include the responsibility for World War II, the attack on the
Soviet Union in 1941 (a recent topic), the debate about the number of victims of
the Holocaust. In the seventies, the historian Martin Broszat described that movement as "running amok against reality" (Broszat 1976). Pseudohistorical writers—
many of them right-wing publishers or people who quite rapidly turned to right-
wing extremists—try to prove that certain historical events have not taken place,
or have occurred differently than generally acknowledged, as if they were able to
undo or redo events by denying or reinterpreting them.

To simply call this a conception of "negationism" (Auerbach 1993a, Fromm and
Kernbach 1994a: 9, Landesamt für Verfassungsschutz Berlin 1994) or "Holocaust
denial" (Lipstadt 1993: 20) would neglect other components of "revisionism" that
are logically connected with the denial of the Holocaust (the latter being the extreme variant). As Auerbach puts it, World War II "revisionists" are, in truth, apologists of National Socialism (1993a: 36). Therefore, in this chapter all efforts to
rewrite history with the aim of apologizing for or decriminalizing National Socialism for personal or political purposes will be called "revisionism." In Austria and
Germany the word "revisionism" has a historical background quite different from

that in the United States. In the latter it is connected to a historical tradition of the twenties when historians reinterpreted the history of the United States' entry into World War I (discussed later). In the German-speaking countries, the word is sometimes also associated with a reform-Marxist trend in the German labor movement at the beginning of the twentieth century (J. Bailer 1992, Landesamt für Verfassungsschutz Berlin 1994).[2]

"Revisionism" is mostly connected with right-wing extremists or neo-Nazism. Even if some authors do not regard themselves as right-wing extremists, their publications are being used and instrumentalized by those political groups. Since National Socialist ideology is inseparably associated with the atrocities committed by the Nazi regime, all groups that try to revive its ideology have to eliminate remembrance of its crimes. They have to whitewash the leading National Socialists and their politics in order to win followers. The historical roots of "revisionism" reach back into the late forties and early fifties when tendencies arose to minimize National Socialist crimes and to excuse the starting of World War II by the Hitler regime.

One of the first European "revisionists," Maurice Bardéche—according to Lipstadt "a French fascist" (1993: 50)—mixed the given issues in a way that set the fashion for many of the "revisionist" publications that followed. In 1948, he published *Nuremberg or the Promised Land,* in which he contended that documents concerning the Holocaust had been falsified, that the "Final Solution" merely involved the transfer of the Jews to ghettos in Eastern Europe. Bardéche argued that Jews were not victims of National Socialism but have to be held guilty for the causes and origins of World War II. National Socialist Germany had to defend itself against communism and Stalin's lust for power all over Europe.

Paul Rassinier started his publishing activities in the late forties with his books, *Crossing the Line* and *The Lie of Ulysses,* in which he tried to prove that the accusations against the National Socialists were false and unfair. Later Rassinier specialized in denying the National Socialist genocide of Jews. Both, Bardéche and Rassinier, came directly or indirectly from the ranks of French collaborators with the Nazi occupation power. In fact, one of Bardéche's relatives was executed for collaboration (Fromm and Kernbach 1994a: 10). Bardéche also edited Rassinier's books in France (Baier 1982: 97). The case of Rassinier is more complex. He was originally a French prisoner in the concentration and labor camps of Buchenwald and Dora. Later he wrote that direct contact with the SS had caused him to have an entirely different point of view (Baier 1982: 89 f.).

In Germany and Austria, "revisionism" started with the denial of Hitler's responsibility for World War II and the uncritical glorification of the virtues of German soldiers. Former National Socialists played a leading part in this attempt. Among the first of the "revisionist" books in Germany was Peter Kleist's *Auch du warst dabei* (You Took Part Too) (1952), which became an example for all later authors (Graml 1989). Kleist was a close assistant to National Socialist foreign minister, Joachim von Ribbentrop and the minister of the occupied Eastern territories, Alfred Rosenberg. Kleist presented three types of argument that can be found in many later "revisionist" publications:

1. The accusation that the Treaty of Versailles of 1919 was responsible for almost every brutal measure of National Socialist politics
2. The contention that Western European statesmen supported by "World Jewry" intended to demolish an envied, prospering, and powerful Germany
3. The playing down of National Socialist reality by using euphemisms. (Graml 1989: 68)

One of the first Austrian apologists was Erich Kernmayr (Erich Kern), a former National Socialist and member of the notorious SS. After 1945 he became a prominent activist in a number of right-wing extremist organizations. He started by glorifying German World War II soldiers and their heroic fight against the enemies of the Third Reich and by emphasizing real or alleged Allied war crimes against the German people (Lasek 1994).

From the beginning, European "revisionist" authors clearly showed a tendency toward apology for their own individual past, as well as the German people's past as a national collective. "Revisionism" in the United States, however, claims another tradition. Modern "revisionists" try to exploit the different connotation of *revisionism* in U.S. historiography (see note 2). After World War I, a group of American historians used archival material to argue that, contrary to the prevailing American opinion, Germany had not sought to go to war in 1914. That historiographic movement was called World War I revisionism. One such historian was Professor Harry Elmer Barnes, who "soon surpassed . . . every other revisionist in his vehement criticism of American foreign policy" (Lipstadt 1993: 32). After 1945 Barnes became the "father" of American Holocaust denial. Using similar methods he wrote some of the first attacks on the historiography of the Holocaust and became a promoter of David Hoggan, one of the central contemporary "revisionists." Barnes's influence should not be underestimated because some of his texts and books, especially those on Western civilization, were required reading at prominent U.S. universities (Lipstadt 1993: 67). In other words, right-wing extremist "revisionists" use the traditional term "revisionism," which reaches back to the 1920s U.S. historiography, to camouflage their political background and to claim historical legitimacy. However, there is a personal and methodological tradition of excusing Germany's war guilt in contemporary Nazi "revisionism." After 1945, "revisionism" in the United States became linked with apologetic traditions in Europe. In the sixties both lines of "revisionism" came together when David Leslie Hoggan's book *The Forced War* was published by Herbert Grabert in Germany in 1961. The book is loosely based on Hoggan's Harvard dissertation, in which he stated that Hitler had not wanted war but that Great Britain was to be held responsible for the outbreak of World War II. Later Hoggan published a different version of events, claiming that the Germans were victims of English, American, and Polish efforts to start the war and to destroy a prospering Germany.

Hoggan's book marked a change and progress in "revisionism" compared to the earlier apologetic literature published in Germany. His statements radically criticized the policy of the United States and Great Britain; Hoggan's Hitler is a peace-seeking, almost faultless statesman full of virtues. For the first time Hoggan broke with the "revisionist" tradition of not using archival material. He gave his book a scientific appearance by citing many primary and secondary sources, but most of them were either fake or misinterpretations of authentic documents (Graml 1989: 70 f.). In that way, Hoggan founded a "revisionist" tradition that continues to exist today.

In the following years, apologetic literature of a new kind was published in Germany and Austria. The main topics dwelled on excusing National Socialist policy, accusing the former Allies of responsibility for the outbreak of World War II, and deploring the fate of Germany and the Germans. Udo Walendy published *Truth for Germany* (Wahrheit für Deutschland: Die Schuldfrage des Zweiten Weltkriegs) in 1962, which merely repeated Hoggan's views. According to the historian Hermann Graml (1989: 73), Walendy also shamelessly misinterpreted and falsified historical literature and archival material.

In Austria, Franz Scheidl, a man of academic education but a furious antisemite, published *Geschichte der Verfemung der Deutschen* (History of the Defamation of the Germans) in 1967, stating among other things that World War II was a war between Germans and Jews. International Jewry had declared war on Germany and therefore the Jews themselves were to be held responsible for the atrocities against them (deportation, forced wearing of the yellow star, separation of Jews from Germans). Scheidl did not even mention the mass murders, knowing well that these are the strongest and most eye-opening accusations against National Socialist Germany. In his book *Das Drama der Juden Europas* (The Drama of the Jews in Europe) published in Germany in 1965, Paul Rassinier already doubted the number of 6 million or more Jews murdered, thus taking up an everlasting "revisionist" topic.

Rassinier's argumentation has found a series of followers who not only distort the numbers of murdered Jews cited in serious historical works but even construct "evidence" by citing nonexistent letters of the International Committee of the Red Cross, using pseudostatistics about the Jewish population of the world, or willfully misinterpreting statistics about the number of deaths in concentration camps (Benz 1994; Neugebauer 1992).

In the course of the so-called Hitler wave of the seventies, also books of obvious "revisionist" character were published, as well as books by serious historians with sometimes questionable interpretations (e.g., W. Maser 1971, Fest 1973, 1977). The British revisionist historian David Irving, for example, presented his version of Adolf Hitler by stating that Hitler did not know anything about the so-called Final Solution and the mass murder of Jews and had neither wanted nor ordered these crimes. His book *(Hitler's War)* was followed by a series of biographies about leading National Socialists like Rudolf Hess, Erwin Rommel, and others (Lasek 1994: 543). In 1986, Martin Broszat, a senior historian at the Institute for Contemporary History in Munich, unmasked the pseudoscientific methods Irving used in *Hitler's War.*

During the seventies, Holocaust denial fully came to life. Until then even the most extreme neo-Nazi groups did not totally deny the use of the gas chambers for murdering people. According to Lipstadt, the first generation of "revisionists" "sought to vindicate the Nazis by justifying their antisemitism" (Lipstadt 1993:

52), arguing that the Jews as enemies of Germany had deserved the atrocities inflicted on them. But the second generation of "revisionists" turned to totally denying the intentional murder of European Jewry in the Holocaust and the existence of gas chambers for mass murder in Nazi concentration camps. Therefore the newly published books of the seventies distinctly marked a new quality in "revisionism."

Graml regards this trend as a logical result of the Hitler apology boom of the preceeding years. Hitler could not be presented as a great politician and statesman as long as he was associated with the greatest crime of the twentieth century (Graml 1989: 80). But there are other explanations, too. Although there was an upsurge of right-wing extremist groups in Germany and Austria during the sixties, the political climate favored the Left in the seventies. Thus one can find right-wing extremism and even neo-Nazi extremism alongside left-wing radicalization in the seventies (Bailer and Neugebauer 1994a, Benz 1989). Extreme right-wing ideology had to indicate reasons to excuse National Socialism and the Holocaust in order to popularize neo-National Socialist propaganda. In the second half of the seventies, historians, social scientists, and teachers also began to react to "revisionist" propaganda and publication efforts. Conferences were held ("Internationale Konferenz" 1977) and scholars refuted neo-Nazi lies about historical facts (e.g., Broszat 1976). Nevertheless, standard texts of "revisionist" literature were published in those years by several now prominent "revisionists."[3]

Topics of Contemporary "Revisionist" Writing

The subjects of "revisionist" writing were settled at the end of the seventies. Since then methods have changed, but almost no new topics have been introduced by "revisionists." The main lines of argumentation can be broadly classified as follows, although all of the differences within the categories themselves cannot be listed here. The "revisionists" chose as targets topics that most clearly demonstrated the criminal character of the National Socialist regime, in particular the main responsibility of National Socialism for starting World War II and the planned mass murder on an industrial scale of millions of Jewish people (Bailer-Galanda 1992b, B. Bailer 1994). Symbolizing the worst Nazi crimes, these topics have become the central issues of Nazi "revisionism" since the seventies.

Minimizing and Denying Guilt for and in World War II

As shown earlier, "revisionism" began in the late forties and early fifties with the denial of National Socialist responsibility for the outbreak of World War II. The two main arguments are (1) It is stated that the *Weltjudentum* (World Jewry) had already declared war on Germany in 1933 and therefore Germany herself simply had to react to a formidable external and internal threat (Auerbach 1993b) and (2) that Germany became too powerful during the thirties, and therefore the traditional Great Powers (i.e., the Western Allies) decided to destroy their rival and support Poland in provoking World War II.

Recently, the claim was raised that Hitler's attack on the Soviet Union in June 1941 had a defensive character. According to this assumption, Joseph Stalin had already planned an invasion of National Socialist Germany and Hitler had to defend Germany and the German people by attacking Russia in a preemptive strike. Even though the *Präventivkriegsthese* (Preemptive War Thesis) has found partisans beyond right-wing extremist circles and veterans' organizations in the last few years (Überschär 1987) after the opening of some Soviet archives, such theories should be classified as apologetic. "Revisionists" also try to preserve the patriotic myth of the heroic and brave Wehrmacht soldier who was never involved in any crimes against humanity or the rules of warfare but dutifully and loyally served his country and his people.

In the context of German warfare, some "revisionists"—especially David Irving in his first books—present prominent or leading National Socialists in a positive light. Mainly, Rudolf Hess, depicted as a misunderstood peace-bringer (Emmerer 1993), and Walter Reder, accused of responsibility for the reprisal murder of Italian civilian hostages (Dokumentationsarchiv des österreichischen Widerstandes 1985), were the subjects of right-wing extremist adoration as martyrs to the German cause because both served long prison terms after 1945. It is noteworthy that Reder was placed backstage after his release from Italian imprisonment. His service to the right-wing extremist propaganda cause had obviously lost its importance.

If Nazi crimes are not entirely denied, they are at least set off against Allied atrocities—regardless of truth or fiction—as if Allied misdeeds could minimize Nazi guilt and responsibility. The main topics exploited by extremists are the ethnic cleansing of the German population from the former Eastern provinces of Germany and other German settlements in Central and Eastern Europe (e.g., the Sudetenland in Czechoslovakia, Yugoslavia, Poland, Russia, etc.) and the indiscriminate aerial bombing of German cities during the war, especially the infamous air raid on Dresden in February 1945. Extremists tend to exaggerate the numbers of German victims enormously (Mayr 1993).

Diverting the focus from the fate of Allied—especially Soviet—prisoners of war in camps, in a 1990 book, the Canadian journalist James Bacque claims to have found proof of plans by General Eisenhower and the French to commit war atrocities such as starvation against more than half a million German prisoners of war after the end of World War II. According to Steininger's (1993) critique the proof is weak. Nonetheless the book was used by the far Right and has been advertised or favorably reviewed in numerous Austrian or German right-wing journals.

National Socialist Crimes against Jews

The most important accusations against National Socialism refer to its planned and industrially executed extermination of European Jews. This crime became the central issue of "revisionist" literature during the last twenty years. There are a number of reasons for stressing this subject.

First, the murdering of the European Jews is the strongest accusation against National Socialism since it is a crime of singular dimension in the history of humankind. The only way to revive National Socialist ideology is to minimize or deny that crime.

Second, "revisionists" stress the fact that the Final Solution is a crime of unprecedented and almost unbelievable dimension. They hope that people can easily be convinced that the Holocaust was an invention of Allied propaganda and Jewish revenge. It is certainly easier to imagine that the intentional murder of millions of people has not taken place than it is to recognize the gruesome fact that Auschwitz-Birkenau and the other extermination camps (Treblinka, Sobibor, Chelmno, etc.) were literally slaughterhouses for human beings.

Third, denial of the Holocaust has been labeled a new type of antisemitism. Polls confirm that pockets of active denial—not just lack of knowledge or ignorance—exist not only in Germany and Austria but also in Britain, France, and the United States. According to the Anti-Defamation League in New York City, "revisionism" is a new method of propagating antisemitism (1989, 1993a). As I shall show later, Holocaust denial uses existing antisemitic frames to "prove" that the Holocaust did not take place.

Fourth, denying the Holocaust is used to question the legitimacy of the State of Israel and to criticize the West German restitution of property, reparation payments, and other compensation to the Jewish people.

In sum, minimizing or denying the atrocities against the Jews includes the following lines of argumentation (Spann 1992, Shermer 1994):

- Denial of the intention of genocide primarily based on race
- Denial of the use of gas chambers and crematoria in the course of a highly technical and well-organized extermination program
- Doubting and minimizing the figure of about 5 to 6 million Jews who were killed or perished during World War II (Benz 1991)
- Excusing the atrocities against the Jews as a necessity in the course of the war, insisting that only traitors, criminals, spies, and enemies of National Socialism had been executed
- Stating that the persecution and murdering of the Jews had only been acts of subordinate officials and that Hitler and other leading National Socialists had neither ordered nor intended mass murder
- Making Jews themselves responsible for their fate because they had declared war against Hitler's Germany, thus interpreting World War II as a conflict between World Jewry and Germans
- Questioning the authenticity of Anne Frank's diary, a thorn in the flesh of rightists because the description of the young girl's life in her hiding place in Amsterdam deeply moved hundreds of thousands of readers all over the world. A research project of the Netherlands Institute of War Documentation proved that the diary contains original writings of Anne Frank. But edited versions differ because of omissions and minor corrections by Anne Frank's surviving father, interpreters, and publishers (Rijksinstituut 1988, Bailer-Galanda 1992b).

Conspiracy Theories

All "revisionist" theories are founded on the belief in a worldwide conspiracy that has induced thousands of people to tell the same story about the persecution of Jews and mass murder with poisonous gas in Auschwitz. However, that conspiracy would have had to work very hard to produce the thousands of documents in archives dealing with National Socialist crimes. Conspiracy theories are a tradition of antisemitic agitation that suspects the existence of a plot of Jews, Freemasons, and others to rule the whole world. The so-called *Protocols of the Learned Elders of Zion* (1978), for instance, produced by Russian antisemites a hundred years ago, are still quoted in right-wing extremist literature.

Methods of "Revisionism"

The first to analyze the methods of pseudohistoriographic "revisionist" writing was the director of the Institute for Contemporary History in Munich, Martin Broszat (1986). He was followed by other historians (e.g., Graml 1989, Spann 1992, Lipstadt 1993, Benz 1994).

First, most "revisionists" try hard to give their publications a serious and scientific appearance in order to find their way to a readership outside right-wing extremism. In an effort to hide their propagandistic aims, some deny that they have any contact with neo-Nazi groups or are right-wing extremists themselves. As Lipstadt (1993: 217) puts it, "They attempt to project the appearance of being committed to the very values that they in truth adamantly oppose: reason, critical rules of evidence, and historical distinction." They argue to be just interested in finding the historical truth, but their one-sided use of historical facts unmasks this assertion as pure propaganda.

Second, although the first "revisionists" in Germany and elsewhere did not use any documents for their pseudo-historical writing, their followers examined archival material or at least pretended to use authentic historical materials to add more credence to their publications. One of the first of these "revisionists" was David Irving, who joined the ranks of the deniers some years ago but started as an apologist of leading National Socialists, including the "Führer" himself. He researched archives and found historical material that had been neglected until then. Irving's works called historians on stage to analyze his way of using these newly found documents (Broszat 1986). Irving, Hoggan, and others use the sources to suit their purposes, ironically the same tactic they criticized their predecessors for using—they refer to documents that seem to support their theses and neglect those that contradict their assertions. They interpret documents in a biased way—sometimes even intentionally misunderstanding them. For instance, Irving argues that in National Socialist rhetoric, *ausrotten* and *Endlösung* (final solution) did not mean the extermination but merely the expulsion of Jews.

Third, "revisionists" construct a different and eclectic history *(Geschichtsklitterung)*. They divide the course of historical events into different elements and put them back together in another configuration in order to manufacture their version of historical events. "Revisionists" make use of events that prove their theories and leave out other events that would question their conclusions; this is similar to the previously mentioned method of misusing and misinterpreting documents. In addition, they construct causal relations between historical events that are not supported by closer examinaton of the facts. One example is the claim that atrocities against Jews were a revenge for the indiscriminate firebombing of Dresden in January 1945 (Spann 1992: 17 f.).

The fourth method is the production of "historical" material. Sometimes it is quite difficult for "revisionists" to prove that certain historical events did not happen by using existing materials. Imitating methods used in concentration camp trials, they produce documents or testimonies of witnesses that support their positions. In 1977, the right-wing extremist publisher Druffel Verlag edited the memoirs of Hermann Giesler, a prominent National Socialist architect. Historian Hermann Graml easily proved these "memories" to be very unskillful inventions (1989: 77 ff.). In 1988, Gerd Honsik, an Austrian neo-Nazi, published his book *Freispruch für Hitler: 36 ungehörte Zeugen wider die Gaskammern* (Acquittal for Hitler: Thirty-six until Now Unheard Witnesses against the Gas Chambers), in which he presented interviews or pseudointerviews with more or less prominent National Socialists who deny the Holocaust and the existence of the gas chambers.

In 1987, another Austrian, Emil Lachout, produced a pseudodocument in which he contended that an Allied commission had found out that there were no gas chambers in certain concentration camps. That pseudodocument was published in a series of right-wing extremist magazines in Austria and Germany. Lachout even acted as a witness for the defense in the trial against the Canadian "revisionist," Ernst Zündel.

Fifth, many "revisionist" publications hide behind prominent or pretended authorities by citing an impressive number of references. The authors of these works rely on the reader's confidence in the accuracy of citations in historiographic works. They use this camouflage to cite not only nonexistent documents but also the works of prominent historians like Raul Hilberg. But even when they cite real works, they quote out of context and thus misuse leading historians to buttress their own positions (Graml 1989, Shermer 1994). One standard argument is that the International Committee of the Red Cross stated that only 300,000 Jews died in the course of National Socialist persecution. This lie has been repeated for decades, despite the fact that the Red Cross repeatedly has formally denied ever publishing such a statement. Unfortunately, that does not prevent "revisionists" from continuing to use the authority of the Red Cross for their propaganda (Benz 1994). If there are no authorities to be employed, "revisionists" quote each other, pretending to be serious writers, scientists, and historians.

Sixth, "revisionist" writers use differences in minor details or irrelevant errors of serious historians (whose testimony they ironically accept when it fits their argument) to conclude that the central findings of historical research concerning National Socialist crimes are wrong. Debates between historians such as the Holocaust discussion between "intentionalists" and "functionalists" (Kershaw 1985) are taken for debates about the veracity of the entire field.

Seventh, international "revisionism" makes use of the public's belief in the objectivity of natural sciences by citing supposedly scientific research to "prove" that neither the gas chambers in Auschwitz-Birkenau nor those in Mauthausen could have functioned as instruments for mass murder by poisonous gas. This argument was used for the first time in a trial against Canadian neo-Nazi Ernst Zündel, who was accused of inciting hatred by denying the Holocaust. The French "revisionist" Robert Faurisson engaged Fred A. Leuchter, a self-styled engineer who supposedly constructed gas chambers for executions in American jails, to work on behalf of Zündel. Leuchter traveled to Auschwitz and Majdanek in Poland, where he supposedly took samples from the ruins of the gas chambers and other facilities and had them chemically analyzed for residues of Cyclon-B, although chemically no residue would be expected (J. Bailer 1992). According to the results of his "technical" investigation, Leuchter stated that in his "engineering opinion" the mass murder with Cyclon-B could not have taken place. During cross-examination in a court in Toronto, Leuchter was forced to admit that he had never been an engineer and that he had no historical knowledge about the Holocaust besides some information from Faurisson and other "revisionist" sources. The Canadian court refused to accept Leuchter's report as part of the recorded file. Later, investigations revealed that, contrary to his own assertions, Leuchter was also not an expert in constructing gas chambers (Shapiro 1990, Lipstadt 1993: 169–179). Nevertheless Fred Leuchter became the most famous figure of "revisionism" for some time. His report was sold all over the world, and German translations were widely distributed by the Austrian neo-Nazi Walter Ochensberger and the West German "revisionist" Udo Walendy. The propaganda objective can be easily discerned by comparing the versions in different languages. They even report different versions of Leuchter's calculations (Bailer-Galanda 1992a). Such inconsistencies are ironic, coming from "revisionists" who claimed to be interested only in finding the truth and denounced others for making errors and mistakes.

Recently, several historians have refuted Leuchter's report (Wegner 1990, Auerbach 1993c). Jean-Claude Pressac, a French pharmacist, conducted nearly 10 years of research on the Auschwitz crematoria and gas chambers (Pressac 1989, 1993). He writes that the Leuchter report, "based on misinformation which leads to false reasoning and misinterpretation of data, . . . is unacceptable. It was researched illegally, ignoring the most straightforward of historical data, and found in gross errors of measurement and calculation. What is inexcusable is Leuchter taking historians for idiots. Leuchter's ultimate errors definitively land 'The Leuchter Report' in the cesspool of pretentious human folly" (Pressac 1990: 31).

This new tactic of using natural sciences to deny the Holocaust seemed to be successful and was able to impress less-informed people. It therefore did not take long before Leuchter gained followers. In 1991, in the course of a trial involving the Nazi veteran Otto Ernst Remer, Remer's lawyer engaged Germar Rudolph, a young chemist working with the Max Planck Institute. Rudolph's task was to repeat Leuchter's investigation. Although Rudolph's report, of which several disputed versions exist, appears to be more scientific and serious than Leuchter's, it is scientifically as flawed as Leuchter's (J. Bailer 1995). Rudolph was finally dismissed by the Max Planck Institute and has now found his way into right-wing extremist circles that exploit his report.

The case of the Austrian engineer Walter Lüftl, former president of the Austrian Federal Engineering Association and an expert on structure and buildings, is a bit different. He wrote technically and chemically untenable papers (J. Bailer 1995) arguing that it is impossible to murder human beings with Cyclon-B and carbon monoxide. His papers were distributed to Austrian politicians and journalists. Lüftl was asked by Remer's lawyer to testify as an expert in Remer's trial, but he allegedly refused. He was forced to retreat as soon as his papers became public. The Department of Public Prosecution in Vienna investigated him but dismissed the case, reasoning that Lüftl was not a "revisionist" or a right-wing extremist. Since then, Lüftl has been celebrated as a new hero of international "revisionism." "Revisionists" point to the fact that he is the first "expert" to deny murders in the gas chambers of Auschwitz and that he was not convicted by the Austrian court as proof that Lüftl writes the "truth" (see the "revisionist" *Deutschland in Geschichte und Gegenwart,* March 1994).

The International Network of "Revisionism"

"Revisionism" and Holocaust denial have become central ideological elements of right-wing extremist and neo-Nazi propaganda during recent years. "Revisionist" publications are distributed by these organizations and by the international "revisionist" network. These channels of distribution go hand in hand. As pointed out earlier, since the seventies close connections have existed between "revisionists" in Europe and those in North America.

The organizational center is the Institute for Historical Review (IHR) in California, founded in 1978 by the leader of the antisemitic right-wing extremist Liberty Lobby, Willis A. Carto. The first director was William David McCalden, cofounder of the neo-Nazi British National Party (Lipstadt 1993: 137, Landesamt für Verfassungsschutz Berlin 1994: 19). The IHR organizes regular conferences and publishes the *Journal of Historical Review,* which offers a platform to all apologists and Holocaust deniers. Traditionally, the IHR maintains numerous contacts with "revisionists" in Germany, Austria, Canada, France, Great Britain, and other countries around the world. For instance, the papers of Austrian Walter Lüftl were published in the IHR's *Journal of Historical Review* soon after their release. The institute organizes regular conferences on "revisionism" attended by authors and "revisionists" from the United States, Canada, Germany, Austria, and other countries. It also has ties with like-minded Europeans and Gary Rex Lauck's U.S. organization, the National-Sozialistische Deutsche Arbeiter Partei-Aufbau Organisation (NSDAP-AO). This group spreads neo-Nazi material in Germany and Austria and supports "revisionist" meetings in Europe (Michael Schmidt 1993).

Another overseas "revisionist" center has its seat in Toronto, Canada, and is organized by the German-Canadian Ernst Zündel. His Samisdat publishing house produces newspapers and reprints and distributes "the usual array of antisemitic, racist, and Holocaust denial material" (Lipstadt 1993: 158), including National Socialist music favorites, Hitler's speeches, videocassettes of Leuchter's visit to

Poland, and so on, all over the world. Between 1978 and 1980, 200 shipments of neo-Nazi and "revisionist" material by Samisdat Publications were sent to Western Germany.

In Europe the "revisionist" network has connections in a number of countries. In Spain, Pedro Varela and his CEDADE (Circulo Español de Amigos de Europa) not only publishes and spreads "revisionist" and neo-Nazi material but also gives shelter to legally prosecuted friends. Gerd Honsik, one of Austria's leading activists and a diligent writer of antisemitic, neo-Nazi, and Holocaust-denying books, fled to Spain after being sentenced by an Austrian court because of his neo-Nazi activities. Supported by CEDADE, he still produces his paper *Halt* and sends it home to Austria. Recently, the veteran National Socialist and Holocaust denier Otto Ernst Remer, sentenced by a West German court, also fled to Spain, where he was welcomed by Honsik.

Great Britain's contribution to this group is the "revisionist" historian David Irving, as well as the National Front. Antisemitic and "revisionist" publications by Austrian-born Ditlieb Felderer are distributed from Sweden. Felderer regularly attends IHR conferences, and he supported Ernst Zündel during the latter's trial in Toronto (Landesamt für Verfassungsschutz Berlin 1994). In Switzerland, Max Wahl produces his "revisionist" paper *Eidgenoss* and also distributes it in Austria and Germany. Thies Christophersen, author of *Die Auschwitz-Lüge*, dispatches his magazine *Die Bauernschaft*, which deals with "revisionist" topics and other neo-Nazi subjects, from Denmark.

The networks in Germany and Austria consist of neo-Nazis as well as traditional right-wing extremist organizations and parties that spread their propaganda to sectors of the nonextremist population. Extremist groups and publishers in these two countries traditionally cooperate closely. In Germany, some publishing houses have specialized in "revisionist" topics since the fifties. For instance, the Grabert Verlag, which first published David Hoggan's *Der erzwungene Krieg* and Wilhelm Stäglich's *Der Auschwitz-Mythos*, is still editing the "revisionist" newspaper *Deutschland in Geschichte und Gegenwart*. The Druffel Verlag, which publishes antisemitic and "revisionist" books, has a similar publishing program. Advertisements by these publishing houses can be found in many right-wing extremist newspapers in Austria and Germany. Some of them regularly provide a platfrom for extremists who deny the Holocaust and National Socialist apologists. For many years the *Deutsche National-Zeitung* has denounced "anti-German lies" and has sought to unmask Allied reeducation efforts and propaganda. It takes up current issues, such as the TV series *Holocaust* in 1979. In recent years, it has continued to insist that the number of victims at Auschwitz has been reduced. Recently, it criticized Steven Spielberg's film *Schindler's List* as historically untrue. The paper is sold publicly at newsstands in Austria and Germany even though it was prosecuted by the Austrian courts some years ago. The editor of *Deutsche National-Zeitung*, Gerhard Frey, is a wealthy leader of the right-wing party Deutsche Volksunion (DVU), which gained some seats in regional elections in September 1991 in Bremen and in April 1992 in Schleswig-Holstein (see appendix).

Magazines like *Code*, which was recently sold at Viennese train stations but is now distributed by subscription only (as are most right-wing extremist papers), or

Nation Europa, and the recently founded magazine *Nation,* which is produced in Eastern Europe but written by right-wing extremists in Germany and Austria, often deal with "revisionist" issues. Otto Ernst Remer continues to edit the *Remer-Depesche,* which concentrates on the denial of the mass murder of Jews in National Socialist extermination camps and tries to minimize the number of Jewish victims of Nazi persecution.

Organizational support comes from neo-Nazi groups like the Amt für Volksaufklärung und Öffentlichkeitsarbeit, which is led by the professional West German neo-Nazi, Ewald Bela Althans, one of the successors of the late leader Michael Kühnen, who was himself a "revisionist" activist. Other Kühnen successors who should be mentioned are Christian Worch and his Nationale Liste and the Nationalistische Front, led by Meinolf Schönborn. The Nationaldemokratische Partei Deutschlands (NPD) is an established traditional right-wing party in Germany. It was founded in the sixties and has survived ups and downs in various state elections since then. Currently, the NPD is cooperating with the Deutsche Liga für Volk und Heimat, though this right-wing merger has little significance. During the last few years, all of these political parties and groups organized, supported, or attended "revisionist" meetings in Germany attended by prominent authors like Irving, Faurisson, and Leuchter.

Most of these activities in Germany reach Austria as well. Austrian neo-Nazi organizations and papers traditionally have close connections to like-minded friends in the Federal Republic (Dokumentationsarchiv des österreichischen Widerstandes 1994). Walter Ochensberger with his monthly *Sieg* acted as a center for contacts between Austrian, West German, and international neo-Nazis and "revisionists." Ochensberger is currently in jail for his neo–National Socialist activities, and his periodical has ceased publication. Gerd Honsik is one of the most important Austrian "revisionist" authors on the neo-Nazi scene, though he lost most of his influence after his flight to Spain. The Volkstreue außerparlamentarische Opposition (VAPO) was led by the Austrian neo-Nazi Gottfried Küssel, who had close connections to Germany and was nominated as the successor of the deceased neo-Nazi Michael Kühnen. Küssel was later sentenced because of his contravention of the Verbotsgesetz, and he is currently in prison in Austria. Members of this militant neo-Nazi group took part in demonstrations in Germany in memory of Hitler's deputy Rudolf Hess and attended most of the international "revisionist" meetings during recent years. Besides these militant organizations, traditional far-Right groups in Austria concentrate on cultural activities and organize regular meetings attended by like-minded persons not only from Austria but also from Germany and other European countries. At such meetings, "revisionists" present their ideas. The literature of such organizations regularly contains articles about Holocaust denial or National Socialist apologetic topics. Most outstanding are the Arbeitsgemeinschaft für demokratische Politik (AFP) and the Deutsche Kulturwerk Europäischen Geistes, identical to the German group with the same name.

Aula, a monthly magazine with a more serious appearance, represents the so-called New Right in Austria and tries to build bridges between the New Right and right-wing conservatives. This periodical is associated with the Austrian Freedom Party (Freiheitliche Partei Österreichs [FPÖ]), which gained more than 20% of the votes during the Austrian federal elections of October 1994. Its publishing house (Aula Verlag) is owned by an association of university graduates, most of them members of nationalist student associations *(Burschenschaften)*. *Aula* sometimes publishes positive references to "revisionists" like David Irving, Germar Rudolph, and Walter Lüftl. It celebrated the fact that Lüftl was not charged with a crime for publishing his papers (*Aula* July/August 1994).

Publications of the FPÖ are also not free of "revisionist" tendencies. Party members and representatives have evoked public protests by denying the existence of the Holocaust and by minimizing National Socialist crimes (B. Bailer and Neugebauer 1994b). The party's leader, Jörg Haider, had to resign as head of the provincial government of Carinthia (Landeshauptmann) for publicly praising the management of National Socialist employment policy in June 1991.

"Revisionist" tendencies or sympathy for "revisionist" arguments can be found outside organized right-wing extremism in Austria as well as in Germany. Historians in Germany fought the so-called *Historikerstreit* (historians' debate) in the mid 1980s in which the conservative historian Ernst Nolte played a prominent part. Nolte pleaded for a historicization of National Socialism. He interpreted Nazism as a German reaction to the rise of Stalinism in the Soviet Union. He also implied that National Socialist atrocities were intertwined with Stalinist crimes, thereby (according to his critics) questioning the thesis that the Holocaust was a singular event in our century. Nolte was vehemently opposed by an overwhelming majority of well-known historians and social scientists, such as Jürgen Habermas (Diner 1987, *Historikerstreit* 1987). Since then, Nolte, formerly an honored historian and researcher on fascism, moved further to the Right. In his last book, Nolte (1993) reveals sympathy with "revisionist" authors, some of whom he even grants the status of scientists, though he does not question the facts of the Holocaust except for the exact number of victims. His search for a rationale of the National Socialist policy against European Jewry has raised eyebrows. Lipstadt comments on historians such as Nolte: "Though these historians are not deniers, they helped to create a gray area where their highly questionable interpretations of history became enmeshed with the pseudo-history of the deniers; and they do indeed share some of the same objectives" (Lipstadt 1993: 209). No wonder that some of his theses are exploited by the Right and used by "revisionists." For example, the *Journal of Historical Review* printed a positive review of Nolte's last book and published a long interview with Nolte (January 1994).

Historians like Nolte and people like Herbert Fleissner (the owner of a number of publishing houses in Germany that published books of David Irving, among others) help, in my opinion, to reestablish nationalist feelings by playing down the guilt of Nazi Germany and the Germans (Diner 1987). This is the focus that "revisionists" in Germany and Austria have in common with historians of the Right. The "revisionists" also make use of the fact that 50 years after the end of World War II many Germans and Austrians feel the past as a guilt burden and therefore want to "draw a line" under the continuing and prominent remembrance of the Holocaust and put the National Socialist past and World War II aside. Even persons who are not right-wing extremists, such as veterans' organizations, search for excuses (Benz in Diner 1987). Newspapers like the *Neue Kronenzeitung* (the most widely read newspaper in Austria) sometimes give space to "revisionist" arguments with latent antisemitic undertones (Botz 1994) because they recognize that there is an audience interested in relativizing crimes symbolized by Auschwitz. Also, the revival of nationalist feelings in Germany is supportive of "revisionist" tendencies. To be sure, "revisionism" is not just an issue of right-wing extremists.

The Legal Situation

In 1985, the West German federal diet (Bundestag) passed a law that made the distribution of hate material and denial of the Holocaust punishable. Naturally, the Gesetz gegen die Auschwitz-Lüge was strongly opposed by right-wing supporters in Germany and Austria. But Holocaust denial could only be prosecuted if uttered in close connection with intent to defame Jews. That condition led to a series of unequal and contradictory sentences of the West German Bundesgerichtshof (Federal High Court) and the Bundesverfassungsgericht (Federal Constitutional Court). Whereas the Bundesgerichtshof stated that simple denial of the Holocaust without intention of defamation or the propagating of National Socialist ideology was not punishable, the Bundesverfassungsgericht reasoned that denial itself was an attack on the dignity of man, notably of Jews living today. Therefore, amending the law became necessary, supported by a great majority of all parties in the national German parliament. The amendment was enacted on December 1, 1994.

In Austria, neo-Nazi activities can be punished according to the Verbotsgesetz, which dates back to 1945. This law was passed to prohibit a revival of the NSDAP or its ideology. As a result of problems in the forties, it became more and more difficult to execute the law in connection with neo-National Socialist activities. Besides, the law contained no passage clearly stating that denial of the Holocaust meant activity in a National Socialist sense—although Austrian courts and judges interpreted the law that way. When "revisionism" also became a central argument of neo-Nazi propaganda in Austria, it took long and various discussions until the law was finally amended in February 1992. In addition to other changes, a new section was added to the law that explicitly forbids the denial or gross minimizing of Nazi genocide or of other Nazi crimes against humanity. This amendment makes it easier for the courts to deal with neo-Nazi propaganda and "revisionism." Sentences against leading Austrian right-wing extremists like Ochensberger, Honsik, and Küssel show that the discussions about the National Socialist past and the amendment of the Verbotsgesetz helped to change the public views of neo-Nazi and right-wing extremist activities.

Summary

"Revisionism" is not a recent phenomenon. It started in the first years after the end of World War II but has changed its character since then. With growing distance from the reality of the National Socialist dictatorship, it became easier for the remaining devotees of that ideology to play down crimes and guilt until they turned to denial and a diversion of focus from the main crime, the Holocaust. The movement for a "revisionist" historicization of the years 1933–1945 appeals to those who want to put an end to the so-called *Vergangenheitsbewältigung,* or discussions of the Nazi past. But it is essential that the memory of the Holocaust not be buried not only to protect political morality but also to avoid the danger of neo-Nazism, racism, and antisemitism. In the aftermath of the fundamental changes in Europe since 1989, new political and economic challenges have arisen, among them an increase in right-wing extremism and "revisionism." States and politicians can cope with these problems by using laws and courts. But developing a sensible public conscience, providing constant information, and educating people about prejudice and the dangers of forgetting the past will be as necessary as unmasking the false credibility of right-wing extremism in all of its guises. This problem cannot be solved by historians alone. Governments must be developed that protect citizens' security and liberties, and democratic politicians must ensure that right-wing extremism can never become acceptable and legitimate in public life nor in the government of a democracy willing to defend itself and human rights wherever and whenever they are threatened.

NOTES

The author is indebted to Bonita Samuels and Hermann Kurthen for translations and proof-reading.

1. The word *revisionism* in enclosed in quotation marks to distinguish it from serious efforts of nonapologetic historians to revise some thesis of historiography.

2. Recently, left-wing historians have used the term *historical revisionism* for tendencies of a few historians like Ernst Nolte and Rainer Zitelmann who are not "revisionists" but sometimes unintentionally prepare the ground for "revisionists" (Roth 1994). Critics maintain that a loose use of the term *revisionism* unintentionally minimizes right-wing extremist "revisionism," thus being counterproductive to the well-meaning intention of demasking real "revisionism."

3. Christophersen (1975); App (1973); Harwood (1974), also published in German by Volkstum Verlag in 1974 under the title *Starben wirklich sechs Millionen?;* Butz (1975), published in Germany in 1977; Faurisson (1978); Stäglich (1979), translated as "The Myth of Auschwitz: Legend or Reality? A Critical Survey."

9

ELLIOT NEAMAN

A New Conservative Revolution?

Neo-Nationalism, Collective Memory, and the New Right in Germany since Unification

> Finally it has to do with a tragedy that has so far been completely covered up—the tragedy of the German people and the end of the German nation. All of that has been suppressed. That is why there is no good German literature about the Second World War. The right-wing is now pushing into this vacuum.
>
> —Heiner Müller, *Zur Lage der Nation* (1990)

After the Berlin Wall fell in 1989, a brief wave of optimism engulfed a large number of Western intellectuals who felt that the end of the Cold War would mean not just liberation for Eastern Europe but perhaps a new era of thinking beyond stale ideological confrontations, even leading to a realization of Immanuel Kant's dream of universal world peace. Five years later, much of this early optimism has dissipated as ethnic wars have torn apart the Soviet Union, the Balkans, India, and a host of other countries. The breakdown of the Cold War order galvanized ultraconservative, nationalistic, and right-wing forces in the East and the West. Hans Magnus Enzensberger has recently argued, in a manner reminiscent of conservative cultural pessimism, that civil wars are the anthropological norm rather than a historical contingency that can someday be overcome. The end of the Cold War, of a bipolar world, Enzensberger observes, also means that the more predictable and orderly wars between states will be supplanted increasingly by the breakdown of internal order and the weakening of the monopoly on power claimed by the apparatus of the state (Enzensberger 1994).

Given the traumatic state of the post–Cold War world, one would have expected the peaceful and orderly reunification of Germany to be a cause for celebration by German conservatives and nationalists. One of the most paradoxical developments to emerge, therefore, has been a resurgence of radical conservatism which complains loudly about Germany's lack of national self-determination. Voices are being raised to "draw a line" and stop dwelling on the past and return to a "normal," self-confident nation that does not engage in ritualistic penance for the crimes of National Socialism. The West is from that viewpoint criticized for everything—from contaminating German culture to incapacitating Germany's ability to conduct an independent and self-interested foreign policy. Fears are raised that Germany is embracing pan-Europeanism and multiculturalism and thereby damaging the supposedly homogeneous cultural and ethnic character of the nation, its sovereignty and self-determination. Liberalism is viewed by the radical right-wing as a foreign import that does not respect the cultural, political, and social particularity of the Germans. Finally, unification is seen by some extremists as only a first step to "genuine" unification of all lands from which Germans were exiled or where they still represent sizable minorities.[1]

A parallel might be drawn here between the demands and complaints of the so-called New Right[2] after 1989 and what Fritz Stern has called the cultural despair of the Bismarckian period (Fritz Stern 1961). Far from being satisfied with the smaller-German *(kleindeutsch)* solution of Germany's unification in 1871, which excluded Austrian-Germans, the radical conservatives of the era vociferously attacked the Bismarckian Reich as a soulless, self-satisfied, and philistine state. For them, the Bismarckian revolution did not go far enough, neither geographically nor culturally. Nietzsche's shrill critique of the crass materialism and lack of heroism exhibited by the common German "herd animal" and his evocation of a past aristocratic warrior state, although heard by few at the time, was formulated as a response to the stability and economic success of the Reich. The antisemitic and integrally nationalist writings of Julius Langbehn, Paul de Lagarde, Möller van den Bruck, Guido von List, Jörg Lanz von Liebenfels, and a host of lesser dabblers in German mysticism and Nordic myths remained on the fringes of German intellectual life, but after 1918 their moment came. After the defeat in World War I, a new generation of radical conservatives picked up their mantle and agitated ceaselessly against parliamentary democracy and for the establishment of a German People's State.

The intellectuals who sounded these themes have been cast as part of the Conservative Revolution of the 1920s (Mohler 1950). In contrast to traditional conservatism, which places a high value on stability and order, the radical conservatives of the Weimar period felt that society had become so decadent that holding on to old values would no longer suffice. Möller van den Bruck expressed this sentiment when he rejected the conservatism of the Bismarckian Empire and said values would have to be created that are worth fighting for (Fritz Stern 1961: 256 f.). A leap into the future would have to be made, an arbitrary, but powerful decision that would initiate a German Revolution and sweep aside all foreign (often a code word for Jewish) ideas and institutions. Today's radical conservatives, or the New Right, as the group is often called, explicitly lay claim to the heritage of the Conservative Revolution and its most important exponents, Carl Schmitt, Othmar Spann, Martin Heidegger, Ernst Jünger, Oswald Spengler and others.[3]

Stefan Breuer has argued that the term *Conservative Revolution* encompasses too broad a spectrum of thinkers, movements and political groups to have any coherent signification (Breuer 1993). It is true that Armin Mohler's original classification contains a disparate lot of intellectual and political entities, including the *Bündische* youth groups, various *völkisch* movements, and a wide range of thinkers—many of them obscure and minor figures mixed in with intellectual giants, such as Martin Heidegger. Yet Breuer's suggestion, that these revolutionary impulses be renamed New Nationalism begs other questions and defines the group too narrowly. The ideas of the Conservative Revolution, although diversely formulated, did form a coherent ideology, particularly in the articulation of the adversary: liberalism, social democracy, the Western and European integration, individualism, cosmopolitanism, republicanism—in a word, legacies of the Enlightenment, the labor movement, and the American and French revolutions.

The Generation of 1989

As the self-proclaimed heirs of the Conservative Revolution, the New Right that has emerged since 1989 is a diverse group of intellectuals who are united more by what they oppose rather than a concrete vision of the future. Politically they can be placed somewhere on the spectrum between the ruling Christian Democrats and far right-wing parties, mainly the National Democratic Party (Nationaldemokratische Partei Deutschlands [NPD]), Gerhard Frey's German People's Union (Deutsche Volksunion [DVU]) and Franz Schönhuber's "Republikaner" Party. But since the fortunes of these two right-wing electoral parties have waned, they are in search again for a new political constellation.

The newness of the New Right supposedly consists in its demarcation from neo-Nazism and its claims to offer a chic, updated version of radical conservatism that transcends the social democratic consensus of the major political parties and offers new ideas in contrast to the supposedly liberal and Western-oriented cultural elites of the old Federal Republic (FRG). In its self-understanding the New Right is specifically a generational revolt against the Left of the FRG, in particular against the so-called Generation of 1968, the aging Apo-Opas (grandfathers of the extraparliamentary opposition) whose ideas are viewed as anachronistic and frozen in dogma and who are alleged to be comfortably ensconced in positions of power in the media, education, and other cultural and political institutions (Weißmann 1993: 42–50). But the New Right—sometimes also identified with the Generation of 1989—not only distances itself from the Generation of 1968 *(Achtundsechziger)* but also claims to transcend the politics of the Generation of Yalta, or the founders of the FRG, in particular Konrad Adenauer, who "sacrificed" East Germany and the chance for unification in order to firmly anchor West Germany under the tutelage of the United States and its allies. The New Right questions the utility and wisdom of Germany's one-sided ties to the West after unification in a changed international situation.[4]

The self-image of the generation of 1989 is one of rebellious "Young Turks"— energetic, radical young men with a mission to save Germany. Rejecting the image of stuffy conservatism, the New Right sees itself as the avant-garde for disillusioned leftists whose conversion they actively propagate. As Heimo Schwilk, born in 1952, asserted in an interview:

> The German intellectual who comes over to the camp of the 89ers is following an existential need to avoid soon being buried himself under the old concepts. The year 1989—and this will soon be clear to all intellectuals—has given an entirely new foundation to our intellectual and political reality. This epochal caesura worked like a catalyst, which first made the conversion of many intellectuals possible. (Fenske 1994)

In reality, the "camp of the 89ers" is too diverse a lot and has too many roots in the radical conservative and right-wing political network of the old Federal Republic to be considered an "epochal caesura." The 89ers are part of a New Right that can be traced back to the 1970s and divided into approximately four groups.

The first group, the ethnopluralist New Right, adapted the ideas and programs of the French thinker Alain de Benoist. To clothe old ideas about race and ethnicity in the garb of fashionable rhetoric from the discourse of the Left, they also borrowed Gramscian ideas of cultural hegemony and Jacques Derrida's notion of difference (Taguieff 1993/94). Ethnopluralists assert that ethnic groups are homogenous identities that lose substance when mixed together. Thus ethnopluralists borrow the postcolonial discourse of identity politics to bolster the case for European nationalism and ethnocentrism: Black power to the Blacks; German power to the Germans! The real racists, according to Benoist, are those who would deny ethnic groups their own identity by forcing them into liberal, multicultural (meaning minimal-cultural), and pan-European societies. The French Nouvelle Droite's racism is thus not heterophobic but heterophile (see the sharp analysis by Terkessidis 1995 and Reinfeldt and Schwarz 1994). As early as the 1970s, ethnopluralist arguments were articulated in journals like *Mut, Criticón,* and *Nation Europa.* When the conservative *Junge Freiheit* was first founded in 1986 (discussed later), a regular column was devoted to the subject of ethnopluralism. In the first 1992 issue, the title was changed to "National Questions" (Nationalitätenfragen). Benoist's main think tank, the Research Group for the Study of European Civilization (Groupement de Récherche et d'Etudes pour la Civilisation Européenne [GRECE]), goes out of its way to avoid the language and themes of neo-Nazis and the extreme right in an attempt to appear acceptable to bourgeois intellectuals. At the same time, the boundaries of GRECE's research areas, such as immigration and national traditions, allow xenophobic and antisemitic issues to reenter through the backdoor under the guise of unreprehensible, scientifically sounding language.

Ethnopluralism often refers to mystical, transhistorical foundations of ethnic and cultural groups. A good example of this approach can be found in the German journal *Elemente,* which was the official organ of the Thule Seminar, a now defunct right-wing think tank that had direct connections to Benoist and his journal *Elemente.*[5] The founder and head of the Thule Seminar, Pierre Krebs, published a declaration of principles in 1980, which makes clear why myths and a rejection of history are so important for the ethnopluralists. Krebs writes:

> Myth makes itself manifest in history, and man grows beyond his gods through the solidarity with his ancestors, his earth, the wind and stones, because only the descendants and their actions can lead to eternity. Finally, mankind can only grasp eternity, when it becomes conscious of its identity. Only the interrelatedness between identity and ethnic-cultural diversity creates authenticity. The dialectic of life is a dialectic of evolution, which is subject to the laws of diversity, just as the dialectic of death is a dialectic of decline, for which again the laws of entropy are valid. (Jäger 1988: 86 f.)

Even in this muddy language, one can detect the important elements of a coherent, though closed, naturalistic and vitalist worldview. Ethnopluralists like to buttress their mythical fantasies with bits and pieces of sociobiology and naturalist psychology from the writings of behaviorist scientists such as Hans Eysenck, Konrad Lorenz, Arthur Jensen, Irenäus Eibl-Eibesfeldt, and even the anthropologist Claude Lévi-Strauss.[6] Their ideological enemy is the multicultural society of liberal democracy, because when ethnic and racial groups are mixed, they argue, the natural differences and hierarchies among them cannot develop. Eysenck believes that psychological tests can be used to determine leadership personalities from followers and Lorenz has written extensively on the natural and aggressive drives of human beings, which have been tainted by society. Ethnopluralism is thus a euphemistic name for a theory of quasi-natural hierarchies and a justification of a neo-Darwinist worldview and struggle of cultures, races and tribes.

Second, the group of "Etatisten" or theorists of a strong state is comprised largely of political thinkers influenced by the ideas of Carl Schmitt. This group has adopted Schmitt's notion of the friend/foe determination as the basis of all politics; his critique of liberal democracy as formal, in contrast to an ethnonational community *(Volksgemeinschaft)* as genuine, democracy; and his geopolitical thinking based on sea and land empires.[7] The group includes thinkers ranging from the Left renegade Günther Maschke[8] and the Bochum political science professor Bernard Willms (who died in 1991), to the editor of the far-Right *Staatsbriefe,* Hans-Dietrich Sander, and the self-designated "National Revolutionaries" Henning Eichberg, Günter Barsch, and Wolfgang Strauss (see Mägerle 1994: 124). Most observers agree that Schmitt's influence on the New Right outweighs that of other representatives of the Conservative Revolution because Schmitt's political concepts are abstract, ambiguous, and sophisticated but also can be interpreted in a decidedly undemocratic and nationalistic light. The friend/foe determination, for example, can be read either as a neutral, objective assessment of international politics, or it can be contextualized as a justification for eliminating internal, "foreign" elements inside a homogeneous, "organic" community (see Kriener 1994). Considering Schmitt's stature and relevance for contemporary radical conservatism, it should be noted that his intellectual followers tend to downplay his political involvement in the Third Reich. Schmitt actively engaged himself and his ideas of national homogeneity in the service of the regime and made outspokenly antisemitic remarks. To take but one example, in a speech to a group of National Socialist university teachers he once employed a series of antisemitic caricatures, noting:

> "In relation to our intellectual work, the Jew has a parasitic, tactical, and commercial *[händlerische]* relationship. Because of his commercial talent, he often has a sharp sense for what is genuine; with great cleverness and a good nose *[schnelle Witterung]*, he knows how to hit upon the real thing. That is instinct as a parasite and genuine trader." Schmitt concludes this speech by citing Hitler: "By resisting the Jew, says our Führer Adolf Hitler, I am doing the work of the Lord." (Kriener 1994: 187)

Carl Schmitt's unconventional and at times brilliant political theorizing has even found followers at the institutional centers of German conservatism. As an example of how high in current government circles the ideas of Schmitt have reached, a recent book by the ruling Christian Democratic Party's (Christlich-Demokratische Union [CDU]) general secretary and a possible Helmut Kohl successor, Wolfgang Schäuble, gives some surprising evidence. In his book *Facing the Future,* Schäuble maps out his vision of a CDU politics of the future on central questions, such as the German welfare state, immigration, German history and identity, and the unity of the German state and nation, which he defines as a kind of protective association *(Schutzgemeinschaft)* in an increasingly complex and hard to intellectually penetrate world (Schäuble 1994: 103). Just as Schmitt saw the Leviathan, the omnipotent and apotheosized modern state, in danger of enervation through the private demands of civil society, Schäuble also warns that the modern state is in increasing danger of disfunction because it is "permanently beleaguered by the strong representatives of group interests *[Gruppenegoismen]*" (Schmitt 1976, Schäuble 1994: 99). Schäuble demands a new "will to community," a conscious identification of the state with the nation beyond the "empty" formulations of the liberal state (Schäuble 1994: 44–52).

In a related development, John Eley has also demonstrated how certain key Schmittian concepts are increasingly being applied in the political editorials of the daily national-circulation newspaper *Frankfurter Allgemeine Zeitung (FAZ).* As examples, Eley points out how Schmitt's geopolitical concepts—such as Germany's strategic position *(Standort),* extraterritorial sphere of influence *(Grossraum),* homogeneity, challenge *(Herausforderung),* sovereignty, and decisionism—all increasingly inform *FAZ's* interpretations of Germany's foreign policy options on a global level (Eley 1995).

The third group are spiritual reactionaries,[9] made up of one strand of authors who reacted to the French poststructuralist movement, reaching back to the 1970s, by bemoaning the effects of Americanization (i.e., Hollywood, Coca-Cola, pop music, consumerism, etc.) on German culture. An early exponent of this trend was the filmmaker Hans Jürgen Syberberg, whose postunification book, *Vom Unglück und Glück der Kunst in Deutschland nach dem letzten Krieg* (On misfortune and fortune of the arts in Germany after the last war), had antisemitic undertones. Syberberg blames the lack of a specifically German culture after 1945 on a "Jewish Left aesthetic" in an "unholy alliance" with "throwaway products like punk, pop, and junk" (Syberberg 1990: 14).

Another example of a spiritual reactionary trend is the important playwright, Botho Strauss, whose work in the 1970s was hailed by critics as revolutionary and innovative and who has recently published a number of scathing critiques of German society from a culturally conservative point of view (see Leggewie 1993: 115–119). Although he was a darling of the avant-garde in the late 1970s and early 1980s, his plays, written in a dazzling mixture of Berlin idiom and aesthetic construction, reflected the alienation and insecurity of the late West German republic's intellectual elite. Strauss caused a furor among German intellectuals after he published an article entitled "Anschwellender Bocksgesang" (Swelling Tragedy) in the weekly *Der Spiegel* in February 1993 (B. Strauss 1993).[10] In this aesthetic treatise, Strauss comments, among other things, on the rise of xenophobia and resentment in Germany in 1991–92 and blames the Left, particularly the Generation of 1968, for having created a moral and intellectual vacuum that prepared the social space in which the current younger generation is revolting against a supposedly hypocritical antifascism. Strauss also defended traditions of the intellectual

Right in Germany and lashed out against the supposed debasement of German high culture through television and commercialism. Most disturbingly, Strauss, although claiming to abhor all forms of antisemitism, wrote that ethnocentrism, nationalism, and xenophobia can be thought of as a quasi-anthropological tribal cult ritual that "originally had sacred, order-creating meaning." The writer implied that the hatred of strangers and outsiders, like the sacrificial victims of the Bronze Age, could have a cathartic, uniting, and positive function for communities by unloading aggression on one concentrated target.

In both Germany and France the New Right attempts to attract young intellectuals by occupying the traditional themes of the Left and giving the old issues a new twist. The Munich publishing group of Mathes and Seitz, for example, has been instrumental in translating the most interesting French structuralist and post-structuralist writers such as Georges Batailles, Jean-François Lyotard, and Michel Foucault into German (Diederichsen 1992, 1993). The structuralist discourse on power, consumerism, and bourgeois society can easily be turned into an elitist and conservative-reactionary critique of present society.

The fourth group promote neonationalist historiography. It is composed of historians who have taken the side of the conservative historian Ernst Nolte and, to a lesser extent, Andreas Hillgruber, Thomas Nipperdey, and Michael Stürmer in the so-called Historians' Debate of the 1980s concerning the meaning of the Holocaust. Their critics fear that a historiography that compares the Holocaust to Stalinist Gulags and purges will open the way for new Nationalist paradigms that free historians from concentrating on the crimes of the National Socialist era, either in an anticipatory or consequential sense. In the historical profession, the borders between conservatives, reactionaries, and the radical "revisionist" antidemocratic Right are, in my opinion, somewhat less distinct than in the other areas mentioned earlier because they often argue in a gray area of relativization and nuance.[11] One may count a heterogeneous mixture of more or less prominent historians who support neonationalist historiography, such as Rainer Zitelmann, Karlheinz Weiß-mann, Ansgar Graw, Karl-Eckhard Hahn, and others. Some want to redefine Germany's political and economic ties to the West, and some want to direct their energy to questioning the alleged comparative singularity of the Holocaust and the centrality of racism for explaining the Nazi regime. Others cast Germany in the role of a victim of geography and the desire of other imperialist European powers to keep Germany from becoming hegemonic on the European continent. National Socialism is seen ultimately as an outcome of four centuries of obstruction and interference in Germany's attempt to exercise its national ambitions of self-determination, the most important example of which was French and English "in-transigence" after World War I.[12] This manner of interpreting German history does not deny the extermination of the Jews or Auschwitz, but it tends to recast the origins, causes, and outcome of the two world wars as a set of mainly strategic moves on the chessboard of world politics and thus may recapitulate some of Hitler's own Machiavellian worldview. The Holocaust is reduced to a side effect of Hitler's world strategy or a reflex to situational events.

This new paradigm is not overtly false. As a historical interpretation, it is based on facts and can be weighed against other interpretations. The assertion that German history includes more than 12 years of Nazi rule is, of course, as true as it is banal. Like so many of the arguments of the New Right, straw men are set up and then knocked down (or as the Germans say, open doors are run into). But in my understanding, political and ethical questions remain unanswered: What is the final meaning of the Holocaust for German history and for today's German self-confidence and conscience? (The New Right's answer: Moral lessons and Realpolitik are not identical.) How is German identity to be constituted after Auschwitz? (The New Right's answer: Germany must have a new untainted beginning, which can suggest that the dark lesson of the Holocaust is lost.) How should the experience of the Nazi past influence today's education, personal ethics, foreign policy, questions of citizenship, and other social, political, and economic issues? (The answer of the New Right is, again, that Germany should become a "normal" nation, which begs a definition of normality.)

The Politics of Collective Memory

The new cultural conservatism and its nationalist and ethnocentric undertones in Germany cannot be understood in isolation from the rise of neonationalism in other parts of the world, even though the movement in Germany is, so far, manifested by nonviolence and tactical moderation, if one excepts the brutal neo-Nazi and skinhead offensive against foreigners and asylum seekers, that culminated in fatal attacks in Hoyerswerda, Rostock, and Solingen between 1991 and 1993 (Neaman 1993: 32–35). The battle in Germany is being waged for the most part not in the streets but on the field of collective memory and the self-image of the nation. Zealots of cultural particularism always possess a politics of collective memory, often in the form of radical religious or nationalist claims to historical space, whether symbolic or territorial.

The rise of this form of politics occurs often in the context of questioning which groups belong to the nation and which should be excluded. As an ideology, fascism rejected liberalism not least because universal rationalism seemed to denigrate the heroic, mythological, and unique aspects of a particular people's history and collective memory. The potential for this kind of prerational resurgence remains very much a real danger today. As Jacques Derrida has recently noted in an argument against Francis Fukuyama's position that liberal democracy is the only viable political ideology left for modern states, interethnic wars can erupt anywhere on the planet, driven by the "primitive conceptual phantasm of community, the nation state, sovereignty, borders, native soil and blood" (Derrida 1994: 82). Derrida argues further that the drive for stability, order, and a coherent national narrative is always "rooted first of all in the memory or the anxiety of a displaced—or displaceable—population" (1994: 83). In other words, the politics of cultural particularism is strongest when anxiety about national or religious identity is rising. It is no wonder then that Fukuyama's vision of a liberal world order is interpreted as hegemonic American cultural imperialism by the New Right and as an ideology worth fighting against (see Mohler 1993: 85–89).

Nationalism and History

In Germany the tension between critical Left and liberal scholars on the one hand and conservative-national historians on the other hand has been a consistent characteristic of the post-1945 attempts to grasp the meaning and understand the causes of the Third Reich. Immediately after the war, national liberals like Friedrich Meinecke and Gerhard Ritter were appalled by the generalizing tendency of certain foreign historians, like William Shirer, to see all of German history as contaminated by chauvinism and all Germans as incorrigibly and by nature quasi authoritarian. Conservatives like Reinhold Schneider or Rudolf Alexander Schröder also thought they could separate a contaminated from a benevolent past. For them, the fall from innocence came with the founding of the Reich in 1871 when the heritage of the German classical period and the Reformation was squandered in favor of a suicidal drive for global power. All of these interpretations of German history were attempts to retain positive aspects of German history, its federalism, and high culture, for example, in order to isolate National Socialism as an aberration caused by the crises of imperialism, World War I, and the Weimar Republic. Fritz Fischer's famous condemnation of the German war aims in World War I set off a paradigm shift of historical thinking in the 1960s, not only because the nationalist understanding of Nazism as a foreign element in German culture became less tenable but also because Fischer, a former Nazi Party member, was engaging in a personal form of coping with the past *(Vergangenheitsbewältigung)*, which became a model for a younger generation. The arrival of social history, inspired both by the Annales School and American social science then led to a systematic investigation of the nineteenth century and earlier in a search for the exceptional path of German history that ended inexorably in catastrophe. For much of the 1970s and 1980s this approach arguably has been dominant in West German historiography, and the nationalist historians remained marginalized and even frowned upon. The dominant ethos of the fragmentary West German state was to denigrate national identity, become attached to Europe, and display public guilt about the crimes of the Third Reich. When the Berlin Wall fell in 1989, it became clear that nationalist sentiment, although not particularly rampant, had been bottled up for 40 years.

Up until 1989 it was plausible to insist that Auschwitz was an event that could not "pass into the past" unlike any other event in German history. As Jean-Paul Sartre once said of Marxism, it was the horizon beyond which the twentieth century could not transcend (Stromberg 1994: 260). Jürgen Habermas and others, such as the historians of the Bielefeld School, insisted that the atrocities of the Third Reich serve as the reference point for West German identity: put positively, the FRG should be committed to liberalism, constitutionalism, and ties to the West and Europe so that fascism could never again occur. As long as Germany was a divided nation, the fascist and World War II experience and legacy was, indeed, central and visible to the collective identity of both Germany's. But this is no longer true. As Rainer Zitelmann put it in a recent interview: "Most young people are sick and tired of this exaggerated coping with the past, this ritual of making

amends. The stereotypical repetition of phraselike confessions of guilt bores critical minds" (Stein 1993: 3).

Junge Freiheit: A New Right Avant-garde?

All of the various strands of conservative radicalism and new nationalism came
together in the weekly newspaper *Junge Freiheit,* published in Potsdam for obvious symbolic reasons until 1995, but now published in Berlin. The newspaper was
established with the intent of winning ground in what was viewed to be a cultural
battle for the hearts and minds of young Germans. The strategy of the young men
(there are no women currently on the staff) who run the newspaper is to create a
new image for radical conservatism and avoid the trappings of the old Right, a
dusty and murky hyper-Germanness *(Deutschtümelei)* that led invariably to ideological ghettoization and political impotence. As Karlheinz Weißmann, one of the
avant-gardist thinkers *(Vordenker)* of this group, has written:

> In a pluralistic society, a group's influence is not defined alone and probably not
> even most importantly through its visible participation in political power. What is im-
> portant is to claim ground in pre-political space: in the long run, only a vital sub-
> culture guarantees that one's goals can be realized. The problem for conservatives is
> that one can't just "create" such a sub-culture. An inherent problem exists in regard to
> spontaneous and improvised things. Clearly what is missing are genuine right-wing
> street theaters, right-wing book stores, and finally the mass network of newspapers and
> little publications that the left-wing, alternative scene possesses in order to pass on its
> information and philosophy. (Weißmann 1989: 129)

Weißmann goes on to praise the appearance of the weekly *Junge Freiheit* because it consciously seeks a dialogue with its opponents but also hopes to build
bridges to what it conceives of as the national-Left. The self-image of the men of
the *Junge Freiheit* can be compared to their counterparts at *The Action (Die Tat)*
of the 1920s and 1930s: an avant-garde formation fighting encrusted and anachronistic positions and ideas. But in contrast to the antidemocratic and antiparliamen-
tarian radicals of the young Weimar Right, they are prepared to risk a so-called
"long march through the institutions," just as the Generation of 1968 conceived
its long-term political strategy. The *Junge Freiheit* follows what it considers a
Gramscian strategy, building on its circulation list, offering a "Summer University," salons, E-mail, reading circles, national-conservative advertising, and various
other opportunities for political and social intercourse. This strategy has already
succeeded in placing important New Right intellectuals in key positions at the
Ullstein-Müller publishing house, as well at the leading newspapers *Die Welt* and
the *Frankfurter Allgemeine Zeitung* (see Gessenharter 1992).

The *Junge Freiheit* began in 1986 as an eight-page photocopied newsletter for
youth under the auspices of a splinter party of the "Republikaner," the Freiheitliche Volkspartei (FVP).[13] When the radical FVP folded, the editors of the *Junge*

Freiheit decided to avoid strict party affiliation. In 1988, a national-conservative businessman, Götz Meidinger, founded an Association to Support the Reunification of Germany, (Unitas Germanica), which funded and took over the administrative organization of the newspaper. From 1988 to 1993 it had a letter-sized newspaper format and was available as a monthly throughout the FRG. In January 1994, the newspaper became a weekly and currently estimates its circulation at between 30,000 and 35,000 (see Lange 1993: 104 f.).

The newspaper's main readers are university students, in particular members of conservative student associations and a growing number of conservative traditionalist fraternities *(Burschenschaften)*. A biographical analysis of the staff at *Junge Freiheit* illuminates the social and ideological affinities, as well as the mentality of the young men who run the newspaper. Many are members of the Deutsche Gildenschaft, an elite corporate society with roots in a youth movement, the so-called Bündische Jugend of the 1920s, which Armin Mohler counts as part of the Conservative Revolution of the past.[14] The editor-in-chief, Dieter Stein, as well as the contributing editors Martin Schmitt ("National Questions"), Michael Hageböck ("Youth and Family"), Andreas Molau ("Culture"), and many other occasional contributors to the *Junge Freiheit* are members of the Deutsche Gildenschaft. It represents conservative-reactionary principles with militaristic and *völkisch* undertones. The Gildenschaft affirms the right of unification and self-determination in Austria, the Sudetenland, and other areas previously under German control, such as former East Prussia (Königsberg) and Alsace-Lorraine.[15] All of the *Junge Freiheit* staff did military service (i.e., they were deliberately not conscientious objectors *[Ersatzdienstleistende])*, and Dieter Stein comes from a family with military traditions. His father, Hans-Joachim Stein, joined the Bundeswehr in 1957 and later became a leading military historian in Freiburg, where, according to Kellershohn, he joined the "revisionist, German-national wing" (Kellershohn 1994b: 53).

Furthermore, many of the *Junge Freiheit* circle come directly from the overtly nationalistic fraternities and the newspaper serves as a kind of social conduit for the students, offering message boards, housing for those with national convictions *(nationale Gesinnung)*, and so forth. Hans-Ulrich Kopp, for example, second in command and in charge of the international politics section of the newspaper, is a member of Danubia, known for its right-wing rhetoric. Kopp believes that the large national fraternity network *(Deutsche Burschenschaften)* is an optimal means of placing radical conservatives into leading positions in the world of German finance and politics (Kellershohn 1994b: 71). Other regular contributors are members of fraternities such as Frank Butschbacher (Danubia, Olympia Wien), Alexander Ihls (Germania Marburg), Baldur Jahn (Danubia), Michael Paulwitz (Danubia), Jörg Haider (Silvania zu Wien), Rolf Schlierer (Germania Giessen), and Klaus Kunze (Germania Köln).

Many of the authors who appear in *Junge Freiheit* come from families who were expelled *(Vertriebene)* from their homelands in eastern Germany and East Europe at the end of World War II and the ensuing years. A considerable number of the authors are members, for example, of the Witikobund, one of the most influential interest groups that lobbies on behalf of the families of Sudetendeutsche

(Dietzsch 1994). Thus the mentality and ideological trappings of many young intellectuals associated with the *Junge Freiheit* have roots in nationalist conservatism, elitism, and right-wing traditionalism.

It is not entirely clear who finances the newspaper, though it has been able to sell advertisement space to Coca-Cola and Philip Morris. Recently advertising revenues have been declining as large companies are wary of having their products associated with an ultraconservative right-wing newspaper. Many of the advertisements come from publishers selling reprints, like those by Carl Schmitt, which would seem to appeal to *Junge Freiheit*'s readers. Other revenue is derived from the *Burschenschaften* and small political parties on the far Right. All indicators point to a long-term problem in advertising revenues if the newspaper is to go beyond its dependence on a small number of usually ideologically motivated clients (Hachel 1994).

Besides advertising and sales revenue, the *Junge Freiheit* receives support from various organizations and donors, without whose help the newspaper would hardly be able to survive. The most important group of supporters come from the so-called Tuesday Group in Berlin, a weekly meeting of national conservatives modeled on the long-standing Düsseldorf Herrenrunde (Hundseder 1995). The existence of this rather secretive group came to light in the summer of 1994 when a crisis broke out in the Berlin city government coalition of the SPD and the CDU. It was discovered that Interior senator Dieter Heckelmann's press secretary Christian Bonfert frequently had taken part in the Tuesday Group, which brings together conservative and Right leaders from finance, media, and politics and Right and ultraconservative representatives (Hundseder 1995: 160 ff.). Since the Federal Office for the Protection of the Constitution (Verfassungsschutz) had warned Heckelmann about the visits, he was held responsible for contacts to the far Right. The affair quickly blew over, but the incident threw light on some important connections. The initiator of the group was business consultant Hans Ulrich Pieper, who was a member of the far right-wing National Democratic Party (NPD) and was later active in the ultra-Right populist "Republikaner" Party. Pieper also supports a variety of right-wing think tanks such as the Deutsch-Europäische Studien-Gesellschaft and the Hoffmann-von-Fallersleben-Bildungswerk and occasionally writes for *Criticon*. The Tuesday Group's meetings are held every two weeks in the Berliner Hilton and are regularly visited by top managers such as Wilhelm Nölling of the Deutsche Notenbank, Jörg Schill of Borsig, Ulrich Steger of Volkswagen, and Gerhard Köhler, vice president of the Bundeskriminalamt. Ultraconservative and right-wing politicians such as Austrian Jörg Haider, Alexander von Stahl, and Heinrich Lummer, as well as the historian Ernst Nolte, were regular speakers. Regular guests included Rainer Zitelmann and other *Junge Freiheit* journalists, as well as members of the "Republikaner" Party (Hundseder 1995: 164). The *Junge Freiheit* is circulated at the meetings, and donors to the newspaper are sought out.

The *Junge Freiheit* has adopted all the tactics of the French Nouvelle Droite, attempting to make itself socially acceptable *(salonfähig)* through respectability. The newspaper distances itself editorially from neo-Nazis and the extreme Right, even though it will advertise their books and debate their positions. Any scholarly evaluation of the newspaper must look for indirect and subtle signs of xenophobia and antisemitism, since the editors are, in my opinion, clever enough to cover their traces and use deceptive language when dealing with sensitive issues. The newspaper will not directly join the extreme Right's antiimmigrant campaigns, for example, but every week an entire section of the newspaper is devoted to questions of nationalities ("Nationalitäten Fragen"). Here one will typically find reports from territories previously held by Germany, such as Schlesien/Silesia (a Polish province since Yalta) or East Prussia with its capital Königsberg/Kaliningrad (now a Russian enclave).[16] Instead of overtly supporting Holocaust deniers or "revisionism," "news" reports concerning the legal trials of Fred Leuchter, Ernst Zündel, or Robert Faurisson are given prominent attention.[17] The existence of gas chambers in Auschwitz is never doubted, but the manner in which Jews and others perished or were killed and particularly the exact number of Nazi and war victims are regularly questioned.[18] The kinds of messages that are posted on the Thule-Netz, the *Junge Freiheit*'s on-line computer discussion bulletin board, also indicate that not just a few of the newspaper's readers harbor antisemitic resentment and are addicted to conspiracy theories, viewing the newspaper's moderate tone as a necessary tactical concession to German democracy and its strict laws against public incitement and neo-Nazi propaganda.[19]

The New Version of History

It is of particular interest to scrutinize the manner in which the *Junge Freiheit* treats historical issues. On this terrain, the strategy and intentions of the New Right become more transparent as the politicization of history in the service of current ultranationalist and radical conservative trends becomes apparent. In his contribution to *The Self-Confident Nation* (Selbstbewußte Nation), Ullrich Schacht writes, "It is wrong to stigmatize the Germans with Auschwitz (and thus to misuse Auschwitz). Those who insist on doing so, normally use Auschwitz as a weapon to morally stigmatize those who think differently" (Schwilk and Schacht 1994: 66).

As a programmatic statement, Schacht's position reflects a general tendency in historical thinking of the New Right. The radical conservatives frame neonationalist interpretations of the Nazi past as a refreshing refusal to bow to "political correctness" and a supposedly dominant antifascist thought police in West Germany. Careful scrutiny of the rhetorical strategies of the writers for *Junge Freiheit* discloses how this neonationalism works. Incidental or tangential facts are tendentiously woven together to produce a historical representation that emphasizes the victimization of the German people during the war and stresses the atrocities committed by the Soviets and their Western allies. In a series of articles entitled "Fifty Years After," concerning the memory of World War II, the focus is almost entirely fixated on the suffering of German citizens on the home front and the brave actions of individual German soldiers, as if the Holocaust or other Nazi atrocities against civilians in occupied territories never existed.

In a story entitled "As the Dams Broke," Götz Meidinger discusses the British bombing offensives that began in May 1940: "It is a fact that the first air attack of residential areas in the heart of the enemy's country took place in the early hours of May 11, 1940, by the British royal airforce on Mönchengladbach" (1993: 19). He then describes another British air attack on a dam that was destroyed later during the war, with the result that 1,220 people and civilians were killed, including 718 forced laborers from the Soviet Union. The point of Meidinger's story is to prove that British bombing was militarily useless and "terrorist." By focusing on the suffering of innocent civilians, the author portrays the British as aggressors and the German civilians and Russian POWs as victims. A similar rhetorical strategy is used by Martin Schmidt in an article on a planned memorial statue for British air force general Arthur Harris. Schmidt asks if Harris isn't in fact a "war criminal," a man who was most responsible for a consistent strategy of attacking German cities and civilians instead of concentrating on military targets. Ostensibly out of hatred for Germans and to impress the Soviets, the British carried out "terror bombing" of practically every large German city, with the result of "hurting innocent people and destroying irreplaceable cultural artifacts" (Martin Schmidt 1991: 11). Without denying the fact that the destruction of cities like Dresden was tragic from a human, moral, and cultural point of view, placing German casualties at the center of the story reverses victim and victimizer. It was Hermann Göring's air force that used Blitzkrieg tactics in Poland in the fall of 1939 and began the Battle of Britain in the summer of 1940 by pounding British cities, initiating a practice that made demoralization of citizens a military goal.

The almost exclusive attention paid to the horror of war as experienced by German citizens plays on a number of interrelated levels of the collective memory of the war. As a shield against taking any responsibility for supporting the Hitler state, many Germans who experienced the war, later preferred to see themselves as victims rather than as passive bystanders or collaborators of a criminal regime. Faced with the overwhelming evidence of the atrocities committed by the Nazis, Germans, after the war, reacted by overemphasizing and thereby equating the atrocities committed by the Allies. In popular memory, the firebombing of Hamburg and Dresden and the murder of Polish officers at the hands of the Soviet secret police (Narodny Kommisariat Vnutrennikh Del [NKVD]) in Katyn are often used to support the contention that in war all sides commit equal crimes. The author and filmmaker Wolfgang Venohr even goes so far as to call the British attacks on Germany, beginning in 1942, a "holocaust":

> The German population, which in the next three years would suffer under a continuous holocaust of terror attacks and carpet bombing, the likes of which no other people had to withstand before, and during which 760,000 people, primarily women and children, died, showed a psychological steadfastness that not even the British were able to muster. With their air attacks, the Allies achieved only one thing: they welded the Germans and Hitler together. (Venohr 1992: 15)

Another example of confusing the essential with the peripheral is a story on Karl Dönitz, who is lauded for carrying on the war effort and refusing to join the resistance against Hitler, because as a "good soldier" he felt that it was in Germany's interests to "try and continue fighting as well as one could" (Meidinger 1991:

13). It hardly needs to be added that—from the perspective of the regime's victims—every day that Dönitz fought on as a "good soldier," the concentration camps and Gestapo terror were operating.

Rescuing certain figures of the Third Reich from the taint of ignominy is a regular feature of historical articles in the *Junge Freiheit*. Albert Leo Schlageter, for example, is portrayed by Hans-Ulrich Kopp as a conventional nationalist hero whose memory was distorted by the Nazis and postwar propaganda: "As an unbending fighter for the right of self-determination, he earned a place in the gallery of German ancestors, which can be blackened neither by the propaganda of the National Socialists, nor the propaganda of 'reeducation' " (1994: 18).

Finally, as the "Fifty Years After" memorials were filling up hours of television and hundreds of pages of newspaper print in the summer of 1995, the New Right historians launched an appeal "against forgetting" that sums up the method of inversion whereby the victimization of Germany is placed on the same moral plain as the Nazi war atrocities. The 8th of May was a paradox, the appeal reads, because on that day "we were redeemed and destroyed" at the same time. What has become forgotten, these historians tell us, is that

> this day was not only the end of the National Socialist regime of terror, but also was the beginning of a terror against the exiles in the East and the beginning of the separation of our country. A history that is silent represses or relativizes these truths cannot be the basis for the self-understanding of a self-conscious nation, which we Germans must become in the family of European nations, in order that comparable catastrophes are avoided. (*Junge Freiheit*, May 5, 1995, 16)

The Collision of History and Collective Memory

The one-sided focus on the experience of the Germans during the war did not come about in a historiographical vacuum. The growth of regional studies, microhistory, and grass roots history *(Alltagsgeschichte)* has given historians access to the authentic experiences of common people during the Third Reich, but it has also opened up new possibilities for researchers with political agendas to obscure the essential characteristics of the period. Although many grass roots studies of the Third Reich are legitimate, the danger always lurks of displacing the traditional political narrative, which could not avoid focusing on the Hitler state as racist, expansionist, and self-destructive in favor of so-called split consciousness, by which means the terror and oppression of the regime were ostensibly absent from everyday experience (Schäfer 1981).

Ernst Nolte's so-called phenomenological method, which claims to recapture the intentions and actions of historical actors as they experienced them, is a kind of neohistoricism that, when applied to the Third Reich, for example, carries the danger of elevating elements of the Nazi worldview to the status of a respectable political option. Nolte's often-repeated assertion, for example, that the German invasion of the Soviet Union in 1941 was a preemptive strike against the threat of a Stalinist attack, recapitulates exactly the propaganda that was drilled into young soldiers of the Wehrmacht. Hitler's army was trained to believe, in Omer Bartov's words, in an "inversion of reality": the pillaging, killing, and inhuman treatment perpetrated on Soviet citizens and prisoners of war by the Nazi war and terror apparatus were ascribed as a defense against subhuman Russians and Jewish Bolshevik barbarism (see Bartov 1992: 132 ff.).[20]

Historians of the Generation of 1989 like Rainer Zitelmann have taken the notion of split consciousness, with its inferred premise of normality, one step further, asserting that the Third Reich was actually a modernizing state that bequeathed to the FRG an array of industrial and social accomplishments with which to rebuild after 1945 (Zitelmann and Prinz 1991). In principle, there is nothing new about this thesis. Earlier social historians, such as David Schönbaum, also argued that Hitler's social policies led to a "double revolution": in order to enact the racist, archaic ideology of Nazism, Hitler's social revolution depended on concrete economic and political successes, which entailed concessions toward various classes and economic modernization (Schönbaum 1966). In Zitelmann's analysis, however, modernization is no longer merely an accompanying and unessential aspect of the regime but rather the embodiment of the intentions of the rulers.

The Future of the New Right

In the final analysis, the ideology, motivations, strategies, and rhetoric of the various groups in the New Right in Germany contain a mixture of old *völkisch* cultural traditions, historical relativism, populist nationalist identity rhetoric, and some genuinely challenging questions about Germany's past and future (see Schwagerl 1994). It would also not be fitting to view the New Right as the resurgence of a fascist threat to German democracy, nor would it be wise to pass the phenomenon off as a "normal" aspect of democratic politics.[21] The thematizing of issues such as immigration, an independent foreign policy, an authoritative state, the disadvantages of liberalism, the uniqueness of the Holocaust and so on does not immediately qualify as jack-booted Nazism and can also be observed in other states. On the other hand radical conservatism does not live easily with the mundane, consensus-building, compromising posture of traditional conservatism. The New Right has come into existence because it is dissatisfied with the status quo, meaning the Western and pan-European alliance, orientation, and assimilation of postwar (Western) Germany. But the ultraconservative Right is also discontented with elements of current liberal and pluralist democracy altogether. At the moment, it does not have a viable political party or a mass movement to put forward its program. Jörg Haider's Austrian Free Party (FPÖ) is the closest successful model that exists today.[22] Whether the German New Right can genuinely establish itself as a democratic voice of opposition to the right of the CDU or whether that terrain is so contaminated by the past and by shadowy ideologies and dubious, antidemocratic forces remains to be seen. Whether the emerging attitude of unapologetic and aggressively antiliberal, anti-Western politics contributes to a merely strengthened, albeit strident, national identity, as well as to a natural evolution in generational thinking, or whether the self-centered, nationalist, and in the end destructive politics of the ultraconservatives gains political clout and popular support, remains a lingering question as the just-awakened young and old ideologues of the New Right follow a united Germany briskly treading unforeseen and unaccustomed paths into the next century.

NOTES

1. On the worldview of members of the New Right, in particular their antiliberalism, etatism, sociobiology, and relativizations of the Holocaust, see Assheuer and Sarkowicz (1992: 139–215). For a good example of a pan-German political treatise by one of the New Right's leading intellectuals, see Schöllgen (1992).

2. The term *New Right* is a translation of the French term *Nouvelle Droite,* which is mainly associated with Alain de Benoist's project of a renewal of conservatism in France (see the discussion of Ethnopluralism below). There are at least three intellectual orientations in France: traditional legitimism, conservative revolutionism, and national liberalism (Pierre-André Taguieff). In Germany, the term loosely describes a network of newspapers, journals, think tanks, Internet discussion groups, publishing houses, and independent thinkers united only in the ubiquity of ideas and themes from the intellectual tradition of European conservatism and German radical conservatism. Richard Herzinger and Hannes Stein have argued, I think correctly, that because many of the individuals now considered part of the New Right began ideologically on the Marxist Left and because some of the German Left share certain aversions and dogmas with the New Right, the fault lines dividing liberal and antiliberal, pro-West and anti-West, pluralist and fundamentalist, and rational and apocalyptic better describe the current intellectual divisions in Germany. The Herzinger and Stein argument is convincing, though the amount of convergence between Left and Right is sometimes overstated (Herzinger and Stein 1995).

3. On the connection between today's New Right and the radical conservatives of the Weimar era, see Leggewie (1993). Some may question the inclusion of Heidegger in this list, but almost without exception, intellectual historians have characterized Heidegger as belonging to the philosophical radicals of his day and most would situate his ideas along the broad spectrum known as the Conservative Revolution. In an influential article published initially in French in Sartre's *Les Temps Modernes* in 1946, the Heidegger student Karl Löwith characterized his teacher's writings as "radically revolutionary" (1993: 174). Pierre Bourdieu, in a recent critically acclaimed study, situates Heidegger in relation to Ernst Jünger and Oswald Spengler as conservatives reacting to the extraordinary "revolutionary situation" *(Umsturzsituation)* of the post–World War I era. The result is that Heidegger has become a "conservative revolutionary in philosophy" (Bourdieu 1991: 56). Hans Sluga, in another authoritative reevaluation of Heidegger's politics, describes Heidegger, along with Alfred Bäumler and Ernst Krieck, as "philosophical radicals" in contrast to the old-guard "philosophical conservatives" of the Deutsche philosophische Gesellschaft of the 1920s and 1930s (Sluga 1993: 125–178; see also Neaman 1995).

4. See the collection of essays edited by Rainer Zitelmann, Karlheinz Weißmann, and Michael Grossheim (1993). In particular, see Zitelmann's article (Zitelmann 1993a).

5. The original Thule Society was founded before World War I by Rudolf von Sebottendorf, who used the swastika as his logo. After the war, the Thule Society became the political arm of the Deutscher Orden (German Order), which early on battled against the Weimar Republic and created a mass movement for antisemitic and small ultranationalist groups of every color and denomination. Pretending to be purely a study group interested in old Germanic languages and symbols, the Thule Society collected weapons, bought up

newspapers, practiced terrorist attacks, and preached antisemitism. Alfred Rosenberg, Rudolf Hess, and Dietrich Eckart were members of the society; essential elements of Nazi ideology, rituals, and symbols were anticipated by the Thule Society and the German Order.

6. Mark Terkessidis points out that, like Lorenz and Eysenck, whose neo-Darwinist biologism has racist undertones, Lévi-Strauss's concept of culture chimes in nicely with the position of ethnopluralists. In particular, Terkessidis points to Lévi-Strauss's articles "Race and Culture" and the section "Race and History" in his book *Structural Anthropology II*. See Terkessidis (1995: 50–63).

7. The literature on Carl Schmitt is already vast, though all the archival material is not yet available. For a good overview of the current debates; see the special issue, "Schmitt's Testament and the Future of Europe," *Telos* (Spring 1990).

8. For a good example of Schmitt's influence on the New Right, see Maschke's critique of the U.S. invasion of Iraq in 1991, which also appealed to many on the pacifist German Left (Maschke 1991).

9. The term *spiritual reactionaries* is used in Diedrich Diederichsen (1993). An English version of this article was also published in Diederichsen (1992).

10. "Anschwellender Bocksgesang" was reprinted in Schwilk and Schacht (1994) and includes reactions to Strauss from the intellectual Right.

11. For links between Holocaust "revisionism" and the radical conservative Right, see chapter 8. On the American revisionists and their influence on Holocaust deniers, see Lipstadt (1993).

12. This is most clearly stated in Weißmann (1993). Other important works in this vein are Mechtersheimer (1991) and Backes, Jesse, and Zitelmann (1990).

13. For a comprehensive overview of the history of the *Junge Freiheit,* see Kellershohn (1994a).

14. The biographical information is from Kellershohn (1994b).

15. From the Preamble of the constitution of the German fraternity, (Verfassung der deutschen Gildenschaft,) 1960, cited in Kellershohn (1994b: 67).

16. The *Junge Freiheit* runs regular advertisements from a group calling itself Unitas Germanica that describe the taking and plundering of Königsberg in April 1945 by Russian troops as a "Holocaust in Ostpreussen."

17. See, for example, Jakob Sprenger's coverage of the Zündel trial in Canada (1993: 18).

18. A good example is an article by Götz Meidinger describing, with evident Schadenfreude, how U.S. historians are in vast disagreement over the number of Jews killed at Babi-Jar, near Kiev, on September 29–30, 1941. Going beyond the statistical dispute, Meidinger compares Babi-Jar to Katyn, suggesting that like the latter, the Russians blamed the Germans for their own atrocities (1992: 27).

19. Samples from Thule-Netz on-line: "It is about time we started an archive on the crimes of the Jews." "Hello comrades, finally the invitation to the Rudolf Hess march 1993 has arrived. According to the arrangement made with Althans, I'm publishing the invitation here: the pseudodemocracy BRD made a martyr out of Hess by betraying him, and he should never be forgotten" (cited in Kellershohn 1994: 132.)

20. Brumlik, one of the most radical critics, accuses Nolte openly of unveiled antisemitism and sees in his work even the projection of a fascist dictatorship as a political option (see Brumlik 1995).

21. The 1,600 French intellectuals who signed an "Appeal to Vigilance" in the summer of 1993 are not convinced of the democratic intentions of the Nouvelle Droite. The document states: "These ideologues have tried for a long time to make us believe that they have changed. In order to achieve this goal, they have developed a seductive strategy aimed at

democratic celebrities and intellectuals, among whom many are known as coming from the Left. Because they are not informed about the activities or the net of extreme Right circles, or do not know these people, they let themselves get published in journals edited by these ideologues. These publications are then presented to the public as proof that the supposed metamorphosis has become reality."

This appeal first appeared in *Le Monde* on July 13 signed by Pierre Bourdieu, Jacques Derrida, and other notables, then resurfaced exactly a year later, signed by 1,600 other intellectuals. For a polemic against the appeal, see Adler (1993/94).

22. According to a recent analysis of extreme Right tendencies among German voters based on extensive questionnaires, an electoral potential definitely exists: 17% of German voters have a "relatively hardened extreme Right worldview," and 5% have "hard-core extreme Right views" (see Falter 1994: 156).

III

AMERICAN, JEWISH, AND GERMAN PERCEPTIONS OF AND REACTIONS TO ANTISEMITISM AND XENOPHOBIA

RAINER ERB

Public Responses to Antisemitism and Right-Wing Extremism

Antisemitic propaganda in the ultraright-wing press,[1] the increasing number of militant attacks on Jews and Jewish institutions since 1991 committed mainly by right-wing extremists (Erb 1994), motivational analyses of ultraright-wing voters, and attitude surveys (Bergmann and Erb 1991b, 1996) all serve to demonstrate the extent to which right-wing extremism and antisemitism are intertwined. The concentration of the splintered right-wing spectrum into two political parties has given antisemitism a new organizational base; a further increase in aggressive, antisemitic demonstrations can thus be expected. Furthermore, collective offenders cannot hide their opinions as well as individuals can; indeed, political parties need to express themselves publicly in fulfilling their function of shaping public opinion. This is why the long-term presence on the political stage of ultraright-wing parties is expected to bring with it an increase in the number of antisemitic scandals, especially since, as in the case of the "Republikaner" Party, their supporters exhibit the greatest density of antisemitic and right-wing extremist attitudes (Stöss 1993b, Falter 1994).

Despite these developments, researchers have paid little attention to society's reactions to antisemitism and right-wing extremism,[2] even though the success of such extremism is largely dependent on changes in basic structural conditions over time and the way in which society responds to the electoral success of right-wing parties.[3] Social processes affect every development phase of a movement, influencing its course, momentum, and direction (Bergmann and Erb 1994c). The only type of analysis that is able to adequately grasp the process nature of the escalation of ultraright-wing, xenophobic, and antisemitic actions is one that integrates social reactions as a constitutive element of the examination, taking into account the dynamic interactive relationships between democratic center and extremist periphery (see Backes and Jesse 1993, Jaschke 1994). An analysis of counterforces in society has been largely neglected, particularly in incident-related publications on right-wing extremism. This is why it is necessary to direct attention to the ways in which central political institutions and organs of social control deal with antisemitism and right-wing extremism. I will attempt to do this concentrating on four areas: the mainstream media, public protest, democratic political parties, and the justice system.

Inherent in the subject matter are a normative problem and a problem of democratic theory. First, in order to avoid a normative, voluntaristic point of view, an attempt will be made to interpret social responses from the perspective of their specific interactions. Thus, behavior should not be interpreted on the basis of preference for either correct (i.e., normatively expected) or incorrect (i.e., disappointing) actions, but on the basis of social interrelationships. Second, the concept of "no freedom for the enemies of freedom" within the scope of a militant democracy *(streitbare Demokratie)* leads to a democratic dilemma (see Michalka 1987). On the one hand this concept aims to assure that extremist efforts never again will gain the upper hand in Germany; on the other hand, it has to make sure that in defending itself the republic is not changed to such an extent that it begins to employ repressive and undemocratic means. The precautions against extremism laid down in the constitution and criminal code of the Federal Republic of Germany (FRG) are intended to strengthen internal security and political stability, but their application must comply with civil liberties, the constitutional dictates of appropriateness of means, and tactical considerations.

Media Reporting

Antisemitic scandals have to reach a certain level before they are recognized in the public as a social problem. Only then can political mobilization against antisemitism be achieved.[4] In Germany, the public debate about the danger and degree of antisemitism usually follows an antisemitic incident or an antisemitic statement by a public figure. Publicity is a stimulus to political action that politicians can hardly avoid. Because of Germany's National Socialist history, antisemitic incidents quickly become subjects of public debate.[5] Antisemitic incidents have the status of a taboo, and the public reacts very sensitively to its breach. The way the public in Germany explains, reacts to, and deals with antisemitism is determined by the fact that German history is intertwined and identified with Nazism and the Holocaust.[6] Those guilty of violating normative loaded issues by ignoring politically correct rules of interaction *(Sprachregelungen)* suffer a loss of both credibility and political support. Prominent public figures[7] who go too far by making antisemitic statements are usually pressured either to publicly dissociate themselves from their statements or to step down. The case of antisemitic statements made by the former ultraright-wing "Republikaner" Party leader Franz Schönhuber illustrates how the violation of taboos not only can hurt the image of a political party but also is used by other democratic parties to denounce their rivals and their leaders. In the case of Schönhuber, commentators of all political camps called for ostracism of the "Republikaner," demanding that the party be classified as right-wing extremist and hostile to the constitutional order, thereby prompting proceedings before the Federal Constitutional Court aimed at an official prohibition of the party.

Using theoretical labeling models, one can explain how media, parties, dominant groups, and so on, can define antisemitic rhetoric and action as "deviant" on the background of a common consensus and then deal accordingly with those subjected to such stigmatization (Lamnek 1994: 45 ff.). Negotiations on what is to be considered "deviant" in each case take place among the various factions within the stigmatizing majority, without direct participation of those stigmatized. The discussion that defines the social problem of antisemitism is closed to antisemites,[8] taking place instead among competitors in the defining process, that is, Jewish representatives, the press, politicians, and researchers.

News coverage of antisemitism, xenophobic violence, and right-wing extremism represents a conflict of goals for the media. On the one hand they report on violent groups of young people and right-wing extremist organizations in accordance with their duty to inform, thus documenting relevant incidents; on the other hand they lend these groups greater public visibility than they would normally receive considering their size, power, and public legitimacy and thus may encourage subsequent incidents and unwillingly mobilize potential supporters. Since particularly antisemitic incidents are considered to have great news value, the reports stand a very good chance of being published and even minor events almost inevitably become media attractions. The factors contributing to their becoming news items include degree of confrontation and provocation, use of violence, element of surprise, number of persons involved, actual or potential damage, negative impact of the event at home and abroad, and connection to other current issues and events.[9] The greater the news value, the greater the pressure on competing media to report on these issues too, simply in order to keep up with the competition. The logic of reporting based on violence and confrontation requires comprehensive coverage; the resulting dynamic process of feedback often inadvertently strengthens such behavior.[10] Adolescents and right-wing extremist leaders quickly learned that the use of violence and neo-Nazi provocation could bring them (worldwide) attention in the media and politics. When such behavior is successful—and receiving publicity per se is a form of success—it will more likely be maintained than discarded, and the probability of its occurrence rises. The negative bias of the coverage is secondary to the perpetrators; even critical and condemning reports are welcomed. The important thing is to be mentioned in the media, television being seen as most significant. Coverage thus internally legitimates and strengthens extremist groups and individuals and is credited as a triumph.[11]

But publicity has a twofold effect. On the one hand it may motivate and encourage perpetrators; on the other hand it can serve to provoke resistance by democratic citizens and a militant democracy. Important forms of radio and TV publicity are interviews and participation in talk shows. After scandalous, riotlike events in East and West Germany in the early 1990s, teams of reporters from all over the world traveled to the scenes in search of "real right-wing extremist offenders" to interview for the sake of authenticity. Such interviews are extremely harmful to efforts to dismantle extremist attitudes and behavior. In the process of defining deviant roles, the interviewees attain and strengthen a self-image and public status that does not necessarily exist to such an extreme degree outside of the interview situation. Participation on talk shows has great publicity value, creating a media career for the person involved. Editorial offices have now recognized this advertising and mobilization effect, however, and, following a critical debate on the issue in Germany, have increasingly stopped inviting right-wing extremist politicians, musicians, and journalists to speak on their shows since mid-1993.

News coverage can generally be said to be incident-related. Because reporting only deals with specific time-related events, the complex long-term origins and causes of events tend to be neglected. Even individual chains of events are not covered completely.[12] Moreover, since antisemitism is by no means a perpetual media issue, no journalistic specialization has emerged in this area. Thus, when new incidents are appraised, knowledge of previous events, their context, and prior experience in dealing with such occurrences is lacking.

Public Protest

Motivated by the wave of xenophobic violence and the success of right-wing parties in elections, numerous informal grass roots organizations and activities emerged in Germany that were dedicated to tolerance, protection of refugees, and fighting racism. These were impressive signals, showing the right-wing mob that it represented only a tiny minority doomed to political failure.[13] The antiracist coalition ranged from professional associations (e.g., pharmacists and physicians) to artists, athletes, business people, and academics. It included financial, business, and cultural institutions such as the Deutsche Bank and the Deutsche Oper, as well as activities of local administrations and citizens' groups. To a large degree the protest and its organizers developed spontaneously, was situation-related, and was disbanded after a short phase of activity. For modern pluralistic individualistic societies with middle-class, private interests, and freedom from obligatory social participation, it is, indeed, structurally difficult to mobilize the public on specific issues. This is one reason for the somewhat delayed start of mass protests against violence in unified Germany. Specialists—that is, groups specializing in opposition to right-wing extremism and racism (such as the Left), organizations dealing with the concerns of foreigners, segments of the trade unions and the churches, antifascist organizations, Jewish communities, and so on—protested immediately and repeatedly, predominantly in major cities. However, it was not until well-known, politically neutral journalists and artists started dedicating their cultural capital to the organization of protest actions (such as candlelight vigils, "Rock against the Right" concerts, etc.) that large numbers of people went out onto the streets to demonstrate peacefully in mass rallies against hate and violence. Millions of people participated in the candlelight vigils in order to show that the violent criminals could not base their actions on their Germanness by using slogans like "Germany for the Germans! Foreigners get out!" and that they were mistaken if they thought their political crusade against foreigners expressed the general will of the German public. The demonstrators wanted to correct this assumption, refusing to be drawn into the atrocious actions or thought of as silent accomplices.

The public's demands sent signals that were interpreted and reinforced in the media by sympathetic journalists (gatekeepers and multipliers). However, in the end it was the fact that the public felt incapable of taking individual action that led to demonstrations and protests that instigated a political debate. The government, in particular, was accused of not taking up the public's wishes, the latter of which the electronic media[14] had been publicizing for months, thereby also helping to organize public opinion and shape pro-immigrant action groups. But in the debates on the so-called asylum compromise, even the opposition Social Democratic Party failed to take advantage of the broad-based support and favorable timing to reform not only the asylum law but also citizenship, naturalization, and immigration regulations and improve the protection of immigrant minorities through detailed antidiscrimination legislation (see Kurthen and Minkenberg 1995). The delayed and somewhat cautious response of the political class to the challenges of immigration and right-wing violence was due to the self-induced counterproductive fact that in 1991–92, the government had led a large-scale, aggressive campaign against the abuse of the very liberal right of political asylum by so-called economic refugees. In multiparty democracies, the instrumentalization of xenophobia and ethnocentrism in one or the other way appears to be a reliable tool of last resort for conservative parties to appeal to disgruntled voters. Politicians must have firmly rooted moral convictions to withstand the temptation to take this path (see Thränhardt 1993).

Although hostility toward asylum seekers and foreigners was politically instrumentalized by mainstream democratic parties,[15] only ultraright-wing parties have used antisemitism (albeit unsuccessfully) in an attempt to gain votes and popular support. The democratic parties have learned the historical lesson that antisemitism should not in any case be tolerated or exploited for political gain. They are persistent, however, in their refusal to apply this insight with the same clarity to other minorities—in this case, immigrants and refugees—and to reject any expression of xenophobia, hatred, and prejudice against minority groups within their own ranks.

It is doubtful whether state institutions on all levels, from which action is often first demanded, are indeed capable of taking appropriate action. The federal government has declared its underlying view of society time and time again—namely, that "Germany is not a country of immigration." This description, which belies the facts, hinders any long-term integrative policy toward long-term foreign residents and their offspring born in Germany. Democrats have succeeded in dissociating themselves from xenophobic positions at the cost of partial agreement with antiimmigration demands—that is, no changes in the social and legal policy toward foreign nationals. Even the debate on the problematic concept of *nation* has been used to deny immigrants the right of full political participation and easy access to citizenship, in contrast to a world characterized by increasing transnational mobility (see Hoffmann 1994: 46 ff.).

When somewhat contradictory preferences are expressed by politicians—for example, "Germany is not a country of immigration" but "Germany is friendly to foreigners"—this ambiguity provides occasions and motives for extremists to propagate their versions of a nonimmigration Germany. Simple right-wing slogans such as "Germany for the Germans" are good examples of how extremists use ambiguous public declarations of democrats for their own purposes. Xenophobic resentment can count on the legitimacy of inconsistent official policies of democrats. Xenophobia is not just a regrettable psychological trait or deviation of some individuals that can be explained by human nature.

Responses among Political Parties

Federal and state governments and established democratic political parties have repeatedly voiced their willingness to take active measures to fight right-wing extremism, antisemitism, and xenophobic violence.[16] The democratic parties are dedicated to the fight against extremism, but it is a paradoxical task. They may fight political rivals, but they must also pay a certain amount of attention to the attitudes and resentments of their own supporters. By distinguishing between more or less unconstitutional ultraright-wing parties and their protest voters, democrats have created a bridge facilitating the reintegration of right-wing voters. Because the behavior of right-wing voters at the polls is perceived as a disruption of the legitimate democratic order and stability, efforts are made to reintegrate right-wing voters. They are asked to voluntarily resume voting for a democratic party. To facilitate this "homecoming," democratic parties use a political rhetoric that incorporates some right-wing issues into their political agenda, thereby blurring the boundary between extremists and democrats. On the other hand such a tactic makes it easier for established democratic parties to keep voters that sympathize with right-wing slogans (see Herz 1991). However, functionaries and dedicated members of right-wing parties (the so-called uneducable) are not included in this voter recovery strategy. The latter are excluded step-by-step and forced onto the fringes of society via political stigmatization, administrative controls,[17] repression, and criminal justice.

Instead of a collective, public discussion about the origins and causes of antisemitism, xenophobia, and right-wing extremism, institutions of social control respond with professional technical-coping mechanisms. One can observe an increasing police role in the struggle against right-wing extremism. Both the problem itself and the solution to the problem are thus limited to individual acts; professional specialists deal with a social problem on behalf of the society as a whole.

Extremists react to this growing pressure by either becoming politically inconspicuous or joining together to confront the threat, declaring their deviant behavior a virtue and creating an alternative morality with corresponding interpretations to justify a resistance campaign based on the principle of counterjustice. They challenge repression, calling it the negation of justice or the "unmasking of the pseudodemocracy," which must be resisted.[18] These countermaneuvers also are used to justify resentment against certain groups and allegedly "supranational powers." Jews in particular are easy scapegoats for extremists. They are suppos- edly "pulling the strings." The external and invisible conspirators of "international Jewry" exert tangible power over politicians and (television) journalists, bringing disaster to "nationally conscious Germans." Such conspiracy theories perpetuate familiar interpretation patterns of threat and conflict; extremist violence and re- sentment is legitimized as self-defense of innocent victims against powerful ene- mies. The extremist energy is directed outward, toward the core of the conspiracy and its helpers. Antisemitic conspiracy theories satisfy this pattern very well and have become more popular in ultraright-wing literature than they have been for years. This has had a paradoxical impact: the stronger right-wing extremists expe- rience social ostracism, the greater they perceive the presence of "the Jews!" [19]

Actions of democratic parties against right-wing rivals are limited by constitu- tional and democratic standards and are clearly influenced by tactical considera- tions. International protests, Germany's fear of losing face abroad, concerns about the country's economic competitiveness, and the fact that 1994 was an election year all contributed to the fact that democratic political parties issued firm declara- tions of right-wing incompatibility with constitutional values. All democratic par- ties also refused publicly to cooperate with the "Republikaner" Party. Also, the Federal Office for the Protection of the Constitution classified the "Republikaner" as a right-wing extremist party in December 1992,[20] and there have also been calls for a ban on the party. This was not always the case in years past. The establish- ment of the "Republikaner" Party was sometimes seen as a normalization of the party spectrum, and the party was viewed as a potential coalition partner of the CDU/CSU. Even today there are some conservative, right-wing Christian Demo- crat politicians who hold onto such ideas.[21]

The isolation of the "Republikaner" Party on local and state levels had a deci- sive impact during more than a dozen national and state elections in 1993–94. The social inhibitions against voting for the "Republikaner" have increased, and right- wing party officials in public service are being warned not to deviate from disci- plinary standards. Such symbolic sanctions have clearly demonstrated the political ineptitude of the "Republikaner" Party's activists, restrained their activities in the ultraright-wing milieu, and created public awareness of the incompetence of right- wing representatives in the European and state parliaments. Furthermore, scandals involving the "Republikaner" and tactical mistakes of the party leadership have damaged their image. In order to direct public attention in his favor following the arson attack on the synagogue in Lübeck on March 25, 1994, Franz Schönhuber, the then "Republikaner" Party head, verbally attacked Ignatz Bubis, head of the Central Council of Jews in Germany, calling him "one of the worst inciters of racial hatred" and accusing him of being responsible for the spread of antisemit- ism. The political and media response to this attack was consistently negative, showing a degree of rejection that had never been expressed in Germany in re- sponse to similar slanderous attacks.[22] All of these measures, actions, and re- sponses led to the demise of the "Republikaner" Party after 1992. Public opinion surveys show a steady decline in voters' support of the "Republikaner" at the end of 1993 (from approximately 3% to 2%, then down to 1% in August 1994). Only an extremist core is still interested in voting for the "Republikaner." Schönhuber's aggressive statements against Jewish representatives are certainly not the only factor responsible for his party's drop in popularity, but they can definitely be assumed to play some role. The waning prospects of the "Republikaner" at the polls clearly show that the debate over immigration and political asylum between 1990 and 1993 was the central issue of protest. Once political institutions of the democratic mainstream proved capable of taking action in these areas, voters were no longer willing to support the program and political goals of right-wing extremists.

It is increasing political pressure, however, that has triggered an undesirable side effect: ultraright extremists have been forced to put aside rivalries and animosities within their own camp, making agreements, forming defensive coalitions, and reforming action alliances. Even neo-Nazis are once again becoming more palatable in the so-called nationalist camp. New methods of networking by extremists via electronic communications make monitoring more difficult, requiring greater shows of strength by the state during public appearances, such as the annual Rudolf Hess memorial march.

The Legal System

Antisemitism is perceived by German society as a breach of rules. It is relatively easy to exert social control in this case because the issue is not the making of rules but the carrying out of already existing, sanctioned ones. There is little desire to reach any consensus with the violator of the rules, and the authorities' legitimacy in such instances is very high. In public opinion surveys, right-wing extremists and antisemites are among the most unpopular groups.[23] There is public support for the courts and police to apprehend, prosecute, and convict violent right-wing extremists and antisemites. Institutions of social control are subjected to severe criticism if their investigations are not carried out speedily or if there is public disagreement with their judgment, justification, or supposedly inaction. The public, both within and outside Germany, are third parties observing the legal proceedings, verifying their correctness, determining how much discretion will be allowed, and setting areas of emphasis.

One simple reason that crimes motivated by antisemitism are clearly being followed up more vigorously and are generally made public immediately, is the fact that information about such incidents is prioritized in authorities' internal communications. It is now directly passed on to the responsible ministers of the interior or mayors, who then declare the incidents top priority, instruct the police, and issue press releases that express outrage at such "disgraceful antisemitic or xenophobic acts." German law regarding political crimes aims to keep everyday politics free of any form of National Socialist and antidemocratic organization and propaganda.[24] The laws are oriented, first of all, toward the prohibition of such political parties and organizations, including use of any right-wing symbols or uniforms, and second against racism, antisemitism, and historical revisionism. They are generally considered adequate.[25]

Public opinion about the legitimacy of criminal prosecution of antisemitism and neo-Nazism cannot be assessed with precision for the past because no systematic polls or analyses of relevant criminal trials exist as yet. But a shift in opinion is observable. Mild treatment of perpetrators of right-wing motivated crimes by the courts at the beginning of the xenophobic wave in 1990–91 quickly led to accusations from the public that the justice system was "blind in the right eye"—that is, that judges sympathized with opinions of the offenders. In fact, the opposite is more likely the case. Most of the present generation of judges are liberal and skeptical about the effectiveness of deterrence that amounts to nothing more than punishment. Judges make use of the insights of modern criminology and a reformed justice system that has proclaimed penal reform as its aim—a reform that generally mistrusts traditional penal methods and long sentences without taking into account efforts toward rehabilitation. In particular, juvenile justice, which gives priority to education over punishment, is regarded as the cornerstone of this reform. Long sentences are only considered desirable if a realistic criminal profile exists.[26]

Nevertheless, the causes and significance attributed by the public to acts of violence have changed. Pogromlike riots are no longer perceived as the actions of frustrated or bored adolescents but are defined as crimes. This new perception is now associated with the idea that a perpetrator responsible for a crime should be charged as guilty and held accountable for his or her act. By being held responsible, punishment is more legitimate than someone not held accountable, such as an intoxicated hooligan. In fact, in the years after 1990, the prosecution of politically motivated violent crimes has been better enforced and punishment has been more severe. In other words, the costs of such deviance are increasing.[27] In 1992, over 12,000 preliminary proceedings were initiated; in 1993, the figure rose to over 23,000; in the first quarter of 1994, there were 4,163.[28]

The activities of right-wing extremists also provide an impetus to adapt the criminal code to new developments.[29] The international dimension is of particular significance here. National law encounters barriers when right-wing extremists become part of an international network and exploit differences in legislation in other European countries and abroad. In the FRG, ultraright-wing propaganda has often encountered decisive barriers when extremist or revisionist authors were not able to find places to publish their propaganda. For this reason, criminal and offensive material is now more frequently printed outside the country, and propaganda centers are being relocated beyond Germany's borders. In this way, right-wing extremists avoid the publication ban as well as criminal prosecution in Germany. Although modern communications techniques (e.g., electronic mailboxes and cellular telephones) can be monitored domestically, albeit at considerable expense, it is very simple and inexpensive to set up a mailbox in Poland or Denmark, thereby evading the German justice system. Nationally oriented criminal prosecution is seriously threatened in view of the international right-wing extremist network.

Summary

The perspective of the justice system focuses on the deviant individual as the source of a crime or offense, whereas the social sciences consider a causal relationship or interaction between individual and society responsible for the emergence of deviant attitudes and behavior. Accordingly, problem-solving intervention into social relationships must follow. In the end, some sociological criticism expresses doubt as to whether political authorities and institutions of social control are capable of adequately responding to violence, right-wing extremism, and antisemitism at all because institutions are themselves part of a causal chain that leads to prejudice and violence (Heitmeyer 1994a: 11). Consequently, such social criticism in Germany now focuses more on extremism at the center rather than on extremism at the margins of society. But such theoretical approaches do not relieve society as a whole from its responsibility to take care of its extremists and processes of radicalization. Aside from the question whether such theory is consistent and empirically valid, such deterministic social criticism lacks a practical purpose. Reasons for how it came to be may be reconstructed, but they provide no guidelines on where to go from here and what to do with those who have been apprehended and adjudicated for deviant extremist behavior.

The course taken in response to antisemitism is typically a confrontational one. Usually, it is not the antisemitism itself that is in dispute but the identification of its origins, the assessment of its threat to society, and the appropriateness of countermeasures. Such measures are most often limited to educational recommendations and symbolic political acts through which the norm of anti-antisemitism is reconfirmed and strengthened. The often-criticized ineffectiveness of such appeals is to some extent due to the fact that on the one hand fighting antisemitism is not a private matter and on the other hand society does not have any institution[30] specifically empowered to educate and dismantle prejudices. There is no appropriate organization or occupational group to deal with such problems, employing professional problem-solving strategies, and serving as a social advocate, a communication and negotiation partner for politics, ministerial administrations, and any others concerned with the issue. The social problem of antisemitism or xenophobia is thus passed on to established task-related systems such as political and social education, the schools, and the justice system, all of which deal with the issue as one of many tasks to carry out, after first making internal decisions as to what is socially appropriate and objectively justified. Due to insufficient organization, capabilities, and the prevailing public individualism, the appeal to every man and woman to stand up against right-wing extremism and antisemitism gradually loses its strength. Media interest and sensationalist reports decline and social institutions return to their task-specific routines until new scandals or violence demand renewed attention.

NOTES

Translated from German by Allison Brown.

1. The "Auschwitz lie" is a major focus of such literature. On its prevalence, see Landesamt für Verfassungsschutz Berlin (1994) and chapter 8.
2. Scientists often do not draw specific conclusions from their research but instead make

general recommendations, based on everyday experience, regarding politics and education (see Bergmann 1988).

3. The "Republikaner" Party was supported by 5% of the respondents in the surveys of November 1993; in the 1994 election year, it had a voter share of up to 15% according to the Institut für Demoskopie Allensbach (cited in *Die Tageszeitung,* November 24, 1993). However, the "Republikaner" actually received only 1.9% of the vote in the Bundestag elections of October 1994.

4. On media impact, see Bergmann (1994b); for a case study of a well-meaning but unsuccessful talk show, see Schröder and Tykwer (1994).

5. Robert Goldmann, the European representative of the Anti-Defamation League of B'nai B'rith, wrote in an Anti-Defamation League memorandum of September 1, 1994: "It is this continuing process of coming to grips with the burden of history that has provided greater opportunities for Jews to find allies in Germany in fighting against discrimination and bigotry than in other countries."

6. Works on the subject of antisemitism often refer back to the Nazi persecution of the Jews. This is succinctly expressed by the slogan "Wehret den Anfängen!" (Nip this in the bud, or literally, Fight the beginnings!). A majority of the population identifies right-wing extremism with Nazism. Whether or not this fixation is justified; it forms a strong taboo against the Right wing. For example, according to a Forsa poll in May 1994, 74% of the population supported fully or to some extent the statement, "Today's right-wing radicals in Germany want the same thing that the Nazis did" (Forsa 1994).

7. This includes, for example, politicians as well as historians (e.g., Ernst Nolte), writers (e.g., Hans-Jürgen Syberberg), and artists (e.g., Alfred Hrdlicka).

8. The media career of former head of the "Republikaner" Party, Franz Schönhuber, as a television talk show host in Bavaria came to an abrupt end when he proved to be better prepared than the journalists interviewing him. Schönhuber appeared on television least often of all politicians, in terms of number of appearances and total time, although he benefited during the 1994 election year from the constitutional guarantee in article 3 of the Federal Basic Law that all legal political parties must be equally treated (*Der Spiegel* 1994: 29).

9. Besides violence and ideology, another phenomenon also brings media attention: warlike skinheads and neo-Nazis (shaved heads, boots, uniforms, flags, paramilitary marches, etc.) are a photogenic image, easy to convey visually. The aesthetics of photographic reporting also sets an example for imitators worldwide.

10. The waves of violence in recent years (e.g., the severe rioting in Rostock in August 22–28, 1992) clearly show the connection between an event, its dissemination through the mass media, and the resulting series of subsequent incidents.

11. Statement by a neo-Nazi in 1992: "Any publicity is motivation for us. You don't get a reputation without publicity."

12. For example, the desecration of the Jewish cemetery in Leipzig in December 1992, including graffiti like "Adolf lives, Sieg Heil" and "Jew, perish," was reported in detail, whereas reports virtually ignored the fact that residents cleaned the gravestones, the city hired three stonemason companies to restore the overturned gravestones, and all damage to the cemetery was repaired within days. See *Frankfurter Rundschau,* December 22, 1992, including an announcement by the Jewish Community of Leipzig.

13. The streets never belonged to right-wing extremists. Only up to 2,000 supporters could be mobilized at any one time. However, up to 300,000 people participated in demonstrations protesting right-wing extremism.

14. After several right-wing extremist organizations were banned and after the mass demonstrations in November–December 1992 in Berlin, Cologne, Munich, Hamburg, Frankfurt

am Main, and elsewhere, a change in media coverage could be observed; for the first time since the outbreak of a wave of violence in 1991, there was more extensive coverage of actions *against* racism than of attacks and violent crimes themselves.

15. Unfortunately, representatives of all democratic parties have made statements such as, "Asylum seekers are welfare spongers."

16. For example, Brandenburg's state minister of the interior Alwin Ziel stated: "Right-wing extremists don't have a chance in the state of Brandenburg! This is the position of the state government" (*Soko ReGa* 1993: 5). The senator for internal affairs in Bremen, Friedrich von Nispen, declared: "The Senate of the Free Hanseatic City of Bremen will use all available constitutional means to fight right-wing extremism. A number of measures are being passed to proscribe it socially" (foreword to Senator für Inneres 1993). Of course, these selected statements do not address the difference between the goal and its implementation. However, such political commitment becomes a question of political credibility, and this commitment can be used to judge a state's actions.

17. Newly founded parties are obligated to submit a certain number of signatures along with their election proposal. This rule ensures that there is at least a minimum of support for a new party among the population. Also, local agencies tend to refuse right-wing parties access to meeting places and arrange media blackouts of their public party activities. Nevertheless, if right-wing parties receive at least 5% of all votes in an election and are able to send elected representatives to the Landtag (State Assembly), other rules of representation in parliamentary committees serve as obstacles to gaining access to publicity, power, and influence.

18. Right-wing extremists are organizing this campaign, using the slogan, "Where right becomes wrong, resistance becomes a duty."

19. The following is a recent example. An ultraright-wing "press office" in Bingen, a city on the Rhine River, announced the publication of an information pamphlet in the winter of 1994–95 that traces so-called manipulated attacks, locating the "responsible ones pulling the strings in a demimonde where Stasi, Mossad, and West German government agents work hand in glove with each other. . . . Attacks for which German 'right-wing radicals' have been receiving the blame for decades have more than once been planned and perfectly carried out by officials in the 'antifascist' SED [East German communist] state. Television stations throughout the world, in the battle for audience ratings, pay hard cash for violence and 'Sieg Heil' chants. 'Foreign citizens' set their own businesses on fire for the generous insurance spoils awaiting them, Orthodox Jews vandalize Mosaic cemeteries personally, and in their free time, so-called antifascists and suntanned guest workers from southern Europe decorate their homes with swastikas" (leaflet in the archive of the Research Center on Anti-Semitism, Technische Universität Berlin).

20. The decision by the Federal Office for the Protection of the Constitution also created suspicion among members and potential followers of the "Republikaner" Party, which functioned as an additional sanction. Furthermore, the latent threat of a party ban signalizes to fellow travelers a state commitment and activates the potential to impose penalties without actually doing so.

21. The CDU/CSU politicians Heinrich Lummer and Max Streibl met with Schönhuber on various occasions. For both politicians, this had negative consequences, and they had to forfeit their high party positions.

22. See the recent debate on antisemitism as Schönhuber's political strategy initiated by the CDU parliamentary party of the state legislature (Landtag von Baden-Württemberg 1994).

23. In a December 1992 poll measuring social distance of socially stigmatized groups like drug addicts, alcoholics, immigrants, left-wing radicals, Jews, and so on, right-wing

extremists were rejected most frequently as neighbors by 77% of West Germans and 79% of East Germans (see Institut für Demoskopie 1992b).

24. The display of the German Imperial War Flag (Reichskriegsflagge), often used by right-wing groups at demonstrations, has been outlawed as "disturbing public peace" in 9 of 16 federal states. According to the law, the display is not a criminal act, but its use is judged to be a detriment to civic coexistence.

25. See the only extensive analysis on criminal proceedings against the Right in Kalinowsky (1993). Empirical research on antiracist efforts in the police and the military is just as inadequate (see Jaschke 1994).

26. In 1991–92, of all suspects in xenophobic crimes, 75% were younger than 20 years old and about 90% were younger than 25 (Willems 1993: 110).

27. The percentage of solved criminal cases has continued to increase: in 1994, approximately 70% of violent crimes were solved and about 18% of arson cases were solved, a considerably lower figure due to the nature of the crime (see Bundesminister des Innern 1994: 91).

28. Press release of the German Federal Ministry of Justice in Bonn, June 1994.

29. This was the position of the former liberal federal minister of justice, Sabine Leutheusser-Schnarrenberger (1994).

30. There is no organization in the FRG comparable to the Association for Resistance to Antisemitism (Verein zur Abwehr des Antisemitismus) of the Weimar Republic or to the Anti-Defamation League in the United States. This task should not be considered the responsibility of the Jewish community; instead, it lies in the well-understood self-interest of the majority of society. A democratic society that does not attack its prejudices and lets them penetrate the foundation of its politics destroys itself.

ANNA J. MERRITT AND RICHARD L. MERRITT

Berlin's Jews after Unification

Challenges to Community

"Something there is," Robert Frost told us, "that doesn't love a wall." Westerners were quick to cite this image when in August 1961 East Germans built walls that split their country and its capital city, Berlin, between East and West. It was cited again almost three decades later when the socialist German Democratic Republic (GDR) broke these walls open. The image was apt. However, to the surprise of many Germans and non-Germans alike, the removal of cinder blocks and barbed wire did not lead back immediately and easily to a prewall existence. Indeed, the end of the Berlin Wall exacerbated a number of problems facing Germany and even led to new and problematic divisions. Berliners in particular quickly realized that a new integration of East and West Germany would be difficult to achieve after Germans had lived for four decades in separate, hostile political systems.

Berlin's Jews no less than their gentile neighbors were stunned by the turn of events. What happened demonstrated once again that communities are far from immune to the unanticipated and variable impact of social change. It also reminded us that external structures and processes, as well as isolated events operating outside the community can help determine what that community can become and what it will do.

Social change from without has strongly shaped the character and behavior of Berlin's Jewish community[1] both before and after the transformation of 1989. East or West, for instance, the Holocaust's enduring presence has plagued Jewish community members. Merely having survived the death camps did not guarantee them either popular acceptance in postwar Germany or a trouble-free life. On the contrary, German Jews must continuously perform, must bear witness to the authenticity of the past, for their gentile audiences and also for their fellow Jews. This means repeatedly and sometimes publicly coming to terms with their own past and often explaining how they can possibly live in the land that spawned the Holocaust. Jews and their communities in postwar West Germany were an ever-present reminder of guilt and the need for reparation.

Dealing with the past and the reality of social change has been but one challenge confronting German Jews. Another comprises the traumas of subtle as well as overt antisemitism. Not long after the "velvet revolution" of 1989, a new danger swept through Germany: a resurgent xenophobia replete with hate crimes, swastikas daubed on Jewish gravestones, Nazi symbols and slogans, racial violence, and new groups espousing extreme right-wing sentiments. Such developments were, most assuredly, not unique to Germany. And German governments, churches and other social institutions, and private citizens stood up to defend the victims and excoriate the perpetrators. Nevertheless, Germany, with its dismal record of genocide, bore the brunt of the world's alarm and scorn.

Berlin Jews understood, perhaps too well for their own mental well-being, that right-wing extremism and xenophobic outbursts, targeted initially at asylum seekers and foreign workers but soon bearing antisemitic overtones, endangered their individual and communal security. But political, religious, and other groups both at home and abroad ensure that the world is aware of and can help fend off new assaults. The nature and consequences of such extraordinary and threatening circumstances originating outside of the Jewish community are the subject of several chapters in this volume.

Beyond such exogenous events, which jeopardize Jewish security, there are important endogenous events that deserve our attention: normal processes initiated within the Jewish community that change it. Why, Jews and gentiles alike have asked, did the Nazis find it so easy to deport and slaughter the Jews? A common response, one that became dogma in postwar West Berlin's Jewish community, was that their own disunity kept them from mounting a successful defense. Jews, this perspective says, were so busy competing and squabbling with each other that they could not attend to the dangers from outside. Conclusion? It follows that the Jewish community has an absolute imperative: Jews must eschew dissension, divisiveness, and divisions lest they be exposed once again to their enemies.

Not unexpectedly, then, West Berlin Jews saw the transformation of 1989 as a golden opportunity to expand their integrative network within the entire city. This network enabled local Jewish leaders to realize a self-imposed mission hearkening back to earlier days: to create for the first time since 1869 a united Jewish community in Berlin. This united community would enhance its members' social integration as Jews, and hence their own self-realization, and protect Jewish society as a whole. But, as we shall see, events conspired against the integrators. Indeed, Berlin's Jewry seems to be headed toward a threshold of enervating conflict that could severely damage not only the mission but the community as a whole. This chapter addresses this proposition of internal conflict by exploring two dimensions of changing Jewish life in post-1989 Berlin: reforming the structure of Jewish communal life in united Berlin; and defusing the approaching population time bomb that threatens the community itself.

Uniting Jews in Berlin

Although Jews reached Berlin as early as 1295, seven decades after the city's existence was first documented, an organized Jewish community did not develop until 1671. The Jewish Community of Berlin (Jüdische Gemeinde zu Berlin [JCoB]), as it came to be called, thrived in a generally tolerant environment and grew from 3,000 members in 1812 to 24,000 a half century later and 173,000 in 1925.

National Socialists did their best to destroy the JCoB as well as every other form of Jewish life in Germany and elsewhere. They created a National Representation of the Jews in Germany (Reichsvertretung der Juden in Deutschland), which, among other things, sought to co-opt Jewish communities into the service of the Third Reich and to encourage the eventual transfer of Jews to a Zionist homeland (Nicosia 1991). It was replaced in 1939 by the National Association of the Jews in Germany (Reichsverband der Juden in Deutschland), which dissolved all Jewish communal bodies and provided for the confiscation of Jewish property (Kulka 1979). In 1939, all such communal bodies disappeared as legal entities.

Only days after the European phase of World War II ended, Berlin Jews, with the help of Germany's foreign occupiers, set about reconstructing their religious life. December 1945 saw the formal creation of the new Jewish Community of Greater Berlin.[2] Its first years were rocky. The city's 6,556 Holocaust survivors differed on major issues: how to marshal their social forces, how to guarantee the security of both individual Jews and their communities, and how to select new leaders. Differences notwithstanding, on one point the emerging leaders were virtually unanimous: the need for Jewish unity. An earlier splintering of Berlin's Jewry, they thought, had been a cause of their people's fate under Nazism. For example, it was imperative that the JCoB provide its members with Orthodox as well as Reformed services. West Berlin's government for its part felt quite comfortable dealing with and responding to a single—and hierarchically structured— Jewish community. Such symbiosis strengthened a community of fate among Berlin's Jews and gentiles.

One of the architects of unified Jewry, Heinz Galinski, was elected in June 1950 to preside over the JCoB's board of directors. For more than four decades, until he died in July 1992, Galinski acted promptly and forcefully to prevent any new splintering of his community. A hard-line anti-Communist, he also staunchly maintained that the GDR had acted illegally in 1952 when it instructed eastern communities to separate from their western counterparts.[3] This stance ensured that in any eventual German unification, East German Jewish communities would "return" to their "natural" home in the West. But Galinski's enduring leadership position and increasingly dogmatic style had multiple effects. Cold War pressures and Galinski's own forceful personality made it difficult to contest his emphasis on unity. An abating Cold War nevertheless raised questions about the alleged evils of pluralism, and years of squelching those who did not share his views added strength to his critics' complaints.[4]

Indicative of Galinski's leadership style was his response to East Germany's breakdown after the fall of the Berlin Wall on November 9, 1989. Complete German unification, he said, would not serve Jewish interests. He was, of course, not alone in this view. Around the world important Jewish and non-Jewish intellectuals and political leaders also voiced their concern about, if not their opposition to, the reemergence of a single German state. But Galinski soon saw the writing on the wall. Irrespective of what isolated voices at home or abroad desired, the German people, East and West alike, wanted unification and were willing to pay a high price to get it. Galinski bowed to what was becoming inevitable. There remained no doubt in his mind, however, about the future of East Germany's Jewish community. As rapidly as possible, he wanted the JCoB locally and the CCJG nationally to incorporate their eastern brothers and sisters.[5]

The corporate takeover staged in 1990—in which about 180 East Berlin JC/B members led by their president, Peter Kirchner,[6] were swallowed up by over 6,000 West Berlin JCoB members—had some unexpected consequences. The East Berlin community had reached an almost paralyzed state in which it was dominated by leaders trying to keep it on an even keel, comfortable with its geriatric members who did not want change, and, although agreeing on the need to attract young Jews, unsure how such needed change might be brought about. On more than one occasion Galinski and Kirchner had also crossed swords. Thus the merger, effective on January 1, 1991, saw not Kirchner but Hans Rotholz, a more pliable easterner, co-opted to serve on the unified JCoB board of directors.

The Jewish Cultural Association

Impetus for change in the East came from outside of the JC/B. Formal community membership in early 1989 stood at 360 in the whole of the GDR, with half in East Berlin. In addition, an unknown number, perhaps 3,000 of unaffiliated Jews lived in eastern Germany. Many were Communists and intellectuals who had forsaken the synagogue, or, indeed, Judaism itself, in favor of a new political faith. Their children grew up with, at best, a tenuous relationship to their Jewish heritage. Some learned only from outsiders that their families had Jewish backgrounds and others had participated in services during the High Holidays, but few had a clear notion of what it meant to be Jewish, especially in a country whose former leaders had fashioned the Holocaust. Some made overtures to the JC/B but felt unwelcome in Kirchner's hidebound community.[7]

One such person undertook an initiative that is both intrinsically interesting and historically significant. Irene Runge, born in New York City in 1942 into a German emigré family that returned to Germany seven years later to serve the GDR's version of Marxism/Leninism, has spoken of her experience as a politically engaged young Jewish woman: "Most of our friends and acquaintances were Jewish, but none of them were religious. We talked a lot about being Jewish and we told Jewish jokes, but the Jüdische Gemeinde seemed to be very religious, and we had no contact with it because our people weren't members" (Ostow 1989b: 46 f.).

Persuaded by an Australian friend that communism and Judaism were mutually compatible, Runge said that she "also began to think that if you're Jewish, it makes sense to really identify as a Jew and to do more about it: though I never was a very religious Jew." Her next step was to take on a more active role in the JC/B: initiating cultural Sundays, serving on the JC/B's board of directors, and even beginning to attend services. In 1987, after drawing up a list of 50 young East Berliners who were probably Jews but who took no part in the JC/B's life, Runge contacted them to see if they would be willing to participate in her Sunday forums, which, she promised, would be heavy on culture and politics but light on religion.

Runge's activities coincided with two other efforts to rejuvenate the JC/B. First, in September 1987, tedious negotiations among the U.S. Department of State, the GDR government, and the World Council of Jews finally brought to East Berlin an American rabbi—the GDR's first full-time rabbi (see R. L. Merritt 1989). Rabbi Isaac Neuman had long served the Sinai Temple in the university town of Urbana-Champaign, Illinois. Not surprisingly, then, one of his primary goals in East Berlin was to revitalize the JC/B's youth program, trying especially to bring new blood into the community. This was not to be fully realized, however. Conflict among Neuman, Kirchner, and the GDR government led the dynamic—some would say excessively dynamic—rabbi to return home abruptly after less than nine months in the city. His brief tenure, nevertheless, left more than a blip in the post-1945 history of Jewish life in East Berlin. The pragmatic but by no means formal link between Neuman's emphasis on youth and Runge's inchoate cultural organization is particularly noticeable.

Second, however, and in a rather different context, Runge's cultural organization fell victim to institutional progress. Since the early 1980s, GDR politicians—including even the head of state, Erich Honecker—and Jewish functionaries had hinted at ideas that might improve their relationships. The government's hope was that accommodating Jewish interests would pave the way toward the GDR's greater international acceptance. Ideas that surfaced included better pensions for Jewish victims of Nazism, subsidies to Jewish communities, improved ties with Israel, and permitting the JC/B to raise overseas money to refurbish its New Synagogue (R. L. Merritt 1989). The GDR visit in October 1988 by Edgar M. Bronfman, president of the World Jewish Congress, was treated by Honecker as a major propaganda success.

The visit of foreign dignitaries and the fiftieth anniversary celebration of the Night of Broken Glass (Reichskristallnacht, November 9, 1938) provided the occasion to promulgate the New Synagogue Berlin–Centrum Judaicum (Ostow 1990b: 375 f.). The plan was to turn the synagogue in the eastern borough of Mitte[8] and its neighboring building into a major cultural center, one that could establish East Berlin as Germany's preeminent site for the study of Jewish history and culture. When finished, it would include (among other facilities) a library, chapel *(Stiebel),* seminar rooms, conference center, and home for the historically important Comprehensive Archive of the German Jews (Gesamtarchiv der deutschen Juden). But, with the Centrum Judaicum's focus on East Berlin and the JC/B, how could alternative organizations advance even remotely similar ventures?

More specifically, what role was to be played by Runge's alternative organization, now called the (Jewish Cultural Association [JCA]) Jüdischer Kulturverein Berlin? The following year's push toward German unification answered this question. If unification meant the JC/B's absorption into the JCoB and if the JCoB continued to maintain its anti-Communist stance, then Runge's cultural organization had no role to play.[9] Overweening West Germans, Runge and others feared, would decimate if not directly ban the Communist Socialist Unity Party (Sozialistiche Einheitspartei Deutschlands [SED]) to which Runge adhered and would punish those who had collaborated with the Communist regime.[10] It was just as clear that, as soon as possible, the JCoB would absorb East Berlin's Jewish community. In these circumstances, Runge would find it extremely difficult to gain support for her programs.

Runge found a deus ex machina in the interim East German governments that followed the collapse of the Berlin Wall and preceded unified elections. For their own reasons, interim leaders hoped to protect some socialist accomplishments carved out during the regime's forty-year existence. By maintaining the JCA, they could ensure that at least some leftist Jews in East Berlin would continue to play a role, despite the dominant JCoB faction's anti-Communist bias. Moreover, JCA's formal recognition as a cultural entity together with some modest funding ensured that, whatever the new unified government in Berlin had in mind, the JCA could continue to operate.

In part because of these systemic changes, Runge's JCA shifted its initial focus somewhat. The Sunday program continues to function regularly, but two elements suggest eventual expansion. One is the steady stream of ultra-Orthodox rabbis and other Jewish functionaries invited to address or otherwise participate in the program's proceedings. Second, the JCA forum offers more than political and cultural discussions; it also provides a substantial number of normal religious services. The JCA seems set to become a full-scale religious community that will be independent of the JCoB. In this regard, however, the JCA may be competing with yet another breakaway group: Adass Jisroel, or the Israelite Synagogue Community. As West Berlin Jews slowly accepted the political changes that would unify the city's Jewish community, Adass Jisroel reemerged as another community to claim its right to serve the city's Jews.

Annihilating a Community

Adass Jisroel dates back to 1869 when some dissatisfied Berlin Jews broke off from the established community to form a more Orthodox community. It very soon achieved permanent status. Adass Jisroel received a royal patent in 1885 as the second independent Jewish community in Berlin; and in Siegmundshof (located in the western borough of Tiergarten), as well as Artillerie (now Tucholsky) Street (located in the eastern borough of Mitte) they founded synagogues, schools, a rabbinical seminary, a hospital, a senior citizens' home, a cemetery, and ritual baths. By 1930, the community, constituting 30,000 of Berlin's 170,000 Jews, seemed firmly situated in German society.

But, of course, they were not so firmly situated. In 1932, even before Hitler's accession to power, Nazi mobs smashed the windows of the community's cultural center in Siegmundshof. Destruction during the Night of Broken Glass, aerial bombardments, and intense street fighting left its buildings severely, though not irreparably, damaged. At the same time, the Nazi government directed pressure against all Jews, including Adass Jisroel members. March 1939 saw financial support lifted from Jewish community schools; August 1939 the closing of schools not linked to the Reichs Association of the Jews in Germany; May 1941 the forced union of all Jewish groups into the Reichs Association; and June 1942 the closing of all Jewish schools. By then, many Jews had already fled the country, and the Adass Jisroel leaders had been marched to the Sachsenhausen concentration camp in Berlin's northern outskirts. Most who remained in the city faced horrifying ends in one death camp or another. The Nazis literally annihilated Adass Jisroel as an organization and scattered around the world the few members who survived the Holocaust. Only a handful chose to return to Berlin after the war's end.

Picking Up the Scattered Pieces

Two members who made their way to postwar Berlin were Ari Abraham Offenberg, grandson of an Adass Jisroel founder, and his Israeli-born son, Mario. Born in 1946, Mario Offenberg was too young to have experienced at firsthand the Community's glory and demise, but the family's traditional role of leadership was deeply ingrained. He arrived in Berlin in the mid-1960s as a student of political science and economics at the Free University.

The Offenbergs played critical roles in reestablishing Adass Jisroel. September 1985 found them bringing surviving Adassians and their relatives to Berlin to pay tribute to the defunct organization by honoring a monument raised in Siegmundshof. The following year, Mario Offenberg organized a major exhibition at West Berlin's Provincial Archive (Landesarchiv Berlin) and the Berlin Museum; the placement of a commemorative plaque in East Berlin's Tucholsky Street, the site of the Community's former home; and a public ceremony at the reopened cemetery in the eastern borough of Weissensee at which East German State Secretary for Church Affairs Klaus Gysi spoke (Offenberg 1986: 324). He also formed the Friends of Adass Jisroel Society, serving as a representative with power of attorney, and the Jewish Community Adass Jisroel (JCAJ), in which Ari Offenberg served as chair and Mario Offenberg as executive director.

These initiatives did not produce an enthusiastic response from all members of the Jewish community in Berlin or elsewhere. Most seemed to welcome Adassians and their relatives only as long as they maintained their nostalgic aura. Galinski and his JCoB, however, were not at all pleased that the Offenbergs were unwilling to seek or follow their lead.[11] More significantly, the changing logic of the situation pointed clearly toward efforts to restore Adass Jisroel as an entity that, while succoring the Community's members, could also make claims on Berlin's Jewry and government—precisely the situation that Galinski wanted to forestall! Shmuel Auerbach, honorary president of the Friends of Adass Jisroel Society, vigorously denied that the society had any such intent, and cited his own preference for preventing sectarian fragmentation. Galinski, for his part, turned his attention to defusing Adass Jisroel's efforts to disrupt the JCoB's position of uncontested primacy.

For instance, one of Galinski's first acts in 1950 when he became the JCoB's executive director was to lay claim to Adass Jisroel's cultural center at Siegmundshof. Since no Adass Jisroel Community members filed a competing claim, Berlin authorities awarded the property by default to Galinski's Jewish community—which promptly sold it at a ridiculously low price ($23,000 for property that Mario Offenberg later valued at $450,000) to a commercial developer who flattened the remaining buildings and constructed a large apartment house for students. Thus Adass Jisroel property that the Nazis had seized was now gone forever—and the proceeds had gone to the JCoB.

Property, and hence money, became a major point of dispute. Mario Offenberg filed a lawsuit in 1988 claiming that his JCAJ was in fact the legitimate successor of the Adass Jisroel that the Nazis had closed down in 1939. Accordingly, the Siegmundshof property, which is likely to soar in value after united Germany's capital moves from Bonn to Berlin, rightfully belongs to and must be reclaimed by the successor Community. Reversing the 1950 decision and the JCoB sale of the real estate would undoubtedly cost millions. Not surprisingly, Galinski's staff bitterly—and initially quite successfully—contested the claim.[12] The combination of the JCoB's obduracy and the West Berlin government's acceptance of the established community seemed to block the revitalization of Adass Jisroel—at least as far as West Berlin was concerned.

Shift from West to East

Were prospects in East Berlin any better? In 1986 Mario Offenberg, besides placing a memorial plaque in Tucholsky Street, gained a promise from the East German regime that it would not shut down the Adass Jisroel cemetery in Weissensee[13] in order to build new housing. Another major breakthrough came in 1989. Together with Lothar de Maizière[14] and Gregor Gysi,[15] two prominent church-affiliated attorneys who wanted to reform East German society, Offenberg approached the GDR's head of state to seek official support on several issues.[16] At stake were direct government funding[17] and the "return" to Adass Jisroel of its Tucholsky Street and other East Berlin properties. But Honecker's evident willingness to act fell victim to the sands of time when on October 18, 1989, reformers forced him out of office. Two months later Premier Hans Modrow, nevertheless, formally recognized the JCAJ's legitimacy and provided it with provisional funding.

The dramatically changing situation in East Germany gave Mario Offenberg the window of opportunity he needed to move ahead decisively toward stabilizing the JCAJ's status. On the one hand it became increasingly clear that the West Berlin community would swallow up what was left in the GDR. In these circumstances Galinski—now president of both the JC/B and the CCJG—would be in a position to isolate Adass Jisroel and block its reemergence as a religious force in Berlin.[18]

This possibility created among Adass Jisroel members a sense of urgency. On the other hand in December 1989 two important Eastern German allies—Gysi, who now headed the post-Communist Party of Democratic Socialism (PDS), and de Maizière, soon to become the GDR's last premier—acted on its behalf. Offenberg was permitted as early as December 18, 1989, to reconsecrate the Tucholsky Street synagogue. Three months later Premier de Maizière formally recognized the JCAJ as a religious entity. He not only transferred to the JCAJ ownership of the Tucholsky Street property and a former Jewish hospital nearby but also guaranteed an annual subsidy of $1.9 million. The GDR's waning days thus gave to the JCAJ the status that West Berlin had denied it.

Despite the JCAJ's official recognition, Galinski and Mario Offenberg publicly snarled at each other until Galinski died in July 1992 (Beringer 1989). Were Adassians legitimately seeking to regain their plundered status and property, or were they only freebooters trying to get their hands on monies rightfully belonging to the established Jewish community? Was Galinski historically justified in demanding a unified Jewish community, or was he simply wielding a heavy hand to avoid keeping up with changing times? At one point, the Berlin Senate tried to reverse de Maizière's ruling that had accorded legal status to the Adass Jisroel Community. The JCoB's stance after Galinski's death has been mainly to ignore Adass Jisroel and deny its legitimacy as a representative of Berlin's Jewish community.[19] But it faced a serious setback in October 1994 when Berlin's Administrative Court declared the JCAJ to be the earlier Adass Jisroel's legal successor.

The drive for Jewish confessional unity in Germany was strong only so long as the Cold War and Germany's division pressured German institutions to stick together. When that situational glue began to dissolve, however, paths toward independence became more attractive and eventually individual groups began to test the waters. Circumstances of time and place enabled both Runge and Offenberg to make significant inroads while East-West German relations were still flexible. Both the JCA and the JCAJ gained institutional footholds that may well endure the counterrevolutionary pressures emanating from the established Jewish community in Berlin. But institutional restructuring is not the only source of change in Berlin's Jewish community. Another is social: the influx of literally thousands of foreign Jews wishing to call Berlin their home.

Soviet Jews

After 1945 few Jews who had escaped the Holocaust wanted to return to Germany, and large numbers of Germans, whether antisemitic or simply afraid that Germans might again run amok, thought it better that the Jews not return (R.L. Merritt 1995). From 564,000 community affiliates in 1925 and 500,000 eight years later, before the Nazi onslaught, the number of Jews in Germany dwindled to 25,300 in 1950 and stabilized in the late 1960s at about 27,000. Berlin's Jewry declined from 173,000 in 1925 to as few as 6,500 Jews in the city's eastern and western parts in 1965.[20] Increasingly, Germany's aging Jewish population was not finding replacements through new births or young immigrants. The fierce demographics alone seemed to be realizing Hitler's dream of a Germany free of Jews. Could anything be done to stop the trend?

Changing Soviet Policy

A far distant event, Mikhail Gorbachev's *glasnost,* provided one way out of this population dilemma. Even before Gorbachev changed the modern world, of course, Soviet leaders were trying to deal with their own "Jewish problem": from 2 to 5 million Jews, many of them highly skilled and professionally qualified, were Soviet citizens. Several factors—including Soviet hostility toward religion, heavy-handed treatment of dissidents, propagandistic skills of foreign groups that supported dissident Soviet Jews, the relative weakness of an overcommitted military regime—contributed to a Soviet decision in the late 1960s to relax its restrictions on exit visas. At least some Jews seeking to leave the USSR would be granted exit visas to Israel (via Vienna, since the USSR and Israel did not enjoy formal diplomatic relations).[21]

Increasing numbers of Soviet Jews jumped at the opportunity. The trickle of 229 people who left the USSR in 1968 became an incipient flood of 32,000 in 1972 and 51,000 in 1979 (Runge 1993: 26). But things did not work out as Israeli and Soviet officials had planned. More than a few emigrants ended up not in Israel but somewhere else. In 1972 only 251 people (0.8%) violated their pledge to go to Israel, but by 1979 as many as 34,000 (66%) did so. Emigrants increasingly, much to the distress of Israel and Zionist organizations in Germany, had no intention of going to Israel; they got off an airplane in Vienna and promptly made arrangements to go on to their targeted site—which for many was, if not the United States, West Berlin. Others went to Israel, decided that they did not want to spend the rest of their days there, and moved on, some to Frankfurt am Main.

West German officials found themselves in a quandary. The liberal asylum law and the country's antisemitic past made them reluctant to deny access to Soviet Jews, whatever their immediate point of origin. But few wanted to see a large influx of these immigrants. They dealt with this ambivalence by trying to impose strict controls: permitting de facto entry to Jews who came directly from the Soviet Union but prosecuting and even deporting those who had violated German law or international agreements, such as Austria's obligation to ensure that Soviet emigrants to Israel actually ended up there. Their hard-line policy,[22] though, eventually gave way to pressure at home and abroad for a more lenient treatment of the "Israeli dropouts" (*Tagesspiegel* 1985). After all, said Jewish leaders such as Heinz Galinski as well as many non-Jews, each year witnessed only 200 to 300 such cases, most of them from Israel. Besides, Germany's Jewish communities needed invigoration.

Circumstances changed in the late 1980s. One reason for this was a more open Soviet (and, after 1991, CIS) policy that came with *glasnost.* Soviet emigration offices began handing out exit visas to practically all applicants who could claim a tie to Judaism or a Jewish community and letting them depart for whatever country they wished. For most of the half-million applicants, this meant going to

Israel, which welcomed them, and the United States, which did not. (In fact, the United States tightened its quota to restrict entry by USSR/CIS Jews.) A substantial number, perhaps 17,000 during the 5 years up to 1994, went to Germany.[23]

Changing East German Policy

Officials of the GDR followed the Soviet lead. As long as Soviet authorities remained punctilious in insisting that emigrants go to Israel, few Soviet Jews made their way into East Germany. But in the 1990s things were different. Gorbachev seemed intent on opening boundaries; and in the GDR, even before November 1989, men such as Gysi and de Maizière sought to persuade the GDR government to ease its own barriers. The transition months of 1990 saw strong efforts to enhance international linkages: particularly, to convince worldwide Jewry that the German leopard had truly changed its spots and to convince Germans that inviting more professionally qualified Jews into their country would improve the quality of their own life. In fact, almost at the outset of his tenure, premier de Maizière apologized publicly for Nazi Germany's crimes against Jews and Jewry and the GDR's long-standing refusal to deal openly with the consequences of such crimes. He also sought to demonstrate that his government would aid the country's Jewish communities by acting decisively rather than merely offering polite homilies.

It was increasingly clear, however, that the GDR was losing ground to a political unification that would end its independent authority. Did accepting an ever larger number of Soviet Jews continue to make sense? The five new provinces in eastern Germany paid heed to the old provinces of western Germany: all of them did their best to prohibit any new so-called economic refugees.[24] But East Berlin continued to accept all who applied—and even those contingency refugees who did not apply but who somehow managed to appear personally in Berlin.[25] The Berlin connection became the gateway to the West.

East Berlin Jews, too, were of different minds on this issue. Some took a very practical view. Leading GDR members of the JC/B expressed the fear that a large influx of Soviet Jews would intolerably tax their capacity to meet communal needs.[26] Others were ideologically motivated. They would doubtless have preferred to postpone any German unification whatever or at least to ensure an interim confederation that would permit East Germans to retain their form of government and their other "socialist accomplishments." But unification was not to be deterred. The best such ideologues could do was to strengthen East German independence, thereby slowing down the assimilative process that would inevitably lead to co-optation by established structures in West Germany.

Yet another group, the institution builders whose primary interest was maintaining East Berlin's status quo, saw the influx of Soviet Jews as a way to further their own aims. If the newcomers could be housed in East Berlin, they said, and if at least a substantial number of immigrants could be committed early to the entrepreneur's own community, then their influx could significantly change the existing balance of power among Berlin's various Jewish communities.

Runge's Jewish Cultural Association and Offenberg's Adass Jisroel followed precisely this strategy to maximize the ingress of Soviet Jews. In February 1990, Runge even wrote openly to encourage government acceptance of as many Soviet Jews as were willing to come to the GDR (Runge 1993). The stakes were high: JCA and JCAJ wanted to recruit the newcomers not only to ease them into their lives but, more importantly, to demonstrate materially that, contrary to what their critics claimed, the institutions appealed to more than a handful of communicants.[27] Having already achieved formal legitimization, JCA and JCAJ wanted this legitimization socially reinforced.

This is not to suggest that either group was solely self-serving. Both offered important social services. They have worked closely with government offices to help the Soviet Jews find housing, jobs, short-term financial support, religious instruction, German and Hebrew language training, intellectual enrichment, and counseling[28]—in short, most of the support services normally provided by governments and their religious communities. Unquestionably, however, a quid pro quo existed: support services in exchange for a legitimization that would endure beyond Germany's formal unification. Critics viewed this arrangement as an unholy alliance among Communists (or at least Communist sympathizers) and power-hungry Jews, supporters as an effective means to accomplish practical goals that both freed oppressed co-religionists and made feasible the acceptance by Germans of Soviet Jews.

The GDR government under Premier de Maizière moved quickly to realize the reform. Ordering rapid processing of applications was an important step. On April 12, 1990, the government proclaimed that it would accept *all* persecuted Jews rather than quibble over their status. Three months later the GDR Council of Ministers announced that it would "grant Jews arriving from the USSR residence rights, housing, upkeep, language training, and work permits" (Ostow 1992: 378). Not surprisingly, the rate of Soviet Jews entering East Berlin increased from 40 per week in spring and summer, reaching 2,900 in 1990 as a whole.

Changing West Berlin Policy

For their part, the West Berlin government and Heinz Galinski originally balked at changes being carried out in the soon-to-be-immersed GDR. The apparently unending invasion by Soviet Jews was a common problem that both saw as a potential obstacle to their own political goals. The German government's concern was fairly clear. Already faced with hundreds of thousands of ethnic Germans calling for "repatriation" and refugees seeking political asylum, it was wary of opening the gateway to any large body of people, Jews or anyone else—particularly if the government could not exercise its own discretion regarding timing, individual acceptability, numbers, and the like. The FRG first requested that the GDR government cease its open policy. It then ordered its own consulates in the USSR to refuse new applications. But these measures were to no avail. Immigrants continued to register with startling regularity at East Berlin's refugee reception center.

Less immediately comprehensible was Galinski's concern. His voice was initially conservative. German unification, he said, was neither necessary nor, from the perspective of world Jewry, desirable. Jews had already suffered too much from a unified Germany during its Nazi past. Who needed a new one? Moreover, following official German complaints about masses of refugees, he remarked that the country's existing Jewish communities could not accommodate large numbers of newly arriving Soviet Jews, most of whom spoke neither German nor Hebrew, nominal Jews who had grown up in an atheistic state that hindered their assimilation into Jewish culture.

Galinski soon changed his tune. One reason is that it became increasingly clear that he was barking up the wrong tree as far as his overall policy goals were concerned. Germans, East and West, wanted unification. Prominent Jews, besides seeing the futility of trying to block unification, also saw the value of bringing to an end the Cold War's ugliest manifestation. Another more practical consideration also caught his attention. Would Galinski's JCoB, by shunning unification and the changes that were taking place in East Germany, thereby scuttle an opportunity to shape the future? Turning control of the eastern territories over to the independent and perhaps untrustworthy members of the JCA and Adass Jisroel and permitting them to attract ever more Soviet Jews would clearly be self-destructive for the JCoB. But the JCoB had to become a player before it could influence the game's outcome.

Galinski then donned the garments of active participant and decision maker. This went beyond merely incorporating the East German community, a step begun in February and concluded in December 1990. Galinski also insisted that West Germany open its border to Soviet Jews, set up procedures for accommodating those already in Berlin, and, after October 2, the day before formal German unity became effective, ensured that the new FRG policy closing the borders did not apply in Berlin. A major JCoB program emphasizing social support and culture sharply restricted the influence of East Berlin's other Jewish communities. By July 1992—shortly before Galinski's death—the JCA and Adass Jisroel were struggling to maintain their position in a changing Jewish community.

Limits of Stability

Heinz Galinski's stance against national unification created an interesting but difficult situation. Some German intellectuals and the international Jewish community were doubtless impressed. It made other Germans ask questions, however. Of what value is a unitary Jewish community, which Germans had supported so steadfastly, if its leaders speak out against what four decades of Germans had claimed as their nearest and dearest goal, namely, German unification? Was having pluralistic Jewish communities in Berlin such a bad idea after all?

Perhaps Berlin Jews were seeking a stultifying hyperstability. Berlin as a pawn in the Cold War could afford its sometimes languid Jewish community; and it could resist destabilizing changes by suppressing or co-opting the occasional maverick reformer. But the Cold War was over. The world after November 1989 was different. Certainly few would now fault the FRG's chancellor, Helmut Kohl, for seizing the opportunity to merge the two Germanys. Taking a similar step to integrate the JC/B into the JCoB was also historically consistent and practically sensible. But should all Berlin Jews have to adhere to the integrated JCoB? Wasn't it equally consistent historically and practically to support an independent community such as Adass Jisroel or even the JCA? By the same token one could treat the influx of 6,000 Soviet Jews[29] as a blessing rather than a curse.

The institutional and personal events of 1989–90 had an enduring but far from expected impact on Berlin's Jewish community. The jewel in the crown was unquestionably the merged JCoB and JC/B, torn asunder in 1952 by the GDR regime. But even unification had its problems—a bloodletting that reflected personal animosities rather than substantive issues and conflicts about property rights and the effective use of resources and facilities. Strength in numbers and resources ensures that West Berlin Jews will dominate the community for many years. The unified JCoB has pushed toward institutional normality.

At the same time, however, other developments pressed for significant change. One is the emergence of two new Jewish communities that are capturing the attention of at least some Berlin Jews. Adass Jisroel represents a neo-Orthodox religious orientation, the JCA combines religiosity with left-wing politics, and both have made a strong pitch to incorporate Jews migrating from the USSR/CIS (Commonwealth of Independent States). The new communities may never threaten the JCoB's dominant position. They can, nevertheless, be a constant source of irritation and occasionally even woo away entire groups of members.

The second major development was the arrival in Berlin of several thousand USSR/CIS Jews. Initial efforts to limit their ingress gave way to competition aimed at accommodating them. Meanwhile, their sheer numbers began posing a challenge, particularly in East Berlin and its immediate suburbs where most of them resided because of policies implemented in 1990. Recently, an elderly Jewish woman in East Berlin wrote a poignant letter to the JCoB (Brück 1994) in which she expressed the feeling that the community had betrayed her and her friends. For forty years they had steadfastly supported their community. Now, however, they saw foreign Jews and the Russian language flooding the synagogue, its meeting rooms, and even the informal gatherings of the women's group. They saw the newcomers receiving various kinds of economic and social assistance, whereas those who had been deprived under the GDR continued to suffer.[30] This image of disparity cripples any popular sense of the system's legitimacy.

In time the large number of USSR/CIS Jews can change the nature of the JCoB. For example, in 1991 twelve Soviet Jews joined a German Jew in bolting from Berlin's "mother" community to create their own community in neighboring Potsdam.[31] Again, in March 1993, voting by USSR/CIS Jews almost helped the opposition topple Galinski's successor, Jerzy Kanal, as chair of the JCoB's Representative Assembly (Repräsentantenversammlung). In other words, sociocultural integration has not proceeded as smoothly as community members had hoped. But the more the USSR/CIS Jews become oriented to working and living in Berlin, the more they and other immigrants may take active roles in Jewish communal life.

The case of Berlin's Jewish community suggests some other components of social change. First, the key role in encouraging or discouraging such change derives from leadership, communication, and especially identity formatioi?. Where the community is heading now in this respect is not clear. Second, advocates and opponents of social change will encounter internal as well as external challenges that have probably not been seen since 1945.

Recent events offer a number of examples of such social change. For instance, contrary to what Berlin Jews may have hoped, reuniting the city's divided political communities did not create a smoothly running and integrated religious community. Indeed, the normality of the new status quo poses a greater challenge to Berlin's Jewish community than do such extraordinary events as overt antisemitism. The latter's open assault can unite a people, both Jewish and gentile, to combat its effects and limit its recurrence. The principle of equal protection under the law effectively restrains those who would carry their personal antisemitism into the public arena. But decisions about who is Jewish, how the scriptures are to be read, what is to be eaten (and when), or how communal resources are to be distributed are potentially divisive issues for the Jewish community that give its members an unwelcome image of querulousness. The end of the Cold War and the FRG's control over the whole of post-1945 Germany has greatly eased pressure for social conformity as a protective device. But the new era of plurality does not promise Berlin Jews a conflict-free environment.

NOTES

The authors are indebted to the late Heinz Galinski and to Dr. Eva Grünstein, Jerzy Kanal, Konstantin Münz, Rabbi Isaac Neuman, Dr. Mario Offenberg, and Dr. Irene Runge who generously shared their time and thoughts.

1. The word *Gemeinde* translates as both *community* and *congregation,* but the latter translation gives the incorrect impression that a Jewish *Gemeinde* in Germany is the same as a Jewish congregation in the United States. Here we use the term *community,* capitalizing it when referring to a specific institution (e.g., Jewish Community of Berlin) and using lowercase when referring to several individual groups or to generic, that is, noninstitutional, entities (e.g., Jewish community in East Germany).

2. "Greater Berlin" dates back to the city's incorporation in 1920. Since our focus is on the period beginning in 1989, we shall not distinguish between the appellation Jewish Community of Greater Berlin (JCoGB), which existed until the late 1960s, and the subsequent Jewish Community of Berlin (JCoB).

3. In 1952, the GDR's Jewish community left the all-German Central Council of Jews in Germany (Zentralrat der Juden in Deutschland [CCJG]) to form the Alliance of Jewish Communities in the German Democratic Republic (Verband der Jüdischen Gemeinden in der Deutschen Demokratischen Republik), and East Berlin Jews abandoned the JCoB in favor of a GDR-rooted Jewish Community Berlin (Jüdische Gemeinde Berlin [JC/B]).

4. In these regards Galinski's success paralleled that of West Germany's (sometimes autocratic) leader Konrad Adenauer. Both thrived on international tension. The chancellor's policy of strength brought him admiration and acceptance during the years that saw a Soviet threat, but his inability to adapt to changing times proved to be problematic.

5. Perhaps unfairly, critics have compared Galinski's strategy in 1989–90 to the forcing

into line *(Gleichschaltung)* imposed on Jewish organizations in the late 1930s by the Nazis' Jewish *Reichsvertretung* and later a *Reichsverband.* Generally speaking, even his colleagues complained about Galinski's authoritarian tendencies and rigidities *(Der Spiegel* 1988), and his difficulty in dealing with important political leaders, such as Chancellor Helmut Kohl, rubbed critics and supporters the wrong way (Bodemann 1990: 361, 370).

6. Dr. Kirchner, a physician, also ruled with an iron fist. His situation differed from Galinski's, however, since Kirchner knew that any political mistake made by him or his community members would incur the GDR's wrath. Kirchner has been generally blamed for programs that unwittingly drove potential members away from the community.

7. For an interesting account by an East Berlin Jew who migrated to the West in the mid-1980s, see Ostow's interview with Thomas Eckert (1989b). Kirchner seemed to be more interested in preserving relationships among the increasingly aged East German Jews than in making political waves or emphasizing religious doctrine—however, see Ostow's interview with Kirchner (1989b).

8. The New Synagogue Berlin on Oranienburger Street, completed in 1866, was extensively damaged during the Reichskristallnacht and especially later in World War II by Allied bombing raids. Getting state support for raising funds overseas promised a durability of Jewish institutions that the GDR had earlier been unwilling to accept.

9. In 1989, of the 150 members of Runge's cultural group, many were SED members and less than 25 had actually joined the JC/B (Ostow 1989a: 351).

10. Although West Germany's judicial sweep of the GDR's Augean stable did not reach the proportions some feared, people such as Runge nevertheless suffered personally from unification. The two merging German states agreed that individuals who had worked for the GDR's Ministry for State Security (Stasi) even in an informal capacity would be denied access to jobs in the public sector. Runge, with a doctorate in economics and sociology and a research position at East Berlin's Humboldt University, found herself out of work. When her linkage to Stasi became known publicly, she resigned from her role in the JCA—even though today she continues to carry out its leadership functions, especially coordinating programs and fund-raising because of her extensive international contacts.

11. Mario Offenberg also had problems with the JC/B in East Berlin. At one point Kirchner obtained a government order that declared Offenberg was a persona non grata to be expelled from the eastern part of the city.

12. In July 1989, the West Berlin Senate confirmed an earlier court ruling that the JCAJ had ceased to exist in 1939. Therefore, a newly formed group, however much it claimed to represent the defunct Community, had no legal standing regarding the latter's property *(Der Spiegel* 1989). Mario Offenberg tartly remarked that, first, the Nazis broke up the Community and confiscated its property; and then, supported by new Berlin authorities, the JCoB took advantage of its postwar prominence to gain control of the property and ensure that wreckers would demolish the last remnants of Adass Jisroel in western Berlin. The decision was reversed on October 10, 1994, by the Berlin Administrative Court, which formally established the JCAJ as a public corporation succeeding the 1869–1939 Adass Jisroel. It is not difficult to predict a spate of new lawsuits on contested property.

13. This cemetery is located slightly north of the Jewish Community's larger cemetery which is also in the borough of Weissensee.

14. Lothar de Maizière, besides serving as vice president of the GDR Protestant church's synod in 1986, had gained a reputation for defending political dissidents. He was deputy prime minister under Hans Modrow's governments of November 18, 1989, and February 5, 1990, and after April 9, 1990, he was prime minister. In unified Germany, he became a Bundestag member and deputy chair of the Christian Democratic Union (CDU) but resigned because of his implication in a Stasi scandal.

15. Gregor Gysi, whose father, Klaus Gysi, was until 1988 state secretary for church affairs, also defended highly visible dissidents. His family background was half Jewish, although he was himself not a practicing Jew. On December 9, 1989, he accepted the chairmanship of the SED, soon transformed it into the reformed Party of Democratic Socialism (Partei des Demokratischen Sozialismus [PDS]); eventually he won Bundestag seats in December 1990 as a PDS delegate and in October 1994 as an elected constituency member.

16. It is noteworthy that Offenberg gained the support and even sponsorship of two of the most powerful and respected politicians of post-1989 eastern Germany.

17. The FRG's tax system makes funds available to religious entities, such as the JCoB, recognized as public corporations. This system did not exist in the GDR. In united Berlin, then, the JCAJ did not gain access to public funding until the administrative court's decision of October 1994; two months later the Berlin Senate agreed to provide JCAJ with about $1.5 million annually. Appeals, however, particularly on the disposition of property earlier owned by JCAJ, mean that such issues remain outstanding.

18. For instance, after the JCAJ gained formal standing from the GDR government, Offenberg received no response to his call for the JCoB's assistance in obtaining a Torah, even though it has many in its possession.

19. In July 1994, when President Bill Clinton visited Berlin, he asked his staff to arrange for a representative visit to a synagogue. The staff and Berlin government authorities decided that an appropriate venue would be the JCoB's New Synagogue. No one seems seriously to have considered a stop at Adass Jisroel's synagogue on Tucholsky Street, located right around the corner. An irate Mario Offenberg interpreted this omission as unfriendly collusion between the U.S. and Berlin governments at the cost of Adass Jisroel.

20. The area that became the GDR claimed 4,639 Jews in 1946 (including 2,465 East Berliners). By 1988 emigration and death had reduced these numbers to about 360 overall, half of them in East Berlin, and with an estimated average age in the upper sixties. For more complete data see R.L. Merritt (1989: 167).

21. Much to the distress of critics, the influx of USSR/CIS Jews strongly aided Adass Jisroel in its struggle for recognition. Offenberg's JCAJ needed more members to authenticate the community's existence as a bona fide religious body (rather than the private family association cynics saw) and Klaus Gysi and Lothar de Maizière needed to legitimate the earlier decision that gave political life to the resurrected infant (see Broder 1991).

22. A celebrated case in 1980 sentenced a Lithuanian to five months probation for having migrated to Israel in 1971, buying false Soviet papers there, and then flying to West Berlin and applying for refugee status (*Tagesspiegel* 1980). From August 1973 to June 1980, the number of Soviet Jews who obtained refugee status was 2,414 in Berlin—about 300 of them with false papers.

23. This figure is closer to 25,000 if we include those who did not ascribe to Jewish law (*halakhah*) or who did not formally belong to a Jewish community (see *Der Spiegel* 1993).

24. Later, after unification, the German federal government imposed acceptance quotas on all the provinces, new and old.

25. The term *contingency* in this context has taken on a bureaucratic meaning of its own. It refers to USSR/CIS Jews who could probably not have met strict quotas had they applied but who, by simply showing up in Berlin, were granted residency permits because of Germany's desire to deal with USSR/CIS Jews as a special category of refugees. Contingency refugees got expedited processing and rapid approval. The FRG tightened procedures again in early 1991, although the real impact was minimal.

26. This proved not to be a fanciful concern. For instance, in 1990 East German authorities assigned 100 new Soviet immigrants to the care of Magdeburg's Jewish community,

which at that time comprised only 34 members, all of them pensioners (Ostow 1992: 379).

27. In August 1994, Offenberg reported that the JCAJ included about 200 families, or about 960 individuals; and Runge reported that the JCA had about 600 members plus as many as 100 to 150 Russian Jews.

28. Support also came from the GDR Office for Foreigners and the Protestant church (Ostow 1992: 378).

29. Berlin had 6,500 Jewish affiliates in 1968 and about 10,000 in late 1994. Estimated death rates of the overaged population in 1968 suggest that 60% of Berlin's Jews today came from the USSR/CIS.

30. A related problem that may abate with time is persuading oldsters to change their ways, for example, to attend religious services and other meetings in distant parts of the city.

31. Jews in Potsdam, the provincial capital of Brandenburg, even before 1939 had been attached to the community in Berlin. From 1945–91 Brandenburg did not have its own Jewish community.

HOLLI A. SEMETKO AND WOLFGANG G. GIBOWSKI

The Image of Germany in the News and U.S. Public Opinion after Unification

The November 1992 presidential election in the United States signaled important changes. The year-long campaign focused on domestic problems and issues, which candidate Bill Clinton promised to make his priorities. The election result signaled the public's preference for a shift away from foreign affairs, President George Bush's forte, to more pressing problems at home. The last Cold War president left office and a new generation entered the White House in January 1993. The climate of opinion in the United States when President Clinton took office was largely one of looking inward, one preoccupied with events and problems at home, with little interest in developments abroad.

Just four years earlier, in November 1989, U.S. news was saturated with information about events abroad. For at least a week, NBC, ABC, and CBS news anchors broadcast their main evening bulletins live from Berlin. The fall of the Berlin Wall, the bloodless revolutions in Eastern Europe, and the consequences of these events for a new world order captured public attention that was usually reserved for domestic news. During this time of dramatic change in Europe, U.S. television news was an especially important conveyor of images and information because it influenced public perceptions of many foreign countries (Semetko et al. 1992).

The amount of foreign news reported in American news media ebbs and flows with crises and world events (Graber 1994). Foreign affairs normally account for a small proportion of U.S. news coverage (Wilhoit and Weaver 1983). American news media generally devote less time and space to foreign news in comparison with the news media in many other countries. Foreign news coverage in the American press was much less prevalent than in Europe in the 1960s, for example, and this continues to a great extent today (Hart 1966). Television, an important source of foreign news, has expanded the size of the attentive audience substantially, particularly at times of crisis (see Almond 1960). Graber notes that without television most people skip foreign affairs reports if they encounter them solely in newspapers (Graber 1994). But exposure does not in itself necessarily result in gaining knowledge or learning. Despite high levels of exposure to foreign affairs news, the public has a relatively low level of knowledge about foreign affairs; this is explained by the lack of audience interest (Graber 1988, Sahin et al. 1982). Attention to or interest in news is a stronger predictor of effects on opinions than is mere exposure. (McLeod and McDonald 1985, Chaffee and Schleuder 1986, Drew and Weaver 1990).

The research on the association between media use and opinion about foreign countries is mixed with regard to the effects of exposure on the direction of opinions. Exposure has been associated with relatively positive evaluations of all countries (Chaffee and Miyo 1983, NcNelly and Izcaray 1986), as well as with negative attitudes (Korzenny, del Toro, and Gaudino 1987). If there is a relationship between the visibility of a foreign country in the news and public opinion about that country, then we might expect the direction of opinion to reflect the predominant tone of that coverage (see Semetko et al. 1992). A study of television news and public opinion about the Arab-Israeli conflict in the 1970s and 1980s, in fact, found a positive relationship, at the aggregate level, between the images of the countries in the news and the subsequent direction of public opinion about those countries (Adams and Heyl 1981).

Previous research on the image of Germany in U.S. news media suggests a lingering persistence of associations with the Third Reich and the Nazi period (Stapf, Stroebe, and Jonon 1986, Marten 1989, Trautmann 1991). Such images, however, were absent in the coverage of the fall of the Berlin Wall and the dramatic developments in central Europe and the Soviet Union in late 1989 and early 1990, when there was especially heavy foreign news coverage in the United States. In live broadcasts from Berlin in November 1989, the evening news programs of the three major television networks relayed emotionally powerful images and reports from East Germany and other eastern bloc countries. A study of the effects of this unusual period of foreign news coverage on American public opinion about Germany and other countries found that TV played a more important role than newspapers (Semetko et al. 1992). A significant and positive association was found between the visibility of foreign countries in the U.S. news, and TV news in particular, and public opinion about those countries. The more visible a country was on TV news, the stronger the survey measures of attention and exposure as predictors of opinions about that country, even after controlling for key demographic characteristics such as education, gender, and age, as well as political interest in and travel to Europe. During this period of dramatic and positively depicted change in Germany and central Europe, greater attention to foreign affairs news on TV was also consistently associated with more positive opinions of a country.

By 1992–93, however, a number of attacks against foreigners and a resurgence of activities among right-wing radicals in Germany had occurred. The optimism of public opinion that predominated in eastern Germany in the period leading up to the 1990 German national election had disappeared (see Semetko and Schönbach 1994). A study was undertaken to determine whether the news concerning right-wing radicals and violence against foreigners in Germany had an influence on U.S. public opinion about Germany and its people.

This chapter presents the results of this study, which involved a content analysis of American mainstream news media coverage of foreign countries and a national survey in March/April 1993 to address three questions. (1) How visible was Germany in the U.S. news media relative to other countries in the early 1992–93 period? (2) What were the main themes or topics in the news about Germany? (3) What influence, if any, did news and information about Germany have on public opinion?

This chapter draws on two sources of data. One is a content analysis of U.S. media coverage of a number of foreign countries over a twelve-month period (March 1992–March 1993). The Lexis/Nexis on-line database was used to obtain news reports about these countries in twenty-six major U.S. metropolitan daily newspapers, as well as on TV news programs on the ABC network.[1] Second, from March 26 to April 9, 1993, a nationally representative survey of 1,203 adults (aged 18 and over) throughout the continental United States was fielded. The survey included questions on U.S.-German relations, the future of German democracy, attitudes about foreign countries and international political leaders, and interest in developments abroad. The survey was designed to be broadly comparable with two previous studies of U.S. attitudes toward Germany, one conducted in March 1990, just before the East German parliamentary elections, when few expected that German unification would be achieved so quickly, and the other in September 1991 in the aftermath of the Gulf War. This chapter provides comparisons with the 1991 data when relevant.[2]

Foreign Countries in the U.S. News Media: March 1992–March 1993

The visibility of thirteen foreign countries and a number of international political leaders (including Helmut Kohl, François Mitterrand, Boris Yeltsin, and Mikhail Gorbachev) in the U.S. news was assessed over the twelve-month period preceding the survey. There was little variation across media in the visibility of international political leaders. Of stories mentioning political leaders, Russia's Boris Yeltsin (71%) and Mikhail Gorbachev (17%) were the most visible in the press, and they were also the subject of 56% and 19% of ABC television coverage, respectively. German chancellor Helmut Kohl, though visible, was far down the list both on TV (14%) and in the press (8%). Only French president François Mitterrand was less visible, appearing in 11% of TV stories and 4% of stories in the press). Television and the press, however, differed substantially in terms of the visibility of certain foreign countries in the news.

The content analysis showed that Germany was less visible than other countries in the U.S. news media. Overall, in twenty-six metropolitan daily newspapers, Japan, Russia, Mexico, Britain, Israel, and Canada each received more coverage than Germany. Newspapers also varied greatly in the amount of coverage devoted to Germany, with the *New York Times,* the *Chicago Tribune,* the *Los Angeles Times,* and the *Washington Post* offering substantially more news about Germany than other newspapers. On TV, Germany ranked among the top four foreign countries in the news, following Russia but preceding Japan and Israel. Foreign news, however, generally accounts for only a small part of U.S. news coverage (see, e.g., Graber 1994). This was especially so during the time of this study, given that 1992 was a presidential election year and 1993 was the first year of a new administration.

The news stories about Germany on TV and in the press concerned a range of topics, though extremism and violence against foreigners were the most common themes. As a consequence, this should have an effect on the American public's responses to questions about Germany in the March/April 1993 survey. The rank order of the visibility of foreign countries on ABC television programs, as a percentage of all coverage given to thirteen foreign countries between March 1992 and March 1993, was Russia (21%), Germany (13%), Japan and Israel (each 12%), Britain and France (each 9%), Mexico (8%), Canada (6%), Italy (4%), Poland and Czechoslovakia (each 2%), and Hungary and Austria (each 1%). The rank order in major newspapers was Japan (21%), Russia (18%), Mexico (11%), Britain and Israel (each 10%), Canada (9%), Germany (8%), France (7%), Italy (4%), Poland (2%), Hungary and Czechoslovakia (each 1%), and Austria (less than 0.5%). Although Germany occupied a higher position in the rank order on ABC television (where it came second) than in the press (where it came seventh), the proportion of news about Germany in both media was not dramatically different. Although the number of stories about Germany varied from month to month in the press, the four-month period from September to December 1992 included the greatest number of stories. This period corresponded with an increase in right-wing violence particularly in the new Bundesländer. A total of 499 stories in the press in which Germany featured in the headline and the lead paragraph were analyzed for their subject matter from September 1, 1992, to March 31, 1993. There was great variation across newspapers. The number of stories about Germany during this period ranged from a high of 77 in the *New York Times* to a low of 1 in the *Arizona Republic,* as is shown in table 12.1. In addition to the *New York Times,* substantial coverage of Germany appeared in three other newspapers—the *Chicago Tribune* (72 stories), the *Los Angeles Times* (61 stories), and the *Washington Post* (60 stories).

The subjects of stories were classified into the following seven categories: economy (business and industry, finance, banking, world economy, investment, and the Bundesbank); refugees (refugees, asylum laws, immigration, Romanians/Gypsies, deportation); Europe (the Maastricht Treaty, European unification, European Community, currency crisis in Europe, European monetary system, relations between European countries); extremism (extremist activity, violence and attacks on foreigners, neo-Nazis, Nazism, fascism, antisemitism, Jewish/Israeli reactions); world (Germany and the world, but excluding stories about the economy, the United Nations, and international relations); domestic (internal domestic affairs, unification, Kohl's popularity, domestic policies, politics, parties, and political leaders); other (tourism, travel, fashion, art, sports, environment, schools and education,

TABLE 12.1. Number of Stories about Germany in
U.S. Newspapers, September 1, 1992–March 31,
1993

Newspaper	Number of Stories
New York Times	77
Chicago Tribune	72
Los Angeles Times	61
Washington Post	60
Houston Chronicle	30
Atlanta Journal Constitution	29
Star Tribune	19
Washington Times	17
USA Today	16
Christian Science Monitor	15
Dallas Morning News	14
St. Petersburg Times	13
New York Newsday	13
Boston Globe	11
Cleveland Plain Dealer	11
Orlando Sentinel	11
San Francisco Chronicle	10
Buffalo News	5
Seattle Times	4
Hartford Courant	3
San Diego Union-Tribune	2
Phoenix Gazette	2
St. Petersburg Times Picayune	2
Sacramento Bee	1
Arizona Republic	1

Source: Major Papers Database on Lexis/Nexis.

health care). Figure 12.1 displays the visibility of two issues—refugees and extremism—month by month in all of the newspapers listed in table 12.1.

A closer look at the four newspapers that devoted the most coverage to Germany during this seven-month period shows that the pattern of extensive coverage
about extremism in November and December 1992 was true for each. The subjects
of stories over time are presented for each paper as follows: *New York Times* (table
12.2), *Chicago Tribune* (table 12.3), *Los Angeles Times* (table 12.4).

In the *New York Times,* the subjects, in order of importance, were: extremism,
the economy, refugees and domestic news. In the *Chicago Tribune,* extremism
topped the list, followed by the economy, domestic news, Europe and refugees. In
the *Los Angeles Times,* economic news topped the list, followed by extremism,
domestic news and refugees. Finally, in the *Washington Post,* extremism far out-
paced the economy as the most important subject of German stories over the
seven-month period. In sum, of the four newspapers that devoted the most coverage to Germany in the period under study, extremism ranked among the top two
subjects. Figure 12.2 displays these four newspapers' coverage of extremism and
refugees. The tables and figures include all stories about Germany that appeared
in these newspapers—news stories, editorials, Op Ed pieces (commentaries), let-

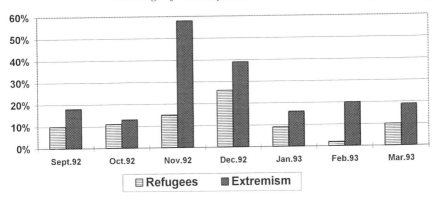

FIGURE 12.1. Percentages of All Stories about Germany with Main Topic of Refugees or Extremism in U.S. Newspapers

ters to the editor, as well as news in other sections such as style, travel, and book reviews.

When one considers news stories only, that is, excluding the Op Ed pieces, letters to the editor, editorials, and so on, it is noteworthy that from one-third to nearly one-half of such stories concerned the subject of extremism or refugees: 36% in the *New York Times,* 46% in the *Washington Post,* 48% in the *Chicago Tribune,* and 34% in the *Los Angeles Times.* The majority of Op Ed pieces and editorials also concerned extremism or refugees in each of these four newspapers, though the number of such stories was very small (less than five) in each news-paper.

Of the stories about Germany appearing on ABC television news and current affairs programs between March 1992 and March 1993, only a portion were actu-ally in the main evening news program, *World News Tonight,* anchored by Peter Jennings. A total of 74 stories about Germany were aired on this program over the twelve months preceding the survey, and these were content analyzed for their subject matter, based on the transcripts of the stories. The visibility of Germany

TABLE 12.2. Main Subjects of U.S. Newspaper Stories about Germany over Time: *New York Times,* September 1, 1992–March 31, 1993 (N = 77)

Subject	Sept. 92	Oct. 92	Nov. 92	Dec. 92	Jan. 93	Feb. 93	Mar. 93
Economy	22%	20%	10%	11%	17%	100%	27%
Refugees	28	—	10	21	—	—	—
Europe	6	—	—	—	—	—	—
Extremism	11	10	60	47	17	—	9
World	11	—	—	—	33	—	18
Domestic	6	40	10	10	—	—	18
Other	17	30	10	10	33	—	27
Total	100	100	100	100	100	100	100
Base	18	10	10	19	6	3	11

TABLE 12.3. Main Subjects of U.S. Newspaper Stories about Germany over Time:
Chicago Tribune, September 1, 1992–March 31, 1993 (N = 72)

Subject	Sept. 92	Oct. 92	Nov. 92	Dec. 92	Jan. 93	Feb. 93	Mar. 93
Economy	39%	7%	—	—	—	20%	25%
Refugees	11	14	20	25	67	—	—
Europe	17	7	—	13	—	—	—
Extremism	22	21	67	38	—	20	50
World	6	21	—	13	33	10	25
Domestic	—	14	7	—	—	—	—
Other	6	15	7	12	—	50	—
Total	100	100	100	100	100	100	100
Base	18	14	15	8	3	10	4

in the main evening news varied from month to month, ranging from a high of 9 stories in July 1992 to a low of 1 story in January 1993 (8 in April, September, and November 1992; 6 in May and December 1992 and March 1993; 5 in August 1992 and February 1993; and 4 in March, June, and October 1992). Overall, this shows that extremism also ranked among the top two subjects on TV news over the twelve-month period. There were 18 stories about Germany and the world, 11 about extremism, 10 about the economy, 8 about domestic politics and issues, 8 about Europe, 3 about refugees, and 18 about other topics.

In comparison with an earlier content analysis of U.S. news from 1991, news about extremism and violence in Germany increased as these events became more commonplace. A content analysis of news from September 1990 to September 1991 showed that stories about Germany's problems with right-wing radicals were so few in number that they were combined with stories about World War II crimes; together these amounted to only 3 stories (1% of news about Germany) over the one-year period. During the same period, the Associated Press wire service material (an indicator of what was likely to appear in major metropolitan newspapers in the country) contained only 23 stories about right-wing radicals or neo-Nazis

TABLE 12.4. Main Subjects of U.S. Newspaper Stories about Germany over Time:
Los Angeles Times, September 1, 1992–March 31, 1993 (N = 61)

Subject	Sept. 92	Oct. 92	Nov. 92	Dec. 92	Jan. 93	Feb. 93	Mar. 93
Economy	41%	36%	—	—	25%	60%	20%
Refugees	—	27	9	25	—	—	20
Europe	18	—	9	25	—	—	—
Extremism	24	—	46	13	50	20	20
World	12	—	—	13	—	—	40
Domestic	—	27	27	25	—	—	—
Other	6	9	9	—	25	20	—
Total	100	100	100	100	100	100	100
Base	17	11	11	8	4	5	5

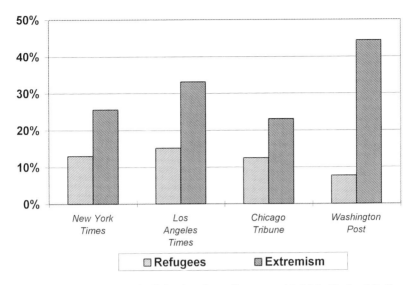

FIGURE 12.2. Percentages of All Stories about Germany with Main Topic of Refugees or Extremism, September 1, 1992–March 31, 1993

and World War II crimes, and this was less than 3% of stories about Germany (see Semetko et al. 1992).

U.S. Public Opinion: March/April 1993

The survey began with the open-ended questions: "Looking back over the past year, in your opinion, what was the most important event in the news? And what was the second most important event in the news?" The presidential election and inaugural were the most important events; nearly 69% of respondents named these as either the first or second most important events in the news (*IPOS* 1993: 1). The majority of respondents agreed, regardless of age, gender, education, or interest in foreign affairs news. Only those with no interest in politics were less apt to name the election as the most important event in the news though many (43%) in this group did so. Other domestic events in general were named by 25% in addition to the 6% who named the Los Angeles riots and the Rodney King trial. Natural disasters at home—storms and hurricanes—were mentioned by nearly 7%. Other domestic events were named by nearly 25%. Overall, then, domestic events in-cluding the election, inaugural, riots, natural disasters, and the Rodney King trial, as well as other events at home, were by far considered the most important in the news. Of foreign events mentioned, the civil war in the former Yugoslavia was named by 5%; 7% named Somalia, where U.S. troops were stationed; and 16% named events in the former Soviet Union. Events in Germany were not named as important events in the news over the previous year. All other foreign events taken together were mentioned by only 3% of respondents. (These figures sum to more that 100% because multiple responses were permitted.)

A range of domestic problems were on the minds of most Americans. There was no single overarching domestic problem named by a majority of respondents, though the economy would come closest to this if all economic-related responses were taken together. The ten most often named problems facing the country, in response to questions about the two most important problems, were in order of importance: the economy (31%), the health system (25%), jobs (20%), the deficit (20%), poverty and homelessness (11%), law and order (10%), taxes and the budget (7%), education (6%), drugs (5%), and family values (5%). In the spring of 1993, therefore, Americans were looking inward. They looked back on the events in the news over the past year and pointed to domestic problems, as well as the presidential election and the change in power in the White House. This is in stark contrast to the two previous U.S. survey findings from the fall of 1991 and the spring of 1990, when events abroad featured at the top of the list of most important events in the news and when Germany featured separately in this list (*IPOS* 1991a: 1, 1990a: 1). In March 1990, for example, events related to Germany were named by over 40% of U.S. respondents, and the fall of the Berlin Wall accounted for most of this. In 1991, 69% named the Gulf War as one of the two most important events in the news, whereas events in Germany were named by 6%. By 1993, events in Germany did not feature in the public mind as important events in the news. This corresponds with what we know from the content analysis of press and TV news over 1992 and early 1993 when Germany was not, in fact, highly visible in U.S. news.

Opinions about Germany and the Germans

Despite this, over the early 1990s, Germany came to be seen by an increasing number of Americans as the leading power in Europe. When asked the open-ended question, "In your opinion, which European country is the leading power in (Western) Europe?," the percentage naming Germany rose from 27% in 1990 to 30% in 1991 and 34% in 1993. Those naming Britain dropped from 26% in 1991 to 24% in 1993, and the number responding "don't know" went up from 21% in 1991 to 29% in 1993 (*IPOS* 1993: 5). In 1993, as well as in 1991, older Americans (over 40) were more likely than younger Americans to name Germany, as were those with higher education (beyond high school), men, those with a strong interest in politics, and those who were highly attentive to foreign news.

Nevertheless, most Americans continued to believe that Britain is the country that the United States can rely on most in the event of a problem, though this was on the decline by 1993. When asked the open-ended question, "If there was a problem, which [West] European country could the United States rely on most?," 8% said Germany in 1991 and 1993; 5% in 1991 and 8% in 1993 said France; 4% said Russia or the Soviet Union in both surveys; 6% in 1991 and 4% in 1993 named another country and the number of those responding "don't know" increased from 17% in 1991 to 22% in 1993. Among those who named Germany, there was no consistent pattern in demographic characteristics, though those who had been to Germany, who said they were very interested in German developments, or who said they liked the Germans were more likely to name Germany as a reliable partner in case of a problem (*IPOS* 1993: 9).

The number of Americans who believed that unified Germany could be a danger to peace in Europe increased substantially between 1991 and 1993. This follows what appeared to have been a slight decline between 1990 and 1991. In September 1991, when asked, "Do you believe that a united Germany could become a danger to peace in Europe?," 64% said no (up nearly 4 percentage points from 1990) and 30% said yes (down nearly 5 percentage points) (*IPOS* 1991a: 64). In March 1990, prior to unification, American respondents were asked a slightly different question, "Do you believe that a reunified Germany could become a danger to peace in Europe?," though it seems unlikely that the minor change in wording resulted in a significant change in public opinion. By the spring of 1993, however, when asked the same question as in the 1991 survey, only 46% responded no and 41% responded yes, with 13% saying "don't know."

Those 41% who said yes in 1993 were asked why and were given a number of possible options—"Is it because Germany might try to expand its territory again, or because the German economy might become too strong, or because it might lead to a revival of fascism, or for some other reason?" Whereas in 1991 responses were fairly evenly distributed among all categories (*IPOS* 1991a: 64), by 1993 a revival of fascism was named most often, followed by the economy, and then territory. Of the entire sample in 1993, including the 46% who believed Germany does not present a danger to peace in Europe, as well as the 13% who said "don't know," a full 15% pointed to a possible revival of fascism, 11% named the strong economy, and 9% named territorial expansion (*IPOS* 1993: 62). By contrast, in 1991 only 7% mentioned a possible revival of fascism, 7% named the economy, and 10% named territorial expansion. The fact that the number of Americans naming a possible revival of fascism nearly doubled between 1991 and 1993 is probably largely due to the emphasis on violence and extremism in U.S. news coverage.

Sympathy with (or liking) Germany remained relatively high in 1993, though it declined slightly from 1991 as it had for nearly all foreign countries. In each survey, respondents were asked to rate a number of countries on a $+5$ to -5 (like/dislike) scale. Germany's mean rating in 1993 was 1.9 and in 1991 it was 2.4; this compares with 2.3 for West Germany and 1.1 for East Germany in 1990. Britain's mean rating was 2.7 in 1993, 3.3 in 1991, and 2.9 in 1990. The rank order of countries, based on mean sympathy ratings ranging from highest to lowest in March 1993, with September 1991 in parentheses, was Canada 3.5 (3.8), Britain 2.7 (3.3), Germany 1.9 (2.4), France 1.9 (2.1), Austria 1.8 (not asked in 1991), Italy 1.8 (2.2), Poland 1.2 (1.6), Japan 1.0 (1.4), Mexico 0.9 (1.1), Russia/Soviet Union 0.9 (1.4), Hungary 0.7 (1.1), Israel 0.7 (1.4), and the Czech Republic/ Czechoslovakia 0.1 (1.1), (*IPOS* 1991a: 14–25; 1993: 22). More countries were included in the 1991 survey than in 1990, which makes it problematic to compare rank order. Mean sympathy rating in 1990 were Britain 2.9, West Germany 2.3, France 2.1, Poland 1.6, Japan 1.5, East Germany 1.1, Hungary 1.0, Israel 0.9, and the Soviet Union 0.6.

The general decline in sympathy rating for all countries between 1991 and 1993 may be symptomatic of an inward-looking citizenry. As a consequence, there was a decline in those willing to give an evaluation, so the less informed or less educated were simply opting out of answering these questions. The proportion of those offering no rating increased for all countries, for example, whereas nearly 4% offered no rating of Germany in 1991, this increased to nearly 9% in 1993 with roughly similar increases for Britain, France, Italy, Russia, Mexico, Canada, Israel, and Japan. The proportion of those offering no evaluation of Poland, the Czech Republic and Hungary nearly tripled from 1991, to reach 16%, 22%, and 20%, respectively. An inward-looking citizenry unable to evaluate foreign countries also corresponds with the increase in the number of respondents giving "don't know" answers to the earlier questions concerning the leading power in Europe and a reliable partner.

Using the same +5 to −5 scale, respondents were asked to rate a number of international political leaders. But a substantial portion of Americans were unable to rate British prime minister John Major (46%), German chancellor Helmut Kohl (50%) and French president François Mitterrand (51%)—more often because they did not recognize the name than because they had a lack of sufficient information about the leader to evaluate him (IPOS 1993: 34). This corresponds with the September 1991 survey, which was conducted shortly after the failed Russian coup, when more than 48% of Americans were unable to rate these three leaders (IPOS 1991a: 26–35). Many more recognized Russian president Boris Yeltsin in 1993, and only 18% did not offer an evaluation of him compared with 10% for Yeltsin predecessor Mikhail Gorbachev and 3% for Bill Clinton.

Of all the leaders, newly elected U.S. president Bill Clinton was most highly rated with a mean of 2.0 (compared with 3.2 for his predecessor George Bush in 1991), followed by Boris Yeltsin at 1.9 (2.2 in 1991), and Mikhail Gorbachev at 1.6 (2.4 in 1991). Of the lesser known leaders, the mean ratings were John Major 2.3 (2.5 in 1991), Helmut Kohl 1.6 (1.8 in 1991), and François Mitterrand 0.9 (1.2 in 1991) (IPOS 1991a: 30–32, 1993: 31). Overall there has been a decline in the ratings of all the international political leaders since 1991; this corresponds with the decline in sympathy ratings for foreign countries.

Most Americans believed that German democracy is at least somewhat endangered by right-wing and left-wing extremism. Asked in 1993, "How strongly do you think German democracy is endangered by right-wing radicals or neo-Nazi extremism? Would you say very strongly endangered, strongly endangered, somewhat endangered, or not at all endangered?," 9% said very strongly, 19% said strongly, 50% said somewhat, and only 9% said not at all—with 13% saying "don't know." Slightly less believed Germany democracy was strongly endangered by left-wing radicals: 4% said very strongly, 11% strongly, 52% somewhat, and 16% not at all—with 17% saying "don't know" (IPOS 1993: 65). In 1993, people under the age of 24, as well as those between 40 and 60 years of age, were more inclined to believe Germany was strongly endangered by right-wing extremism, as were those with less education and those who pay a great deal or a lot of attention to foreign affairs news in the press or on television (IPOS 1993: 65–67). In 1991, the question was asked slightly differently: "Do you think that German democracy is seriously endangered by right-wing radicals and neo-Nazis or is it not endangered?"; 55% said it is not endangered, 33% said it is seriously endangered, and 12% said "don't know." Asked in 1991, "Do you think that German democracy is seriously endangered by left-wing radicals or is it not endangered?," 62% said it is not endangered, 21% said it is seriously endangered, and 18% said "don't know" (*IPOS* 1991a: 70).

The most disturbing result of the 1993 survey emerged from a new question that had not been asked in previous studies. When asked, "Do you believe there is a danger in Germany that Nazism will return, or does this danger not exist?," a full 54% said there is a danger Nazism will return and only 36% believed this danger does not exist—with nearly 10% responding "don't know" (*IPOS* 1993: 73). Older people (over 30) were slightly, but not substantially, more likely to believe Nazism will return, women (61%) were far more likely than men (46%) to believe this, and those with some college education (59%) were somewhat more likely than the high school educated (52%) or college graduates (48%) to believe this. Respondents in the U.S. West were least likely to believe Nazism will return to Germany (50%), and those in the Midwest were most likely (58%). As interest in politics increased, so did one's likelihood of believing that Nazism will return. Those who paid a great deal of attention to TV news about foreign affairs (61%) were more likely to believe this in comparison with those who paid less attention (50%). The highly attentive to TV (61%) were also more likely to believe this than those who paid a great deal of attention to foreign affairs news in the press (50%). Not surprisingly, those who believed that there is a danger Nazism will return to Germany were also far more likely to believe Germany is very strongly or strongly endangered by right-wing or left-wing radicals.

Most Americans view themselves as patriotic, trustworthy, and friendly to foreigners. Germans are viewed as patriotic, trustworthy, but arrogant. Respondents were asked whether a number of characteristics describe themselves: "Please tell me whether you think the following qualities describe Americans—are Americans friendly to foreigners? (trustworthy, arrogant, violent, hostile to Jews, patriotic)." They were then asked the same series of questions about Germans. Americans' perceptions of themselves in 1993 follow, with Americans' perceptions of Germans in parentheses: friendly to foreigners 73% (43%); trustworthy 74% (54%); arrogant 63% (54%); violent 57% (43%); hostile to Jews 27% (52%); patriotic 89% (77%). Americans are thus far more likely to view themselves than Germans as friendly to foreigners and far more likely to view Germans than themselves as hostile to Jews. These perceptions are likely to have been influenced by the presence of news stories about extremism in Germany. It is worth noting, however, that in 1991 when the survey used the term "friendly" instead of "friendly to foreigners," the gap between American's self-perceptions and their perceptions of Germans was just as great (30 percentage points).

That said, most Americans said they like Germans: 72% said they like the Germans, 15% said they don't like them, and 13% said "don't know." By contrast, 61% said they like the Japanese in 1993, whereas 30% said they don't like them—with 10% saying "don't know" (*IPOS* 1993: 83). A not insubstantial portion of Americans (22%) report having friends or relatives currently living in Germany.

And perhaps surprisingly, 39% claim to have German ancestors or relatives (*IPOS* 1993: 151). More than one-quarter (27%) of the respondents have been to Europe, including 16% who have been to Germany or Berlin (*IPOS* 1993: 149).

Summary

The content analysis shows that in the year preceding the March 1993 survey, Germany was hardly the most visible foreign country in the U.S. press. Japan, Russia, Mexico, Britain, Israel, and Canada appeared more often than Germany. Germany was one of the most visible countries on ABC television news and current affairs programs, following only Russia, but in ABC's prime-time news program over the twelve months, there were only 74 stories about Germany, an average of 6 per month or 1.4 stories per week. Given that the average length of a TV news story is between one and two minutes, this is roughly equivalent to about 90 seconds on Germany in 110 minutes of main evening news on ABC each week, with most of the 22-minute daily program devoted to domestic affairs.

Nevertheless, the problems Germany then had with extremism, violence against foreigners, and refugees were among the most prominent themes in the mainstream news media during this period, particularly between September and December 1992. News about the German economy, Germany's domestic politics, and international relations was also important. News about extremism and violence in Germany increased substantially between 1991 and 1993 because of the increased occurrence of these events. Between September 1990 and September 1991, for example, there was almost no news about extremism or right-wing radicals, and the subject ranked at the bottom of the list of themes of stories about Germany in the American news media.

The survey data provide a somewhat mixed account of U.S. public opinion concerning Germany in early 1993. On the one hand Americans continued to have a positive view of Germany, giving it one of the highest sympathy ratings among the many countries included in the survey. Americans rated only Canada and Britain more highly than Germany. Germany also came to be seen by more Americans as the leading power in Europe. United States–German relations were viewed positively by most Americans in 1993, and the majority wanted relations to become even closer. Americans also expressed interest in following developments in Germany, more than in the former Yugoslavia, despite the civil war in that region.

Americans also clearly like Germans. In fact, substantially more Americans like Germans than the Japanese—in part because many believed Japan presented a greater threat to the U.S. economy. But Americans also have a high degree of contact with Germany and the Germans, with friends or relatives living there. Many also feel a connection to Germany via ancestors. On the other hand, however, the number of Americans who believed that unified Germany could be a danger to peace in Europe increased substantially since 1991, by 11 percentage points to 41% in 1993. A not insubstantial number of Americans in 1993 also believed German democracy was endangered by threats from right-wing and left-wing extremists, though substantially more believe there is a strong threat to democracy from right-wing radicals than from the Left. Finally, a majority of Americans in 1993 said they believed there is a danger in Germany that Nazism will return. This response was associated with high levels of interest in politics and high attention to foreign affairs news on TV and in the press, though there was no clear linear relationship with education. Those with some college education were more likely to believe this than those with only high school or with postcollege (graduate) education. Women were also much more likely than men to believe this.

These evaluations, however, must be viewed in the context of the climate of opinion in the United States in early 1993. It was one of looking inward, one preoccupied with events and problems at home, with little interest in developments abroad. When asked to name the most important events in the news over the past year, domestic issues, events, and problems dominated the list. Events abroad were hardly mentioned, apart from the occasional reference to Russia and Somalia, and events in Germany did not even emerge on the list. Domestic problems also predominated in response to the open-ended questions regarding the most important problems facing the country today, including the economy, health care, jobs, the deficit, poverty, and homelessness. Although substantially more Americans in 1993 expressed high levels of interest in politics than in 1991, this was limited to national and local issues. Nearly half of the respondents were unable to rate leading international political leaders—including Chancellor Helmut Kohl, Prime Minister John Major, and President François Mitterrand—using a $+5$ to -5 (eleven-point) sympathy scale because they did not recognize them or did not know enough about them to offer an evaluation. Many more Americans recognized and felt able to rate Mikhail Gorbachev and Boris Yeltsin, but this, too, was lower than in 1991 when these leaders had received substantial attention in the news shortly before the 1991 survey began.

A study based on a similar survey conducted in early 1990, within three months after the fall of the Berlin Wall, found that the more visible Germany was on the U.S. network TV news, the stronger the media attention and exposure measures were as predictors of liking or disliking that country (Semetko et al. 1992). There appears to be a base level of positive attitudes toward Germany among the U.S. public, and this is related to the contact people have with Germany via travel, friends, relatives, and ancestors (Gibowski and Semetko 1992).

But Germany's comparatively low visibility in the sea of news about domestic problems in 1992–93 meant that attention to news was not as important a predictor of the country's sympathy ratings as it had been in the past.[3] Nevertheless, the news about violence and extremism was associated with a significant change in opinion about unified Germany being a possible danger to peace in Europe due to the possible revival of fascism. This news also contributed to the view held by many politically interested Americans in early 1993 that Nazism could return to Germany one day. Even during this time of Germany's comparatively low visibility in the U.S. media, the news about these events struck a chord with many Americans. People are likely to interpret current events in Germany in the context of historical memory. The images of Germany's twelve years of Nazi rule beginning in the 1930s are replayed often on American TV movie channels and surfaced again in U.S. news and foreign affairs commentary when there was a resurgence of violence against refugees and foreigners. Although the events in the fall of 1992 were short-lived, the historical memory remains.

NOTES

This chapter is based on a Gallup survey conducted by telephone. The survey and content analysis were supported by a grant from the German Federal Press and Information Agency to the author at the Center for Political Studies, Institute of Social Research, University of Michigan. An earlier version of this chapter was presented at the International Studies Association annual meeting in Chicago, at a panel on "International News and Foreign Policymaking" of the Foreign Policy Analysis Section, February 23–25, 1995. Research assistance and computer support were provided by the S. I. Newhouse School of Public Communications and the Global Affairs Institute at the Maxwell School of Citizenship and Public Affairs, Syracuse University. The research assistance of James McQuivey, a doctoral student in public communications at Syracuse University, is gratefully acknowledged. Also, the research assistance of Jaqui Chmielewski on the 1990 study is much appreciated.

1. Findings from an earlier study are reported in Semetko, Brzinski, Weaver, and Willnat (1992) which was awarded the Robert Worcester Prize and named the article of the year in the *International Journal of Public Opinion Research*.

2. The 1990, 1991, and 1993 U.S. surveys were conducted in collaboration with IPOS in Mannheim, which fielded comparable surveys of publics in the old and new Bundesländer in the same periods. IPOS also produced the table volumes on the U.S. surveys. These include "American Attitudes about Germany in an Age of Transition," Study Number 670, March 1990; "American Attitudes toward German in a Changing Europe," Study Number 777, October 1991; "American Attitudes toward Germany in a Changing Europe," Study Number 850, March/April 1993.

3. In regression analysis, the measures of exposure to news and attention to foreign affairs news in 1993 did not emerge as significant predictors of sympathy with Germany (using the -5 to $+5$ scale as the dependent variable).

HERMANN KURTHEN, WERNER BERGMANN, AND RAINER ERB

Concluding Remarks

Questions for Further Research in Comparative Perspective

The wave of xenophobic violence, the electoral successes of far-right parties, and the upsurge of aggressive antisemitic incidents between 1991 and 1994 alarmed the German and international public. This book itself is a reaction to those events and reflects academic attempts to describe and explain these challenges to united Germany from historical, political, and sociological perspectives. The intention of this book is to shed more light on the causes and origins of societal transformations that promote the escalation of xenophobic and ethnocentric violence and antisemitic resentment. In the first part of this volume (chapters 2–5), empirical facts and findings are presented that cover the origins and the extent of antisemitism and xenophobia in East and West Germany. In chapters 6–9, roots and motives of specific social forces, movements, groups, and organizations propagating hate and prejudice are analyzed. Finally, chapters 10–12 cover the reactions of German society and the Jewish community in Germany, as well as the response of the media abroad.

The focus on Germany in this study might give the impression that the types of events analyzed are unique and essentially "German" in their character. However, if we put these incidents into a wider comparative and historical perspective, it becomes clear that the upsurge of nationalist and xenophobic resentment and right-wing violence in combination with large-scale societal transformations and migration movements is a phenomenon that can be observed in other European and Western countries as well. In fact, since 1990 the academic debate in Europe has reflected this broader scope and has already produced an impressive range of literature. Prominent theoretical approaches try to explain trends of a renationalization and ethnicization of politics by referring to the Janus-face of societal development and modernization (Heitmeyer 1994a, 1994b) or changes in the political culture. Other explanations are found in the tradition of studies in authoritarianism

(Adorno et al 1950, Lederer et al. 1991, Oesterreich 1993), individual psychology and socialization theory, group sociology and political deviance (Hagan, Merkins, and Boehnke 1995; for an overview see Wahl 1993). Important new impulses also come from youth research that analyzes, for example, the construction of enemy-images and violent acts among young male gangs (Kersten 1994). A relatively new field studies the involvement of women in the right-wing scene (Birsl 1994). Research about the violence of adolescents stresses the importance of misguided and anomic processes of individualization resulting in isolation, indifference, and violent behavior as a means to express identity (Heitmeyer 1995).

Another central issue of ongoing research, not only in Germany but also in other Western nations, is the question of historical continuity and the persistence of traditional extremist right-wing ideologies and prejudice. How persistent is the wave of violence and resentment? Is it a youth and social movement or only a short-lived surge based on contingent opportunity structures? Have antisemitism, ethnocentrism, and xenophobia taken on characteristics that transcend links with National Socialism and fascism? How "new" is the New Right? Has it been able to successfully absorb populist demands and resentment that exist among the mainstream population? Are right-wing parties, such as the "Republikaner" Party in Germany and the National Front in France, protest or *Weltanschauungs* parties, and how far have they departed from democratic principles? Also, the actual role of the New Right in promoting racist violence and xenophobic movements, in setting the agenda of European immigration policy, and in breeding extremist right-wing parties and deviant youth violence is subject to controversy (see Björgo 1995, Björgo and Witte 1993, Butterwegge and Jäger 1992, Ford 1992, Hafeneger 1990, Hainsworth 1992, Hargreaves and Leaman 1995, Minkenberg 1993, Ignazi and Ysmal 1992, Kowalsky and Schroeder 1994, Merkl and Weinberg 1993, Miles 1993, and Wrench and Solomos 1993).

Four dimensions should be taken into account in analyzing the emergence of right-wing movements, violence, and prejudice in modern Western societies. They are (1) general societal trends, (2) ideological drifts in Western democracies, (3) political cultures, and (4) societal opportunity structures.

1. The crisis in postwar affluent welfare states is an international phenomenon. In the mid-1970s and especially in the 1980s, Western democracies underwent sweeping changes in their socioeconomic, technological, political, and ethnocultural makeup. In the economic realm, conservatives have tried to overcome the dilemmas of modern welfare states by down-sizing welfare and social security provisions. But Reaganomics and Thatcherism have led only to an increase in social inequality without removing indebtedness, inflation, unemployment, labor market segmentation, and polarization between losers and winners of modernization. In the political realm, the emergence of new political cleavages has led to the unfolding of crosscutting catchall parties, electoral shifts, and voter apathy or protest. Reorganization of society in the cultural sphere is characterized by sweeping changes in mass communications, the evolution of a global media culture, and the dissolution of traditional social and cultural milieus, lifestyles, values, and

normative orientations. In addition, mass immigration of an unprecedented extent and large-scale refugee movements have changed the demographic composition and ethnocultural map of Western countries. They have increased diversity and pluralism, but they have also led to tensions and resentment. The struggle for scarcer resources has created a partially real, partially imagined competition between natives and immigrants. Hostile antiimmigrant attitudes question the participation of newcomers in the social system of the host country. Also, demands for a limitation of immigration or even the return of immigrants have gained ground. The Right in Western Europe in particular cultivates a fortress mentality that wants to fend off migration by all means.

Immigration also fostered the ethnicization of social conflicts and gave rise to contested issues that are currently exploited by populist right-wing parties and used as vehicles to propagate further ranging radical political and social changes. Unfortunately, at the same time, the established party systems became paralyzed and ties to the electorate weakened. Parties and politicians are now seen as incompetent, indecisive, or alienated from the everyday worries of their electorate. The established elites have contributed to this image by fostering internal disarray and corruption, by not reacting efficiently and sufficiently to new challenges, and by polarizing voters for short-sighted political gain. Everywhere, one can observe signs of delegitimization and an increase in political distrust, apathy, and protest voting.

2. The end of the Cold War, with the breakdown of Communist regimes in Central and Eastern Europe, has left many to question universalist or internationalist ideologies and to reject the subduing of national interests under an East-West confrontation that was withering away. But a political climate that favors a renaissance of nationalism, regionalism, particularism, and ethnocentrism is in stark contrast to the facts of integration of nation-states into global and regional economies, supranational security networks, and the establishment of ethnic and minority communities in former ethnoculturally more homogenous nations. The economic, political, and cultural dynamics of these controversial transformations gave far-right parties and antidemocratic movements opportunities to popularize their resentment and to feed it to protest movements. The Right hopes to find more resonance with topics like curtailment of immigration, the rejuvenation of national interests and regionalism, and retreat from supranational alliances (such as the European Union and NATO). They slow down the dynamics of ongoing societal and transnational changes by demanding national-particularistic autonomy, economic autarky, ethnocultural identity, and political sovereignty. Intellectual leaders, publishers, and charismatic populists play a decisive role in developing, legitimating, and propagating antimodern theories, Western cultural racism, and neonationalist ideologies. However, the impact of this New Right on the intellectual, cultural, and political mainstream is contested in politics and science and needs to be studied more closely.

Besides historical and general societal and ideological trends that characterize current Western democracies, one has to consider specific political cultures and fluctuating opportunity structures that foster in a given time period the wavelike emergence of protest movements, violence, and prejudice. In the case of Germany, unification and mass immigration, national traditions and identities, collective mentalities and memories, political cultures, and the legal framework that deals with political deviance are of importance in the attempt to explain how and why this society reacted differently to the challenges of the Right than did neighboring countries (see Almond and Verba 1963, Dalton 1988, and Reichel 1981).

3. The German political culture is characterized by a sharp difference between the extent and expression of antisemitism and xenophobia. Xenophobic resentment can count on a much broader societal acceptance than antisemitism. Germany's attempts to distance itself from National Socialist ideology had a formative influence on the political culture and the German elite in postwar Germany. Auschwitz more than anything else stands in the way of an unbroken identification of Germans with German history and the German nation. It is common consent for Germans to harshly sanction antisemitic remarks in public, to refrain from patriotic sentiments and national chauvinism, to denounce the Nazi past, and to express guilt, shame, and remorse for what has been done in the name of Germany. Therefore, antisemitic actions and the display of Nazi paraphernalia inside and outside Germany are highly provocative. Antidemocratic opponents of the liberal political system of the Federal Republic know about these taboos and use the symbolic value of Nazism and antisemitism to express their opposition and hostility (Erb 1994). Taking their provocation at face value plays into the hands of these extremists by destroying the image of a new and democratic Germany and its postwar accomplishments within the community of civilized nations.

In the case of hostility toward foreigners and ethno(cultural)-centrism, the picture is not so clear. It certainly contains elements of common Western racism against people from non-Western cultures and civilizations. In Germany, xenophobia is also nurtured by the weakened but among certain groups still existing *völkisch* understanding of nationhood as a homogeneous community based on common descent and a shared destiny in good and bad times *(Abstammungs- und Schicksalsgemeinschaft)*. Such perceptions are a barrier to accept politically and psychologically the fact that after the war Germany has become a country of immigration with a comparatively large ethnocultural minority of almost 10% of its population (Kurthen 1995, Kurthen and Minkenberg 1995). Although the heterogeneous group of labor migrants with their families and offspring, recognized asylum seekers, naturalized former resident aliens, and ethnic German resettlers are economically and socially more or less integrated, many remain culturally excluded and isolated. Empirical surveys since the 1970s confirm that feelings of mutual distance and rejection prevail (Geiger 1991, Bade 1992). Among the indigenous population, immigrants are often associated with stereotypes and traits that are assigned conventionally to members of lower classes (dirty, lazy, noisy, promiscuous, and deviant). This perception significantly differs from the Jewish stereotype, which has an upper-class profile (wealthy, powerful, smart, and intelligent) (see *Der Spiegel* 1992: 63 and Bergmann and Erb 1991a).

The specific historical experience of Germany with National Socialism, postwar reeducation, and vigilance of democratic forces also determined the marginalization and isolation of right-wing extremism. In comparison to France, Italy, and Belgium, the far-right in West Germany (organized in political parties) was relatively unsuccessful, except for two short periods in 1949–52 and 1965–69 (Stöss

1989). The extremists' attempts to gain a foothold on the political stage in Germany was blocked by their stigmatization as successors of the National Socialist terror regime. Right extremism was pushed into hiding and became a subculture that was divided into a multitude of sectarian splinter groups.

4. The reference to the political culture of the Federal Republic, however, is insufficient to explain the violent wave that shook Germany after unification and raised eyebrows all over the world. We believe, it is necessary to refer to theories of collective action and the political agenda approach (Cobb and Elder 1983, Leenen 1992) to explain the interaction of a multitude of institutions and levels of action over time during a given period of action.

Because immigration in the context of unemployment and housing shortages became an issue of public contention after 1989, the newly founded far-Right "Republikaner" Party, a splinter of the Bavarian Christian Social Union (CSU), was able to overcome the 5% threshold in some state and local elections. Similarly, militant neo-Nazis and skinheads increased their activities and membership in the late 1980's (see table 1.1). Both trends were thrust into significance by two unexpected events: the domestic problems and uncertainties created by unification and the rising numbers of immigrants. The strains and costs of unification in combination with a deep economic recession, inflation, rising taxes, and unemployment for a moment brought to a halt tendencies toward postnationalist attitudes and more cultural pluralism. The sudden increase of asylum seekers combined with increased East-to-West immigration led to a backlash in public opinion, although hundreds of thousands of East Germans had been welcomed enthusiastically when the Wall came down. The immigration issue was exacerbated by the inability of democratic parties to sensitively tackle asylum and related issues of citizenship and cultural pluralism. Together, these conditions gave right-wing mobilization a momentum and public attention it lacked during earlier periods (Kurthen and Minkenberg 1995)

Our interpretation is supported by the different developments in the fields of xenophobia and antisemitism. Opinion polls between 1990 and 1994 indicate relatively stable attitudes in the population at large (Hill 1993, Wiegand 1992, Schnabel 1992). Therefore, changes in electoral behavior can be interpreted as a protest vote responding to issues that are perceived as acute, for example, asylum reform and integration of foreigners. But organized right-wing extremists and youth subculture, mostly responsible for xenophobic violence and antisemitic propaganda, were able to use the given opportunity structure after 1990 to express public feelings that ranged from uneasiness to open resentment (see Bergmann 1994c, Bergmann and Erb 1994c and 1994a, and Willems 1994). At one point a concurrence existed among the majority of the population, right-wing protest voters, and extremist militants: all wanted to limit immigration, in particular that of asylum seekers. When after a difficult process of decision making among the democratic parties the asylum law was reformed, this overarching issue—as many surveys clearly show—lost its relevance for the population and even for many former protest voters. They were clearly not willing to support the more far-reaching radical objectives of right-wing parties or of militant neo-Nazis, which were also directed against foreign residents living and working for many years in Germany, as well as against the relatively small Jewish community in Germany. These different political objectives and motivations led to the formation of a somewhat delayed, but resolute, societal response against the excesses of the Right fringe on three levels. The democratic political parties and government retained their authority and competence to act; the population demonstrated and publicly expressed their dislike of violence, xenophobia, and antisemitism; and the judiciary and police put the violent Right extremists into place with punitive methods.

These reactions stopped a further escalation of violence and resentment and initiated a slow process of deescalation. However, up to now neither the membership of right-wing organizations, the percentage of voters of far-Right parties, nor the number of racist and violent crimes is back down to the lower levels of the late 1980s. External pressure on the Right also has promoted attempts among the Right fringe to overcome personal and ideological differences and to modernize their movement, that is, to protect their cadres and subcultural organizations against prosecution via autonomous networks and to improve their opportunities for action and access to the public by modernizing their communications via electronic media.

For the time being, the issue of xenophobia and antisemitism has subsided and a similar upsurge of violence and resentment in the near future is unlikely. Singling out Germany as atypical does not solve the underlying problems of the reemergence of nationalism, xenophobia, and antisemitism in Western countries. Instead, a rational discussion is needed about the origins of and remedies for the phenomena analyzed in this book. The case of Germany is a stern lesson for other Western societies that indicates the need for constant vigilance, education, and coordinated action by the democratic public, the media, the government, and the judiciary; the maintenance of a healthy political culture; and the continued observance of the dynamics of political opportunity structures. Because recent events in Germany also reflect global problems, such as the rise of nationalism, huge migration movements, and the establishment of international right-wing networks and subcultures, Western societies need concerted responses on local, regional, national, and supranational levels regarding migration, labor market, and welfare policies to control and roll back any further outgrowth of violence and resentment from the beginning.

Appendix

Selected Chronology of Antisemitic and Extreme Right-Wing Events in Germany during and after Unification, 1989–1994

1989

January 7: The memorial to the deportation of Berlin Jews at the Putlitzbrücke, the memorial prison at Plötzensee, and the Rosa Luxemburg Monument are desecrated with pigs' heads. The Movement of April 20 (Adolf Hitler's birthday) takes responsibility. On August 28, 1989, and March 15, 1990, the Putlitzbrücke memorial again becomes the target of attacks.

January 29: During the West Berlin city council election, the right-wing "Republikaner" Party receives 7.5% of all votes.

February 9: The minister of the interior in Bonn bans the National Alliance (Nationale Sammlung) of the neo-Nazi Michael Kühnen.

March 12: During the local government elections in Hesse, the right-wing National Democratic Party (NPD) wins in Frankfurt am Main 6.6% of all votes and is represented in the city parliament by seven NPD city assemblymen.

March 13: Supporters of Michael Kühnen found the neo-Nazi state party, National List (NL), in Hamburg. Christian Worch becomes head of the organization, Thomas Wulff party chairman. The NL, with a total of thirty members, is banned by the Hamburg state on February 24, 1995. The decision argues that the organization intends to remove the Federal Basic Law (Grundgesetz) and has policy goals inspired by the Third Reich.

April 20: Police arrest about one hundred persons in Berlin and twenty-one persons in Bremen during disturbances on the centennial of Adolf Hitler's birthday.

April 22: During a campaign speech for the European election, the "Republikaner" Party demands the removal of the concentration camp memorial in the Bavarian city of Dachau.

May: Supporters of Michael Kühnen found the German Alternative (Deutsche Alternative [DA]) as a national protest party in Bremen.

May 22: Unknown persons assault neo-Nazi Christian Worch in his Hamburg apartment and rob him.

May 29: The honorary Frankfurt NPD city councilman Erich Gutjahr precludes his party suspension by resigning from the party and giving up his city office. Gutjahr denounced the German president Richard von Weizsäcker as "the greatest scoundrel in this country" and maintained that Jews "loot us again."

June 18: The "Republikaner" win 7.1% of all votes in West Germany during their first participation in a European election. In Bavaria they receive 14.6%. Despite a costly advertisement campaign, the German People's Union [DVU–Liste D]) receives only 1.6% of all votes.

July 27: Two skinheads who are brothers injure a 59–year-old homeless person so badly that he dies soon after in Gelsenkirchen (North Rhine–Westphalia). The district court in Essen sentences one of the brothers to 5 years and the other to 6 years in youth detention for manslaughter.

August 8: Once more, unknown persons desecrate the memorial prison at Berlin-Plötzensee with photographs of pigs' heads.

October 9: The beginning of "Monday demonstrations" against the regime in Leipzig(Saxony) and other cities of the German Democratic Republic.

October 11: The public prosecutor's office at the district court in Amberg charges a 20-year-old neo-Nazi with arson. The defendant is suspected of committing an incendiary attack at a house in Schwandorf (Bavaria) that resulted in the deaths of three members of a Turkish family and a German.

October 18: After 18 years, the secretary general of the East German Socialist Unity Party (Sozialistische Einheitspartei Deutschlands [SED]), Erich Honecker, is ousted from office. His successor is Egon Krenz.

November 7: The government of East Germany resigns.

November 9: The Berlin Wall and other border crossings from East to West Germany are opened.

November 22: The Turkish cemetery in Berlin-Neukölln is desecrated.

About 35,900 persons in West Germany are members of extremist right-wing organizations according to a report by the Federal Office for the Protection of the Constitution (Amt für Verfassungsschutz). The number has increased by 27% or by 7,600 persons from the previous year. The increase is explained by the continuous expansion of the DVU–Liste D. For 1989 the report also cites 1,853 violations of law by the extremist right wing, including 254 violent acts.

1990

February 1: Six skinheads associate with Ingo Hasselbach's National Alternative, a party that sees itself as the Berlin branch of the German Alternative, in Berlin-Lichtenberg. The new party gives as the date of its foundation January 30.

March 8: A neo-Nazi attack on an asylum home in Essen causes considerable material damage.

March 18: The first free election in the German Democratic Republic is held. According to East German law, extreme right-wing parties from West Germany are not allowed to participate in the election.

March 28: The Hamburg district court fines neo-Nazi Edgar Geiss 6,000 DM because of his assertion that the diary of Anne Frank was forged.

March 31: About twenty skinheads attack a Tamil in Nienburg (Weser). Four passersby who stop to help are seriously injured.

April 28: At a rock concert in Nordhausen near the East German–West German border, skinhead groups initiate riots.

May: Thorsten Heise, a militant neo-Nazi, tries to drive over a Lebanese asylum seeker in Nörten-Hardenberg (Lower Saxony). On July 5, 1991, the district court in Göttingen sentences Heise to two years in prison for this attempt and other offenses.

May 6: Unknown neo-Nazis desecrate the Dorothenstädtische cemetery in East Berlin with antisemitic slogans. Among the graves are those of Bertolt Brecht and Rosa Luxemburg.

May 12: Three skinheads desecrate a concentration camp cemetery in Türkheim (Bavaria). In January 1991, the district court in Memmingen sentences the skinheads to between 10 and 18 months in prison.

May 25: Franz Schönhuber resigns from his office as party chairman of the "Republikaner" Party.

July 3: Former activists of the Free Workers' Party (FAP) who are disappointed about the party's internal quarrels found the National Offensive (NO).

July 7–8: Once again Schönhuber is elected as party chairman by a majority of delegates at the party convention of the "Republikaner" in Ruhsdorf (Lower Bavaria).

July 28: The Jewish cemetery in Stuttgart–Bad Cannstatt is desecrated. On January 27, 1992, the district court in Stuttgart sentences a 24-year-old skinhead to three years in prison for disturbing the dead and for public incitement. The two other defendants each receive a suspended youth detention sentence with two years of probation. About 1,500 citizens protest against the desecration of the Jewish cemetery with a silent march through the inner city of Stuttgart.

August 25: Out of about 200 tombstones, 177 are desecrated at the Jewish cemetery in Ihringen (Baden-Württemberg).

August 31: The Jewish cemetery in Hechingen (Baden-Württemberg) is desecrated.

September 6: The state of Baden-Württemberg's minister of the interior, Dietmar Schlee, orders increased security at about 150 Jewish cemeteries and memorials.

September 12: Foreign minister talks in Moscow conclude. The Two-plus-Four-Treaties regulating the full sovereignty of united Germany are signed.

October 3: The German Democratic Republic joins the Federal Republic according to article 23 of the Federal Basic Law (constitution).

October 7: Special party convention of the National Democratic Party (NPD) is held in Erfurt. The independent NPD of the former German Democratic Republic is admitted. Its chairman, Dr. Rainer Prigge, becomes the fourth deputy chair of the united party.

October 8: Three extreme right-wingers seriously mistreat three Poles in Lübbenau (Brandenburg). The state court in Cottbus imposes prison sentences of three years and nine months against one and three years against two of the perpetrators.

October 13: Four skinheads desecrate the Jewish cemeteries in Vaihingen an der Enz and Markgröningen-Unterriexingen (Baden–Württemberg). For the following night, they had planned an arson attack at an asylum-seeker home in Großsachsenheim. In February 1991 the district court in Stuttgart hands down sentences of between two years and nine months and three years and nine months in prison.

October 14: State elections are held in the five new East German Länder: Saxony, Saxony-Anhalt, Thuringia, Brandenburg, and Mecklenburg-Vorpommern. The "Republikaner" Party receives between 0.6% and 1.9% of all votes.

November 25: Right-wing radicals mistreat Angolan Amadeu Antonio Kiowa in Eberswalde (Brandenburg); he dies of his injuries on December 16. In September 1992, the state court in Frankfurt/Oder sentences four juveniles to between three years and six months and four years in prison for inflicting lethal bodily injuries. A fifth defendant receives a suspended prison sentence and two years probation. The behavior of policemen who observed the attack but did not intervene was not fully resolved.

November 25: Skinheads throw stones and Molotov cocktails at a Turkish mosque in Herten (North Rhine–Westphalia).

December 2: The first all-German national election for the federal diet (Bundestag) is disappointing for the "Republikaner" Party. It receives 2.4% of all votes in the western election districts and 1.3% of all votes in the eastern districts—or a total of 2.1.%.

December 5: Skinheads throw Molotov cocktails at an asylum seeker's home in Würselen (Kreis Aachen).

December 13: The cemetery of the Jewish community Adass Jisroel at Berlin-Weissensee is desecrated by unknown persons.

December 16: Martin Mussgnug resigns from his post as party chairman of the NPD in reaction to the weak results of his party (0.3%) during the German national elections on December 2. Günter Deckert is elected as his successor.

December 28: Skinheads kill a 17-year-old Kurd in Hachenburg (Westerwald). In February 1992 the district court in Koblenz sentences the 20-year-old Alexander T. to six years in youth detention for manslaughter with conditional intent.

For all of 1990, the Federal Office for Protection of the Constitution registered 1,380 extreme right-wing-motivated violations of law, among them 308 violent acts.

1991

January 14 and 30: Arson attacks are made on the central reception center for asylum seekers in Eisenhüttenstadt (Brandenburg).

January 15: Once again, the Jewish cemetery in Ihringen (Kreis Breisgau-Hochschwarzwald in Baden-Württemberg) is desecrated.

January 18: The German Alliance Association of the United Right is established in Munich as a "large collection center of all national people," following the activities of Ewald Althans.

February 24: Several persons are injured during a raid of right-wing radicals on the refugee home in Leisnig (Saxony). Occupants have to be evacuated because all the furnishings are damaged.

March 5: About thirty right-wing radicals attack an asylum-seeker home in Klötze (Saxony) and seriously injure three occupants.

March 23: Ernst Zündel intends to hold the International Revisionist Congress or Leuchter Congress in Munich. About four hundred participants protest in front of the German Museum (Deutsches Museum) after the congress is prohibited and Zündel arrested.

March 31: Skinheads throw a 28-year-old Mozambique citizen, Jorge Gomondai, out of a moving tram in Dresden (Saxony). He dies of his injuries one week later. On October 29, 1993, several suspects aged 19 to 22 are sentenced to up to two years and six months in youth detention.

April 8: On the occasion of the introduction of visa-free traffic between Germany and Poland, extreme right-wing activists commit various violent acts along the Polish border.

April 13: In Görlitz several neo-Nazis assail a Polish couple in their car. In the following weeks frequent aggressive acts against Polish travelers occur.

April 22: A third arson attack occurs on the asylum-seeker home in Schwalbach (Hesse) within one week, damaging property.

April 24: A group of high-school students from Haifa (Israel) are attacked by skinheads in Bremen.

April 25: Neo-Nazi leader Michael Kühnen dies. At first it seems as if Gottfried Küssel, an Austrian, will replace him, but after criticism from Küssel's own followers, however, and his arrest in Vienna in January 1992, the Hamburg neo-Nazi Christian Worch rises into the highest ranks of the leadership.

May 3: An attack of armed right-wing radicals in Wittenberge (Brandenburg) injures two Namibians, one of them critically. On March 26, 1992, the district court in Perleberg sentences four defendants to prison for between 15 and 18 months because of breach of public peace and trespass in a particularly serious case. The direct participation of the defendants in the act could not be proven.

May 8: A 21-year-old member of the German armed forces fires at five foreigners in Munich; two are seriously wounded.

May 8: Rainer Sonntag, the Dresden neo-Nazi leader and cofounder of the Association of Saxonian Werewolves, the Protection Squadron East (Schutzstaffel Ost), and the Defense Sports Group Peiper (Wehrsportgruppe Peiper), is shot to death in Dresden during a clash in the pimp milieu.

June 8: The Hessian state party, Covenant of the New Front—German Hesse (Gesinnungsgemeinschaft der Neuen Front—Deutsches Hessen [GdNF/DH]), is founded.

June 8 and 9: Günter Deckert is confirmed as party chairman of the National Democratic Party at its national party convention.

June 15: A 19-year-old skinhead stabs a 34-year-old Angolan to death in Friedrichshafen (Baden-Württemberg). On December 12, 1992, the district court in Ravensburg sentences the perpetrator to five years in youth detention for manslaughter with conditional intent.

June 15: On the occasion of the murder of neo-Nazi leader Rainer Sonntag, there is a demonstration by neo-Nazis in Dresden (Saxony).

July 6: The Bavarian state party of the GdNF, National Block (NB), is founded.

July 20: In Hamburg skinheads critically injure a Turk.

July 20: Three skinheads assault and seriously injure three foreigners in their car in Northeim (Lower Saxony).

August 5: Three disguised perpetrators deface information signs with Nazi slogans at a memorial in the former concentration camp of Sachsenhausen near Berlin.

August 17: A neo-Nazi demonstration takes place in Bayreuth after the so-called Rudolf Hess memorial march has been prohibited in Wunsiedel (Bavaria).

Mid-August: The Jewish cemetery in Dresden (Saxony) is desecrated.

August 24: Right-wing radicals injure several occupants of the foreigner residence in Wurzen near Leipzig (Saxony) and destroy all furnishings.

August 25: The Baden-Württemberg state party of the GdNF, List of People's Loyalists (Volkstreue Liste [VL]), is founded.

August 31: The Saxon state party of the GdNF, Saxonian National List (SNL), is founded.

September 17–22: Right-wing radicals riot against a foreigner residence and an asylum seeker home in Hoyerswerda (Saxony). More than 30 persons are injured, some of them seriously. Neighbors express approval of the acts. On September 21 and 22, the attacks reach a climax. The asylum seekers are finally evacuated on September 24.

This incident has a signal effect. Numerous arson attacks and assaults on foreigners and asylum seeker homes occur in Germany in the following weeks, in which more than 100 persons are injured. The distribution of criminal offenses of foreigner hostility in 1991 is as follows: August, 104; September, 314; October, 961; November, 420; and December, 224.

September 19: An arson attack on a residence in Saarlouis kills a Ghanaian. Two Nigerians are injured during their escape from the burning building.

September 21: Several foreigners are injured during assaults of right-wing radicals on the asylum-seeker home in Thiendorf (Saxony) and Jesteburg (near Hamburg).

September 25: Two Nigerians are seriously injured during an arson attack on an asylum-seeker home in Münster (North Rhine–Westphalia).

September 28 and 29: On this weekend, the police register 43 aggressive acts against foreigners, 22 of them in North Rhine–Westphalia.

September 29: In the Bremen state elections, the German People's Union (DVU) receives 6.2% of all votes and 6 mandates.

October 2: A 30-year-old man stabs a 47-year-old Turk in Mönchengladbach (North Rhine–Westphalia). On July 10, 1992, the district court in Mönchengladbach sentences the attacker to twelve years in prison.

October 3: Two Lebanese children are critically injured during an arson attack on the asylum-seeker home in Hünxe (North Rhine–Westphalia). On May 26, 1992, the Duisburg district court sentences each of the two main defendants to five years in prison and another young man to three years and six months in youth detention.

October 3: The German League for People and Homeland (Deutsche Liga für Volk und Heimat) is founded as the Party of the National Congregation in Villingen-Schwenningen (Baden-Württemberg). The national committee members are former functionaries of the NPD and the "Republikaner" Party (Harald Neubauer, Jürgen Schützinger, Rudolf Kendzia, and Martin Mussgnug).

October 4: About 150 persons armed with stones and Molotov cocktails attack an asylum-seeker home in Zwickau (Saxony) and seriously injure seven foreigners.

October 5: Under the leadership of a member of the local branch of the NPD in Brühl (Baden-Württemberg), about twenty right-wing extremists assail three Nigerians, seriously injuring them.

October 5 and 6: The violence against asylum seekers and foreigners is continuous during the weekend. The police register about fifty cases of aggressive acts on persons or residences in which several persons are injured, some of them seriously.

October 8: In Karlsruhe (Baden-Württemberg) right-wing radicals beat up three Romanians, who must be hospitalized.

October 12: Four Turks are seriously injured in Kaufbeuren (Baden-Württemberg) after they jump out of a window to escape a fire that has been set by right-wing radicals.
     About thirty right-wing radicals beat and injure a Moroccan student in Greifswald (Mecklenburg–Hither Pomerania).

October 13: An arson attack totally destroys the asylum-seeker home in Immenstadt (Allgäu). On March 26, 1992, the district court in Kempten sentences three skinheads to serve from three years and six months to five years in youth detention for serious arson and dangerous bodily injury.

October 14: Skinheads critically wound a Vietnamese in daylight on a busy street in Berlin-Hellersdorf. Nobody helps.

October 16: Seven foreigners and a German child suffer from smoke inhalation during an arson attack at their home in Bad Vilbel (Hesse).

October 22: Five skinheads beat up two German passengers who tried to protect two Blacks on a public bus.

October 26: Three juveniles critically injure Mete Eksi, a 19-year-old Turk, with baseball bats in Berlin. He dies on November 12 as a result of the attack.

November 2: An Albanian asylum seeker is seriously injured by knife wounds in Hagen (North Rhine–Westphalia).

November 4: After a soccer game between the Greifswalder Sports Club and the Berlin Soccer Club, about 200 Berlin fans rampage and attack an asylum-seeker home in Greifswald (Mecklenburg-Hither Pomerania). Several asylum seekers and fifteen policemen are injured.

November 5: In an arson attack on a building mostly occupied by foreigners in Nürnberg, seven occupants are injured, and twenty-one are evacuated.

November 7: Once again the memorial for the deportation of Jewish Berliners at the Putlitzbrücke is desecrated with a pig's head.

November 8: The neo-Nazi German League of Comrades Wilhelmshaven (Deutscher Kameradschaftsbund Wilhelmshaven) is founded, under the leadership of Thorsten de Vries.

November 9: Youngsters shoot a Mozambique citizen in the face with an air rifle in Weimar (Thuringia).

November 13: Six disguised persons assault a Vietnamese family in their home in Leipzig (Saxony). The father is seriously injured.

November 17: Skinheads in Dresden (Saxony) want to force a 34-year-old man to use the Hitler salute and to shout "Heil Hitler." When the man refuses, the skinheads throw him into the Elbe River, and he is critically injured.

November 18: The Viking Youth group organizes, as in the previous year, a War Hero Memorial Celebration at the military cemetery in Halbe (Brandenburg). About 400 supporters participate from the NPD, JF, NF, and FAP.

November 20: Right-wing–oriented soccer fans riot during a qualification game of the German national soccer team for the European Cup in Brussels; 799 fans are arrested.

November 23: A skinhead is seriously injured during clashes between Turks and skinheads in East Berlin.

November 30: Unknown perpetrators vandalize the Jewish cemetery in Weiden (Upper Franconia).

December 3: Neo-Nazis kill a 30-year-old man in Hohenselchow (Mecklenburg–Hither Pomerania).

In 1991 the Federal Office for Protection of the Constitution registers 1,483 violent acts and 2,401 other violations of law with a proven or suspected extreme right-wing background. Three persons were killed in a total of 383 arson attacks. About 39,800 members of extreme right-wing organizations were counted (the "Republikaner" Party excluded). East German states are included in the statistics of the Amt für Verfassungsschutz for the first time.

1992

January 4 and 5: During assaults of skinheads in several cities in Thuringia, eight persons are injured, some of them seriously.

January 6: An arson attack on an asylum-seeker home in Waldkirch near Freiburg/Breisgau critically injures a Lebanese. Twenty other asylum seekers are hospitalized due to smoke inhalation.

January 28: Three young men torch an Iranian restaurant in Kassel (Hesse) and mistreat the proprietress.
The district court in Stuttgart sentences three defendants for the desecration of tombstones at five Jewish cemeteries in Baden-Württemberg between December 1989 and August 1990. One defendant receives three years in prison; the other two get suspended sentences of two years in youth detention with probation.

January 31: A Sri Lankan couple and child die during a fire in the asylum-seeker home in Lampertheim (Hesse).

March 14: Public concert of skinhead rock bands is held near Weimar (Thuringia) with the German rock groups Radikahl, Störkraft, Märtyrer, Wotan, and Kraftschlag and the American bands Bound for Glory and Final Solution.

March 15: Twenty-five youngsters assault the asylum-seeker home in Saal near Rostock (Mecklenburg–Hither Pomerania) and beat an 18-year-old Romanian to death.

March 18: Two skinheads kill 53-year-old Gustav Schneeclaus in Buxtehude (Lower Saxony) because he called Hitler a criminal. On September 8, 1992, the district court in Stade sentences both previously convicted perpetrators for joint manslaughter to six years in youth detention and eight years and six months in prison.

March 28: Two right-wing extremists seriously injure a 15-year-old Turk with knife wounds in Worms (Rhineland-Palatinate).

April 4: A German loses his life during an arson attack on the asylum-seeker home in Hörstel (North Rhine–Westphalia).

April 5: The "Republikaner" Party receives 10.9% of all votes and 15 mandates at the state elections in Baden-Württemberg. This represents their best election results since the foundation of the party in 1983.

April 5: With 6.3% of all votes, the German People's Union becomes the third largest political power in the state of Schleswig-Holstein, after the Social Democratic Party and the Christian Democratic Union.

April 19: The neo-Nazi German National Party (Deutsch Nationale Partei [DNP]) in Wechselburg (Saxony) is founded, under the leadership of Thomas Dienel, a former secretary of the Communist Free German Youth (Freie Deutsche Jugend [FDJ]). Dienel was NPD party chairman in Thuringia from October 1990 to January 1992.

April 21: The memorial to the deportation of Jews in Halberstadt near Magdeburg (Saxony-Anhalt) is desecrated.

April 25: A 21-year-old German stabs 29-year-old Vietnamese Nguyen Van Tu to death in Berlin-Marzahn.

End of April: Once again the Jewish cemetery in Berlin-Weissensee is desecrated.

May 8: Two skinheads knock down a Nigerian in a discotheque in Wendisch Rietz (Brandenburg) and throw him unconscious into a lake. He is saved by a bouncer but is in a coma for three weeks. On December 10, 1992, the district court in Frankfurt/Oder sentences a 24-year-old perpetrator to eight years in prison for attempted murder.

May 9: About 60 armed neo-Nazis raid a birthday party of punks in the Magdeburg restaurant, Elbterrassen. Eight persons are seriously injured and 23-year-old Torsten Lamprecht dies. On December 14, 1992, the Magdeburg district court sentences several skinheads to between two years on probation and eight years in prison. The court was unable to determine who killed Lamprecht.

May 24: The "Republikaner" Party receives 8.3% of all votes during the Berlin local elections; in East Berlin 5.4% and in West Berlin 9.9%.

May 25–29: Up to 400 youngsters maintain a continuous uproar in front of the asylum-seeker home in Mannheim (Baden-Württemberg) because of supposedly "sexual abuse of German women" by asylum seekers.

July: The extreme right-wing Sponsorship Middle German Youth (Förderwerk Mitteldeutsche Jugend [FMJ]) is founded Berlin and Brandenburg.

July 5: During clashes between right-wing radicals and asylum seekers in Zittau (Saxony), a German youngster is killed and several asylum seekers are injured, some of them seriously. After the fights, the extremists attack an asylum-seeker home.

July 8: Assaulting a labor hostel in Ostfildern-Kemnat (Baden-Württemberg), skinheads kill a 55-year-old Kosovo-Albanian and seriously injure his 46-year-old fellow countryman. On May 13, 1993, the district court in Stuttgart sentences the repeat offender, Thomas Wede, to prison for life and Michael Drigalla to nine years in youth detention. The other five defendants receive prison or youth-detention sentences of between six months and seven years. Three defendants are put on probation.

July 20: After the death of Heinz Galinski, chairman of the Central Council of Jews in Germany, Thomas Dienel, leader of the German National Party (DNP), and three others shout malicious diatribes against Galinski and throw a pig's head cut in half into the front garden of the Jewish community center in Erfurt. On December 1992, the state court in Rudolstadt (Thuringia) sentences Dienel to two years and eight months in prison because of public incitement and disparagement of the remembrance of deceased persons.

August 1: Two skinheads stab and trample to death a 49-year-old homeless man, Klaus Dieter Klein, in Bad Breisig (Rhineland-Palatinate). On June 30, 1993, the district court in Koblenz sentences one to eight years and three months and the other to six years and three months in youth detention.

August 3: Two skinhead bouncers beat up and kick to death a 24-year-old Pole, Ireneusz Szyderski, in a discotheque in Stotternheim (Thuringia).

August 15: About 2,000 neo-Nazis from Germany and abroad participate in the so-called Rudolf Hess memorial march in Rudolstadt (Thuringia).

August 22–28: Applauded by the local population, hundreds of youngsters rampage in front of an asylum-seeker home in Rostock-Lichtenhagen (Mecklenburg–Hither Pomerania) and set the home on fire on the night of August 25, threatening the life of 115 Vietnamese guest workers and a TV crew. The events are broadcast on the TV news, and a wave of similar incidents unfolds in united Germany. The hesitant intervention of the police triggers fierce criticism at the leadership of the police and responsible politicians. About 200 persons are temporarily arrested and charges are brought against more than 30 persons. In most proceedings, only small sentences of youth detention and youth arrest are given because of a lack of documentation of proof. After long arguments, the Mecklenburg–Hither Pomerania's minister of the interior and the mayor of Rostock are forced to resign.

August 29: Two unemployed juveniles, 18 and 19 years old, throw Molotov cocktails at an asylum-seeker home in Bad Lauterberg/Harz. The district court in Göttingen sentences them to four years in youth detention each for attempted murder and serious arson.

August 29–September 2: Serious rampaging occurs in front of an asylum-seeker home in Cottbus (Brandenburg).

August 30: A bomb attack is made on the memorial for deported Jews at the Berlin Putlitz-brücke. On March 17, 1993, the Berlin district court sentences the 31-year-old principal defendant to five years and nine months and the 35-year-old codefendant to two years and nine months in prison.

September: The number of daily arson attacks on asylum-seeker homes and foreigners' residences in Germany are as follows: July, 126; August, 235; September, 536; October, 364; November, 344; and December, 283.

September 3: Arson attack is made on the asylum-seeker home in Ketzin (Brandenburg). The building is completely burned out. The state court in Potsdam sentences the 20-year-old defendant, to four years in youth detention and the 21-year-old to seven years in prison for serious arson.

September 4: Street fights break out between right-wing extremists and the police in front of the central reception camp for asylum seekers in Eisenhüttenstadt (Brandenburg).

September 5: Skinheads harass foreigners in Hamminkeln (Lower Rhine); two refugees are injured, one seriously.

September 8–12: Rioting in front of the asylum-seeker home in Quedlinburg (Saxony-Anhalt) is applauded by neighbors. On September 12, the police arrest 41 persons. On September 14, the Saxony-Anhalt minister of the interior transfers the asylum seekers to an unknown location.

September 15–22: Arson attacks and violent aggressive acts are directed against the asylum-seeker home in Wismar (Mecklenburg–Hither Pomerania). The most brutal attack occurs on September 19, and it takes 200 policemen to repel the assailants. On September 22, the Schwerin Ministry of the Interior and the state parliament decide to evacuate the asylum-seeker home.

September 21: An Iranian born Green party/Alternative List member of the Berlin-Neukölln citizen council withdraws from his mandate out of fear of racist attacks after continuing telephone harassment.

September 26: Arson attack is made on the Jewish barrack in the Sachsenhausen concentration camp memorial near Berlin. On October 5, 1995, an appeal hearing by the criminal division of the Youth Court of Appeals and the Federal Supreme Court (Jugendstrafsenat) sentences at the district court in Potsdam the 19- and 22-year-old defendants to three years and two and a half years in youth detention, respectively, after they were originally acquitted in a three-month trial in 1993 because of lack of proof.

October: Otto Ernst Remer sends a 114-page brochure, "Expertise about the Origin and Proof of Cyanide Compounds in the 'Gas Chambers' of Auschwitz," edited by chemist

Germar Rudolf, to the "Jew leader Bubis" (Ignatz Bubis, Chairman of the Central Council of Jews in Germany) and to scientists, mostly professors of inorganic chemistry. The pamphlet intends to prove that in Auschwitz "deadly amounts of Cyclon-B have never been discharged." In August 1993, after Remer also sends his "report" to the Christian Democratic Union (CDU) in the state parliament of Mecklenburg–Hither Pomerania, the CDU parliamentary faction institutes legal proceedings against Remer for public incitement.

October: A 20-year-old skinhead critically wounds a Nigerian with a knife in Frankfurt/ Oder (Brandenburg). On July 26, 1993, the district court in Frankfurt/Oder sentences him to seven years in youth detention.

October 2: About twenty youngsters throw incendiary compounds at a home for the disabled in Leipzig (Saxony).

October 7: Skinheads assault a German whom they mistake for a foreigner with a knife in Köthen near Magdeburg (Saxony-Anhalt).

October 10: After deciding "to spank gays," skinheads brutally beat a man in Saarbrücken (Saarland).

October 15: Right-wing radicals shouting antiforeigner slogans seriously hurt a 50-year-old Italian in Saarbrücken (Saarland).

October 21: Arson attack is made on the concentration camp memorial at Ravensbrück. On April 29, 1993, the state court in Potsdam sentences the 17- and 19-year-old perpetrators to 18 months and 2 years on probation.

October 21–25: Night attacks are made on a dormitory for foreign students in Greifswald (Mecklenburg–Hither Pomerania).

October 22: During an arson attack on an asylum-seeker home in Adenstedt (Lower Saxony), two Lebanese children who are two weeks and eight months old suffer from smoke inhalation.

October 22: Ten children of asylum seekers given refuge in a Turkish restaurant are injured during an arson attack in Hameln (Lower Saxony).

October 22: The district court in Schweinfurt convicts the 80-year-old Nazi, Otto Ernst Remer, to 22 months in prison without probation for public incitement and instigation of racial hate.

October 24: A cemetery of deported laborers from the former Dachau concentration camp in Überlingen (Lake Constance) is desecrated.

November 2: Rostock city councilman Karl-Heinz Schmidt asks Ignatz Bubis, the chairman of the Central Council of Jews in Germany, during his visit: "Mr. Bubis, you are a German citizen of Jewish faith. Your homeland is Israel. Is that right? How do you judge the daily violence between Palestinians and Israelis?" Schmidt is forced to resign because his comment denies Bubis the right of a German homeland.

November 4: The Jewish cemetery in Wuppertal-Barmen (North Rhine–Westphalia) is vandalized.

November 5: A 22-year-old South African is seriously injured by two juveniles in Wolgast (Hither Pomerania).

November 8: Under the patronage of German president Richard von Weizsäcker, about 300,000 persons demonstrate in Berlin against hostility toward foreigners. Some hundred hooligans disturb the final rally. In the preliminary planning of the demonstration, Bavarian minister president Max Streibl had declined to participate.

November 13: In a Wuppertal bar (North Rhine–Westphalia), two skinheads seriously injure and set on fire 53-year-old Karl-Hans Rohn. They drive their victim over the border into The Netherlands, where the body is found the next morning. Before the deadly clash, the men had been drinking together and several times Rohn had been labeled a Jew. On February 1994, the skinheads were sentenced to between eight and fourteen years in prison and the bar owner received ten years in prison for jointly committed murder.

November 13: The district court in Mannheim (Baden-Württemberg) sentences Günter Deckert (NPD chairman) to one year in prison on probation and fines him 10,000 DM for public incitement, defamation of character, disparagement of the remembrance of the deceased, and instigation of hate. Deckert had the rabble-rousing lecture of the revisionist Fred A. Leuchter translated into German and denied that Jews had been killed in gas chambers by the National Socialist regime.

November 15: A large police contingent prevents the War Hero Memorial Celebration at the military cemetery in Halbe (Brandenburg).

November 21: Two hooligans stab to death 27-year-old Silvio Meier, who was said to belong to the squatter movement in Berlin-Friedrichshain. Two other juveniles are seriously injured. On October 1, 1993, the Berlin-Moabit juvenile court sentences a 17-year-old apprentice to four years and six months in youth detention.

November 23: Violence against foreigners reaches a new climax with the neo-Nazi arson attack in Mölln (Schleswig-Holstein). Three Turkish females aged 51, 14, and 10 are killed in the fire; nine other persons are injured. On December 8, 1993, the provincial high court and court of appeals in Schleswig convicts 26-year-old Michael Peters to life imprisonment for three murders, thirty-nine attempted murders, and serious arson. Twenty-year-old Lars Christiansen gets the highest possible sentence, ten years in youth detention.

November 25: The district court in Oldenburg sentences Thorsten de Vries, the leader of the German League of Comrades Wilhelmshaven to sixteen months in prison without probation because of threats, coercion, resistance to the authority of the state, slander, and disturbance of public peace.

November 27: The federal minister of the interior prohibits the Nationalist Front (NF), led by Meinolf Schönborn, because of its offense against the constitutional order of the Federal Republic of Germany.

December 6: More than 400,000 people participate in the first candlelight protest march against hatred of foreigners and violence in Munich. In the following weeks, similar candlelight protests are held in almost all large German cities.

December 9: The federal government files a claim, based on article 18 of the Federal Basic Laws in the Federal Constitutional Supreme Court to forfeit the rights of neo-Nazis Thomas Dienel and Heinz Reisz to freedom of speech, freedom to publish, freedom of assembly, and the freedom to organize because of their outrageous public comments and activities.

December 10: The federal minister of the interior bans the neo-Nazi group, German Alternative (chairman, Frank Hübner, Cottbus), which had concentrated its activities in the new East German states since 1990.

December 21: The extreme right-wing German League of Comrades Wilhelmshaven, under the leadership of Thorsten de Vries, is banned by the interior minister of Lower Saxony.

December 22: The federal minister of the interior prohibits the National Offensive, led by Michael Swierczek, which was particularly active in Bavaria and Saxony.

December 27: Two skinheads seriously injure a tram driver in Frankfurt/Main because he gave two Turks some information.

December 31: The Federal Association of Soldiers of the Former Waffen-SS (Bundesverband der Soldaten der ehemaligen Waffen-SS [HIAG]), often accused of harboring former Nazis, dissolves itself.

In 1992 the Federal Office for Protection of the Constitution registers 7,684 criminal acts with a proven or suspected extreme right-wing background, among them 2,639 violent acts. Seventeen persons died as a result of extreme right-wing attacks. About 41,900 members were counted in 82 extreme right-wing organizations.

1993

February 3: Nationwide action is taken against radical right-wing music groups. Records, videos, uniforms and ammunition are confiscated during house searches.

February 16: Two 14-year-old students desecrate the Jewish cemetery in Märkisch Buchholz (Brandenburg) out of a "thirst for adventure and boredom."

March 7: The "Republikaner" Party wins 8.6% of all votes in the Hessian local elections.

March 9: A 56-year-old Turk dies of an apparent heart attack shortly after a clash with two Germans. The perpetrators threatened him with a charged gas pistol. On September 17, the district court in Duisburg sentences each of the Germans to four years in prison because of lethal bodily harm injuries.

April 1: The Jewish cemetery in Eisenhüttenstadt (Brandenburg) is desecrated.

April 20: About 300 neo-Nazis celebrate the birthday of Hitler in Mainz (Hesse). At the same time, more than 1,000 people demonstrate against them on a march through the city.

May 12: The district court in Itzehoe (Schleswig-Holstein) sentences four members of the skinhead rock band Powerbeat (*Kraftschlag*) to seven months on probation because two of their songs constitute public incitement and the instigation of racial hatred.

May 29: Five Turkish women and girls die during an arson attack on a house occupied by Turks in Solingen (North Rhine–Westphalia). The police arrest four young men, aged 18, 19, 22, and 25, one of whom admits responsibility. The provincial high court and court of appeals in Solingen sentence three of the defendants on October 13, 1995, to fifteen-year prison terms and one to a ten-year prison term. The defense announce that they will appeal the decision.

The Solingen arson attack triggers a renewed wave of violence against foreigners and asylum seekers in united Germany, as reflected in these figures: April, 155; May, 206; June, 283; July, 179; August, 144; September, 118; October, 140; and November, 126.

June 8: Arson attacks are made on homes occupied by foreign families and on Turkish restaurants in Hamburg, Wülfrath and Oberhausen-Rheinhausen (Baden). At least fifteen persons are injured.

June 11: The Bavarian Ministry of the Interior bans the extreme right-wing organization Nationaler Block.

June 15: Arson attacks are made on a house occupied by Italians in Waldshut-Tiengen (South Baden) and a house of a Moroccan family in Wegberg (North Rhine–Westphalia).

June 19: About 800 right-wing skinheads attend a skinhead concert in the district of Königs Wusterhausen (Brandenburg). Although neighbors complain, the police do not intervene.

June 29: A Romanian asylum seeker is stabbed to death in Mühlhausen (Thuringia).

June 30: Arson attacks are made on apartments of Turkish families in Cologne and Erbendorf (Upper Palatinate). Two persons are injured.

July 1: The reform of the asylum-law comes into force.

July 14: The Baden-Württemberg Ministry of the Interior prohibits the extreme right-wing Association of Faithfuls to the German Homeland (Heimattreue Vereinigung Deutschlands [HVD]).

July 27: The Jewish cemetery in Hechingen (Baden-Württemberg) is desecrated.

August 14: About 500 neo-Nazis, including delegations from France, Belgium, and the United Kingdom, arrive unhindered at the sixth Rudolf Hess memorial march in Fulda (Hesse) after officially announced meetings had been prohibited in Saxony, Thuringia, and Bavaria. The Hessian police, who prevent a simultaneous demonstration against the march, are criticized for their passive stance toward the neo-Nazis. On August 20 Hessian minister president Eichel dismisses the secretary of state, holding him politically responsible for the incident.

August 24: A Berlin newspaper reports that the public prosecutor's office in Potsdam (Brandenburg) is investigating the 260 inhabitants of the village of Dolgenbrodt (south of Berlin) because they are suspected of having hired a skinhead arsonist and collected 2,000 DM for the torching of a home planned for asylum seekers on November 1992.

August 30: Brandenburg is the first state to ban the public display of the naval war ensign of the German Empire (Reichskriegsflagge) because "it has become a symbol of neo-Fascist confusion, hate against foreigners and racism." In the following days, Hesse, North Rhine–Westphalia, Rhineland-Palatinate, Saxony-Anhalt, and Berlin impose the ban.

August 30: Two men desecrate a sculpture in front of a concentration camp memorial at Sachsenhausen with swastikas. The 19- and 20-year-old perpetrators are caught in the act and arrested.

September 2: The North Rhine–Westphalian interior minister bans the extreme right-wing and antisemitic Friends of Freedom for Germany (Freundeskreis Freiheit für Deutschland [FFD]) and confiscates its assets.

September 2: The federal government instructs the federal minister of the interior to prepare to file a claim with the Federal Constitutional Supreme Court to ban the Free Workers' Party (FAP) as unconstitutional. After the Federal Constitutional Supreme Court decides the FAP and its 430 members do not fulfill the criteria of a legal party, the federal minister of the interior in Bonn bans the organization on February 24, 1995. The court's decision states that the organizational structure of the FAP is not feasible for continuous party activity and that it is instead an association. Federal minister of the interior Kanther further explains that the FAP is related in character to the goals of the former Nazi Party. Leading Nazis are honored, human rights are disrespected, democratic institutions are defamed, and antisemitic and antiforeigner hate propaganda is disseminated.

September 2: Jörg Petritsch, lead singer of the skinhead rock band Störkraft, is sentenced to two years on probation for public incitement, Nazi propaganda, and distribution of literature liable to corrupt the young.

September 7: The Jewish cemetery in Wriezen (Brandenburg) is desecrated by three 14-year-old students.

September 19: The "Republikaner" Party and German People's Union (DVU) compete separately for the Hamburg state parliament election. Both parties fail to achieve the 5% threshold and receive 4.8% and 2.8%, respectively, of all votes.

September 28: The Jewish cemetery in Dresden (Saxony) is desecrated.

September 29: The Vienna district court sentences 35-year-old Austrian neo-Nazi Gottfried Küssel (temporarily regarded in April 1990 as a successor of the late Michael Kühnen) to ten years in prison—the highest sentence ever given to a neo-Nazi in Austria—for "reactivating National Socialist convictions."

October 2: Three persons are seriously injured during clashes between left- and right-wing radical youth in Suhl (Thuringia) after a skinhead assault on two Angolans.

October 21: The memorial for the remembrance of the deportation of Berlin Jews at the suburban train station (S-Bahn) in Grunewald is desecrated by unknown persons.

October 24: A worker fires at and critically wounds a 26-year-old Lebanese in Lüneburg (Lower Saxony).

October 29: Police in Cologne arrest U.S. citizen Fred A. Leuchter because he is suspected of public incitement and disparagement of the remembrance of the deceased. In November 1991, at a revisionist meeting of the National Democratic Party (NPD) in Weinheim, he maintained that the mass murder of Jews in Auschwitz could not have happened because the technical installations were not suitable. His lecture was translated by NPD chairman Deckert. Leuchter was set free on bail. In September 1994, he failed to appear for his trial.

October 29: Skinheads assault an American Olympic bobsled-team member in a discotheque in Oberhof (Thuringia) and injure a team member coming to his aid. The police investigate the four suspects of the act and fourteen other persons involved. In January 1994, two principal defendants (16 and 21 years old) receive sentences of a year in youth detention and two years and eight months in prison.

November 7: A 23-year-old German throws an incendiary compound into a trailer home occupied by Kurds in Küssaberg-Rheinheim (Baden-Württemberg). The occupants escape unharmed.

In 1993 the Federal Office for Protection of the Constitution registers 10,561 criminal acts with a proven or suspected extreme right-wing background, among them 2,232 violent acts. Eight persons died as a result of attacks. About 64,500 members were counted in 78 extreme right-wing organizations.

1994

January 2: Four right-wing radicals, one policeman, and one Turk are injured during a brawl between right-wing radicals and foreign youth in Frankfurt/Main (Hesse).

January 13: Three juveniles assault a 23-year-old pregnant woman from Nigeria and kick her in the abdomen at the central station in Erfurt (Thuringia). Police arrest all of the perpetrators.

January 16: Four persons are injured during an arson attack at an asylum-seeker home in Ludwigshafen (Rhineland-Palatinate). Police arrest a 34-year-old man.

January 20: Unknown perpetrators assail an asylum-seeker home near Ludwigshafen (Rhineland-Palatinate). The homemade bomb cause considerable damage.

January 26: A 38-year-old homeless person is set on fire while asleep in Karlsruhe (Baden-Württemberg). The man suffers serious injuries.

February 7: Unknown perpetrators commit an arson attack at an asylum-seeker home in Geisenheim.

February 28: Unknown persons throw an incendiary compound into the synagogue in Essen (North Rhine–Westphalia), which serves as a documentation center and memorial.

March: The movie *Schindler's List* premieres in German cinemas and becomes a big media event.

March 10: In Duisburg (North Rhine–Westphalia), a leading member of the FAP shoots signal flares at a residential building of ethnic German resettlers.

March 13: State elections are held in Lower Saxony. The "Republikaner" Party fails to achieve the 5% threshold, receiving 3.7% of all votes.

March 23: Twenty local juveniles mistreat eight high school students from Berlin on an excursion to Rügen (Mecklenburg–Hither Pomerania). A dark haired German boy and some foreign students are the targets of the assailants.

March 25: Unknown persons commit an arson attack on the synagogue in Lübeck (Schleswig-Holstein), endangering the lives of people living above the prayer hall. The attack is condemned by politicians, the media, and the public. The population reacts by holding public vigils. A special police commission is able to arrest four suspects from the extreme right-wing skinhead milieu. The trial of the defendants (aged 20, 20, 22, and 25) is scheduled for November, with charges of five attempted murders and serious arson.

March 25: According to opinion polls, the support for the extreme right-wing "Republikaner" dwindles to 1% of all persons interviewed. Their electoral defeat in October becomes apparent.

March 28: The Jewish cemetery in Guben (Brandenburg) is desecrated.

March 31: The Jewish cemetery in Pretzfeld (Bavaria) is desecrated.

March–June: Extreme right-wing parties receive between 0.1% and 3.4% of all votes at the local government elections in Schleswig-Holstein, Baden-Württemberg, Mecklenburg–Hither Pomerania, Rhineland-Palatinate, Saarland, Saxony, Saxony-Anhalt, and Thuringia. They obtain a noteworthy result with 5.4% of all votes only at the city parliament election in Munich on June 12.

April: The parties in the federal parliament debate a tightening of the criminal law against the "Auschwitz lie." The amended law passes and comes into force on December 1.

April 9: A 30-year-old man sets a fire in front of an asylum-seeker home in Limburg and is apprehended.

April 13: Four African asylum seekers are attacked in Ludwigslust (Mecklenburg). They report to the police that they were chased by several youngsters on motorbikes and assaulted with stones and sticks. Two refugees were seriously injured.

April 19: In Göttingen four extreme right-wing juveniles attack a young Israeli with a hatchet. Because the attacker was obviously too drunk to handle the weapon, the victim received only slight injuries.

April 20: Youngsters assail a foreigner's residence in Leipzig (Saxony), firing at occupants with a gas pistol. A 14-year-old student who is arrested gives as the motive, "hostility against foreigners."

April 20: Juveniles set a house occupied by Turks on fire in Bielefeld. Firefighters save the occupants. Police arrest six youngsters, age 14 to 16.

April 24: The Jewish cemetery in Dortmund (North Rhine–Westphalia) is desecrated.

April 25: Unknown persons push a 33-year-old Vietnamese man out of a moving train somewhere between Ruhland and Hoyerswerda (Saxony), resulting in injuries.

May 5: The Jewish cemetery in Bad Kreuznach is vandalized.

May 12: Right-wing radicals chase foreigners through the inner city of Magdeburg (Saxony-Anhalt). Police only hesitantly intervene. The violent attackers are released soon after their arrest. Serious investigations of the perpetrators start only after national protests. The police chief of Magdeburg is forced to resign after the Saxony-Anhalt government changes following the elections in June.

May 13: Unknown perpetrators desecrate the Jewish cemetery in Bad Kissingen.

May 15: The Jewish cemetery in Dresden (Saxony) is desecrated.

May 17: According to reports from the Federal Criminal Police Office (BKA), radical right-wing-motivated arson attacks are aimed more and more against the apartments and businesses of foreigners. In 1992, racist arson attacks in 70% of all cases were directed against asylum-seeker homes: in 1993 this percentage fell to 45%.

June 6: Four neo-Nazis assault and injure an asylum seeker in Luckenwalde (Brandenburg). The perpetrators escape unidentified.

June 12: The "Republikaner" Party candidates receive only 3.9% of all votes for the European Parliament and are not able to take up their seats again because they fail to meet the 5% threshold.

June 23: In an appeal hearing, the chairman of the National Democratic Party (NPD), Günter Deckert, is again sentenced by the district court in Mannheim (Baden-Württemberg) to one year of probation and is fined 10,000 DM for public incitement and instigation of racial hatred. In August, when the reasoning of the verdict is made public, the reaction is worldwide anger, a long debate, and a judicial scandal. The ruling reveals unusual understanding for right-wing extremist Deckert and grants him a "legitimate interest" because he allegedly wants "to ward off claims against Germany resulting from the Holocaust." Deckert is certified to have a "strong character and to be a responsible personality," and his political convictions are described as "an affair of his heart" *(Herzenssache)*. All three judges call in sick after protests from German chancellor Helmut Kohl to the German Association of Judges: "Those who argue like the court turn the value hierarchy of the Basic Law upside down." In interviews, Judge Rainer Orlet defends the sentence. When he returns on November 14 to his office, a public demonstration is staged in front of the district court in Mannheim.

The faction of the Social Democratic Party (SPD) in the Baden-Württemberg state legislature investigates whether Judge Orlet can be dismissed from his office by instituting juridical proceedings through the Federal Constitutional Supreme Court. The Munich lawyer Rolf Bossi institutes legal proceedings against all three judges because of public incitement, "lest the Nazi chumminess within the judiciary ends."

On April 21, 1995, the Karlsruhe district court sentences Deckert to two years in prison without probation for public incitement. Deckert appeals the decision. The court's decision meets with general public approval. In addition, the state parliament of Baden-Württemberg considers removing Judge Orlet from office because of violating professional rules of conduct. Under public pressure, Orlet resigns his post and applies for early retirement at the beginning of May 1995.

June 26: The "Republikaner" Party wins 1.4% of the vote during the state elections in Saxony-Anhalt.

July 9: A 17-year-old Bosnian boy is pushed out of a moving suburban train in Berlin and is injured.

July 14: Unknown persons desecrate the Jewish cemetery in Baden (Baden-Württemberg).

July 18: A group of about fifteen juveniles assails an asylum-seeker home near Cottbus (Brandenburg). No one is injured.

July 23: Twenty-three skinheads desecrate the concentration camp memorial in Buchenwald (Thuringia). The group had been previously under surveillance by police. Because of this and other examples of police misjudgment, the public debates the question: Are the police and judiciary blind when it comes to right-wing activities? The perpetrators are eventually found and sentenced on probation in October.

August: After several state offices of the Verfassungsschutz had already classified the "Republikaner" Party as right-wing extremist and unconstitutional, the Federal Office for Protection of the Constitution in Bonn also reaches this conclusion.

August: In remembrance of the death of Rudolf Hess (the former deputy of Adolf Hitler), neo-Nazis call for a National Week of Action between August 13 and August 20. Eighteen meetings are registered nationally. All planned demonstrations are banned by the authorities. On August 13, the neo-Nazis move over the border into Luxembourg after a massive nationwide police contingent prevents extreme right-wing appearances in united Germany. Luxembourg arrests about ninety neo-Nazis and sends them back to Germany.

August 15: A Chinese family is chased by two juveniles through the streets of Erfurt. The pursued family is able to reach police headquarters, and the assailants are arrested.

August 22: In Gotha two youngsters beat a 41-year-old Azerbaijani unconscious.

August 29: The Jewish cemetery in Mühlhausen (Thuringia) is desecrated.

September 3: An arson attack is made on an asylum-seeker home in Romrod (Hesse). No one is injured; a 26-year-old man is arrested.

September 11: State elections are held in Brandenburg. The "Republikaner" Party receives 1.1% of the vote—the same percentage as in 1990.

September 11: State elections are held in Saxony. The "Republikaner" Party receives 1.2% of the vote. In 1990, the party was not involved in the election.

September 13: Extreme right-wing juveniles assail three 17- to 18-year-old asylum seekers in Magdeburg (Saxony-Anhalt) and seriously injure them. One victim is hospitalized.

September 17: An asylum seeker from Ghana is seriously injured by knife wounds and thrown out of a moving S-Bahn train in Berlin. Several passengers supposedly observed the act without intervening. The next morning the victim is found almost dead. The unidentified perpetrators are sought by the media and a large police contingent. In December more and more evidence is collected that the refugee was the victim not of an assault but of an accident and fantasized the story of a skinhead attack following media attention.

September 22: About ten skinheads brutally assail a group of illegal Vietnamese cigarette traders in Berlin.

September 25: State elections are held in Bavaria. The "Republikaner" Party receives 3.9% of the vote (compared to 4.9% in 1990).

October 6: Unknown persons desecrate the Jewish cemetery in the Berlin district of Prenzlauer Berg.

October 16: Of all extreme right-wing parties, only the "Republikaner" Party has candidates for the German national election. They win 1.9% of all votes (compared to 2.1% in 1990), and do not win any mandates in the parliament.

October 16: State elections are held in Thuringia. The "Republikaner" Party gains 1.3% of the vote (compared to 0.8% in 1990).

October 16: State elections are held in Mecklenburg–Hither Pomerania. The "Republikaner" Party wins 1.0% of the vote (compared to 0.9% in 1990).

October 16: At the state election in Saarland, the "Republikaner" Party receives 1.4% of the vote (compared to 3.4% in 1990).

October 20: Juveniles hostile to foreigners attack a house occupied by Portuguese in Wurzen (Saxony). Five persons are injured. Eleven suspects are arrested.

November 8: Police prohibit a meeting of the extreme right-wing organization The Nationals at the anniversary of the Night of Broken Glass (Reichskristallnacht) in front of the concentration camp memorial at Sachsenhausen near Berlin.

November 10: The Viking Youth, an imitation of the Hitler Youth, is banned forty-two years after its founding. Federal minister of the interior Manfred Kanther orders that the organization, with about 400 members, be disbanded and its assets seized.

November 25: The trial of the Lübeck synagogue arson attack of March 25 begins in the provincial high court and the court of appeals in Schleswig (Schleswig-Holstein). The public prosecutor accuses four juvenile defendants from lower-class backgrounds and without political affiliation of arson and five counts of attempted murder on the people who lived on the upper floors of the attacked synagogue. Three of the defendants confess. On April 13, the young men are convicted of arson. The murder charge is dropped because the attackers claim they believed the synagogue was not occupied. Stephan Westphal (age 25) is sentenced to four and a half years in youth detention; Nico Trapiel (20) and Boris Holland-Moritz (20) are each sentenced to three years and nine months in youth detention. Dirk Brusberg (22), who refused to confess and claimed he was not involved in the attack, receives two and a half years in youth detention as an accessory. He appeals the decision but the Federal Supreme Court in Karlsruhe (Baden-Württemberg) upholds the legality of all sentences on October 12, 1995.

December 1: Tightened requirements of criminal law are enacted regarding such matters as public incitement and the use of symbols of unconstitutional organizations.

In 1994, the Federal Office for the Protection of the Constitution registers 7,952 violations of law with a proven or suspected extreme right-wing background and 1,489 violent acts. Although in 1994 no homicides were registered, the characteristics of perpetrators have not changed much in comparison with previous years. Young men still represent the majority of attackers: less than 2% are female and 78% are aged 14 to 20. Only 3% of all persons investigated are older than 30. The report also confirms the existence of 82 right-wing extremist organizations with an estimated 56,600 members.

In 1990–1994, the numbers of applications of asylum seekers and the percentages of applications approved are as follows: in 1990, 193,063 applications, 4.4% approved; in 1991, 256,112 applications, 6.9% approved; in 1992, 438,191 applications, 4.3% approved; in 1993, 322,599 applications, 3.5% approved; and in 1994, 127,210 applications, 7.3% approved. The asylum law was reformed on July 1, 1993.

NOTE

This chronology has been prepared and compiled by Rainer Erb, supported by Angelika Königseder and Alexander Piccolruaz at the Center for Research on Antisemitism, Technical University of Berlin. It was translated from German by Hermann Kurthen. The compilation is based on the center's archives. The following documents were used: annual reports of the federal and state offices for the Protection of the Constitution (Verfassungsschutzämter), police statistics, and reports in regional and nationally circulated newspapers, such as the *Frankfurter Rundschau, Süddeutsche Zeitung, Frankfurter Allgemeine Zeitung,* and *Taz Berlin.*

References

Abella, Irving. 1994. "Antisemitism in Canada: New Perspectives on an Old Problem." In *Approaches to Antisemitism,* edited by Michael Brown. New York: American Jewish Committee and International Center for University Teaching of Jewish Civilization, pp. 46–56.

Abramson, Paul R. 1983. *Political Attitudes in America.* San Francisco: W. H. Freeman.

Ackerman, Nathan W., and Marie Jahoda. 1950. *Anti-Semitism and Emotional Disorder: A Psychoanalytic Interpretation.* New York: Harper & Row.

Adams, William C., and Philip Heyl. 1981. "From Cairo to Kabul with the Networks, 1972–1980." In *Television Coverage of the Middle East,* edited by William C. Adams. Norwood, N.J.: Ablex, pp. 11–26.

Adler, Frank. 1993/94. "Left Vigilance in France." *Telos* 98–99. (Winter/Spring), pp. 23–33.

Adorno, Theodor W., et al. 1950. *The Authoritarian Personality.* New York: Harper Row.

ALLBUS (Allgemeine Bevölkerungsumfrage der Sozialwissenschaften). 1980, 1984, 1988, 1990. Durchgeführt vom Zentrum für Umfragen, Methoden und Analysen (ZUMA). Mannheim.

Allport, G. W. 1954. *The Nature of Prejudice.* Cambridge, Mass.: Cambridge University Press.

Almond, Gabriel. 1960. T*he American Public and Foreign Affairs.* New York: Praeger.

Almond, Gabriel, and Sidney Verba. 1963. *The Civic Culture.* Princeton, N.J.: Princeton University Press.

Anti-Defamation League of B'nai B'rith New York, ed. 1989. *Holocaust "Revisionism": Reinventing the Big Lie.* ADL Research Report. New York: Anti-Defamation League.

———. 1993a. *Hitler's Apologists: The Anti-Semitic Propaganda of Holocaust "Revisionism."* New York: Anti-Defamation League.

———. 1993b. *1992 Audit of Anti-Semitic Incidents.* New York: Anti-Defamation League.

App, Austin. 1973. *The Six Million Swindle: Blackmailing the German People for Hard Marks with Fabricated Corpses.* Takoma Park, Md.: Boniface Press.

Assheuer, Thomas, and Hans Sarkowicz. 1992. *Rechtsradikale in Deutschland: Die alte und die neue Rechte.* Munich: Beck.

Auerbach, Hellmuth. 1993a. "Auschwitz-Lüge." In *Legenden, Lügen, Vorurteile: Ein Wörterbuch zur Zeitgeschichte,* edited by Wolfgang Benz. Munich: Deutscher Taschenbuch Verlag, pp. 36–37.

———. 1993b. " 'Kriegserklärung' der Juden an Deutschland." In *Legenden, Lügen, Vorurteile: Ein Wörterbuch zur Zeitgeschichte,* edited by Wolfgang Benz. Munich: Deutscher Taschenbuch Verlag, pp. 122–126.

———. 1993c. "Leuchter-Report." In *Legenden, Lügen, Vorurteile; Ein Wörterbuch zur Zeitgeschichte,* edited by Wolfgang Benz. Munich: Deutscher Taschenbuch Verlag, pp. 147–149.

Backes, Uwe, and Eckhard Jesse. 1993. *Politischer Extremismus in der Bundesrepublik Deutschland.* Bonn: Bundeszentrale für politische Bildung.

Backes, Uwe, Eckhard Jesse, and Rainer Zitelmann. 1990. *Die Schatten der Vergangenheit: Impulse zur Historisierung des Nationalsozialismus.* Frankfurt am Main: Ullstein.

Bade, Klaus J. 1992. *Ausländer, Aussiedler, Asyl in der Bundesrepublik Deutschland.* Bonn: Bundeszentrale für politische Bildung.

Baier, Lothar. 1982. *Französische Zustände: Berichte und Essays.* Frankfurt am Main: Europäische Verlagsanstalt.

Bailer-Galanda, Brigitte. 1992a. "Der Leuchter-Bericht." In *Amoklauf gegen die Wirklichkeit: NS-Verbrechen und "revisionistische" Geschichtsschreibung,* edited by Bundesministerium für Unterricht und Kunst und Dokumentationsarchiv des österreichischen Widerstandes. Vienna: Dokumentationsarchiv des österreichischen Widerstandes, pp. 41–46.

———. 1992b. "Die Leugnung der Echtheit des Tagebuches der Anne Frank." In *Amoklauf gegen die Wirklichkeit: NS-Verbrechen und "revisionistische" Geschichtsschreibung,* edited by Bundesministerium für Unterricht und Kunst und Dokumentationsarchiv des österreichischen Widerstandes. Vienna: Dokumentationsarchiv des österreichischen Widerstandes, pp. 89–92

———. 1992c. "Der 'Revisionismus': Pseudowissenschaftliche Propaganda." In *Amoklauf gegen die Wirklichkeit: NS-Verbrechen und "revisionistische" Geschichtsschreibung,* edited by Bundesministerium für Unterricht und Kunst und Dokumentationsarchiv des österreichischen Widerstandes. Vienna: Dokumentationsarchiv des österreichischen Widerstandes, pp. 11–14.

Bailer, Brigitte. 1994. "Der 'Revisionismus': Pseudowissenschaftliche Propaganda." In *Handbuch des österreichischen Rechtsextremismus,* edited by Dokumentationsarchiv des österreichischen Widerstandes. Vienna: Deuticke, pp. 530–536.

Bailer, Brigitte, and Wolfgang Neugebauer. 1994a. "Abriß der Entwicklung des Rechtsextremismus in Österreich." In *Handbuch des österreichischen Rechtsextremismus,* edited by Dokumentationsarchiv des österreichischen Widerstandes. Vienna: Deuticke, pp. 97–102.

———. 1994b. "Die FPÖ: Vom Liberalismus zum Rechtsextremismus." In *Handbuch des österreichischen Rechtsextremismus,* edited by Dokumentationsarchiv des österreichischen Widerstandes. Vienna: Deuticke Verlag, pp. 357–494.

Bailer, Josef. 1992. "Der Leuchter-Bericht aus der Sicht eines Chemikers." In *Amoklauf gegen die Wirklichkeit: NS-Verbrechen und "revisionistische" Geschichtsschreibung,* edited by Bundesministerium für Unterricht und Kunst und Dokumentationsarchiv des österreichischen Widerstandes. Vienna: Dokumentationsarchiv des österreichischen Widerstandes, pp. 47–52.

———. 1995. "Die 'Revisionisten' und die Chemie." In *Wahrheit und "Auschwitzlüge":*

Zur Bekämpfung "revisionistischer" Propaganda, edited by Brigitte Bailer-Galanda, Wolfgang Benz, and Wolfgang Neugebauer. Vienna: Deuticke, pp. 99–118.

Baldwin, Peter, ed. 1990. *Reworking the Past: Hitler, the Holocaust, and the Historians' Debate.* Boston: Beacon Press.

Bar-On, D., F. Beiner, and M. Brusten. 1988. "The Holocaust and Its Relevance to Current Social Issues in the Federal Republic of Germany and Israel." In *Der Holocaust: Familiale und gesellschaftliche Folgen,* edited by D. Bar-On, F. Beiner and M. Brusten. Wuppertal: Universität Wuppertal, pp. 211–220.

Bar-On, D., P. Hare, M. Brusten, and F. Beiner. 1993. " 'Working Through' the Holocaust: Comparing the Questionnaire Results of German and Israeli Students." *Holocaust and Genocide Studies* 2, pp. 230–246.

Bartov, Omer. 1992. *Hitler's Army.* New York: Cambridge University Press.

Bauer, Yehuda. 1994. "In Search of a Definition of Antisemitism." In *Approaches to Antisemitism,* edited by Michael Brown. New York: American Jewish Committee and International Center for University Teaching of Jewish Civilization, pp. 10–23.

Bauer, Yehuda, and Menachem Z. Rosensaft. 1988. *Antisemitism: Threat to Western Civilization.* Jerusalem: Hebrew University of Jerusalem, Vidal Sassoon International Center for the Study of Antisemitism.

Beck, Ulrich. 1986. *Risikogesellschaft.* Frankfurt am Main: Suhrkamp.

Beck, Ulrich, and Elisabeth Beck-Gernsheim, eds. 1994. *Riskante Freiheiten.* Frankfurt am Main: Suhrkamp.

Benz, Wolfgang. 1987. "Die Abwehr der Vergangenheit: Ein Problem nur für Historiker und Moralisten?" In *Ist der Nationalsozialismus Geschichte?: Zu Historisierung und Historikerstreit,* edited by Dan Diner. Frankfurt am Main: Fischer Taschenbuch Verlag, pp. 17–33.

———. 1989. "Die Opfer und die Täter: Rechtsextremismus in der Bundesrepublik." In *Rechtsextremismus in der Bundesrepublik: Voraussetzungen, Zusammenhänge, Wirkungen,* edited by Wolfgang Benz. Frankfurt am Main: Fischer Taschenbuch Verlag, pp. 9–37.

———. 1994. "Die 'Auschwitz-Lüge.' " In *Der Umgang mit dem Holocaust: Europa—USA—Israel,* edited by Rolf Steininger. Vienna: Böhlau, pp. 103–115.

———, ed. 1991. *Dimension des Völkermords: Die Zahl der jüdischen Opfer des Nationalsozialismus.* Munich: Oldenburg.

———. 1992a, 1993, and 1995a. *Jahrbuch für Antisemitismusforschung. Vols. 1, 2, 4.* Frankfurt am Main: Campus.

———. 1992b. *Legenden, Lügen, Vorurteile: Ein Wörterbuch zur Zeitgeschichte.* Munich: Deutscher Taschenbuch Verlag.

———. 1995b. *Antisemitismus in Deutschland: Zur Aktualität eines Vorurteils.* Munich: Deutscher Taschenbuch Verlag.

Bergmann, Werner. 1988. "Combatting Prejudice." In *Error without Trial: Psychological Research on Antisemitism,* edited by Werner Bergmann. Current Research on Antisemitism 2. Berlin: Walter de Gruyter, pp. 519–526.

———. 1990a. "Der Antisemitismus in der Bundesrepublik Deutschland." In *Der Antisemitismus der Gegenwart,* edited by Herbert A. Strauss, Werner Bergmann, and Christhard Hoffmann. Frankfurt am Main: Campus, pp. 151–166.

———. 1990b. "Sind die Deutschen antisemitisch?: Meinungsumfragen von 1946–1987 in der Bundesrepublik Deutschland." In *Antisemitismus in der politischen Kultur nach 1945,* edited by Werner Bergmann and Rainer Erb. Opladen: Westdeutscher Verlag, pp. 108–130.

———. 1992. "Antisemitismus und Fremdenfeindlichkeit: Eine empirische Überprüfung ihres Zusammenhangs." In *Zwischen Nationalstaat und multikultureller Gesellschaft,* edited by Manfred Heßler. Berlin: Hitit, pp. 115–131.

———. 1994a. "Effekte öffentlicher Meinung auf die Bevölkerungsmeinung: Der Rückgang antisemitischer Einstellungen als kollektiver Lernprozeß." In *Öffentlichkeit, Öffentliche Meinung, Soziale Bewegungen,* edited by Friedhelm Neidhardt. Opladen: Westdeutscher Verlag, pp. 296–319.

———. 1994b. "Medienberichterstattung über Rechtsextremismus und Rassismus." *Jahrbuch für Antisemitismusforschung* vol. 3, edited by Wolfgang Benz. Frankfurt am Main: Campus, pp. 13–25.

———. 1994c. "Ein Versuch, die extreme Rechte als soziale Bewegung zu beschreiben." In *Neonazismus und rechte Subkultur,* edited by Werner Bergmann and Rainer Erb. Berlin: Metropol, pp. 183–208.

Bergmann, Werner, and Rainer Erb. 1986. "Kommunikationslatenz, Moral und öffentliche Meinung." *Kölner Zeitschrift für Soziologie und Sozialpsychologie* 38, pp. 223–246.

———. 1991a. *Antisemitismus in der Bundesrepublik Deutschland: Ergebnisse der empirischen Forschung von 1946 bis 1989.* Opladen: Leske & Budrich.

———. 1991b. "Extreme Antisemiten in der Bundesrepublik Deutschland." *Jahrbuch Extremismus und Demokratie,* vol. 3, edited by Uwe Backes and Eckhard Jesse, pp. 70–93.

———. 1994a. "Kaderpartei, Bewegung, Szene, kollektive Episode oder was?: Probleme der soziologischen Kategorisierung des modernen Rechtsextremismus." *Forschungsjournal Neue Soziale Bewegungen* H7(4), pp. 26–34.

———. 1994b. *Neonazismus und rechte Subkultur.* Berlin: Metropol.

———. 1994c. "Eine soziale Bewegung von rechts?: Entwicklung und Vernetzung einer rechten Szene in den neuen Bundesländern." *Forschungsjournal Neue soziale Bewegungen* 7(2), pp. 80–98.

———. 1995. "Wie antisemitisch sind die Deutschen?: Meinungsumfragen, 1945–1994." In *Antisemitismus in Deutschland: Zur Aktualität eines Vorurteils,* edited by W. Benz. Munich: Deutscher Taschenbuch Verlag, pp.47–88.

———. 1996. *Anti-Semitism in Germany: The Post-Nazi Epoch from 1945 to 1995.* New Brunswick, N.J.: Transaction.

———, eds. 1990. *Antisemitismus in der politischen Kultur nach 1945.* Opladen: Westdeutscher Verlag.

Bergmann, Werner, Rainer Erb, and Albert Lichtblau, eds. 1995. *Schwieriges Erbe: Der Umgang mit Nationalsozialismus und Antisemitismus in Österreich, der DDR und der Bundesrepublik Deutschland.* Frankfurt am Main: Campus.

Beringer, Johannes. 1989. "Zertrümmerte Grabsteine und eine planvoll vergessene Geschichte: In Berlin kämpft die zweite jüdische Gemeinde 'Adass Jisroel' um ihre Anerkennung." *Frankfurter Rundschau,* July 6, p. 14.

Bettelheim, Bruno, and Morris Janowitz. 1964. *Dynamics of Prejudice.* New York: Harper & Row.

Beyme, Klaus von. 1988. "Right-Wing Extremism in Post-War Europe." *West European Politics* 11(2), pp. 1–18.

Birsl, Ursula. 1994. *Rechtsextremismus: weiblich—männlich? Eine Fallstudie.* Opladen: Leske & Budrich.

Björgo, Tore. 1995. *Terror from the Extreme Right.* London: Frank Cass.

Björgo, Tore, and Rob Witte, eds. 1993. *Racist Violence in Europe.* New York: St. Martin's.

Bodemann, Y. Michal. 1989–92. "Federal Republic of Germany." In *American Jewish Year Book,* vols. 89–92, edited by David Singer and Ruth R. Seldin. New York: American Jewish Committee and Jewish Publication Society.

Bodemann, Y. Michal, and Robin Ostow. 1993. "Federal Republic of Germany." In *American Jewish Year Book 1993,* vol. 93, edited by David Singer and Ruth R. Seldin. New York: American Jewish Committee and Jewish Publication Society, pp. 282–300.

Bortfeldt, Heinrich. 1991. "The German Communists in Disarray." *Journal of Communist Studies* 7(4), pp. 522–532.

Bortfeldt, Heinrich, and Wayne C. Thompson. 1993. "The German Communists." *Western European Communists and the Collapse of Communism,* edited by David S. Bell. Oxford, England: Berg, pp. 139–156.

Botz, Gerhard. 1994. " 'Neonazismus ohne Neonazi?': Inszenierte NS-Apologetik in der 'Neuen Kronen-Zeitung.' " In *Handbuch des österreichischen Rechtsextremismus,* edited by Dokumentationsarchiv des österreichischen Widerstandes. Vienna: Deuticke, pp. 595–615.

Bourdieu, Pierre. 1991. *The Political Ontology of Martin Heidegger.* Stanford: Stanford University Press.

Bourdieu, Pierre, Jacques Derrida, et al., eds. 1993. "Appeal to Vigilance." *Le Monde,* July 13, p. 14.

Braham, Randolph L. 1994. "Antisemitism and the Treatment of the Holocaust in Post-Communist East Central Europe." *Holocaust and Genocide Studies* 8(2), pp. 143–163.

Bredehöft, Sonja, and Franz Januschek. 1994. *Doppelzüngler: Die Sprache der "Republikaner."* Duisburg: Diss.

Breuer, Stefan. 1993. *Anatomie der konservativen Revolution.* Darmstadt: Wissenschaftliche Buchgesellschaft.

Broder, Henryk M. 1991. "Tote Seelen in Berlin." *Die Zeit* 45(40), p. 52.

Broszat, Martin. 1976. "Zur Kritik der Publizistik des antisemitischen Rechtsextremismus." *Aus Politik und Zeitgeschichte* 19, pp. 3–7.

———. 1986. "Hitler und die Genesis der 'Endlösung': Aus Anlaß der Thesen von David Irving." In *Nach Hitler: Der schwierige Umgang mit unserer Geschichte,* edited by Martin Broszat. Munich: Oldenburg, pp. 187–229.

———. 1990. "A Plea for the Historicization of National Socialism." In *Reworking the Past: Hitler, the Holocaust, and the Historian's Debate,* edited by Peter Baldwin. Boston: Beacon, pp. 77–87.

Brown, Michael, ed. 1994. *Approaches to Antisemitism: Context and Curriculum.* New York: American Jewish Committee and International Center for University Teaching of Jewish Civilization.

Brück, Eva. 1994. "Ostberliner Gemeindemitglieder an letzter Stelle?" *Berlin-Umschau* 5(1), pp. 4–5.

Brumlik, Micha. 1995. "Geisteswissenschaftlicher Revisionismus: auch eine Verharmlosung des Nationalsozialismus." In *Rechtsextremismus: Ideologie und Gewalt,* edited by Richard Faber, Hajo Funke, and Gerhard Schoenberner. Berlin: Hentrich, pp. 178–187.

Brusten, M. 1992. "Die Bedeutung des Holocaust für die Einstellung der deutschen Jugend zu aktuellen sozialen und politischen Fragen." In *Entwicklungsperspektiven von Kriminalität und Strafrecht,* edited by Uwe Ewald and Kersten Woweries. Bonn: Forum, pp. 289–331.

Brusten, M., and B. Winkelmann. 1992. "The Understanding of the Holocaust and Its Influence on Current Perspectives of German Youth: An Overview of a Quantitative Research Project on Attitudes of Pupils and Students." *Soziale Probleme* 1, pp. 1–27.

———. 1993. "Einstellung von Studenten zum Holocaust: Unterschiede nach parteipolitischer Grundorientierung und im deutsch-israelischen Vergleich." In *Polen und Deutschland: Belastungen der Vergangenheit und Chancen künftiger Kooperation,* edited by Landeszentrale für politische Bildung Nordrhein-Westfalen. Düsseldorf, pp. 186–220.

———. 1994. "Wie denken deutsche Studenten in 'West' und 'Ost' nach der Wiedervereinigung über den Holocaust?: Erste empirische Ergebnisse zu den Auswirkungen unterschiedlicher 'politischer Sozialisation' und parteipolitischer Grundorientierung." *Tel Aviver Jahrbuch für Deutsche Geschichte,* vol. 23. Gerlingen: Bleicher, pp. 461–486.

Brusten, Manfred. 1995. "Wie sympathisch sind uns die Juden?: Empirische Analysen zum Antisemitismus aus einem Forschungsprojekt über Einstellungen deutscher Studenten in Ost und West." In *Jahrbuch für Antisemitismusforschung,* vol. 4, edited by Wolfgang Benz. Frankfurt am Main: Campus, pp. 107–129.

Bundesminister des Innern, ed. 1993. *Extremismus und Gewalt.* Vol. 2. Bonn.

———. 1994. *Extremismus und Gewalt.* Vol. 3. Bonn.

Bundesministerium des Innern. 1991. *Verfassungsschutzbericht 1990.* Bonn.

———. 1992. *Verfassungsschutzbericht 1991.* Bonn.

———. 1993. *Verfassungsschutzbericht 1992.* Bonn.

———. 1994. *Verfassungsschutzbericht 1993.* Bonn.

———. 1995. *Verfassungsschutzbericht 1994.* Bonn.

Buruma, Ian. 1994. *The Wages of Guilt: Memories of War in Germany and Japan.* New York: Farrar Straus Giroux.

Butterwegge, Christoph. 1990. "Gesellschaftliche Ursachen, Erscheinungsformen und Entwicklungstendenzen des Rechtsradikalismus." In *Rechtsextremismus im vereinigten Deutschland,* edited by Christoph Butterwegge and Horst Isola. Bremen: Steintor, pp. 181–201.

———. 1994a. "Mordanschläge als Jugendprotest: Neonazis als Probestbewegung." *Forschungsjournal Neue soziale Bewegungen* 4, pp. 35–41.

———. 1994b. "Rechtsextremismus/Rassismus im vereinten Deutschland." In: *Europa: Zukunft eines Kontinents,* edited by Margit Pieber. Münster: Westfälisches Dampfboot, pp. 144–157.

Butterwegge, Christoph, and Horst Isola, eds. 1990. *Rechtsextremismus im vereinten Deutschland.* Berlin: LinksDruck.

Butterwegge, Christoph, and Siegfried Jäger, eds. 1992. *Rassismus in Europa.* Cologne: Bund Verlag.

Butz, Arthur R. 1975. *The Hoax of the 20th Century.* Richmond, England: Historical Review Press.

Cesarani, David. 1991. "Antisemitism in the 1990s: A Symposium." *Patterns of Prejudice* 25(2), pp. 13–16.

Chaffee, Steven H., and Yuko Miyo. 1983. "Selective Exposure and the Reinforcement Hypothesis: An Intergenerational Panel Study of the 1980 Presidential Campaign." *Communications Research* 10, pp. 3–36.

Chaffee, Steven H., and Joan Schleuder. 1986. "Measurement and Effects of Attention to Media News." *Human Communications Research* 13, pp. 76–107.

Chanes, Jerome A. 1994. "Antisemitism in the United States, 1993: A Contextual Analysis." In *Approaches to Antisemitism,* edited by Michael Brown. New York: American Jewish Committee and International Center for University Teaching of Jewish Civilization, pp. 32–45.

Christians, Georg. 1990. *"Die Reihen fest geschlossen Die FAP: Zu Anatomie und Umfeld einer militant-neofaschistischen Partei in den 80er Jahren.".* Marburg: Arbeit & Gesellschaft.

Christophersen, Thies. 1975. *Die Auschwitz-Lüge: Ein Erlebnisbericht.* Mohrkirch: Kritik.

Claußen, Bernhard. 1989. "Überlegungen zur Entwicklung des autoritären Sozialcharakters in industriellen Massengesellschaften: Perspektiven für eine international vergleichende Theorie und Praxis der politischen Sozialisation." In *Politische Sozialisation Jugend-*

licher in Ost und West, edited by Bernhard Claußen. Bonn: Bundeszentrale für politische Bildung, pp. 287–319.

Cobb, Roger W., and Charles D. Elder, eds. 1983. *Participation in American Politics: The Dynamics of Agenda-Building.* 2d ed. Baltimore: The Johns Hopkins University Press.

Cohen, Renae, and Jennifer Golub. 1991. *Attitudes toward Jews in Poland, Hungary, and Czechoslovakia: A Comparative Study.* Working Papers on Contemporary Anti-Semitism. New York: American Jewish Committee.

Crick, Bernard. 1971. "Toleration and Tolerance in Theory and Practice." *Government and Opposition* 6(2), pp. 144–171.

Curtis, Michael, ed. 1986. *Antisemitism in the Contemporary World.* Boulder: Westview.

Dalton, Russell J. 1988. *Citizen Politics.* Chatham, N.J.: Chatham House.

Derrida, Jacques. 1994. *Specters of Marx: The State of the Debt, the Work of Mourning and the New International.* New York: Routledge.

Deutsches Jugendinstitut, ed. 1992. *Schüler an der Schwelle zur deutschen Einheit.* Opladen: Leske & Budrich.

Diederichsen, Diedrich. 1992. "Spiritual Reactionaries after German Reunification: Syberberg, Foucault, and Others." *October* 62, pp. 65–83.

———. 1993. *Freiheit macht arm: Das Leben nach dem Rock 'n' Roll, 1990–93.* Cologne: Kiepenheuer & Witsch.

Dietzsch, Martin. 1994. "Kader gegen die Fünfundvierziger: Die völkische Gesinnungsgemeinschaft Witikobund." In *Das Plagiat: Der völkische Nationalismus der Jungen Freiheit,* edited by Helmut Kellershohn. Duisburg: DISS-Verlag, pp. 133–142.

Diner, Dan, ed. 1987. *Ist der Nationalsozialismus Geschichte? Zu Historisierung und Historikerstreit.* Frankfurt am Main: Fischer Taschenbuch Verlag.

Dokumentationsarchiv des österreichischen Widerstandes, ed. 1985. *Am Beispiel Walter Reder: Die SS-Verbrechen in Marzabotto und ihre "Bewältigung."* Vienna: Dokumentationsarchiv des österreichischen Widerstandes.

———. 1990. *The Lachout "Document": Anatomy of a Forgery.* Vienna: Dokumentationsarchiv des österreichischen Widerstandes.

———. 1994. *Handbuch des österreichischen Rechtsextremismus.* Vienna: Deuticke.

Drahtzieher im braunen Netz: Der Wiederaufbau der NSDAP. 1992. Berlin: Edition ID-Archiv.

Drew, Dan, and David Weaver. 1990. "Media Attention, Media Exposure, and Media Effects." *Journalism Quarterly* 67, pp. 740–748.

Dudek, Peter. 1992. " 'Vergangenheitsbewältigung' Zur Problematik eines umstrittenen Begriffs." *Aus Politik und Zeitgeschichte,* 1–2, pp. 44–53.

———. 1994. "Die Auseinandersetzungen mit Nationalsozialismus und Rechtsextremismus nach 1945." In *Rechtsextremismus,* edited by Wolfgang Kowalsky and Wolfgang Schroeder. Opladen: Westdeutscher Verlag, pp. 277–301.

Eley, John. 1995. "The Frankfurter Allgemeine Zeitung and Contemporary National Conservatism." *German Politics and Society* 13(2, Summer), pp. 80–121.

Elsässer, Jürgen. 1992. *Antisemitismus: Das alte Gesicht des neuen Deutschland.* Berlin: Dietz.

Emmerer, Brigitte. 1993. "Heß Englandflug." In *Legenden, Lügen, Vorurteile: Ein Wörterbuch zur Zeitgeschichte,* edited by Wolfgang Benz. Munich: Deutscher Taschenbuch Verlag, pp. 94–95.

Emnid-Institut. 1954. *Zum Problem des Antisemitismus im Bundesgebiet.* Bonn: Bundeszentrale für Heimatdienst.

———. 1989. *Zeitgeschichte.* Bielefeld.

———. 1992. *Antisemitismus in Deutschland.* Bielefeld.

Enzensberger, Hans Magnus. 1994. *Civil Wars from L.A. to Bosnia*. New York: New Press.

Epstein, Simon. 1993. "Cyclical Patterns in Antisemitism: The Dynamics of Anti-Jewish Violence in Western Countries since the 50's." *Acta No. 2: Analysis in Current Trends in Antisemitism*. Jerusalem: Hebrew University.

Erb, Rainer. 1994. "Antisemitismus in der rechten Jugendszene." In *Neonazismus und rechte Subkultur,* edited by Werner Bergmann and Rainer Erb. Berlin: Metropol, pp. 31–76.

Eurobarometer 1970, 1988, 1990, 1991, 1992. Studies conducted by order of the Commission of the European Community, Brussels.

Falter, Jürgen W. 1994. *Wer wählt rechts?: Die Wähler und Anhänger rechtsextremistischer Parteien im vereinigten Deutschland*. Munich: Beck.

Falter, Jürgen, and Markus Klein. 1994. "Die Wähler der PDS bei der Bundestagswahl 1994: Zwischen Ideologie, Nostalgie und Protest." *Aus Politik und Zeitgeschichte* 51–52, pp. 22–34.

Falter, Jürgen, Hans Rattinger, and Klaus G. Troitzsch, eds. 1989. *Wahlen und politische Einstellungen in der Bundesrepublik Deutschland*. Frankfurt am Main: Peter Lang.

Farin, Klaus, and Eberhard Seidel-Pielen. 1992. *Rechtsruck: Rassismus im neuen Deutschland*. Berlin: Rotbuch.

———. 1993. *Skinheads*. Munich: Beck.

Faurisson, Robert. 1978. *Es gab keine Gaskammern*. Witten: Deutscher Arbeitskreis.

Fein, Helen, ed. 1987. *The Persisting Question: Sociological Perspectives and Social Contexts of Modern Antisemitism*. Berlin: Walter de Gruyter.

Feingold, Henry. 1985. "Finding a Conceptual Framework for the Study of American Antisemitism." *Jewish Social Studies* 47 (Summer/Fall), pp. 313–326.

Feist, Ursula. 1991. "Zur Politischen Akkulturation der vereinten Deutschen: Eine Analyse aus Anlaß der ersten gesamtdeutschen Bundestagswahl." *Aus Politik und Zeitgeschichte* 11–12, pp. 21–32.

Feldman, Lily Gardner. 1984. *The Special Relationship between West Germany and Israel*. Boston: Allen & Unwin.

Fenske, Wolfgang. 1994. "Die Freiheit des Denkens zurückgewinnen" (interview with Heimo Schwilk). *Junge Freiheit* 45 (November 4), p. 3

Fest, Joachim C. 1973. *Hitler: Eine Biographie*. Frankfurt am Main: Propyläen.

Fest, Joachim C. and Christian Herrendorfer. 1977. *Hitler: Eine Karriere*. Frankfurt am Main: Ullstein.

Ford, Glyn, ed. 1992. *Fascist Europe: The Rise of Fascism and Xenophobia*. London: Pluto.

Forsa. 1994. "Die Deutschen und der Nationalsozialismus: Kenntnisse, Einschätzungen, Urteile." Survey sponsored by the magazine *Die Woche*. Hamburg.

Förster, Peter, and Walter Friedrich. 1995. *Schuljugend in Sachsen*. Leipzig: Leipziger Institut für praktische Sozialforschung e.v.

Förster, Peter, Walter Friedrich, Harry Müller, and Wilfried Schubarth. 1993. *Jugend Ost: Zwischen Hoffnung und Gewalt*. Opladen: Leske & Budrich.

Friedrich, Walter. 1990. "Mentalitätswandlungen der Jugend in der DDR." *Aus Politik und Zeitgeschichte* 16–17, pp. 24–37.

———. 1993. "Einstellungen zu Ausländern bei ostdeutschen Jugendlichen: 'Autoritäre Persönlichkeit' als Stereotyp." In *Rechtsradikale Gewalt im vereinigten Deutschland,* edited by Hans-Uwe Otto and Roland Merten. Opladen: Leske & Budrich, pp. 189–199.

Friedrich, Walter, and Wilfried Schubarth. 1991. "Ausländerfeindliche und rechtsextreme

Orientierungen bei ostdeutschen Jugendlichen." *Deutschland Archiv* 24(10), pp. 1052–1065.

Friedrich, Walter, and Hartmut Griese, eds. 1991. *Jugend und Jugendforschung in der DDR.* Opladen: Leske & Budrich.

Frings, Ute. 1991. "Nicht alle erfreut die wiederbelebte Gemeinde: Ein Berliner Streit um die Einheit der gläubigen Juden—und um Millionenwerte." *Frankfurter Rundschau*, August 24, p. 5.

Fromm, Rainer. 1992. *Rechtsextremismus in Thüringen.* Erfurt: Landeszentrale für politische Bildung.

———. 1993. *Am rechten Rand: Lexikon des Rechtsradikalismus.* Marburg: Schüren.

Fromm, Rainer, and Barbara Kernbach. 1994a. *Europas braune Saat: Die internationale Verflechtung der rechtsradikalen Szene.* Bonn: Aktuell.

———. 1994b. *". . . und morgen die ganze Welt?": Rechtsextreme Publizistik in Westeuropa.* Marburg: Schüren.

Fuchs, Dieter, Jürgen Gerhards, and Edeltraud Roller. 1993. "Wir und die anderen: Ethnozentrismus in den zwölf Ländern der europäischen Gemeinschaft." *Kölner Zeitschrift für Soziologie und Sozialpsychologie* 45, pp. 238–254.

Funke, Hajo. 1989. *"Republikaner"—Rassismus, Judenfeindschaft, nationaler Größenwahn: Zu den Potentialen der Rechtsextremen am Beispiel der "Republikaner."* Berlin: Aktion Sühnezeichen.

Gabriel, Oscar W. 1993. "Institutionenvertrauen im vereinigten Deutschland." *Aus Politik und Zeitgeschichte* 43, pp. 3–12.

Gauly, Thomas M., ed. 1988. *Die Last der Geschichte: Kontroversen zur deutschen Identität.* Cologne: Verlag Wissenschaft und Politik.

Geiger, Klaus F. 1991. "Einstellungen zur multikulturellen Gesellschaft: Ergebnisse von Repräsentativbefragungen in der Bundesrepublik." *Migration* 9, pp. 11–48.

German Information Center. 1994. *German-Israeli Relations.* New York.

Gessenharter, Wolfgang. 1992. *Kippt die Republik? Die neue Rechte und ihre Unterstützung durch Politik und Medien.* Munich: Beck.

Gibowski, Wolfgang G., and Matthias Jung. 1993. "Economic Perceptions and System Support: Germany Three Years after Reunification." Paper presented at the annual meeting of the American Political Science Association, Washington, D.C., September 2–5.

Gibowski, Wolfgang G., and Max Kaase. 1991. "Auf dem Weg zum politischen Alltag: Eine Analyse der ersten gesamtdeutschen Bundestagswahl vom 2. Dezember 1990." *Aus Politik und Zeitgeschichte* 11–12, pp. 3–20.

Gibowski, Wolfgang, and Holli A. Semetko. 1992. "Amerikanische öffentliche Meinung und deutsche Einheit." In *The USA and the German Question, 1945–1990*, edited by Wolfgang-Uwe Friedrich. Frankfurt am Main: Campus, pp. 391–406.

Giesen, Bernd, and Claus Leggewie, eds. 1991. *Experiment Vereinigung: Ein sozialer Großversuch.* Berlin: Rotbuch.

Gilman, Sander L., and Steven T. Katz, ed. 1991. *Antisemitism in Times of Crisis.* New York: New York University Press.

Ginzel, Günter B., ed. 1991. *Antisemitismus, Erscheinungsformen der Judenfeindschaft gestern und heute.* Bielefeld: Verlag Wissenschaft und Politik.

Giordano, Ralph. 1987. *Die zweite Schuld, oder von der Last Deutscher zu sein.* Hamburg: Rasch und Röhring.

———. 1992. *Ich bin angegelt an dieses Land: Reden und Aufsätze über die deutsche Vergangenheit und Gegenwart.* Hamburg: Rasch und Röhring.

Glazer, Nathan. 1986. "Is Anti-Zionism a New Form of Anti-Semitism?" In *Anti-Semitism in the Contemporary World,* edited by Michael Curtis. Boulder: Westview, pp. 155–163.

Golub, Jennifer. 1993. *British Attitudes toward Jews and Other Minorities.* Working Papers on Contemporary Anti-Semitism. New York: American Jewish Committee.

Golub, Jennifer. 1994. *Current German Attitudes toward Jews and Other Minorities.* Working Papers on Contemporary Anti-Semitism. New York: American Jewish Committee. (Survey by Emnid-Institut, January 12–31, 1994, Bielefeld.)

Golub, Jennifer, and Renae Cohen. 1993a. *What Do the Americans Know about the Holocaust?* Working Papers on Contemporary Anti-Semitism. New York: American Jewish Committee.

———. 1993b. *What Do the British Know about the Holocaust?.* Working Papers on Contemporary Anti-Semitism. New York: American Jewish Committee.

———. 1994. *What Do the French Know about the Holocaust?* Working Papers on Contemporary Anti-Semitism. New York: American Jewish Committee.

Graber, Doris A. 1988. *Processing the News: How People Tame the Information Tide.* New York: Longman.

———. 1994. *Mass Media and American Politics.* Washington, D.C.: Congressional Quarterly Press.

Graml, Hermann. 1989. "Alte und neue Apologeten Hitlers." In *Rechtsextremismus in der Bundesrepublik: Voraussetzungen, Zusammenhänge, Wirkungen,* edited by Wolfgang Benz. Frankfurt am Main: Fischer Taschenbuch Verlag, pp. 63–92.

Greiffenhagen, Martin. 1991. "Die Bundesrepublik Deutschland von 1945 bis 1990: Reformen und Defizite der politischen Kultur." *Aus Politik und Zeitgeschichte* 1–2.

Groll, Klaus-Michael. 1990. *Wie lange haften wir für Hitler: Zum Selbstverständnis der Deutschen heute.* Düsseldorf: Droste.

Grosser, Alfred. 1990. *Ermordung der Menschheit.* Munich: Hanser.

Gudkov, Lev and Alex Levinson. 1992. *Attitudes toward Jews in the Soviet Union: Public Opinion in Ten Republics.* Working Papers on Contemporary Anti-Semitism. New York: American Jewish Committee.

———. 1994. *Attitudes toward Jews in the Commonwealth of Independent States.* Working Papers on Contemporary Anti-Semitism. New York: American Jewish Committee.

Hachel, Heinz. 1994. "Poor Impact: Werbeträger Junge Freiheit." In *Das Plagiat: Der völkische Nationalismus der Jungen Freiheit,* edited by Helmut Kellershohn. Duisburg: DISS-Verlag, pp. 143–152.

Hafeneger, Benno. 1990. *Die "extreme Rechte" und Europa: Herausforderungen für eine multikulturelle Gesellschaft.* Frankfurt am Main: Verlag für akademische Schriften.

Hagan, John, Hans Merkens, and Klaus Boehnke. 1995. "Delinquency and Disdain: Social Capital and the Control of Right-Wing Extremism among East and West Berlin Youth." *American Journal of Sociology* 100(4), pp. 1028–1052.

Hainsworth, Paul, ed. 1992. *The Extreme Right in Europe and the USA.* London: Pinter.

Halbwachs, Maurice. 1992. *On Collective Memory.* Chicago: University of Chicago Press.

Hargreaves, Alec G., and Jeremy Leaman, eds. 1995. *Racism, Ethnicity, and Politics in Contemporary Europe.* Aldershot, England: E. Elgar.

Hart, James. 1966. "Foreign News in U.S. and English Daily Newspapers: A Comparison." *Journalism Quarterly* 43, pp. 443–449.

Harwood, Richard E. 1974. *Did Six Million Really Die?: The Truth at Last.* Richmond, England: Historical Review Press.

Heitmeyer, Wilhelm. 1991. "Individualisierungsprozesse und Folgen für die politische Sozialisation von Jugendlichen." In *Politische Sozialisation und Individualisierung,* edited by Wilhelm Heitmeyer and Juliane Jacobi. Weinheim: Juventa, pp. 15–34.

————. 1994a. "Der Blick auf die 'Mitte' der Gesellschaft." In *Das Gewalt-Dilemma: Gesellschaftliche Reaktionen auf fremdenfeindliche Gewalt und Rechtsextremismus,* edited by Wilhelm Heitmeyer. Frankfurt am Main: Suhrkamp, pp. 11–26.

————. 1994b. "Das Desintegrationstheorem." In *Das Gewaltdilemma,* edited by Wilhelm Heitmeyer. Frankfurt am Main: Suhrkamp, pp. 29–69.

Heitmeyer, Wilhelm, et al. 1992. *Die Bielefelder Rechtsextremismus-Studie: Erste Langzeituntersuchung zur politischen Sozialisation bei männlichen Jugendlichen.* Weinheim: Juventa.

————. 1995. *Gewalt: Schattenseiten der Individualisierung bei Jugendlichen aus unterschiedlichen Milieus.* Weinheim: Juventa.

Hennig, Eike. 1988. *Zum Historikerstreit: Was heißt und zu welchem Ende studiert man Faschismus?* Frankfurt am Main: Athenäum.

Henningsen, Manfred. 1989. "The Politics of Memory: Holocaust and Legitimacy in Post Nazi-Germany." *Holocaust and Genocide Studies* 4(1), pp. 15–26.

Herbst, Ludolf, and Constantin Goschler eds. 1989. *Wiedergutmachung in der BRD.* Munich: Oldenbourg.

Herf, Jeffrey. 1994. "Antisemitismus in der SED: Geheime Dokumente zum Fall Merker aus SED- und MfS-Archiven." *Vierteljahrshefte für Zeitgeschichte* 42, pp. 635–667.

Herz, John. 1990. "Bürde der Vergangenheit oder: Wie die Deutschen mit der Nazihinterlassenschaft fertig wurden." *Tel Aviver Jahrbuch für deutsche Geschichte* 19, pp. 13–32.

Herz, Thomas. 1991. "Rechtsextreme Parteien und die Reaktionen der Gesellschaft." *Sozialwissenschaftliche Informationen* 4, pp. 234–240.

Herzinger, Richard, and Hannes Stein. 1995. *Endzeit-Propheten oder die Offensive der Antiwestler: Fundamentalismus, Antiamerikanismus und Neue Rechte.* Hamburg: Rowohlt.

Hill, Paul B. 1993. "Die Entwicklung der Einstellungen zu unterschiedlichen Ausländergruppen zwischen 1980 und 1992." In *Fremdenfeindliche Gewalt: Einstellungen, Täter, Konflikteskalation,* edited by Helmut Willems et al. Opladen: Leske & Budrich, pp.25–68.

"Historikerstreit." 1987. *Die Dokumentation der Kontroverse um die Einzigartigkeit der nationalsozialistischen Judenvernichtung.* Munich: Piper.

Hoffmann, Christa. 1990. "Die justitielle 'Vergangenheitsbewältigung' in der Bundesrepublik Deutschland." In *Die Schatten der Vergangenheit: Impulse zur Historisierung des Nationalsozialismus,* edited by Uwe Backes, Eckhard Jesse, and Rainer Zitelmann. Frankfurt am Main: Ullstein, pp. 497–521.

Hoffmann, Lutz. 1994. *Das deutsche Volk und seine Feinde: Die völkische Droge.* Cologne: PapyRossa.

Hoffmann-Lange, Ursula. 1995a. "Determinanten politischer Gewaltbereitschaft Jugendlicher in Deutschland." In *Jugend und Gewalt: Devianz und Kriminalität in Ost und West,* edited by Siegfried Lamnek. Opladen: Leske & Budrich, pp. 57–74.

————. 1995b. *Jugend und Demokratie in Deutschland: DJI-Jugendsurvey 1.* Opladen: Leske & Budrich.

Hundseder, Franziska. 1995. *Rechte machen Kasse: Gelder und Finanziers der braunen Szene.* Munich: Knauer.

Hurrelmann, Klaus, and Dieter Ulich. 1991. *Neues Handbuch der Sozialisationsforschung.* Weinheim: Beltz.

Husbands, Christopher T. 1991. "Neo-Nazis in East Germany: The New Danger?" *Patterns of Prejudice,* 25(1), pp. 3–17.

ID-Archiv im ISSG, ed. 1992. *Drahtzieher im braunen Netz. Der Wiederaufbau der "NSDAP."* Berlin: Edition ID-Archiv.

Ignazi, Piero, and Colette Ysmal. 1992. "Extreme Right-Wing Parties in Europe." *European Journal of Political Research* 22(1), special issue.

Inglehart, Ronald and Jacques-Rene Rabier. 1986. "Political Realignment in Advanced Industrial Society: From Class-Based Politics to Quality-of-Life Politics." *Government and Opposition* 21, pp. 456–479.

Innenminister des Staates Thüringen, ed. 1992. *Verfassungsschutzbericht Thüringen.* Erfurt.

Institute of Jewish Affairs, ed. 1994. *Antisemitism World Report.* London.

Institut für angewandte Sozialforschung. 1992. *Jugend und Rechtsextremismus in Schleswig-Holstein.* Hamburg: Norddeutscher Rundfunk.

Institut für Demoskopie. 1949. *Ist Deutschland antisemitisch?* Allensbach.

———. 1986. *Deutsche und Juden vier Jahrzehnte danach.* Allensbach.

———. 1992a. *IfD-Surveys No. 5056, 5064, 5069.* Allensbach.

———. 1992b. *IfD-Survey No. 5074.* Allensbach.

"Internationale Konferenz gegen Neonazismus und zur Immunisierung der Jugend." 1977. Unpublished manuscript, Vienna, April 22–24.

IPOS. 1988, 1989, 1990, 1991. *Einstellungen zu aktuellen Fragen des Innenpolitik in Deutschland.* Mannheim.

———. 1990a. "American Attitudes about Germany in an Age of Transition." Study no. 670 (March). Mannheim.

———. 1991a. "American Attitudes toward Germany in a Changing Europe." Study no. 777 (October). Mannheim.

———. 1993. "American Attitudes toward Germany in a Changing Europe." Study no. 850 (March/April). Mannheim.

Jacobsen, Hans-Adolf. 1982. "Anmerkungen zum Deutschlandbild in den USA und zum Amerikabild in der Bundesrepublik Deutschland." *Internationale Schulbuchforschung* 4(2–3). pp. 109–112.

Jäger, Siegfried. 1988. *Rechtsdruck: Die Presse der Neuen Rechten.* Berlin: Dietz.

———. 1992a. *BrandSätze.* Duisburg: Diss-Verlag.

———. 1992b. "Wie die Deutschen die Fremden sehen." In *Rassismus in Europa,* edited by Christoph Butterwegge and Siegfried Jäger. Cologne: Bund Verlag, pp. 230–247.

Jarausch, Konrad H. 1988. "Removing the Nazi Stain?: The Quarrel of the German Historians." *German Studies Review* 11(2), pp. 285–301.

Jaschke, Hans-Gerd. 1990. *Die Republikaner: Profile einer Rechtsaußen-Partei.* Bonn: Dietz.

———. 1991. *Streitbare Demokratie und innere Sicherheit.* Opladen: Westdeutscher Verlag.

———. 1993. "Formiert sich eine neue soziale Bewegung von rechts?: Über die Ethnisierung sozialer und politischer Konflikte." *Institut für Sozialforschung, Mitteilungen,* no. 2, pp. 28–44.

———. 1994. "Rechtsextremismus, Fremdenfeindlichkeit und die Polizei." In *Rechtsextremismus und Fremdenfeindlichkeit: Studien zur aktuellen Entwicklung,* edited by Institut für Sozialforschung. Frankfurt am Main: Campus, pp. 167–209.

Jesse, Eckhard. 1990. "Philosemitismus, Antisemitismus und Anti-Antisemitismus: Vergangenheitsbewältigung und Tabus." In *Die Schatten der Vergangenheit: Impulse zur Historisierung des Nationalsozialismus,* edited by Uwe Backes, Eckhard Jesse, and Rainer Zitelmann. Frankfurt am Main: Ullstein, pp. 543–567.

———. 1991. "Vergangenheitsbewältigung." In *Handwörterbuch zur deutschen Politik,* edited by Werner Weidenfeld and Karl-Rudolf Korte. Bonn: Bundeszentrale für politische Bildung, pp. 715–722.

References 299

Jodice, David A. 1990. *United Germany and Jewish Concerns: Attitudes toward Jews, Israel, and the Holocaust.* New York: American Jewish Committee.

———. 1991. *United Germany and Jewish Concerns: Attitudes toward Jews, Israel, and the Holocaust.* Working Papers on Contemporary Anti-Semitism. New York: American Jewish Committee.

Jung, Matthias, and Dieter Roth. 1994. "Kohls knappster Sieg: Eine Analyse der Bundestagswahl 1994." *Aus Politik und Zeitgeschichte* 51–52, pp. 3–15.

Kaase, Max. 1971. "Demokratische Einstellungen in der Bundesrepublik Deutschland." In *Sozialwissenchaftliches Jahrbuch für Politik,* vol. 2, edited by Rudolf Wildenmann. Munich: Olzog, pp. 119–326.

Kalinowsky, Harry H. 1993. *Kampfplatz Justiz: Politische Justiz und Rechsextremismus in der Bundesrepublik Deutschland, 1949–1990.* Pfaffenweiler: Centaurus.

Karmasin, Fritz. 1992. *Austrian Attitudes toward Jews, Israel, and the Holocaust.* New York: Working Papers on Contemporary Anti-Semitism. American Jewish Committee.

Kaufman, Theodore N. 1979. *Germany Must Perish!* Newark: Argyle, 1941. Reprint, New York: Gordon.

Kellershohn, Helmut. 1994a. "Das Projekt Junge Freiheit." In *Das Plagiat: Der völkische Nationalismus der Jungen Freiheit,* edited by Helmut Kellershohn. Duisburg: DISS-Verlag, pp. 17–50.

———. 1994b. "Die selbsternannte Elite: Herkunft und Verständnis der 'Jungen Freiheit.'" In *Das Plagiat: Der völkische Nationalismus der Jungen Freiheit,* edited by Helmut Kellershohn. Duisburg: DISS-Verlag, pp. 51–116.

———. 1994. *Das Plagiat: Der völkische Nationalismus der Jungen Freiheit.* Duisburg: DISS-Verlag.

Kershaw, Ian. 1985. *The Nazi Dictatorship: Problems and Perspectives of Interpretation.* London: Edward Arnold.

Kersten, Joachim. 1994. "Feindbildkonstruktionen und Gewalthandlungen bei Gruppierungen junger Männer." In *Neonazismus und rechte Subkultur,* edited by Werner Bergmann and Rainer Erb. Berlin: Metropol, pp. 125–142.

Kielmannsegg, Peter Graf. 1989. *Lange Schatten: Vom Umgang der Deutschen mit der nationalsozialistischen Vergangenheit.* Berlin: Siedler.

Kinder, Donald R., and D. Roderick Kiewiet. 1981. "Sociotropic Politics: The American Case." *British Journal of Political Science* 11, pp. 129–161.

King, Preston. 1971. "The Problem of Tolerance." *Government and Opposition* 6(2), pp. 172–207.

———. 1976. *Toleration.* London: Allen and Unwin.

Kittel, Manfred. 1993. *Die Legende der "Zweiten Schuld": Vergangenheitsbewältigung in der Ära Adenauer.* Berlin: Ullstein.

Klein, Stefan. 1984. "Von den Schwierigkeiten der Justiz im Umgang mit KZ-Schergen und Neonazis." In *Rechtsextremismus in der Bundesrepublik: Voraussetzungen, Zusammenhänge, Wirkungen,* edited by Wolfgang Benz. Frankfurt am Main: Fischer Taschenbuch Verlag, pp. 97–114.

Klingemann, Hans-Dieter, and Richard I. Hofferbert. 1994. "Germany: A New 'Wall in the Mind?'" *Journal of Democracy* 5(1), pp. 30–44.

Köcher, Renate. 1987. *Ausmaß und Form des heutigen Antisemitismus in der Bundesrepublik Deutschland.* Allensbach: Institut für Demoskopie.

———. 1994. "Auf einer Woge der Euphorie: Veränderungen der Stimmungslage und des Meinungsklimas im Wahljahr 1994." *Aus Politik und Zeitgeschichte* 51–52, pp. 16–21.

Königseder, Angelika. 1994. "Zur Chronologie des Rechtsextremismus." In *Rechtsextremismus in Deutschland: Voraussetzungen, Zusammenhänge, Wirkungen,* edited by Wolfgang Benz. Frankfurt am Main: Fischer Taschenbuch Verlag, pp. 246–315.

Kopp, Hans-Ulrich. 1994. "Mutiger Kämpfer der Gegenrevolution." *Junge Freiheit* 32 (August 5), p. 18.

Korzenny, Felipe, Wanda del Toro, and James Gaudino. 1987. "International News Media Exposure, Knowledge and Attitudes." *Journal of Broadcasting and Electronic Media* 31(1), pp. 73–87.

Kowalsky, Wolfgang, and Wolfgang Schroeder, eds. 1994. *Rechtsextremismus: Einführung und Forschungsbilanz.* Opladen: Westdeutscher Verlag.

Kriener, Klaus. 1994. "Plettenberg-Freiburg-Potsdam: Über den Einfluß Carl Schmitts auf die 'Junge Freiheit.' " In *Das Plagiat: Der völkische Nationalismus der Jungen Freiheit,* edited by Helmut Kellershohn. Duisburg: DISS-Verlag, pp. 181–213.

Krisch, Henry. 1993. "From SED to PDS: The Struggle to Revive a Left Party." In *The New Germany Votes: Unification and the Creation of a New German Party System,* edited by Russell J. Dalton. Providence: Berg, pp. 163–186.

Kuechler, Manfred. 1992. "The Road to German Unity: Mass Sentiment in East and West Germany." *Public Opinion Quarterly* 56, pp. 53–76.

———. 1994. "The Germans and the 'Others': Racism, Xenophobia, or 'Legitimate Conservatism?' " *German Politics* 3(1), pp. 47–74.

Kulka, O. D. 1979. "The 'Reichsvereinigung of the Jews in Germany' (1938/9–1943)." *Patterns of Jewish Leadership in Nazi Europe, 1933–1945: Proceedings of the Third Yad Vashem International Historical Conference, Jerusalem, April 4–7, 1977.* Jerusalem: Yad Vashem, pp. 45–58.

Kurthen, Hermann. 1995. "Germany at the Crossroads: National Identity and the Challenges of Immigration." *International Migration Review* 29(4), pp. 914–938.

Kurthen, Hermann, and Michael Minkenberg. 1995. "Germany in Transition: Immigration, Racism and the Extreme Right." *Nations and Nationalism* 1(2), pp. 175–196.

Kushner, Tony. 1991. "The Social and Cultural Roots of Contemporary Antisemitism." *Patterns of Prejudice* 25(1), pp. 18–31.

Lamnek, Siegfried. 1994. *Neue Theorien abweichenden Verhaltens.* Munich: Fink.

Landesamt für Verfassungsschutz Berlin. 1994. "Die internationale Revisionismus-Kampagne." *Durchblicke* 1(3).

Landtag von Baden-Württemberg. 1994. *Antisemitism as Schönhuber's Political Strategy.* 11th legislative period, plenary minutes, April 13, 1994, cols. 3346–3362. Stuttgart.

Lange, Astrid. 1993. *Was die Rechten lesen: Fünfzig rechtsextreme Zeitschriften—Ziele, Inhalte, Taktik.* Munich: Beck.

Langmuir, Gavin. 1990. *Toward a Definition of Antisemitism.* Berkeley: University of California Press.

Lasek, Wilhelm. 1994. "Verzeichnis 'revisionistischer' Autoren und deren Publikationen." In *Handbuch des österreichischen Rechtsextremismus,* edited by Dokumentationsarchiv des österreichischen Widerstandes. Vienna: Deuticke, pp. 537–551.

Lederer, Gerda, Joachim Nerger, Susanne Rippl, Peter Schmidt, and Christian Seipel. 1991. "Autoritarismus unter Jugendlichen der ehemaligen DDR." *Deutschland Archiv* 24(6), pp. 587–596.

Leenen, Wolf Rainer. 1992. "Ausländerfeindlichkeit in Deutschland: Politischer Rechtsruck oder Politikversagen?" *Deutschland Archiv* 25(10), pp. 1039–1054.

Leggewie, Claus. 1993. *Druck von rechts: Wohin treibt die Bundesrepublik?* Munich: Beck.

———. 1994. "Rechtsextremismus—eine soziale Bewegung." In *Rechtsextremismus,* edited by Wolfgang Kowalsky and Wolfgang Schroeder. Opladen: Westdeutscher Verlag, pp. 325–338.

Lepsius, M. Rainer. 1989. "Das Erbe des Nationalsozialismus und die politische Kultur der Nachfolgestaaten des 'Großdeutschen Reiches.' In *Kultur und Gesellschaft: Verhandlungen des 24. Deutschen Soziologentags,* edited by Max Haller et al. Frankfurt am Main: Campus, pp. 247–264.

Leuthcusser Schnarrenberger, Sabine. 1994. *Innere Sicherheit: Herausforderung an den Rechtsstaat.* Karlsruhe: C. F. Müller.

Levkov, Ilya, ed. 1987. *Bitburg and Beyond: Encounters in American, German and Jewish History.* New York: Shapolsky.

Lillig, Thomas. 1994. *Rechtsextremismus in den neuen Bundesländern.* Mainz: Forschungsgruppe Deutschland der Universität Mainz.

Linz, Juan J., and Alfred Stepan. 1989. "Political Crafting of Democratic Consolidation or Destruction: European and South American Comparisons." In *Democracy in the Americas: Stopping the Pendulum,* edited by Robert A. Pastor. Boulder, Colo.: Westview, pp. 41–61.

Lipset, Seymour Martin. 1960. *Political Man.* Garden City, N.Y.: Anchor.

Lipset, Seymour Martin and Earl Raab. 1978. *The Politics of Unreason,* 2d ed. Chicago: University of Chicago Press.

Lipset, Seymour Martin, and William Schneider. 1983. *The Confidence Gap.* New York: Free Press.

Lipstadt, Deborah E. 1993. *Denying the Holocaust: The Growing Assault on Truth and Memory.* New York: Free Press.

Löwith, Karl. 1993. "The Political Implications of Heidegger's Existentialism." In *The Heidegger Controversy,* edited by Richard Wollin. Cambridge: Massachusetts Institute of Technology Press.

Lübbe, Hermann. 1983. "Der Nationalsozialismus im politischen Bewußtsein der Gegenwart." In *Deutschlands Weg in die Diktatur: Internationale Konferenz zur nationalsozialistischen Machtübernahme,* edited by Martin Broszat et al. Berlin: Siedler, pp. 329–349.

Lüdtke, Alf. 1993. " 'Coming to Terms with the Past': Illusions of Remembering—Ways of Forgetting Nazism in West Germany." *Journal of Modern History* 65(3), pp. 542–572.

Lutz, Felix Philipp. 1991. "Geschichtsbewußtsein." In *Handwörterbuch zur deutschen Einheit,* edited by Werner Weidenfeld and Karl-Rudolf Korte. Bonn: Bundeszentrale für politische Bildung, pp. 348–356.

———. 1993. "Verantwortungsbewußtsein und Wohlstandschauvinismus: Die Bedeutung historisch-politischer Einstellungen der Deutschen nach der Einheit." In *Deutschland: Eine Nation—doppelte Geschichte,* edited by Werner Weidenfeld. Cologne: Verlag Wissenschaft und Politik, pp. 157–173.

Mägerle, Anton. 1994. "Criticon: Die 'Junge Freiheit' im Zeitschriftenformat: Ein rechtsintellektuelles Stategieorgan." In *Das Plagiat: Der völkische Nationalismus der Jungen Freiheit,* edited by Helmut Kellershohn. Duisburg: DISS-Verlag, pp. 117–132.

Maier, Charles S. 1988. *The Unmasterable Past: History, Holocaust, and German National Identity.* Cambridge: Harvard University Press.

Markovits, Andrei S. 1990. "Coping with the Past: The West German Labor Movement." In *Reworking the Past: Hitler, the Holocaust, and the Historian's Debate,* edited by Peter Baldwin. Boston: Beacon, pp. 262–275.

Marrus, Michael R. 1986. "Is There a New Anti-Semitism?" In *Antisemitism in the Contemporary World,* edited by Michael Curtis. Boulder: Westview, pp. 172–181.

Marten, Eckhard. 1989. *Das Deutschlandbild in der amerikanischen Auslandsberichterstattung: Ein kommunikationswissenschaftlicher Beitrag zur Nationenbildforschung.* Wiesbaden: Deutscher Universitätsverlag.

Martire, Gregory, and Ruth Clark. 1982. *Anti-Semitism in the United States: A Study of Prejudice in the 1980's.* New York: Praeger.

Maschke, Günther. 1991. "Frank B. Kellogg siegt am Golf." *Siebte Etappe* 10 (October), pp. 5–35.

Maser, Peter. 1995. "Juden und Jüdische Gemeinden in der Innenpolitik der DDR." In *Schwieriges Erbe: Der Umgang mit Nationalsozialismus und Antisemitismus in Österreich, der DDR und der Bundesrepublik Deutschland,* edited by Werner Bergmann, Rainer Erb, and Albert Lichtblau. Frankfurt am Main: Campus, pp. 339–368.

Maser, Werner. 1971. *Adolf Hitler: Legende, Mythos, Wirklichkeit.* Munich: Bechtle.

Mayer, Karl Ulrich. 1991. "Soziale Ungleichheit und Lebensverläufe." In *Experiment Vereinigung: Ein sozialer Großversuch,* edited by Bernd Giesen and Claus Leggewie. Berlin: Rotbuch.

Mayr, Monika. 1993. "Dresden." In *Legenden, Lügen, Vorurteile: Ein Wörterbuch zur Zeitgeschichte,* edited by Wolfgang Benz. Munich: Deutscher Taschenbuch Verlag, pp. 61–62.

McLeod, Jack, and Donald McDonald. 1985. "Beyond Simple Exposure: Media Orientations and Their Impact on Political Processes." *Communications Research* 12, pp. 3–24.

McNelly, John T., and Fausto Izcaray. 1986. "International News Exposure and Images of Nations." *Journalism Quarterly* 63(3), pp. 546–553.

Mead, W. R. 1990. "The Once and Future Reich." *World Policy Journal* 7, pp. 593–638.

Mearsheimer, John. 1990. "Back to the Future: Instability in Europe after the Cold War." *International Security,* summer issue, pp. 5–56.

Mechtersheimer, Alfred. 1991. *Friedensmacht Deutschland.* Frankfurt am Main: Ullstein.

Meidinger, Götz. 1991. "Der vergessene letzte Kanzler des Reiches." *Junge Freiheit* 12 (December), p. 13.

———. 1992. "Auch Babi-Jar bleibt nicht frei von Zweifeln." *Junge Freiheit* 5 (May), p. 27.

———. 1993. "Vor 50 Jahren: Als die Dämme brachen." *Junge Freiheit* 5 (May), p. 19.

Meier, Christian. 1990. *40 Jahre nach Auschwitz: Deutsche Geschichtserinnerung heute.* Munich: Deutscher Kunstverlag.

Melzer, W. 1992. *Jugend und Politik in Deutschland, gesellschaftliche Einstellungen, Zukunftsorientierungen und Rechtsextremismuspotential Jugendlicher in Ost- und Westdeutschland.* Opladen: Leske & Budrich.

Melzer, Wolfgang, and Wilfried Schubarth. 1993. "Das Rechtsextremismussyndrom bei Schülerinnen und Schülern in West- und Ostdeutschland." In: *Schule, Gewalt und Rechtsextremismus,* edited by Wilfried Schubarth and Wolfgang Melzer. Opladen: Leske & Budrich, pp. 57–79.

Merkl, Peter H., ed. 1989. *The Federal Republic of Germany at Forty.* New York: New York University Press.

———. 1994. *The Federal Republic of Germany at Forty-Five.* London: Macmillan.

Merkl, Peter H., and Leonard Weinberg, eds. 1993. *Encounters with the Contemporary Radical Right.* Boulder: Westview.

Merritt, Anna J., and Richard L. Merritt, eds. 1970. *Public Opinion in Occupied Germany: The OMGUS Surveys, 1945–1948.* Urbana: University of Illinois Press.

———. 1980. *Public Opinion in Semi-Sovereign Germany: The HICOG Surveys, 1949–1955.* Urbana: University of Illinois Press.

Merritt, Richard L. 1989. "Politics of Judaism in the GDR." In *Studies in GDR Culture and Society 9: Selected Papers from the Fourteenth New Hampshire Symposium on the German Democratic Republic,* edited by Margy Gerber et al. Lanham Md.: University Press of America, pp. 163–187.

―――. 1993. "Changing Public Attitudes toward Jews in the Federal Republic of Germany, 1945–93." Paper presented at the German Studies Association Conference, Washington, D.C., October 5–10.

―――. 1995. *Democracy Imposed: U.S. Occupation Policy and the German Public, 1945–49.* New Haven, Conn.: Yale University Press.

Michalka, Wolfgang, ed. 1987. *Extremismus und streitbare Demokratie.* Stuttgart: Wilhelm Fink.

Miles, Robert. 1993. *Racism after "Race Relations."* London: Routledge.

Minkenberg, Michael. 1992. "The New Right in Germany: The Transformation of Conservatism and the Extreme Right." *European Journal of Political Research* 22(1), pp. 55–81.

―――. 1993. "The New Right in Comparative Perspective: The USA and Germany." Western Societies Program, Occasional Paper no. 32, Cornell University.

―――. 1994. "German Unification and the Continuity of Discontinuities: Cultural Change and the Far Right in East and West." *German Politics* 3(2), pp. 169–192.

Minnerup, Günter. 1994. "German Communism, the PDS, and the Re-unification of Germany." In *West European Communist Parties after the Revolutions of 1989,* edited by Martin J. Bull and Paul Heywood. New York: St. Martin's, pp. 178–202.

Mitscherlich, Alexander, and Margarete Mitscherlich. 1975. *The Inability to Mourn: Principle of Collective Behavior.* New York: Grove.

Mohler, Armin. 1950. *Die Konservative Revolution in Deutschland, 1918–1932.* 1st ed. Stuttgart: Vorwerk.

―――. 1980. *Vergangenheitsbewältigung oder wie man den Krieg nochmals verliert.* Krefeld: Sinus.

―――. 1993. "Kondylis—der Anti-Fukuyama." *Criticon* 3/4 (March/April), pp. 85–89.

Moreau, Patrick. 1994. "Das Wahljahr 1994 und die Strategie der PDS." *Aus Politik und Zeitgeschichte* 1, pp. 21–26.

Moreau, Patrick, and Viola Neu. 1994. *Die PDS zwischen Linksextremismus und Linkspopulismus.* Internal Studies no. 76. Sankt Augustin: Konrad-Adenauer-Foundation.

Müller, H. 1991. "Lebenswerte und nationale Identität." In *Jugend und Jugendforschung in der DDR,* edited by W. Friedrich and H. Griese. Opladen: Leske & Budrich, pp. 124–135.

Müller, Richard Matthias. 1994. *Normal-Null und die Zukunft der deutschen Vergangenheitsbewältigung.* Schernfeld: SH-Verlag.

Neaman, Elliot. 1993. "The Escalation of Violence in Germany: Is It Time to Leave?" *Tikkun* 8(6), pp. 32–35.

―――. 1995. "Mutiny on Board Modernity: Heidegger, Sorel and Other Fascist Intellectuals." *Critical Review* 9(3) (Summer), pp. 1–30.

Neugebauer, Wolfgang. 1992. " 'Revisionistische' Manipulation der Zahl der Holocaustopfer." In *Amoklauf gegen die Wirklichkeit: NS-Verbrechen und "revisionistische" Geschichtsschreibung,* edited by Bundesministerium für Unterricht und Kunst and Dokumentationsarchiv des österreichischen Widerstandes. Vienna: Dokumentationsarchiv des österreichischen Widerstandes, pp. 83–87.

Neunter Jugendbericht. 1994. *Bericht über die Situation der Kinder und Jugendlichen und die Entwicklung der Jugendhilfe in den neuen Bundesländern.* Bonn.

Nicosia, Francis R. 1991. "The End of Emancipation and the Illusion of Preferential Treatment: German Zionism, 1933–1938." In *Leo Baeck Institute Year Book, vol. 36.* London: Martin Secker & Warburg, pp. 243–65.

Noelle, Elisabeth, and Erich Peter Neumann. 1965. *Jahrbuch der Öffentlichen Meinung, 1958–1964,* vol. 3. Allensbach: Verlag für Demoskopie.

———. 1967. *Jahrbuch der Öffentlichen Meinung, 1965–1967,* vol. 4. Allensbach: Verlag für Demoskopie.

Noelle-Neumann, Elisabeth. 1984. *The Spiral of Silence: Public Opinion—Our Social Skin.* Chicago: University of Chicago Press.

———. 1992. "Wie belastbar ist die deutsche Demokratie?: Man vertraut dem System, aber mißtraut seinen Repräsentanten und Institutionen." *Frankfurter Allgemeine Zeitung,* December 16, p. 5.

———. 1994. "Problems with Democracy in Eastern Germany after the Downfall of the GDR." In *Research on Democracy and Society. Vol. 2, Political Culture and Political Structure: Theoretical and Empirical Studies,* edited by Frederick D. Weil. Greenwich, Conn.: JAI Press, pp. 213–232.

Noelle-Neumann, Elisabeth, and Renate Köcher, eds. 1993. *Allensbacher Jahrbuch der Demoskopie, 1984–1992.* Vol. 9. Munich: Saur.

Nolte, Ernst. 1987. "Zwischen Geschichtslegende und Revisionismus: Das Dritte Reich im Blickwinkel des Jahres 1980." Speech presented to the Carl Friedrich von Siemens Foundation, 1980. In *Historikerstreit: Eine Dokumentation der Kontroverse um die Einzigartigkeit der nationalsozialistischen Judenvernichtung.* Munich: Piper, pp. 13–35.

———. 1993. *Streitpunkte: Heutige und künftige Kontroversen um den Nationalsozialismus.* Frankfurt am Main: Propyläen.

Oesterreich, Detlef. 1993. *Autoritäre Persönlichkeit und Gesellschaftsordnung.* Weinheim: Juventa.

———. 1994. *Radikalisierung und Krise: Rechtsextremismus bei ost- und westberliner Jugendlichen.* Bielefeld: Research Network no. 1.

Offenberg, Mario, ed. 1986. *Adass Jisroel, Die jüdische Gemeinde in Berlin (1869–1942): Vernichtet und Vergessen.* Berlin: Museumspädagogischer Dienst Berlin.

Olick, Jeffrey K. 1994. "Collective Memory as Discursive Process: The Nazi Past in West German Politics, 1949–1989." Paper presented at the annual meeting of the American Sociological Association, Los Angeles, August 12.

Ostow, Robin. 1989a–1992. "German Democratic Republic." In *American Jewish Year Book, 1989–1992,* vols. 89–92, edited by David Singer and Ruth R. Seldin. New York: American Jewish Committee and Jewish Publication Society.

———. 1989b. *Jews in Contemporary East Germany: The Children of Moses in the Land of Marx.* New York: St. Martin's.

Otto, Hans-Uwe, and Roland Merten, eds. 1993. *Rechtsradikale Gewalt im vereinigten Deutschland.* Opladen: Leske & Budrich.

"Paradoxie des 8. Mai." 1995. *Junge Freiheit,* May 5, p. 16.

Patterns of Prejudice. 1993. Vol. 27. Special Issue on Antisemitism in Europe (with contributions by Hermann Graml, Werner Bergmann, Rainer Erb, and Frank Stern).

Pauley, Bruce F. 1992. *From Prejudice to Persecution.* Chapel Hill: University of North Carolina Press.

Pfahl-Traughber, Armin. 1993. *Rechtsextremismus.* Bonn: Bouvier.

Phillips, Ann. 1994. "Socialism with a New Face?: The PDS in Search of Reform." *East European Politics and Societies* 8(3), pp. 495–530.

Plasser, Fritz, and Peter A. Ulram. 1993. "Zum Stand der Demokratisierung in Ost-Mitteleuropa." In *Transformation oder Stagnation?: Aktuelle politische Trends in Osteu-*

ropa, edited by Fritz Plasser and Peter A. Ulram. Vienna: Schriftenreihe des Zentrums für angewandte Politikforschung, pp. 9–88.

Pressac, Jean-Claude. 1989. *Auschwitz: Technique and Operation of the Gas Chambers.* New York: Beate Klarsfeld Foundation.

———. 1990. "The Deficiencies and Inconsistencies of 'The Leuchter Report.' " In *Truth Prevails—Demolishing Holocaust Denial: The End of "The Leuchter Report,"* edited by Shelly Shapiro. New York: Beate Klarsfeld Foundation and Holocaust Survivors and Friends in Pursuit of Justice, pp. 31–60.

———. 1993. *Les crématoires d'Auschwitz: La Machinerie du Meurtre de Masse.* Paris: CNRS Editions.

Protocols of the Learned Elders of Zion. 1978. Translated from the Russian of Nilus by Victor E. Marsden. Hollywood: New Christian Crusade Church. Reprint, New York: Gordon.

Raab, Earl. 1986. "Attitudes toward Israel and Attitudes toward Jews: The Relationship." In *Antisemitism in the Contemporary World,* edited by Michael Curtis. Boulder: Westview, pp. 288–301.

Rabinbach, Anson. 1990. "The Jewish Question in the German Question." In *Reworking the Past: Hitler, the Holocaust, and the Historian's Debate,* edited by Peter Baldwin. Boston: Beacon, pp. 45–73.

Rabinbach, Anson, and Jack Zipes, eds. 1986. *Germans and Jews since the Holocaust: The Changing Situation in West Germany.* New York: Holmes & Meier.

Reichel, Peter. 1981. *Politische Kultur in der Bundesrepublik.* Opladen: Westdeutscher Verlag.

Reinfeldt, Sebastian, and Richard Schwarz. 1994. "Ethnopluralismus Made in Germany." In *Das Plagiat: Der völkische Nationalismus der Jungen Freiheit,* edited by Helmut Kellershohn. Duisburg: DISS-Verlag, pp. 213–233.

Rijksinstituut voor Oorlogsdocumentatie/Niederländisches Institut für Kriegsdokumentation, ed. 1988. *Die Tagebücher der Anne Frank.* Frankfurt am Main: Fischer.

Rommelspacher, B. 1992. "Rechtsextremismus und Dominanzkultur." In *Ein Herrenvolk voll Untertanen,* edited by A. Foitzik et al. Duisburg: Diss-Verlag, pp. 81–94.

Rose, Richard, and William T. E. Mishler. 1993. *Reacting to Regime Change in Eastern Europe: Polarization or Leaders and Laggards?* Studies in Public Policy no. 210. Glasgow: Centre for the Study of Public Policy, University of Strathclyde.

Roth, Karl Heinz. 1994. "Der historische Revisionismus in Deutschland: Zwischenbilanz und Perspektiven." *1999: Zeitschrift für Sozialgeschichte des 20. und 21. Jahrhunderts* 4, pp. 7–11.

Runge, Irene. 1993. *Vom Kommen und Bleiben: Osteuropäische jüdische Einwanderer in Berlin.* Together: Living in Berlin series. Berlin: Die Ausländerbeauftragte des Senats.

Saalfeld, Thomas. 1994. "Xenophobic Political Movements in Germany, 1949–1994." Paper presented at the 89th annual meeting of the American Sociological Association, August 5–9.

Safran, William. 1986. "Problems of Perceiving and Reacting to Anti-Semitism: Reflections of a 'Survivor.' " In *Anti-Semitism in the Contemporary World,* edited by Michael Curtis. Boulder: Westview, pp. 273–287.

Sahin, Haluk, Dennis K. Davis, and John P. Robinson. 1982. "Television as a Source of International News: What Gets Across and What Doesn't." In *Television Coverage of International Affairs,* edited by William C. Adams. Norwood, N.J.: Ablex, pp. 229–244.

Sallen, Herbert A. 1977. *Zum Antisemitismus in der BRD: Konzepte, Methoden und Ergebnisse der empirischen Antisemitismusforschung.* Frankfurt am Main: Haag und Herchen.

Sana, Heleno. 1990. *Das Vierte Reich: Deutschlands später Sieg.* Hamburg: Rasch & Röhring.

Schäfer, Hans-Dietrich. 1981. *Das gespaltene Bewußtsein: Deutsche Kultur und Lebenswirklichkeit, 1933–1945.* Munich: Hanser.

Schäuble, Wolfgang. 1994. *Facing the Future.* Berlin: Ullstein.

Scheepers, P., A. Felling, and J. Peters. 1990. "Social Conditions, Authoritarianism and Ethnocentrism: A Theoretical Model of the Early Frankfurt School Updated and Tested." *European Sociological Review* 6(1), pp. 15–26.

Schittenhelm, Karin. 1994. "Mahnmal Putlitzbrücke: Ein antisemitischer Bildersturm und seine Folgen." In *Jahrbuch für Antisemitismusforschung,* vol. 3. Frankfurt am Main: Campus, pp. 121–139.

Schmidt, Martin. 1991. "Ehrung für britischen Kriegsverbrecher?" *Junge Freiheit* 11 (November), p. 11.

Schmidt, Michael. 1993. *Heute gehört uns die Straße: Der Inside-Report aus der Neonazi-Szene.* Düsseldorf: Econ.

Schmitt, Carl. 1976. *The Concept of the Political.* New Brunswick, N.J.: Rutgers University Press.

Schnabel, Kai Uwe. 1992. "Ausländerfeindlichkeit bei Jugendlichen in Deutschland: Eine Synopse empirischer Befunde seit 1990." *Zeitschrift für Pädagogik* 39, pp. 799–822.

Schöllgen, Gregor. 1992. *Angst vor der Macht: Die Deutschen und ihre Außenpolitik.* Berlin: Ullstein.

Schönbaum, David. 1966. *Hitler's Social Revolution.* New York: Doubleday.

Schröder, Andreas, and Jörg Tykwer. 1994. "Mit Vorurteilen gegen Vorurteile: Wie eine Fernsehsendung gegen Ausländerfeindlichkeit ankämpft." *Jahrbuch für Antisemitismusforschung,* vol. 3. Frankfurt am Main: Campus, pp. 26–50.

Schubarth, Wilfried, Ronald Pschierer, and Thomas Schmidt. 1991. "Verordneter Antifaschismus und die Folgen: Das Dilemma antifaschistischer Erziehung am Ende der DDR." *Aus Politik und Zeitgeschichte* 9, pp. 3–16.

Schubarth, Wilfried, and Dorit Stenke. 1992. " 'Ausländer'-bilder bei ostdeutschen Schülerinnen und Schülern." *Deutschland Archiv* 12, pp. 1247–1254.

Schwagerl, H. Joachim. 1994. *Rechtsextremes Denken: Merkmale und Methoden.* Frankfurt am Main: Fischer.

Schwilk, Heimo, and Ullrich Schacht, eds. 1994. *Die selbstbewußte Nation.* Berlin: Ullstein.

Segre, Dan V. 1986. "Is Anti-Zionism a New Form of Antisemitism?" In *Anti-Semitism in the Contemporary World,* edited by Michael Curtis. Boulder: Westview, pp. 145–154.

Selznick, Gertrude J., and Stephen Steinberg. 1969. *The Tenacity of Prejudice: Anti-Semitism in Contemporary America.* New York: Harper & Row.

Semetko, Holli A., Joanne Bay Brzinski, David H. Weaver, and Lars Willnat. 1992. "TV News and U.S. Public Opinion about Foreign Countries: The Impact of Exposure and Attention," *International Journal of Public Opinion Research* 4(1), pp. 18–36.

Semetko, Holli A., and Klaus Schönbach. 1994. *Germany's "Unity Election": Voters and the Media.* Cresskill, N.J.: Hampton.

Senator für Inneres. 1993. *Rechtsextremismus und Fremdenfeindlichkeit.* Bremen.

Shapiro, Shelly, ed. 1990. *Truth Prevails—Demolishing Holocaust Denial: The End of "The Leuchter Report."* New York: Beate Klarsfeld Foundation and Holocaust Survivors and Friends in Pursuit of Justice.

Shermer, Michael. 1994. "Proving the Holocaust: The Refutation of Revisionism and the Restoration of History." *Skeptic* 2(4), pp. 32–57.

Silbermann, Alphons. 1982. *Sind wir Antisemiten?: Ausmaß und Wirkung eines sozialen Vorurteils in der Bundesrepublik Deutschland.* Cologne: Verlag Wissenschaft und Politik.

Silbermann, Alphons, and Herbert A. Sallen. 1992. *Juden in Westdeutschland: Selbstbild und Fremdbild einer Minorität.* Cologne: Verlag Wissenschaft und Politik.

Silbermann, Alphons, and Julius H. Schoeps, eds. 1986. *Antisemitismus nach dem Holocaust: Bestandsaufnahme und Erscheinungsformen in deutschsprachigen Ländern.* Cologne: Verlag Wissenschaft und Politik.

Simpson, George Eaton, and Milton Yinger. 1985. *Racial and Cultural Minorities: An Analysis of Prejudice and Discrimination.* 4th ed. New York: Harper & Row.

Sinasohn, Max, ed. 1966. *Adass Jisroel Berlin: Entstehung, Entfaltung, Entwurzelung, 1869–1939.* Jerusalem: Max Sinasohn.

Sluga, Hans. 1993. *Heidegger's Crisis.* Cambridge: Harvard University Press.

Smith, Tom W. 1991. *What Do Americans Think about Jews?* Working Papers on Contemporary Anti-Semitism. New York: American Jewish Committee.

———. 1993. "Actual Trends of Measurement Artifacts?: A Review of Three Studies of Anti-Semitism." *Public Opinion Quarterly* 57, pp. 380–393.

———. 1994. *Anti-Semitism in Contemporary America.* Working Papers on Contemporary Anti-Semitism. New York: American Jewish Committee.

Sniderman, Paul, and Thomas Piazza. 1993. *The Scar of Race.* Cambridge, Mass: Belknap.

Soko ReGa. 1993. Potsdam: Minister des Inneren des Staates Brandenburg.

Spann, Gustav. 1992. "Methoden rechtsextremer Tendenzgeschichtsschreibung und Propaganda." In *Amoklauf gegen die Wirklichkeit: NS-Verbrechen und "revisionistische" Geschichtsschreibung,* edited by Bundesministerium für Unterricht und Kunst and Dokumentationsarchiv des österreichischen Widerstandes. Vienna: Dokumentationsarchiv des österreichischen Widerstandes, pp. 15–28.

Spiegel. 1988. "Er oder ich." 42(47), pp. 34–37.

———. 1989. "Leben eingestellt." 43(29), pp. 43–44.

———. 1992. *Spiegel Spezial Nr. 2: Juden und Deutsche.* Survey by Emnid-Institut, November 30–December 17, 1991, Bielefeld. Hamburg: Spiegel Verlag. Results also published in *Der Spiegel* January 13, 1992, pp. 52–66 and January 20, 1992 pp. 41–50.

———. 1993. "Invaliden des 5. Punkts: Mehr als 15,000 jüdische Emigranten aus den GUS-Staaten leben in Deutschland—für viele Israelis ein Ärgernis." 47(13), pp. 77–81.

———. Vol. 48(40).

Sprenger, Jakob. 1993. "Wie Historisierung behindert wird." *Junge Freiheit* 9 (September), p. 18.

Stäglich, Wilhelm. 1979. *Der Auschwitz-Mythos: Legende oder Wirklichkeit?: Eine kritische Bestandsaufnahme.* Tübingen: Grabert.

Stapf, Kurt H., Wolfgang Stroebe, and Klaus Jonas. 1986. *Amerikaner über Deutschland und die Deutschen: Urteile und Vorurteile.* Opladen: Westdentscher Verlag.

Stein, Dieter. 1993. "Rainer Zitelmann im Gespräch." *Junge Freiheit* 7/8 (July/August), p. 3.

Steininger, Rolf. 1993. "Kriegsgefangenschaft." In *Legenden, Lügen, Vorurteile: Ein Wörterbuch zur Zeitgeschichte,* edited by Wolfgang Benz. Munich: Deutscher Taschenbuch Verlag, pp. 126–128.

Stern, Frank. 1991. *Im Anfang war Auschwitz: Antisemitismus und Philosemitismus im deutschen Nachkrieg.* Gerlingen: Bleicher.

———. 1992. *The Whitewashing of the Yellow Badge: Antisemitism and Philosemitism in Postwar Germany.* Oxford, England: Pergamon Press.

————. 1994. "The Revival of Antisemitism in United Germany: Historical Aspects and Methodological Considerations" In *Approaches to Antisemitism,* edited by Michael Brown. New York: American Jewish Committee and International Center for University Teaching of Jewish Civilization, pp. 78–94.

Stern, Fritz. 1961. *The Politics of Cultural Despair.* Berkeley: University of California Press.

Stöss, Richard. 1989. *Die extreme Recht in der Bundesrepublik.* Opladen: Westdeutscher Verlag.

————. 1993a. *Rechtsextremismus in Berlin 1990.* Berlin Working Papers and Reports on Social Science Research no. 80.

————. 1993b. "Rechtsextremismus und Wahlen in der Bundesrepublik." *Aus Politik und Zeitgeschichte* B 11, pp. 50–61.

Stouffer, Samuel A. 1955. *Communisim, Conformity, and Civil Liberties.* Glouster, Mass.: Peter Smith.

Strauss, Botho. 1993. "Anschwellender Bocksgesang." *Der Spiegel,* no. 6 (February 8), pp. 116–122.

————. 1994. "Anschwellender Bocksgesang." In *Die selbstbewußte Nation,* edited by Heimo Schwilk and Ullrich Schacht. Berlin: Ullstein, pp. 119–140.

Strauss, Herbert A., Werner Bergmann, and Christhard Hoffmann, eds. 1990. *Der Antisemitismus der Gegenwart.* Frankfurt am Main: Campus.

Stromberg, Roland. 1994. *European Intellectual History since 1789.* 6th ed. Englewood Cliffs, N.J.: Simon & Schuster.

Sturzbecher, Dietmar, and Peter Dietrich. 1993. "Jugendliche in Brandenburg: Signale einer unverstandenen Generation 1993." *Aus Politik und Zeitgeschichte* 2–3, pp. 33–43.

Sturzbecher, Dietmar, Peter Dietrich, and Michael Kohlstruck. 1994. *Jugend in Brandenburg '93.* Potsdam: Brandenburgische Landeszentrale für politische Bildung.

Sullivan, John L., James Pierson, and George E. Marcus. 1982. *Political Tolerance and American Democracy.* Chicago: University of Chicago Press.

Syberberg, Hans Jürgen. 1990. *Vom Unglück und Glück der Kunst in Deutschland nach dem letzten Krieg.* Munich: Mathes & Seitz.

Tagesspiegel. 1980. "Die gefälschten Papiere schon in Israel für 2500 Mark bestellt." October 22, p. 9.

————. 1985. "Zuzugsbeschränkung für jüdische Emigranten soll gelockert werden." April 3, p. 2.

Taguieff, Pierre-André. 1993/94. "From Race to Culture: The New Right's View of European Identity." *Telos* 98/99 (Winter/Spring), pp. 99–121.

Telos. 1990. "Schmitt's Testament and the Future of Europe." 83 (Spring), special issue.

Terkessidis, Mark. 1995. *Kulturkampf: Volk, Nation, der Westen und die Neue Rechte.* Cologne: Kiepenheuer & Witsch.

Thränhardt, Dietrich. 1993. "Die Ursprünge von Rassismus und Fremdenfeindlichkeit in der Konkurrenzdemokratie: Ein Vergleich der Entwicklung in England, Frankreich und Deutschland." *Leviathan* 21(3), pp. 336–357.

Trautmann, Günter, ed. 1991. *Die häßlichen Deutschen?: Deutschland im Spiegel der westlichen und östlichen Nachbarn.* Darmstadt: Wissenschaftliche Buchgesellschaft.

Überschär, Gerd R. 1987. " 'Historikerstreit' und 'Präventivkriegsthese.' " *Tribüne: Zeitschrift zum Verständnis des Judentums* 103, pp. 108–116.

Veen, Hans-Joachim. 1993. "National Identity and Political Priorities in Eastern and Western Germany." Paper presented at the annual meeting of the American Political Science Association, Washington, D.C., September 2–5.

Veen, Hans-Joachim, et al. eds. 1994. *Eine Jugend in Deutschland?* Opladen: Leske & Budrich.

Venohr, Wolfgang. 1992. "Vor 50 Jahren: Der Kulminationspunkt wird überschritten." *Junge Freiheit* 9 (September), p. 15.

Wahl, Klaus. 1993. "Fremdenfeindlichkeit, Rechtsextremismus, Gewalt: Eine Synopse wissenschaftlicher Untersuchungen und Erklärungsansätze." In *Gewalt gegen Fremde,* edited by Deutsches Jugendinstitut. Weinheim: Juventa, pp. 11–67.

Watson, Alan. 1992. *The Germans: Who Are They Now?* London: Michelin.

Weil, Frederick D. 1982. "Tolerance of Free Speech in the United States and West Germany, 1970–79: An Analysis of Public Opinion Survey Data." *Social Forces* 60(4), pp. 973–993.

———. 1985. "The Variable Effects of Education on Liberal Attitudes: A Comparative-Historical Analysis of Antisemitism Using Public Opinion Survey Data." *American Sociological Review* 50, pp. 458–474.

———. 1987. "The Extent and Structure of Antisemitism in Western Populations since the Holocaust." In *The Persisting Question: Sociological Perspectives and Social Contexts of Modern Antisemitism,* edited by Helen Fein. Berlin: Walter de Gruyter, pp. 164–189.

———. 1990. "Umfragen zum Antisemitismus: Ein Vergleich zwischen vier Nationen." In *Antisemitismus in der politischen Kultur nach 1945,* edited by Werner Bergmann and Rainer Erb. Opladen: Westdeutscher Verlag, pp. 131–178.

———. 1991. "Structural Determinants of Political Tolerance: Regime Change and the Party System in West Germany since World War II." *Research in Political Sociology* 5, pp. 299–332.

———. 1993. "The Development of Democratic Attitudes in Eastern and Western Germany in a Comparative Perspective." In *Research on Democracy and Society.* Vol. 1, Democratization in Eastern and Western Europe, edited by Frederick D. Weil. Greenwich, Conn.: JAI Press, pp. 195–226.

———. 1994a. "Cohorts and the Transition to Democracy in Germany after 1945 and 1989." In *Solidarity of Generations?: Demographic, Economic and Social Change and Its Consequences,* edited by Henk A. Becker and Piet L. J. Hermkens. Amsterdam: Thesis Publishers, pp. 385–425.

———. 1994b. "Democratic Legitimation in Tough Times: Germany since Reunification." Paper presented at the meeting of the International Political Science Association, Berlin, August 20–25.

———, ed. 1993. *Research on Democracy and Society.* Vol. 1, *Democratization in Eastern and Western Europe.* Greenwich, Conn.: JAI Press.

Weißmann, Karlheinz. 1989. "Die konservative Option: Vorschläge für eine andere Politik." *Criticon* 113, p. 129.

———. 1993. *"Rückruf in die Geschichte"—Die deutsche Herausforderung: Alte Gefahren—Neue Chancen.* Frankfurt am Main: Ullstein.

Wiegand, Erich. 1992. "Zunahme der Ausländerfeindlichkeit?" *ZUMA-Nachrichten* 16(31), pp. 7–28.

Wilhoit, G. Cleveland, and David Weaver. 1983. "Foreign News Coverage in Two U.S. Wire Services: An Update," *Journal of Communication* 33(2), pp. 132–148.

Willems, Helmut. 1993. "Gewalt und Fremdenfeindlichkeit: Anmerkungen zum gegenwärtigen Gewaltdiskurs." In *Rechtsradikale Gewalt im vereinigten Deutschland,* edited by Hans-Uwe Otto and Roland Merten. Opladen: Leske & Budrich, pp. 88–108.

———. 1994. "Kollektive Gewalt gegen Fremde: Historische Episode oder Genese einer sozialen Bewegung von rechts?" In *Neonazismus und rechte Subkultur,* edited by Werner Bergmann and Rainer Erb. Berlin: Metropol, pp. 209–226.

Willems, Helmut, et al. 1993. *Fremdenfeindliche Gewalt: Einstellungen, Täter, Konflikteskalation.* Opladen: Leske & Budrich.

Wisse, Ruth. 1994. "Holocaust, or War against the Jews." In: *Approaches to Antisemitism: Context and Curriculum,* edited by Michael Brown. New York: American Jewish Committee and International Center for University Teaching of Jewish Civilization, pp. 24–31.

Wittenberg, Reinhard, Bernhard Prosch, and Martin Abraham. 1991. "Antisemitismus in der ehemaligen DDR: Überraschende Ergebnisse der ersten Repräsentativumfrage und eine Befragung von Jugendlichen in Jena." *Tribüne: Zeitschrift zum Verständnis des Judentums* 30(118), pp. 102–120.

———. 1995. "Struktur und Ausmaß des Antisemitismus in der ehemaligen DDR." In *Jahrbuch für Antisemitismusforschung,* vol. 4, edited by Wolfgang Benz. Frankfurt am Main: Campus, pp. 88–106.

Wodak, Ruth, et al. 1990. *"Wir sind alle unschuldige Täter!": Diskurshistorische Studien zum Nachkriegsantisemitismus.* Frankfurt am Main: Suhrkamp.

Wolffsohn, Michael. 1991. "Die häßlichen Deutschen?: Israel und die diasporajüdische Welt." In *Die häßlichen Deutschen: Deutschland im Spiegel der westlichen und östlichen Nachbarn,* edited by Günter Trautmann. Darmstadt: Wissenschaftliche Buchgesellschaft, pp. 76–82.

———. 1993. *Eternal Guilt?: Forty Years of German-Jewish-Israeli Relations.* New York: Columbia University Press.

Wrench, John, and John Solomos, eds. 1993. *Racism and Migration in Contemporary Europe.* Oxford, England: Berg.

Zimmermann, Ekkart, and Thomas Saalfeld. 1993. "The Three Waves of West German Right-Wing Extremism." In *Encounters with the Contemporary Radical Right,* edited by Peter H. Merkl and Leonard Weinberg. Boulder: Westview, pp. 50–74.

Zimmermann, Moshe. 1992. "Die Folgen des Holocaust für die israelische Gesellschaft." *Aus Politik und Zeitgeschichte,* 1–2, pp. 33–43.

Zipes, Jack. 1991. *The Operated Jews: Two Tales of Antisemitism.* New York: Routledge.

Zitelmann, Rainer. 1993a. "Neutralitätsbestrebungen und Westorientierung." In *Westbindung: Chancen and Risiken für Deutschland,* edited by Rainer Zitelmann et al. Frankfurt am Main: Ullstein, pp. 173–193.

Zitelmann, Rainer, 1993b. "Wiedervereinigung und deutscher Selbsthaß: Probleme mit dem eigenen Volk." In *Deutschland: Eine Nation—doppelte Geschichte,* edited by Werner Weidenfeld. Cologne: Verlag Wissenschaft und Politik, pp. 235–248.

Zitelmann, Rainer, Karlheinz Weißmann, and Michael Großheim. 1993. *Westbindung: Chancen and Risiken für Deutschland.* Frankfurt am Main: Ullstein.

Zitelmann, Rainer, and Michael Prinz, eds. 1991. *Nationalsozialismus und Modernisierung.* Darmstadt: Wissenschaftliche Buchgesellschaft.

Index